IFIP Advances in Information and Communication Technology 446

IFIP – The International Federation for Information Processing

IFIP was founded in 1960 under the auspices of UNESCO, following the First World Computer Congress held in Paris the previous year. An umbrella organization for societies working in information processing, IFIP's aim is two-fold: to support information processing within its member countries and to encourage technology transfer to developing nations. As its mission statement clearly states,

> IFIP's mission is to be the leading, truly international, apolitical organization which encourages and assists in the development, exploitation and application of information technology for the benefit of all people.

IFIP is a non-profitmaking organization, run almost solely by 2500 volunteers. It operates through a number of technical committees, which organize events and publications. IFIP's events range from an international congress to local seminars, but the most important are:

- The IFIP World Computer Congress, held every second year;
- Open conferences;
- Working conferences.

The flagship event is the IFIP World Computer Congress, at which both invited and contributed papers are presented. Contributed papers are rigorously refereed and the rejection rate is high.

As with the Congress, participation in the open conferences is open to all and papers may be invited or submitted. Again, submitted papers are stringently refereed.

The working conferences are structured differently. They are usually run by a working group and attendance is small and by invitation only. Their purpose is to create an atmosphere conducive to innovation and development. Refereeing is also rigorous and papers are subjected to extensive group discussion.

Publications arising from IFIP events vary. The papers presented at the IFIP World Computer Congress and at open conferences are published as conference proceedings, while the results of the working conferences are often published as collections of selected and edited papers.

Any national society whose primary activity is about information processing may apply to become a full member of IFIP, although full membership is restricted to one society per country. Full members are entitled to vote at the annual General Assembly. National societies preferring a less committed involvement may apply for associate or corresponding membership. Associate members enjoy the same benefits as full members, but without voting rights. Corresponding members are not represented in IFIP bodies. Affiliated membership is open to non-national societies, and individual and honorary membership schemes are also offered.

Bill Doolin   Eleni Lamprou
Nathalie Mitev   Laurie McLeod (Eds.)

Information Systems and Global Assemblages

(Re)Configuring Actors, Artefacts, Organizations

IFIP WG 8.2 Working Conference
on Information Systems and Organizations, IS&O 2014
Auckland, New Zealand, December 11-12, 2014
Proceedings

 Springer

Volume Editors

Bill Doolin
Auckland University of Technology
AUT Business School
Private Bag 92006, Auckland 1142, New Zealand
E-mail: bdoolin@aut.ac.nz

Eleni Lamprou
ALBA Graduate Business School
6-8 Xenias Street, 115 28 Athens, Greece
E-mail: elamprou@alba.edu.gr

Nathalie Mitev
London School of Economics and Political Science
Houghton Street, London WC2A 2AE, UK
E-mail: n.n.mitev@lse.ac.uk

Laurie McLeod
Auckland University of Technology
AUT Business School
Private Bag 92006, Auckland 1142, New Zealand
E-mail: lmcleod@aut.ac.nz

ISSN 1868-4238   e-ISSN 1868-422X
ISBN 978-3-662-52626-2   e-ISBN 978-3-662-45708-5
DOI 10.1007/978-3-662-45708-5
Springer Heidelberg New York Dordrecht London

Typesetting: Camera-ready by author, data conversion by Scientific Publishing Services, Chennai, India

Printed on acid-free paper

Springer is part of Springer Science+Business Media (www.springer.com)

Preface

This book constitutes the proceedings of the 2014 Working Conference of the International Federation for Information Processing (IFIP) Working Group 8.2. The focus of IFIP WG 8.2 (http://ifipwg82.org/) is the interaction of information systems and the organization. The Working Conference took place during December 11-12, 2014, at Auckland University of Technology, New Zealand.

The theme of the conference was "Information Systems and Global Assemblages: (Re)Configuring Actors, Artefacts, Organizations." The theme was intended to encourage researchers to reflect on the performative, processual, and relational aspects of information technology and organizational practices. In particular, we wanted to explore how contemporary information systems are constituted as heterogeneous, emergent, and situated "assemblages" at the intersection between the global and local, the social and the material. The conference provided a forum for a stimulating discussion between researchers from different fields that collectively share an interest in information and communication technologies in organizations and society.

We would like to thank all authors who submitted papers to the conference for their interest in IFIP WG 8.2. We would also like to thank the Program Committee for their support of the conference and for reviewing the submissions. We received 28 submissions, including 22 research papers and six position papers. Each paper was assigned to a program co-chair and forwarded to members of the Program Committee for evaluation using a double-blind review process. At the end of the review period, the program co-chairs reviewed the feedback and scores provided by the Program Committee members and invited the authors of 15 papers to revise and resubmit their papers taking into consideration the reviewers' and editorial comments. One paper was withdrawn before the end of the re-submission period. The remaining 14 papers were finally accepted for presentation at the conference and inclusion in these proceedings. The accepted papers were written by 35 authors from around the world, with 15 authors from institutions in Asia-Pacific, 15 from Europe, and five from North America.

We would like to acknowledge our distinguished keynote speaker, Professor Karlheinz Kautz, and thank him for his contribution to the conference. The topic of his presentation was "From Implementation and Use to Appropriation and Performativity: Sociomaterial Practices and Assemblages." Professor Kautz is Senior Research Professor in IT Management & Innovation and Associate Dean Research in the Faculty of Business at the University of Wollongong, Australia. Previously, he has held academic positions in Germany, Norway, England, and Denmark. He is a founding member and a former chairman of the IFIP WG 8.6 Transfer and Diffusion of IT. His reflections on sociomateriality as a concept to understand information systems have been presented in traditional formats and also made known as a jester's monologue.

The organization of the conference and production of the proceedings are the result of the hard work and commitment of a number of people, whose contributions we would like to acknowledge. In particular, Laurie McLeod edited the proceedings, Serena Gent managed the conference facilities and registration process, and Tingting Zhang developed the conference website. Kevin Crowston, Ulrike Schultze, and Brian Fitzgerald from IFIP WG 8.2 provided invaluable advice and support. We would also like to thank Auckland University of Technology for their support in hosting the conference.

October 2014   Bill Doolin
                                                            Eleni Lamprou
                                                            Nathalie Mitev

Conference Organization

General Chairs

Bill Doolin   Auckland University of Technology, New Zealand

Brian Fitzgerald   University of Limerick, Ireland

Program Co-chairs

Bill Doolin   Auckland University of Technology, New Zealand

Eleni Lamprou   ALBA Graduate Business School, Greece

Nathalie Mitev   London School of Economics and Political Science, UK

Program Committee

Margunn Aanestad	University of Oslo, Norway
Michel Avital	Copenhagen Business School, Denmark
David Avison	ESSEC Business School, France
Vasiliki Baka	IT University of Copenhagen, Denmark
Richard Baskerville	Georgia State University, USA
Deborah Bunker	University of Sydney, Australia
Tom Butler	University of Cork, Ireland
Dubravka Cecez-Kecmanovic	University of New South Wales, Australia
Mike Chiasson	University of British Columbia, Canada
Ioanna Chini	University of Sussex, UK
Kieran Conboy	NUI Galway, Ireland
Kevin Crowston	Syracuse University, USA
Liz Davidson	University of Hawaii, USA
Robert Davison	City University of Hong Kong, SAR China
François-Xavier de Vaujany	Paris Dauphine University, France
Antonio Diaz Andrade	Auckland University of Technology, New Zealand
Philip Dobson	Edith Cowan University, Australia
Aurélie Dudezert	Université de Poitiers, France
Amany Elbanna	University of London, Royal Holloway, UK
Uri Gal	University of Sydney, Australia
Bob Galliers	Bentley University, USA
Michael Gallivan	Georgia State University, USA
Matt Germonprez	University of Nebraska Omaha, USA

Nik R. Hassan	University of Minnesota Duluth, USA
Ola Henfridsson	University of Warwick, UK
Magda Hercheui	University of Westminster, UK
Alan Hevner	University of South Florida, USA
Jonny Holmström	Umeå University, Sweden
Helena Holmström Olsson	Malmö University, Sweden
Dirk Hovorka	University of Sydney, Australia
Netta Iivari	University of Oulu, Finland
Lucas Introna	Lancaster University, UK
Tina Blegind Jensen	Copenhagen Business School, Denmark
Matthew Jones	University of Cambridge, UK
Antonios Kaniadakis	University of Central Lancashire, UK/Cyprus
Helena Karsten	Åbo Akademi University, Finland
Karlheinz Kautz	University of Wollongong, Australia
Julie Kendall	Rutgers University, USA
Ken Kendall	Rutgers University, USA
Ela Klecun	London School of Economics and Political Science, UK
Satish Krishnan	Indian Institute of Management Kozhikode
Lynette Kvasny	Penn State University, USA
Rikard Lindgren	University of Gothenburg, Sweden
Eleni Lioliou	Loughborough University, UK
Attila Marton	Copenhagen Business School, Denmark
Kathy McGrath	Brunel University, UK
Christine McLean	Manchester Business School, UK
Laurie McLeod	Auckland University of Technology, New Zealand
Stephanie Missonier	Université de Lausanne, Switzerland
Eric Monteiro	Norwegian University of Science and Technology, Norway
Benjamin Müller	University of Groningen, The Netherlands
Michael Myers	University of Auckland, New Zealand
Nikos Mylonopoulos	ALBA Graduate Business School, Greece
Peter Axel Nielsen	Aalborg University, Denmark
Jacob Nørbjerg	Copenhagen Business School, Denmark
Wanda Orlikowski	MIT Sloan School of Management, USA
Jessie Pallud	Université de Strasbourg, France
Dimitra Petrakaki	University of Sussex, UK
Jan Pries-Heje	Roskilde University, Denmark
Corina Raduescu	University of Sydney, Australia
Kai Riemer	University of Sydney, Australia
Matti Rossi	Aalto University, Finland
Nancy Russo	Northern Illinois University, USA
Sundeep Sahay	University of Oslo, Norway

Johan Sandberg	Umeå University, Sweden
Suprateek Sarker	University of Virginia, USA
Steve Sawyer	Syracuse University, USA
Ulrike Schultze	Southern Methodist University, USA
Susan Scott	London School of Economics and Political Science, UK
Maha Shaikh	University of Warwick, UK
Harminder Singh	Auckland University of Technology, New Zealand
Carsten Sørensen	London School of Economics and Political Science, UK
Fredrik Svahn	Chalmers University of Technology, Sweden
Tuure Tuunanen	University of Jyväskylä, Finland
John Venable	Curtin Business School, Australia
Geoff Walsham	University of Cambridge, UK
Edgar Whitley	London School of Economics and Political Science, UK
Markos Zachariadis	University of Warwick, UK

Organizing Chairs

Serena Gent	Auckland University of Technology, New Zealand
Laurie McLeod	Auckland University of Technology, New Zealand

Webmaster

Tingting Zhang	Auckland University of Technology, New Zealand

Conference Sponsor

Auckland University of Technology, New Zealand

Table of Contents

Health Care IS

Social Media

IS Design

Information Systems and Assemblages

Eleni Lamprou[1], Nathalie Mitev[2], and Bill Doolin[3]

[1] ALBA Graduate Business School, Athens, Greece
elamprou@alba.edu.gr
[2] London School of Economics, London, UK
n.n.mitev@lse.ac.uk
[3] Auckland University of Technology, Auckland, New Zealand
bdoolin@aut.ac.nz

1   Introduction

The theme for the 2014 IFIP WG 8.2 working conference was 'Information Systems and Global Assemblages: (Re)Configuring Actors, Artefacts, Organizations'. The motivation behind the choice of the conference theme has been the increasing appreciation of notions of emergence, heterogeneity and temporality in IS studies. We found that the conference provided an opportune occasion for inviting scholars interested in exploring these notions, their relevance and promise for IS studies. The concept of the 'assemblage' [1], already referenced in IS studies, as will be discussed below, and with significant popularity in other fields, such as anthropology, geography and cultural studies, provided the stepping stone for approaching the heterogeneous, emergent and situated nature of information systems and organization. In particular, we opted for highlighting the 'global assemblage'[2] as a metaphor to talk about challenging yet often creative tensions that emerge as global imperatives (geographical, intellectual, procedural and others) interact with local arrangements of actors, artefacts and organizations. Here 'global' does not mean universal or everywhere, but mobile, abstractable, and capable of recontextualization across diverse social and cultural situations.

This book provides a collection of contributions by scholars who responded to our invitation, adding depth and breadth to our understanding of the concept and its value for IS studies. At the same time, some contributors chose to discuss emergence, heterogeneity and situatedness in different terms, drawing upon alternative theoretical traditions and concepts. The result has been an engaging and stimulating mix of ideas that points towards the 'multiple' trajectories – current and future – of this exciting stream of research.

2   Information Systems as (Global) Assemblages

Approaches that stress the performative, processual and relational aspects of organizational practice, have received increased attention in recent years. Drawn from diverse philosophical and theoretical traditions, their boundaries are often blurred, intimating the mutability, subversiveness and tentativeness of the very phenomena they study.

B. Doolin et al. (Eds.): IS&O 2014, IFIP AICT 446, pp. 1–7, 2014.
© IFIP International Federation for Information Processing 2014

Discussions of agency and materiality have found a prominent place in the development of these approaches, inviting audiences to reconsider ideas of structure, power and accountability in organizational practice. Emphasis has often been placed on micro-processes of organizing and change, revealing the contribution of interactions at specific localities to the unfolding of the organization as a whole. As such, these approaches problematize the relationship between the social and the technical, the abstract and the specific, the ostensive and the performative, the universal and the particular.

The idea of the assemblage appears to originate in the work of Deleuze and Guattari [3], explicated beautifully by DeLanda [4, 5]. At the same time, Anderson and McFarlane identify another potential reference point in what they call an "'after' actor-network theory literature" [6, p. 125]. What appears to be common in both cases, nonetheless, is that the concept offers an opportunity for subverting prevailing notions of structure by emphasizing movement and the temporary, socially, materially and discursively accomplished "coming-together" of heterogeneous entities into social practices. As Marcus and Saka point out,

> Assemblage is thus a resource with which to address in analysis and writing the modernist problem of the heterogeneous within the ephemeral, while preserving some concept of the structural so embedded in the enterprise of social science research [1, p. 102].

The concept of the assemblage affords insight into the emergence, temporality, spatiality, distributed agency and fragility of social formations [6], the implications of which are revealed vividly and intensely when abstract ideas, routines, technologies and classifications travel to different locations. As Collier and Ong suggest, "As global forms are articulated in specific situations – or are territorialized in assemblages – they define new material, collective and discursive relationships" [2, p. 4]. Examples include various forms of technoscience that, as Sassen suggests "can accommodate multiple particularities" [7, p. 457], such as the human genome, standards regimes, and digital networks.

Hence, the concept of the assemblage emerges as particularly relevant to IS studies that explore the design, development and implementation of abstract technological forms instantiated in particular locations and temporalities. It is not surprising then that the concept has found its place in early technology studies grounded in a practice perspective [8, 9]. The practice turn in social sciences is predicated on an interest with the situated, the local and the relational [10] and the idea of the assemblage serves particularly such purposes. Its use in IS studies became even more popular with the development of the sociomaterial perspective [11, 12] and the ongoing scrutiny of the relation between the social and the material [13, 14]. References to 'sociomaterial assemblages' in IS studies indicate engagement with the perceived heterogeneity, tentativeness and locatedness of the alignment and realignment, configuration and reconfiguration of actors, technological artefacts and organizations. As Orlikowski notes, "The performativity of the sociomaterial assemblage is thus fleeting, fragile, and fragmented, entailing uncertainty and risk, and producing intended and unintended outcomes" [11, p. 1445]. These counterintuitive characteristics appear to consistently attract further attention in IS studies, as demonstrated by the interest in applying the concept of sociomaterial assemblages in both conceptual and empirical studies [15, 16]. Even more so, the idea of the 'assemblage' does not remain limited to the sociomaterial perspective. Instead, it also finds ground in alternative theoretical conceptualizations, as evidenced in recent work [17].

Such increasing interest in "assemblages" suggests this may be a timely opportunity to consider the kind of questions that IS scholars can generate through the application of the concept and how an "assemblage theory" may be of value to the field. Relevant questions have already been posed elsewhere [6], centered on the difference that assemblage thinking can make to studies of relationality and heterogeneity; the relation of the concept to other seemingly familiar concepts, such as network and apparatus; theorizing order and change; and, implications of such an ontological thesis for politics and ethics. Several of these questions have been addressed by contributors to this book, at the same time accentuating particular themes of relevance to IS studies, such as exploring the subjects, rationalities, techniques and practices that constitute information systems as heterogeneous and situated assemblages; discussing temporality and emergence in information systems and organizational change; and, producing alternative insights on the contribution of digital innovation to industry and organizational practices.

3   Overview of the Book

We would like to thank the authors for their contributions to the conference. Some of the papers address directly the theme of the conference, while others address topics relevant to IFIP WG 8.2 beyond the specific call, as per our invitation. In our effort to group the papers, we attempted to identify common underlying issues that could steer discussion and generate insight during the conference sessions.

3.1   IS/IT Implementation and Appropriation

The first group of papers apply alternative theoretical lenses to the study of IS/IT implementation, adoption and use. Lauterbach and Mueller approach what they perceive as terminological heterogeneity in the literature on IT adoption and use it as a starting point for their contribution. They review the development of the field, including positivist and constructivist accounts, and propose a process model of IT adoption with the aim of integrating the field. The authors argue that such an effort brings to the fore questions regarding conceptual clarity, as well as areas available for further investigation. Plumb and Kautz apply a phenomenological approach to the study of IT appropriation in early childhood and care organizations, drawing upon Heideggerian insights. They approach IT artefacts as objects of reflection that through processes of 'place making' become tools and eventually take the role of 'equipment' in organizational practices. The authors understand such a phenomenological theory of appropriation as contributing to the sociomateriality debate, as it portrays technologies as inextricably entangled in practices. Yeow and Faraj propose an alternative vocabulary for studying IS implementation from a sociomaterial perspective. Drawing upon the notion of 'performation' they shift emphasis to how assemblages are rendered performative in the presence of pre-existing sociomaterial contexts. In this light, they bring to the fore the 'invisible work' that is necessary for assemblages to be made to perform, the relevance of discursive practices in stabilizing the meaning of an assemblage as performative and the principle of 'performative exigency' as driving sociomaterial change.

3.2   Ethnographic Accounts of IS Use

A second group of papers offer ethnographic accounts of IS use drawing upon two quite different contexts. Chughtai and Myers present the findings of an ethnographic study of young IT professionals, exploring their 'absorbed' engagement with IT artefacts. The authors propose that the entwinement logic of practices, grounded in Heideggerian insights of 'Being-in-the-World', provides a fruitful, holistic lens for explaining the seemingly comfortable use of IT artefacts by this generation. Such a lens conceptualises practices as sociomaterial and spatiotemporal and technology as entwined in practice – more specifically, as equipment, purposefully used, drawing upon and developing skills. Eades and Zheng wish to contribute to the discussion of Information Systems beyond the realm of business practice and present a study of a commemorative counter-mapping ritual where systems such as Google Earth were employed. The study draws upon the concept of the assemblage to discuss issues of temporality, spatiality and becoming in mapping practices that draw upon translocal technologies and contexts and have transgenerational effects in identity construction.

3.3   Structures and Networks

Another group of papers discuss intra- and inter-organization structures and networks. Aryal, EL Amrani, and Truex employ the concept of the assemblage to approach the development of 'competency centers', namely governance structures and processes that coordinate and facilitate the post-implementation phase of Enterprise Systems. They reach the conclusion that the value of such (fluid and temporary) structures depends on how the constant movement between 'material' and 'expressive' constructs, on the one hand, and forces of 'territorialisation' and 'deterritorialization', on the other, is handled within organizations. Lund dissects the challenges encountered in developing digital innovation drawing upon the case of an e-newspaper initiative. In approaching the subject matter, the author draws the picture of a digital ecosystem as a heterogeneous network of interested parties, with heterogeneous knowledge resources, expectations and requirements that raise political tensions. Concrete ways in which these challenges can been addressed are proposed.

3.4   Health Care IS

A number of papers in the conference are located in the health care context, reflecting an enduring interest of the IFIP WG 8.2 community in health care information systems. Two papers offer a critical eye on developments in that field. Robertson, Nicholas, Rosenfeld, and Travaglia discuss the social and political issues that underlie practices of knowledge production through health information systems. Specifically, the authors question the practices of knowledge production touching upon several issues, such as big data, classificatory systems and digital materiality. Further, they argue that health information systems do not adequately engage with the lived experience of patients and discuss the potential contribution of information on space/place in this direction. Cornford and Lichtner use the concept of the assemblage to approach the digitization of drugs, namely, the integration of digital services into the practices of using drugs. They problematize the seemingly prevalent rationale behind this movement - achieving certainty in medical provision. They produce an 'anatomy' of digital drugs, drawing upon three domains in which issues of their value are raised, (in-)use, research and governance, and point towards relevant questions for the IS community.

3.5   Social Media

Studies of social media with various applications and objectives also found a place in the conference. Pousti, Urquhart, and Linger engage with the role of social media in chronic care management. They identify an affordances perspective as pertinent for the study of social media in healthcare management, as it acknowledges that the meaning of such media and their respective affordances do not reside in the artefact per se, but emerge through material-discursive practices. They move to discuss particular affordances and constraints related to the use of social media in chronic health care management. Dudezert, Fayard, and Oiry draw upon the myth of Asterix and the organization of the inhabitants in the Gaulish village with regards to knowledge, as to explore the tensions and challenges that may occur during the implementation of Knowledge Management Systems 2.0. The authors comment on the relevance of myths for approaching organizational phenomena and engage with the role played by shared national representations in the implementation of Information Systems. Mirbabaie, Ehnis, Stieglitz, and Bunker set out to study communication roles enacted through social media in the face of extreme events. They argue that due to the pervasiveness of social media in everyday life, 'command and control' systems, including governmental agencies, need to engage with information generated on these platforms by organizations, groups and individuals. The research proposed by the authors aims at facilitating effective communication among these parties during an extreme event.

3.6   IS Design

The final group of papers engage with pertinent issues in IS design. Baskerville and Pries-Heje problematize the suitability of criteria such as generalizability and transferability for the evaluation of design theories. They understand design science as different from natural or social studies, as it is materially prescriptive and engages with contexts that may not even presently exist. They propose the criterion of 'projectability' and discuss its relevance, acknowledging two forms of projectability – actual projection into material artefacts or other design theories. Baskerville, Davison, Kaul, and Wong extend an invitation to re-consider the relevance of 'systems' in Information Systems research, a concept which, they argue, has faded in recent studies.

Drawing upon the results of a study on system designer roles, they reach the conclusion that engaging with 'Systems of Information' instead of 'Information Systems' may be more pertinent to new challenges facing systems designers. These challenges emerge from the requirement to preserve the systematicity of information practices in the context of transitions from old to new systems.

4   Conclusion

It is our belief that contributions in this book advance discussions on the notions of emergence, heterogeneity and temporality and mobilise our further engagement with the relevance of (global) assemblages in IS studies. The very heterogeneity of the components of this book; the individual chapters with their distinct objectives, choice of field and conceptual armoury, level of engagement with the theme of the conference; their contingent "coming-together" in this single volume, temporarily stabilizing discussions that have been and instigating discussions that will be; their continuous dispersion, as they seek to develop into different forms and align with further assemblages. These are all valuable mementos of another "coming-together" in beautiful New Zealand, in the forum of the IFIP WG 8.2 working conference, left to remind us of the promise of assemblage theory for IS studies.

References

1. Marcus, G.E., Saka, E.: Assemblage. Theory, Culture & Society 23, 101–106 (2006)
2. Collier, S.J., Ong, A.: Global Assemblages, Anthropological Problems. In: Ong, A., Collier, S.J. (eds.) Global Assemblages: Technologies, Politics and Ethics as Anthropological Problems. Blackwell, Oxford (2005)
3. Deleuze, G., Guattari, F.: A Thousand Plateaus: Capitalism and Schizophrenia. University of Minnesota Press, Minneapolis (1987)
4. DeLanda, M.: Intensive Science and Virtual Philosophy. Bloomsbury, London (2002)
5. DeLanda, M.: A New Philosophy of Society: Assemblage Theory and Social Complexity. Continuum, London (2006)
6. Anderson, B., McFarlane, C.: Assemblage and Geography. Area 43, 124–127 (2011)
7. Sassen, S.: Interactions of the Technical and the Social: Digital Formations of the Powerful and the Powerless. Information, Communication & Society 15, 455–478 (2012)
8. Suchman, L.: Human-Machine Reconfigurations: Plans and Situated Actions, 2nd edn. Cambridge University Press, Cambridge (2007)
9. Pickering, A.: The Mangle of Practice: Time, Agency and Science. University of Chicago Press, Chicago (1995)
10. Schatzki, T.R., Knorr-Cetina, K., von Savigny, E. (eds.): The Practice Turn in Contemporary Theory. Routledge, London (2001)
11. Orlikowski, W.J.: Sociomaterial Practices: Exploring Technology at Work. Organization Studies 28(9), 1435–1448 (2007)
12. Orlikowski, W.J., Scott, S.V.: Sociomateriality: Challenging the Separation of Technology, Work and Organization. Academy of Management Annals 2, 433–474 (2008)
13. De Vaujany, F., Mitev, N. (eds.): Materiality and Space: Organizations, Artefacts and Practices. Palgrave Macmillan, Basingstoke (2013)

14. Leonardi, P.M., Nardi, B.A., Kallinikos, J. (eds.): Materiality and Organizing: Social Interaction in a Technological World. Oxford University Press, Oxford (2012)
15. Doolin, B., McLeod, L.: Sociomateriality and Boundary Objects in Information Systems Development. European Journal of Information Systems 21, 570–586 (2012)
16. Wagner, E.L., Newell, S., Piccoli, G.: Understanding Project Survival in an ES Environment: A Sociomaterial Practice Perspective. Journal of the Association for Information Systems 11(5), 276–297 (2010)
17. Volkoff, O., Strong, D.M.: Critical Realism and Affordances: Theorizing IT-Associated Organizational Change Processes. MIS Quarterly 37, 819–834 (2013)

Adopt, Adapt, Enact or Use?

A Framework and Methodology for Extracting and Integrating Conceptual Mechanisms of IT Adoption and Use

Jens Lauterbach[1] and Benjamin Mueller[2]

[1] University of Mannheim, Chair of Information Systems IV, 68131 Mannheim, Germany
`lauterbach@es.uni-mannheim.de`
[2] University of Groningen, Innovation Management & Strategy Department,
9747 AE Groningen, The Netherlands
`b.mueller@rug.nl`

Abstract. Information Systems (IS) are omnipresent in today's organizations. While much research has been performed on adoption, implementation, and use of IS, still many practitioners are faced with IS change endeavors in organizations that equal "death march" projects and fail before or directly after go-live. Research with a positivist stance has thoroughly studied factors that describe individuals' intentions to adopt or use technology, while largely ignoring social and organizational contexts. Researchers with a constructivist view, on the other hand, have studied how social processes and structures change or emerge in the light of the new IS. We suggest that there is a need to combine what we know from these two streams in an attempt to clarify terminological bafflement that seems to be caused by the different philosophical stances. Our paper contributes by suggesting a framework and methodology for collecting and reassembling scattered conceptual pieces of organizational and individual IT adoption and integrating them into a coherent understanding.

Keywords: IT adoption, information systems, change projects, IT use process, adaptation processes, business value, mechanisms, positivist stance, constructivist stance.

1   Introduction

Information technology (IT) and Information Systems (IS) are omnipresent and indispensable in today's world. Implementation of IS in organizations, such as ERP or CRM, promises a myriad of benefits in terms of standardization of technology-enabled value chains, creation of new business capabilities, efficiency gains, and increased productivity [1, 2]. Many change projects [3] that deal with the implementation of these Enterprise Systems (ES)[1] and the complementary adjustments to the organization [4] and its work systems [5], however, never realize the intended benefits. As a

---

[1] In our paper, we address utilitarian IT and even if not explicitly mentioned in later parts of the paper our understanding fits very well to ES due their complexity, impact and importance for organizations.

B. Doolin et al. (Eds.): IS&O 2014, IFIP AICT 446, pp. 8–29, 2014.

consequence, practitioners, such as managers or sponsors of these change endeavors, often find themselves in "death march" projects [6] that already fail to deliver prior to go-live [7–9]. Even if project management can claim success of releasing the new technology in time, scope, and budget, the chance to realize intended benefits often dies slowly after go-live; for example, due to organizational or individual resistance to adopt the new technology [10–12] or unintended use by some of the system's most important key users [13].

Thus, change projects for the introduction of new systems not only require managers' skills with regard to implementation, project, and change management to deliver expected project results. Their awareness and understanding of individuals' adoption, their responses to the new technology [14], and the emergence of actual IT use processes and dynamic patterns [15] seems equally important. Consequently, it has been suggested that these mechanisms play a vital role in the creation of organizational level benefits [15] or business value [16, 17]. Thus, understanding them is another step towards a better management of technology-related change projects that goes beyond traditional approaches and helps to fully leverage the potential of new technology to add real business value.

By looking at the extant literature, we identified two major streams that rely on a positivist or constructivist paradigm respectively. Both provide deep insights into understanding the phenomenon of technology adoption and use, but have also produced their own idiosyncratic terminology and concepts. Our goal is to reconcile these two camps by suggesting a way of how to resolve their conceptual tension. We argue that both streams do not provide two alternative views, but complementary perspectives on studying adoption and use and respective outcomes of IS in organizations.

With this paper, we want to contribute to building a shared conceptual and terminological foundation for complementing the "traditional" research on technology adoption and use. This can serve as a basis for further empirical investigations.

Our contribution will be to suggest a way of how concepts and terminology can be aligned on a common baseline and to provide an initial synthesis and discussion of our observations and knowledge from the positivist and constructivist paradigms. However, it seems important to highlight that this is a conceptual paper in which we propose a framework, methodology, and initial synthesis of terms and their understanding prevalent in the extant literature. As such, the paper is mainly focused on conceptual reasoning to help piece together the fragmented mosaic of technology adoption and use and advance our understanding (much like, e.g., Ramiller [18]). Others found that such an analysis is warranted as long as the results are dependable and consistent [19]. We suggest that it can inform future empirical research to fill the white spots on the research landscape of one of the most important research streams in the IS field [20].

The remainder of this paper is structured into four sections: The second section motivates the importance of IT adoption and use in the context of creating beneficial outcomes or value for organizations. It then gives a brief historical background on the two major IS research streams of IT adoption research, building on a positivist or constructivist stance respectively. Based on this knowledge, in section three, we suggest a methodology of how to synthesize and align our understanding on IT adoption and use. We then apply the methodology in two iterations by developing and refining an initial process-theoretical framework that incorporates processes, and mechanisms of organizational and individual IT adoption. In section four we conclude with a short summary and discussion of our limitations and contribution.

2   Related Work

2.1   Why Study Adoption and Use of Technology in Organizations?

Probably the most important reason why organizations decide to adopt IT in the first place and create "living" IS [21] is to gain benefits that help them sustain or achieve competitive advantage in their markets. However, many of them seem to struggle in this attempt: Many large change projects that deal with IS implementations have proven to be troublesome and have even led to high losses for the respective organizations [7–9, 22].

Soh and Markus [16] propose a process model that suggests a synthesis of how competitive advantage respectively business value is created from the adoption of IS. Soh and Markus' model shows "how, when, and why IT investment is converted to favorable organizational performance" [16, p. 39]. As an overall outcome, they argue that performance can only emerge if IT supports the business in the *competitive process* in the market. To do so, a company's business units need to be able to create IT impacts, that is, products and services in which IT is meaningfully embodied in a way that makes a difference in the market. This, in turn, is enabled by an appropriate *use process* of IT assets provided to the business units by the IT department. Finally, providing such assets is a result of the *conversion process* in which the IT department converts IT expenditure into assets. Only if a company exhibits the complete process embodying the conversion, use, and competitive processes will it be able to capture value from its IT expenditure [16]. In this model, the importance of time in the different processes and that intermediary results like IT assets are necessary in order to generate performance are major elements or ingredients of Soh and Markus' "recipe" that added explanatory power above and beyond existing models.

For our work, the model's explicit account of the use process as the central stage and necessary condition within the value creation sequence between the IT investment and the organizational performance is important. Since the introduction of the model, actual usage has been described as the "missing link" in the creation of beneficial outcomes for organizations [23].

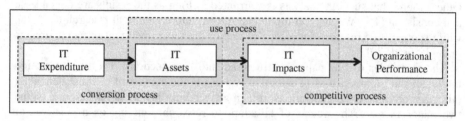

Fig. 1. IT business value process model [16]

The importance of the use process has made research on use of IT one of the most intensively studied areas in the IS field [20]. To that end, research dealing with the organizations' and individuals' decision to adopt [24] and use IT in organizations has been focused to two main research streams that have each intensified and detailed what we know about adoption and use. Empirical research on individual adoption – such as technology acceptance [25–27] or IS success [28, 29] – has shed light on individuals' intentions to adopt and use technology and its presumed individual and organizational outcomes [30]. Many studies in this area, most of which followed a positivist stance, have provided valuable and rich insights. Research has dealt with and conceptualized usage differently, for example IS success, IS acceptance, IS implementation, and IS for decision-making [8, 31]. Empirical studies in the tradition of IS success [29, 32], for example, specifically deal with the relationship between individuals' beliefs, intention to use or actual usage, and net benefits. Here, usage is treated as an independent or mediating variable leading to downstream impacts [31].

However, others suggest that studies in this "traditional" and "static" line of adoption research also have limitations. For example, the examination of the IT usage construct as snapshots of discrete elements [15] with predominantly variance-theoretical and quantitative methods only gives limited attention to the organizational context or the dynamics and emergent nature of technology adoption and its influence on the creation of organizational benefits [e.g., 8, 16, 33–36]. This suggests being particularly difficult when we look at change projects that necessarily take place within complex organizational contexts and are spread across time. As a response, researchers with a constructivist view – in a stream that we call "IT-induced organizational change" – rather understand technology as part of a complex process through which organizing is accomplished by focusing on dynamic interactions between technology and people over time [37]. They study the emergence of technology adoption with qualitative methods as a stream of social action in which people interact and respond to a technology's affordances and constraints [e.g., 4, 38]. But, in the attempt to overcome technological determinism, constructivist research is criticized for not sufficiently conceptualizing technology and for not differentiating between technologies [4]. This suggests being particularly difficult, when we want to understand the adoption and use of complex technologies such as ES. However, both these streams also seem limited to the view and terminology of their respective philosophical paradigm. Even though, this has produced in-depth and valuable insights, it has left us (e.g., researchers dealing with questions of value creation and practitioners in change projects) with no common guideline for identifying and performing empirical research as well as practical work. In order to help overcome this divide, the following two sections shortly discuss the historical evolution and basic paradigms of these streams on adoption and use of technology. This then serves as a basis for proposing an analytical synthesis of the two streams and the suggestion and example of how to build a common understanding necessary to conduct future work in research and practice.

2.2   Evolution of the Positivist Paradigm

Work in this stream looks back at about four decades of research. Lucas et al. [30] describe this research stream as mainly focused on "implementation, innovation, and related themes." Table 1 provides a brief overview of this theme's historical evolution. For more thorough discussions, we point to Lucas et al. [30], Gallivan [24], Fichman [39], or Orlikowski [37] as well as the respective exemplary sources listed in Table 1.

Table 1. Historical development of positivist paradigm

Research Theme	Timeframe	Exemplary References
IT/IS implementation success and failures	early 1970s through 1980s	Lucas [40], Zmud and Cox [41], Swanson [42]
Innovation and its diffusion in the IT context	1980s	Rogers [43, 44], Kwon and Zmud [45]
Individual adoption, acceptance and usage of technology (IT innovations)	late 1980s through early 1990s	Ajzen and Fishbein [46], Davis [25], Delone and McLean [28], Goodhue and Thomson [32]
IT innovation diffusion and infusion	1990s	Cooper and Zmud [47], Zmud and Apple [48], Swanson [49], Kambil et al. [50]
Assimilation of IT innovations	mid 1990s through mid 2000s	Prescott and Conger [51], Fichman [52], Fichman [39], Gallivan [24]
Responses to (disruptive) IT innovations and richer conceptualizations of usage behavior	since early 2000s	Jasperson et al. [20], Beaudry and Pinsonneault [14], Hsieh and Wang [53], Elie-Dit-Cosaque and Straub [54], Hsieh and Rai [55], Sykes et al. [56]

Research on IT implementation in the early 1970s dealt with problems that organizations face when introducing and implementing new IT and how they might be handled [30]. In a sense, the implementation process was seen as a bridge between design and utilization of a system. Until the early 1990s, many popular models were developed based on this work that addressed the issues of adoption, diffusion, or infusion of IT with structural and stage models on the individual or organizational level [45, 47]. Organizational research mainly focused on stage models [e.g., 51] as sub-type of process research models [24]. Rogers defined the first five-stage-model of innovation adoption and implementation in organizations, trying to unify the hitherto fragmented views. Other stage models of information technology innovation and diffusion followed in this line of research [e.g., 47, 57].

At the end of the 1980s, research on individual IT adoption and use started to be centered on theories and applications of theories from socio-psychological models to the IT context [58]. Among these are the theory of reasoned action [46], the diffusion of innovation theory2 [43, 44], the theory of planned behavior [59], the technology acceptance model [25], and task-technology-fit [32]. These models vary in their con-

---

[2] Rogers' (1995) five-stage model of innovation differs from his model of individual adoption, the stages here are: knowledge, persuasion, decision, implementation, and confirmation.

ceptual structures, constructs, and relationships. However, they all address the usage of technology [58]. What these models have in common is that they limit their view on predictors of individuals' beliefs and intentions to adopt and use an IT innovation.

Starting from the 1990s, we saw further diversification of research on innovation in the IT context that developed typologies for IT innovations [e.g., 49] and complemented concepts of diffusion with infusion, finally merging it under the umbrella of assimilation research. Important goals were to understand concepts of IT innovativeness and organizational learning processes and how the depth and breadth of organizations' use of technology alters processes, structures, and organizational culture [52, 60]. Also attempts were made to create integrated models of individual and organizational adoption processes [24].

In the 2000s, research on adoption and use of technology in the positivist stream has become even more diverse with the intention to overcome early issues such as the lack of sufficiently rich technological, institutional, and historical conceptualizations and contexts. Working with and in real organizations, organizational level studies further analyzed the breadth and depth of IT innovation adoption. These were extended by mixed-level analyses as well as by context-rich and multiple methods [30]. This acknowledged that research ought to fully address the wide range of impacts of IT on multiple, complementary levels of analysis across individuals, organizations, and industries with the goal to better describe and explain IT-induced transformations [30]. In this line, criticism has been raised regarding the use of measures limited to behavioral intentions, self-reported use, and a lack of considering organizational dynamics [34]. Arguments have been made that usage as a construct is still rather weakly conceptualized and operationalized [61]. Others claim that usage is a behavior, appropriate for inclusion in a process model but not in a causal model, implicating that usage must precede impacts and benefits [62]. More recent research suggests that the traditional methodological focus on variance theoretical models, quantitative measures, and single levels of analysis [8, 16, 33] only shows one side of the coin. Dealing with the topic in a "greater IT Use leads to greater IT impacts" fashion seems not sufficient [16] and "increased use quantity does not necessarily imply increased individual or organizational benefit" [8, p. 1].

Thus, the "growing complexity of today's organizational IS has resulted in greater user discretion over how – as opposed to whether or how often – an IS is used" [8, p. 1]. Actions, choices, and cognitions of individuals are important elements of the use process [20, 55, 63]. Beyond the rather deterministic and static conceptualization of the relationship between intention to use, usage, and benefits, there is a growing awareness that organizational and individual dynamics (i.e., changes over time) need researchers' attention. It has been suggested that understanding these dynamics can help to further open the "black box of use" [14, 54, 64].

Despite these recent developments in this research stream, the underlying research paradigm can be summarized as depicted in Figure 2. Researchers largely assume that, given certain conditions, whenever X (independent variable) occurs, Y (dependent variable) will follow [65]. That is, quantities of facilitating and inhibiting factors will influence quantities of adoption (identified through joint variation), implementation and use, which in turn will determine quantities of certain outcomes [39]. This understanding is complemented by the idea that respective factors and outcomes can be examined for distinct stages of adoption and use. This empiricist stance is perhaps the dominant form of research in the positivist stream. It leads to studies that primarily focus on observation and measurement, classification, experiment, and statistical analysis. The results of such studies are intended to confirm or falsify pre-specified hypotheses about an objectively observable, independent reality [66].

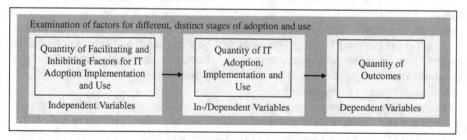

Fig. 2. Positivist research paradigm

2.3   Evolution of the Constructivist Paradigm

Comprehensive summaries of this research stream have just recently been provided by Leonardi and Barley [4] or Orlikowski and Scott [37]. They argue that researchers studying adoption and use of technology with this stance "generally hold that organizational change emerges from an ongoing stream of social action in which people respond to a technology's constraints and affordances, as well as to each other" [4, p. 1]. Table 2 provides a brief historical overview.

Table 2. Historical development of constructivist paradigm

Research Theme	Timeframe	Exemplary References
"Overcoming" technological determinism	Late 1980s or early 1990s	Barley [68], Orlikowski and Gash [69], Markus [70]
Structures embedded in technology shape social processes	Early 1990s	Poole and DeSanctis [71], DeSanctis and Poole [36], Orlikowski [72]
Technologies in practice and enactment and alignment shape social processes and orders	Mid 1990s till mid 2000s	Orlikowski [73], Boudreau and Robey [74]
Sociomateriality and inseparability of the material and social	Since mid 2000s	Orlikowski and Scott [37], Wagner and Newell [75], Ramiller [18]
Critical realist perspective	Late 2000s, early 2010s	Volkoff et al. [76], Mutch [77], Wynn and Williams [78]

Much of the constructivist research tradition we look at today is rooted in criticism towards early positivist studies. As these were often criticized for a techno-determinist view [79], early contributions following a constructivist paradigm aimed at overcoming the one-sided influence of technology on organizations and rather tried to understand organizational change as something that emerges from an ongoing stream of social action [e.g., 68].

Once foundations were laid out, research in this stream started to turn towards the structural properties of technologies and how they interact with established organizational structures. Thus, research posited that structure can be embedded or embodied in technology and individuals such as designers or managers define and shape these structures. Users in turn are influenced by these structures in their actions. Therefore, "once complete, the technology presents an array of social structures for use [...]" that as they are brought into interaction are instantiated in social life [36]. These interactions are defined as appropriations of the technology, that is, "immediate, visible actions that evidence deeper structuration processes" [36, p. 128]. Organizational change, in turn, emerges from social structuring processes that are formed by actors' appropriations of structures embedded in technology.

As a response, a contrasting stream of research soon highlighted that organizational change emerges from social structuring processes in which actors produce, reproduce, and change structures through ongoing situated action (recursive relationship between action and structure as in practice theory). This turn towards practices argued against structures embedded in technology and highlighted that what people do and what their doing so does matters most in our analysis of how technology shapes organizations. For example, Orlikowski [73] theorizes and proposes empirical examples for the introduction of Notes mail technology to different organizations where structuring processes (i.e., specific sets of rules and resources) are enacted in practice and serve to guide future technology use. Structures as "technologies-in-practice" then are integrated in other structures, relevant for guiding individuals' action in the organizational context [73].

However, this understanding seems limited in conceptualizing technology [cf., 4]. More recently, then, the literature started turning towards sociomateriality in an attempt to equally emphasize both technology and structure. It assumes the existence of both material and human agency and suggests that they are interwoven in a way that one cannot exist without the other. They are "constitutively entangled in everyday life" [37, p. 1437], indicating that they only emerge and exist in relation to a practice they are both mangled into or imbricated with. While working with a sociomaterial ontology still seems challenging for many authors [79], the field has seen a number studies in this area. For example, Wagner and Newell [75] study how technological change leads to the need to renegotiate stable work practices across communities of practice. Introna and Hayes [80] or Lewis and Mathiassen [81] are other examples of how a sociomaterial stance is used to inform the study of IT-induced organizational change. They all highlight that, in addition to studying social processes, researchers need to pay attention to what a technology lets users do, what it does not let them do, and the workarounds they develop.

Complementary to sociomateriality, more and more attention seems to be dedicated to the potential role of critical realism. Both special sections in journals (e.g., *Information and Organization*'s January issue in 2013) as well as conference workshops (AIS SIG-Philosophy workshop at ICIS 2013) are currently promoting the debate on the role of this stream of research for studies of technology adoption and use. In it, IT-induced organizational change is described by separation of structure and agency where pre-existing structures enable and constrain agency in social interaction to create new or reinforced structures. Despite its recency, this stream has already produced a number of interesting studies that illustrate its tenets [e.g., 76].

The above illustrates that the constructivist research stream has been equally active and prominent in studying adoption and use of IT. For a more elaborate discussion, we point to the articles mentioned in the introduction of this section. Summarizing the above, and to provide context for the analysis of the various concepts that emerge from the constructivist stream of research, Figure 3 depicts our understanding.

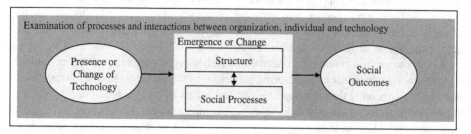

Fig. 3. Constructivist research paradigm

3 Synthesis – Towards a Common Understanding

The summaries of research in the positivist and constructivist paradigms mainly provide the historical context and a rough overview of the evolution of our understanding of the key phenomenon of IT adoption and use. Building on this foundation, we now turn towards our suggestion of how to reconcile the various terms that have been proposed across these two streams. In doing so, we first suggest a methodology and based on it develop a process-theoretical framework. We then show further examples of how to apply the methodology to iteratively refine the framework. Although we do not want to emphasize the philosophical discussion here, we admit our subjectivity while applying our methodology; however, we assume that the mechanisms we extract with it are part of an objective reality. This suggests closeness to the epistemological and ontological views of critical realism [77].

3.1 Foundations and Methodology for a Conceptual Synthesis

As indicated above, we suggest that the process model of how IT creates business value introduced by Soh and Markus [16] provides us with an important frame for our proposed analysis and synthesis. As suggested before it can serve as an overall motivation and frame i.e. a "true north" for the study of adoption and use of IT. Following this orientation, all the various terms the literature uses to describe adoption and use of technology should be analyzed in terms of their contribution to the creation of benefits or value for the organization. In this sense, our analysis aims at understanding how these terms relate to one another as necessary antecedents or preconditions for the overall emergence of benefits, such as competitive advantage, in the context of adopting and using IS in an organization. Following this assumption, our primary interest is in understanding the mechanisms of adoption and use (across both philosophical paradigms) that antecede beneficial outcomes or value, and how they relate to and build upon each other.

This understanding suggests that a process-theoretical stance lends itself as a basis for an integration of the various terms. For this, we see two main reasons. First, as indicated above, we are interested in fundamental mechanisms of adoption and use and their relations and suggest that business value as ultimate outcome (necessary but not sufficient) to be the adequate framework for studying them. This conceptual structure is an inherent property of process theories [82]. Second, our key focus is to better understand the conceptual and particularly temporal sequence of these mechanisms. Their focus on time, in turn, is a property of process theories that makes them a suitable lens for our work [83]. These meta-theoretical aspects [in the sense of 83] are complemented by the fact that we build on the model proposed by Soh and Markus [16] since their work also follows a process-theoretical stance.

While process theories are well defined and established in the IS literature [65, 83], we draw on Machamer [85] for a definition of mechanisms. Thus, mechanisms "are sought to explain how a phenomenon comes about or how some significant process works[; that is, they] are entities and activities organized such that they are productive of regular changes from start or set-up to finish or termination conditions" [85, p. 2]. Mechanisms are needed in many fields of science such as molecular biology to give satisfactory explanations of what holds the world together in its core.

Mechanisms are thus concepts that serve the purpose of explaining the reasons why a phenomenon emerges [66]. According to the definition they can be characterized by *ending/termination conditions or outcomes*, *activities*, that are performed by *entities* (such as the individual or groups or the organization or individuals' cognitions) and a *starting point or starting conditions* [85, p. 2].

With this conceptual foundation, we suggest that it is possible to go through the literature and build a conceptual map in which terms (i.e., mechanisms) can be put in relation to one another. This can be done based on the four characterizing questions for a mechanism depicted in Figure 4 that we derived from the definition of mechanisms suggested by Machamer [85].

This enables us to put concepts on a common ground and relate them to another, more specifically (1) some of the terms that are conceptually close enough can be blended into one overarching term and (2) or concepts can be mapped to each other in terms of their temporal or hierarchical (organizational vs. individual) sequence. This corresponds to our basic process-theoretical stance reported in this paper and allows for arrangement of mechanisms into phases/processes that have similar mechanisms within, and distinct mechanisms across. The methodology we are suggesting is iterative, thus, the resulting conceptual map is in flux, and might have to be revised as new concept is identified. This also applies to the framework that we present in the next paragraph which can be seen as a first step towards conceptual alignment.

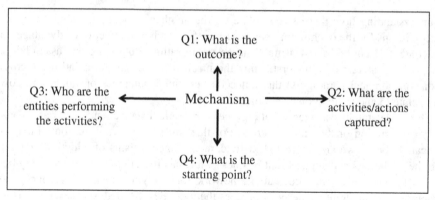

Fig. 4. Questions for characterizing mechanisms

For exemplifying our methodology and deriving our framework, we started a literature analysis with seminal papers and reviews in each of the research streams (such as, e.g., the JAIS 2007 special issue on TAM or the reviews by Orlikowski and Scott [37] and Leonardi and Barley [4]. Then we performed a backward and forward search based on the papers' references. We complemented this by selective database searches via Google Scholar. The mechanisms extracted in a thorough and careful analysis through selective coding [86] from each of the resultant papers were documented in an excel file. We then reviewed and discussed the descriptions and definitions and went back and forth between the original papers and our understanding of their terminology to produce an account of the mechanisms. Since the purpose of this paper is not to show a comprehensive account, but to demonstrate the ability of our approach to foster conceptual alignment, we will only provide and discuss an excerpt of the total mechanisms we extracted.[3]

3.2   Towards a Comprehensive Process-Theoretical Framework

To exemplify the suggested methodology in the last section, we derived a preliminary process-theoretical framework depicted in Figure 5 that we explain in the following. Processes in the framework are high-level representations of the mechanism concept (in italic in the following) that we have introduced above.

Using the model provided by Soh and Markus [16] as a starting point, we can assume that increased organizational performance leading to a competitive advantage for an organization is created in the *competitive process* that builds on impacts that are created in the IT use process. The *use process* involves all actions of individuals in an organization that deal with using and changing the technology or the respective work system to realize the intended impacts and business value. With work system, we refer to the organizational context in which individuals perform their work [20].

---

[3] A table containing a more comprehensive account of mechanisms, their definitions, and a mapping to our preliminary framework can be provided by the authors on request. Taken altogether, our review identified 92 mechanisms across the positivist and constructivist stream.

The use process as such has no defined end. However, it can be assumed that when we turn to the individual level of IT adoption, users need to appropriately use the technology [16]. In this structuring process of appropriations [36, 72] starting with what is often called *initial usage*, users, when they decide for *continued usage* [53, 87], run through several stages of individual *usage* (we used usage here to differentiate individuals' use from the organizational level use), ending with what is often called extension, a behavior where users explore and apply more of the technology's features in order to be able to handle a more comprehensive set of work tasks [88]. *Extension* occurs when users have already reached a stage of *infusion*, which is commonly defined as the IT application being deeply and comprehensively embedded within an individual's (or organization's) work system [60]. Infusion has *routinization* as a prerequisite, where the IT use is no longer perceived as out-of-ordinary but becomes part of an individual's behavioral routine [88]. All these individual level mechanisms are often referred to as *post-adoptive behavior* [20].

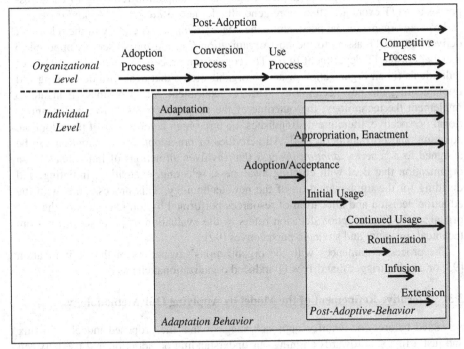

Fig. 5. Process framework of IT adoption and use

Before any of these mechanisms can commence, prospective users first need to make an *adoption* decision on whether they will use the new technology or not. The decision can be in the context of a mandatory *adoption* (e.g., ES adoption), where the organization forces the individual to use the technology, or it can be voluntary (e.g., use of an Enterprise Wiki). This decision is made some time after the adoption decision [20] of the organization in or latest at the end of the *conversion process* when the technology is released or rolled out to the organization and its users. Variations of technology *acceptance* cf. [cf., 89] have dealt with the *cognitive processes* (e.g., resulting in cognitions regarding a technology's usefulness and ease of use) associated with individuals' pre-adoption activities and the adoption decision.

We found some concepts in the literature for the individual level that start before actual adoption and acceptance of the individual takes place. For example user resistance [90]: it is often argued that resistance takes place during the use process, when users start interacting with the technology. However, we can also think of cases in which prospective users already resisted the technology by not supporting the respective implementation endeavors (e.g., lack of support for requirements analysis in the conversion process). Another example are coping mechanisms that users employ to handle the consequences of a technology event. Coping deals with acts that individuals perform in response to disruptive events that occur in their environment. These cognitive or behavioral efforts can already start before the technology has been delivered to the individual user [14]. To account for these concepts, we added the mechanism *adaptation* to our model. Concepts of adaptation referring to users responses to an IT event are often more generally defined as *adaptation behavior* [91].

From an organizational perspective the *conversion process* ends with the release or delivery of the IT assets to the host organization (i.e., business users as opposed to members of the IT department [49]). The conversion process involves all activities of individuals (in an organization or across organizations) that deal with developing and implementing the new technology. The IT department gets a business mandate to implement the technology; the outcome of the adoption process. From an organizational perspective, literature distinguishes the three-high level phases of pre-adoption, adoption, and post-adoption [92]. All activities of pre-adoption and adoption can be assigned to a generic *adoption process* that involves all actions of individuals in an organization that deal with creating awareness, selecting, evaluating, initiating, and deciding for the implementation of the new technology. This process ends with the adoption decision and allocation of resources performed by top managers of the host organization. The adoption decision refers to the evaluation of proposed ideas from technical, financial and strategic perspectives [92].

The process commences with the organizations' awareness of the IT innovation [93] or another trigger that drives IT-induced organizational change.

3.3   Iterative Refinement of the Model by Applying Our Methodology

As stated before, our iterative approach suggests that the proposed model is in flux and just a first step towards aligning our understanding on adoption and use between the two philosophical paradigms. For detailing our preliminary model, we further extracted and analyzed terms of adoption and use from the literature as mechanisms and tried to map them to the initially developed phases and/or refined the model. Due to space restrictions, we focus on a few examples (an explicit application of our methodology to several terms is visible in Table 3) to further show the applicability of our approach. We will focus on concepts that relate to the use process of our initial framework.

After individual users have made their decision to *adopt* respectively *accept*, we find that the positivist research stream applies variations of the usage construct to describe how users employ or change the technology in *actual usage* to perform their work tasks. As opposed to cognitive mechanisms such as intentions to adopt or use a technology, here cognitive or behavioral mechanisms that rather want to capture *initial or continued usage* are important. For *repeated usage* conceptualizing interactions between the technology and the user over time are of essence [58], by describing technology as the independent variable or driving force. Here, researchers with a constructivist stance describe mechanisms such as *patterns of use* where not the technology is the independent variable. Rather the way how a group or individual adapts to a technology is the driving force in the causal effects of technology on human behavior and outcome [71]

We particularly found that the mechanisms that refer to the term *adaptation* in the two streams require explanation. Positivists recently started to use the term *adaptive usage* or *adaptive system use* behaviors to describe individual's behavior to selectively use and extend features offered by the technology [e.g., 94].

Others have also used the term to describe the more generic mechanism of user adaptation that can have several foci for example change the individuals' work system, the technology or the individuals' self – which constructivists refer to as *appropriation* – and from this understanding developed the idea that users can apply different adaptation strategies in response to the technology [14]. Kwon and Zmud [45] used adaptation to describe the process or phase in which an IT application is developed, installed, and maintained (in our model: conversion process).

When researchers with a constructivist view talk about users' adaptations in response to a technology they also describe it as *enactment* to emphasize human actions that create (enact) emergent structures through recurrent interaction with the technology at hand. These structures then guide future use and interaction with the technology in practice. In this structuring process users might come across periods of *resistance* where they try to work around certain functionalities that are then overcome by *accommodations* where individuals deeply deploy the technology in their everyday practice [75]. Then users will be able to use the technology for some parts of their practices up to its full potential (*infusion*) [88]. For other parts of their practices they still or engage in *improvised learning* [74]. Learning might then again lead to *emergent* [24] or *unintended uses* (also *reinventions* or unfaithful appropriations) of technology in workarounds that are *negotiated* as response to technology affordances and constraints [36, 75].

Taken together, these individual efforts in the organizational context, aim at achieving the goal to complete ones work or task with the technology. Research in the positivist stream has lately defined this as *effective use* [99].

Table 3. Examples of extracted and categorized conceptual mechanisms of technology adoption and use

Term/Stream	Starting Conditions	Involved Entities	Activities	Ending Conditions (Outcome)	References
Adoption/Acceptance (*positivist*)	Awareness of the need or opportunity to implement a new technology	Several organizational members/individuals	Activities such as discussions or negotiations of decision makers necessary to come to a decision for or against the implementation of a new technology	Start of implementation activities (conversion process)	Kwon and Zmud [45], Cooper and Zmud [47], Rogers [43, 44]
Enactment (*construct.*)	Acceptance and initial use	Individual in an organization	Interactions of an individual with the technology. These actions are guided by virtual structures that emerge from these interactions	Ongoing until the technology's decommissioning or exit to non-use	Leonardi and Barley [4], Orlikowski and Yates [95], Yates and Orlikowski [96], Orlikowski [73]
Appropriation (*construct.*)	Acceptance and initial use	Individual in an organization	Activities towards deeply incorporating (and using) technology (material affordances and constraints) in an individuals' work practices and behavior at the work place	The technology has been appropriated and use has become routinized or the individual decides for non-use	Poole and DeSanctis [97], Leonardi and Barley [4], DeSanctis and Poole [36], Orlikowski and Yates [98]
Infusion (*positivist*)	The technology has been appropriated and use has become routinized	Individual in an organization	Activities towards using the technology up to its full potential	The individual explores new features and extends his use of the technology or decides for non-use	Hsieh and Zmud [88], Fichman [52]
Emergent Use (*positivist*)	Routinized use	Individual in an organization	Using technology to perform tasks not previously considered possible	Technology's decommissioning or exit to non-use	Gallivan [24], Hsieh and Zmud [88]
Improvised Learning (*construct.*)	Acceptance and initial use	Individual in an organization	Activities towards learning how to use the system that are user-initiated and do not follow method or structure	Routinization of use or reinvention (finding workarounds)	Boudreau and Robey [74]

4   Discussion and Conclusion

As indicated earlier, the paragraphs above only scratch the surface of the discussion and analysis needed to integrate the knowledge from the two philosophical streams. However we wanted to show the need and applicability of our methodology for an integration of positivist and interpretive concepts used in the context of IT adoption and use. Taken altogether, for our review that consisted of two iterations of applying our methodology, we identified more than 90 mechanisms across the positivist and constructivist stream.

The application of our methodology and the resulting conceptual synthesis provides several contributions to research. First and foremost, our approach helps to integrate concepts into a comprehensive nomological net, that at first sight due to their entirely different philosophical foundations seem incommensurable. Here we want to emphasize that we do not attempt to reconcile the philosophical paradigms (which some might find neither possible nor desirable), but suggest a pragmatic approach of how to create a common ground for understanding IT adoption and use, by putting aside the philosophical differences and discussion. Second, we suggest the value creation framework brought forward by Soh and Markus [16] as valuable starting point for analyzing and integrating concepts of IT adoption and use. Third, we borrow the mechanism concept that has been recognized in other scientific disciplines [85] to use it as a meta-theoretical construct for reconciling terminology on IT adoption and use. Fourth, in a first iteration, we provide an initial process-theoretical framework and show in a second iteration how it can be enhanced by applying our methodology that is based on the mechanism concept. In the course of our analysis, we were able to provide a discussion (although limited due to the format of the paper) of concepts and terms on IT adoption and use. This enabled us for example to confirm our initial feeling that there are several concepts or terms used in the context of IT adoption and use (used relatively synonymously, e.g. emergent use and reinvention) to describe similar mechanisms or the same terms are used to describe completely different mechanisms (homonyms, e.g. adaptation as implementing the technology or as changes in individuals' behavior).

In sum, we were motivated by the terminological heterogeneity in the field that often troubled us in our ongoing research work in the context of IS implementation projects in several organizations. So, we tried to start building a common understanding across the two major streams of IT adoption and use that rely on a positivist and constructivist research paradigm respectively. As a frame we suggest the value creation process and the meta-theoretical construct of mechanism for integrating concepts of IT adoption and use.

We are aware that the rather conceptual and methodological nature of our paper deserves discussion. We propose a synthesis of terms and their understanding prevalent in the extant literature and are thus limited to conceptual reasoning. Therefore, we tried to thoroughly build our arguments and construct a solid understanding and history of the extant literature. We were committed to guide the reader through our own sensemaking process and tried to argue and convince why our analysis and synthesis are warranted. However, this paper is only able to provide a snapshot of our complete analysis, understanding, and results. Thus, we focused on showing the suitability and initial results stemming from the application of our suggested methodology.

Keeping these limitations in mind, we provide a contribution by starting a discussion on aligning our understanding on one of the critical phenomena of IS research. We developed a process-theoretical methodology and "meta model" of technology adoption and use in organizations and started to integrate scattered conceptual pieces and terms. Of course, the results we present might be interpreted quite differently by researchers from the paradigms we tapped into. This effect might even be compounded by the rising interest in other paradigms such as realist or pragmatist ones. Nonetheless, we believe that this analysis is not only warranted, but needed, and can be the starting point for future empirical work that, besides all philosophical differences and discussions, can focus on the core phenomenon: What do individuals in organizations actually (need to) do (when and how) to create value when adopting and using IS?

References

1. Brynjolfsson, E., Hitt, L.: Beyond Computation: Information Technology, Organizational Transformation and Business Performance. Journal of Economic Perspectives 14, 23–48 (2000)
2. Shang, S., Seddon, P.B.: Assessing and Managing the Benefits of Enterprise Systems: The Business Manager's Perspective. Information Systems Journal 12, 271–299 (2002)
3. Andersen, E.S.: Toward a Project Management Theory for Renewal Projects. Project Management Journal 37, 15–31 (2006)
4. Leonardi, P., Barley, S.: What's Under Construction Here? Social Action, Materiality and Power in Constructivist Studies of Technology and Organizing. Academy of Management Annals 4(1), 1–51 (2010)
5. Alter, S.: Work System Theory: Overview of Core Concepts, Extensions, and Challenges for the Future. Journal of the Association for Information Systems 14, 72–121 (2012)
6. Yourdon, E.: Death March. Prentice Hall Professional, New Jersey, NJ (2004)
7. Krotov, V., Ives, B.: ERP Implementation Gone Terribly Wrong: The Case of Natural Springs. Communications of the Association for Information Systems 28, 277–282 (2011)
8. Fadel, K.: User Adaptation and Infusion of Information Systems. Journal of Computer Information Systems 52, 1–10 (2012)
9. Bulkeley, W.M.: Technology (A Special Report): Working Together – When Things Go Wrong: FoxMeyer Drug Took a Huge High-Tech Gamble; It Didn't Work. Wall Street Journal, Eastern edn., R25 (November 18, 1996)
10. Burkhardt, M.E., Brass, D.J.: Changing Patterns or Patterns of Change: The Effects of a Change in Technology on Social Network Structure and Power. Administrative Science Quarterly 35, 104–127 (1990)
11. Johnston, W., Zablah, A., Bellenger, D.: Customer Relationship Management Implementation Gaps. Journal of Personal Selling and Sales Management 14, 279–295 (2005)
12. Wen, C., Remus, U., Mills, A.: Understanding and Addressing User Resistance to IS Implementation in a Lean Context. In: ECIS 2011 Proceedings, Paper 171 (2011), http://aisel.aisnet.org/ecis2011/171

13. Bartis, E., Mitev, N.: A Multiple Narrative Approach to Information Systems Failure: A Successful System That Failed. European Journal of Information Systems 17, 112–124 (2008)
14. Beaudry, A., Pinsonneault, A.: Understanding User Responses to Information Technology: A Coping Model of User Adaptation. MIS Quarterly 29, 493–524 (2005)
15. Nan, N.: Capturing Bottom-Up Information Technology Use Processes: A Complex Adaptive Systems Model. MIS Quarterly 35, 505–532 (2011)
16. Soh, C., Markus, M.L.: How IT Creates Business Value: A Process Theory Synthesis. In: ICIS 1995 Proceedings, Paper 4 (1995), http://aisel.aisnet.org/icis1995/4
17. Devaraj, S., Kohli, R.: Performance Impacts Of Information Technology: Is Actual Usage The Missing Link? Management Science 49, 273–289 (2003)
18. Ramiller, N.C.: Reconsidering Resistance in the Post-Human Era. In: Proceedings of the 19th Americas Conference on Information Systems, Chicago (2013), http://aisel.aisnet.org/amcis2013/ISPhilosophy/GeneralPresen tations/3/
19. Lincoln, Y.S., Guba, E.G.: Naturalistic Inquiry. Sage, New York (1985)
20. Jasperson, J., Carter, P., Zmud, R.: A Comprehensive Conceptualization of Post-Adoptive Behaviors Associated With Information Technology Enabled Work Systems. MIS Quarterly 29, 525–557 (2005)
21. Paul, R.J.: Challenges to Information Systems: Time to Change. European Journal of Information Systems 16, 193–195 (2007)
22. Devadoss, P., Pan, S.: Enterprise Systems Use: Towards a Structurational Analysis of Enterprise Systems Induced Organizational Transformation. Communications of the Association for Information Systems 19, 351–385 (2007)
23. Kohli, R., Devaraj, S.: Measuring Information Technology Payoff: A Meta-Analysis of Structural Variables in Firm-Level Empirical Research. Information Systems Research 14, 127–145 (2003)
24. Gallivan, M.: Organizational Adoption and Assimilation of Complex Technological Innovations: Development and Application of A New Framework. Database for Advances in Information Systems 32, 51–85 (2001)
25. Davis, F.D.F.: Perceived Usefulness, Perceived Ease of Use, and User Acceptance of Information Technology. MIS Quarterly 13, 319–340 (1989)
26. Venkatesh, V., Davis, F.D.: A theoretical extension of the technology acceptance model: Four longitudinal field studies. Managemenet Science 46, 186–204 (2000)
27. Venkatesh, V., Bala, H.: Technology Acceptance Model 3 and a Research Agenda on Interventions. Decision Sciences 39, 273–315 (2008)
28. DeLone, W., McLean, E.: Information Systems Success: The Quest for the Dependent Variable. Information Systems Research 3, 60–95 (1992)
29. Delone, W.: The DeLone and McLean Model of Information Systems Success: A Ten-Year Update. Journal of Management Information Systems 19, 9–30 (2003)
30. Lucas, H.J., Swanson, E., Zmud, R.: Implementation, Innovation, and Related Themes Over the Years in Information Systems Research. Journal of the Association for Information Systems 8, 206–210 (2007)
31. Burton-Jones, A., Straub, D.W.: Reconceptualizing System Usage: An Approach and Empirical Test. Information Systems Research 17, 228–246 (2006)
32. Goodhue, D., Thompson, R.: Task-Technology Fit and Individual Performance. MIS Quarterly 19, 213–236 (1995)

33. Pare, G., Bourdeau, S., Marsan, J., Nach, H., Shuraida, S.: Re-examining the Causal Structure of Information Technology Impact Research. European Journal of Information Systems 17, 403–416 (2008)
34. Legris, P., Ingham, J., Collerette, P.: Why Do People Use Information Technology? A Critical Review of the Technology Acceptance Model. Information & Management 40, 191–204 (2003)
35. Orlikowski, W.J.: Improvising Organizational Transformation Over Time: A Situated Change Perspective. Information Systems Research 7, 63–92 (1996)
36. DeSanctis, G., Poole, M.: Capturing the Complexity in Advanced Technology Use: Adaptive Structuration Theory. Organization Science 5, 121–147 (1994)
37. Orlikowski, W., Scott, S.: Sociomateriality: Challenging the Separation of Technology, Work and Organization. Academy of Managemenet Annals 2, 433–474 (2008)
38. Orlikowski, W.: CASE Tools as Organizational Change: Investigating Incremental and Radical Changes in Systems Development. MIS Quarterly 17, 309–341 (1993)
39. Fichman, R.: Going Beyond the Dominant Paradigm for Information Technology Innovation Research: Emerging Concepts and Methods. Journal of the Association for Information Systems 5, 314–355 (2004)
40. Lucas, H.C.: Why Information Systems Fail. Columbia University Press, New York (1975)
41. Zmud, R.W., Cox, J.F.: The Implementation Process: A Change Approach. MIS Quarterly 3, 35–43 (1979)
42. Swanson, E.B.: Information System Implementation: Bridging the Gap Between Design and Utilization. Irwin, Homewood (1988)
43. Rogers, E.M.: Diffusion of Innovations, 3rd edn. Free Press, New York (1983)
44. Rogers, E.M.: Diffusion of Innovations, 4th edn. Free Press, New York (1995)
45. Kwon, T.H., Zmud, R.W.: Unifying the Fragmented Models of Information Systems Implementation'. In: Boland, R.J., Hirshheim, R.A. (eds.) Critical Issues in Information Systems Research, pp. 227–251. Wiley, NY (1987)
46. Ajzen, I., Fishbein, M.: Understanding Attitudes and Predicting Social Behaviour. Prentice-Hall, New Jersey (1980)
47. Cooper, R.B., Zmud, R.W.: Information Technology Implementation Research: A Technological Diffusion Approach. Management Science 36, 123–139 (1990)
48. Zmud, R.W., Apple, L.E.: Measuring Technology Incorporation/Infusion. Journal of Product Innovation Management 9, 148–155 (1992)
49. Swanson, E.: Information Systems Innovation Among Organizations. Management Science 40, 1069–1092 (1994)
50. Kambil, A., Kamis, A., Koufaris, M., Lucas Jr, H.C.: Influences on the Corporate Adoption of Web Technology. Communications of the ACM 43(11es), Article 9 (2000)
51. Prescott, M.B., Conger, S.A.: Information Technology Innovations: A Classification by IT Locus of Impact and Research Approach. Database for Advances in Information Systems 26(2/3), 20–41 (1995)
52. Fichman, R.: The Diffusion and Assimilation of Information Technology Innovations. In: Zmud, R.W. (ed.) Framing the Domains of IT Management: Projecting the Future Through the Past, pp. 105–127. Pinnaflex, Cincinatti (2000)
53. Hsieh, J.J.P.-A., Wang, W.: Explaining Employees' Extended Use of Complex Information Systems. European Journal of Information Systems 16, 216–227 (2007)
54. Elie-Dit-Cosaque, C.M., Straub, D.W.: Opening the Black Box of System Usage: User Adaptation to Disruptive IT. European Journal of Information Systems 20, 589–607 (2011)

55. Hsieh, J.J.P.-A., Rai, A., Xu, S.X.: Extracting Business Value from IT: A Sensemaking Perspective of Post-Adoptive Use. Management Science 57, 2018–2039 (2011)
56. Sykes, T., Venkatesh, V., Gosain, S.: Model of Acceptance with Peer Support: A Social Network Perspective to Understand Employees' System Use. MIS Quarterly 33, 371–393 (2009)
57. Saga, V.L., Zmud, R.W.: The Nature and Determinants of IT Acceptance, Routinization, and Infusion. In: Levine, L. (ed.) Diffusion, Transfer and Implementation of Technology, pp. 67–86. Elsevier, Amsterdam (1994)
58. Chin, W.W., Marcolin, B.L.: The Future of Diffusion Research. Database for Advances in Information Systems 32(3), 7–12 (2001)
59. Ajzen, I.: From Intentions to Actions: A Theory of Planned Behavior. In: Kuhl, J., Beckmann, J. (eds.) Action Control From Cognition to Behavior, pp. 11–39. Springer, Berlin (1985)
60. Apple, L., Zmud, R.: Measuring Technology Infusion/Incorporation. Journal of Product Innovation Management 9, 148–155 (1992)
61. Barki, H., Titah, R., Boffo, C.: Information System Use-Related Activity: An Expanded Behavioral Conceptualization of Individual-Level Information System Use. Information Systems Research 18, 173–192 (2007)
62. Seddon, P.: A Respecification and Extension of the DeLone and McLean Model of IS Success. Information Systems Research 8, 240–253 (1997)
63. Jeyaraj, A., Sabherwal, R.: Adoption of Information Systems Innovations by Individuals: A Study of Processes Involving Contextual, Adopter, and Influencer Actions. Information and Organization 18, 205–234 (2008)
64. Lee, H., Sawyer, S.: Conceptualizing Time, Space And Computing for Work and Organizing. Time & Society 19, 293–317 (2010)
65. Langley, A.: Strategies for Theorizing from Process Data. Academy of Management Review 24, 691–710 (1999)
66. Mingers, J.: Real-izing Information Systems: Critical Realism as an Underpinning Philosophy for Information Systems. Information and Organization 14, 87–103 (2004)
67. Van de Ven, A.: Running in Packs to Develop Knowledge-Intensive Technologies. MIS Quarterly 29, 365–378 (2005)
68. Barley, S.: Technology as an Occasion For Structuring: Evidence from Observations of CT Scanners and the Social Order of Radiology Departments. Administrative Science Quarterly 31, 78–108 (1986)
69. Orlikowski, W.J., Gash, D.C.: Technological Frames: Making Sense of Information Technology in Organizations. ACM Transactions on Information Systems 12, 174–207 (1994)
70. Markus, M.L.: Electronic Mail as the Medium of Managerial Choice. Organization Science 5, 502–527 (1994)
71. Poole, M.S., DeSanctis, G.: Use of Group Decision Support Systems as an Appropriation Process. In: Proceedings of the 22nd Hawaii International Conference on System Sciences (HICSS), pp. 149–157. IEEE (1989)
72. Orlikowski, W.J.: The Duality of Technology: Rethinking the Concept of Technology in Organizations. Organization Science 3, 398–427 (1992)
73. Orlikowski, W.: Using Technology and Constituting Structures: A Practice Lens for Studying Technology in Organizations. Organization Science 11, 404–428 (2000)
74. Boudreau, M.-C., Robey, D.: Enacting Integrated Information Technology: A Human Agency Perspective. Organization Science 16, 3–18 (2005)

75. Wagner, E., Newell, S., Piccoli, G.: Understanding Project Survival in an ES Environment: A Sociomaterial Practice Perspective. Journal of the Association for Information Systems 11, 276–297 (2010)
76. Volkoff, O., Strong, D., Elmes, M.: Technological Embeddedness and Organizational Change. Organization Science 18, 832–848 (2007)
77. Mutch, A.: Actors and Networks or Agents and Structures: Towards a Realist View of Information Systems. Organization 9, 477–496 (2002)
78. Wynn, D., Williams, C.: Principles for Conducting Critical Realist Case Study Research in Information Systems. MIS Quarterly 36, 787–810 (2012)
79. Mueller, B., Raeth, P., Faraj, S., Kautz, K.: On the Methodological and Philosophical Challenges of Sociomaterial Theorizing: An Overview of Competing Conceptualizations. In: ICIS 2012 Proceedings (2012), http://aisel.aisnet.org/icis2012/proceedings/Panels/3/
80. Introna, L.D., Hayes, N.: On Sociomaterial Imbrications: What Plagiarism Detection Systems Reveal and Why It Matters. Information and Organization 21, 107–122 (2011)
81. Lewis, M.O., Mathiassen, L., Rai, A.: Scalable Growth in IT-Enabled Service Provisioning: a Sensemaking Perspective. European Journal of Information Systems 20, 285–302 (2011)
82. Mohr, L.B.: Explaining Organizational Behavior: The Limits and Possibilities of Theory and Research. Proquest Info & Learning, San Francisco (1982)
83. Markus, M., Robey, D.: Information Technology and Organizational Change: Causal Structure in Theory and Research. Management Science 34, 583–598 (1988)
84. Mueller, B., Urbach, N.: The Why, What, And How of Theories in IS Research. In: ICIS 2013 Proceedings (2013), http://aisel.aisnet.org/icis2013/proceedings/ResearchMethods/8/
85. Machamer, P., Darden, L., Craver, C.: Thinking About Mechanisms. Philosophy of Science 67, 1–25 (2000)
86. Glaser, B.G., Strauss, A.L.: The Discovery of Grounded Theory: Strategies for Qualitative Research. Transaction Publishers, New Jersey (2008)
87. Bhattacherjee, A.: Understanding Information Systems Continuance: An Expectation-Confirmation Model. MIS Quarterly 25, 351–370 (2001)
88. Hsieh, J.J.P.-A., Zmud, R.: Understanding Post-Adoptive Usage Behaviors: A Two-Dimensional View. DIGIT 2006 Proceedings, Paper 3 (2006), http://aisel.aisnet.org/digit2006/3
89. Bradley, J.: If We Build It They Will Come? The Technology Acceptance Model. In: Dwivedi, Y.K., Wade, M.R., Schneberger, S.L. (eds.) Information Systems Theory: Explaining and Predicting Our Digital Society, vol. 1, pp. 19–36. Springer, New York (2012)
90. Lapointe, L., Rivard, S.: A Multilevel Model of Resistance to Information Technology Implementation. MIS Quarterly 29, 461–491 (2005)
91. Beaudry, A., Pinsonneault, A.: The Other Side of Acceptance: Studying the Direct and Indirect Effects of Emotions on Information Technology Use. MIS Quarterly 34, 689–710 (2010)
92. Damanpour, F., Schneider, M.: Phases of the Adoption of Innovation in Organizations: Effects of Environment, Organization and Top Managers. British Journal of Management 17, 215–236 (2006)
93. Fichman, R.R.G., Kemerer, C.C.F.: The Assimilation of Software Process Innovations: An Organizational Learning Perspective. Management Science 43, 1345–1363 (1997)
94. Sun, H.: Understanding User Revisions When Using Information System Features: Adaptive System Use and Triggers. MIS Quarterly 36, 453–478 (2012)

95. Orlikowski, W., Yates, J.: Shaping Electronic Communication: The Metastructuring of Technology in the Context of Use. Organization Science 6, 423–444 (1995)
96. Yates, J., Orlikowski, W.J., Okamura, K.: Explicit and Implicit Structuring of Genres in Electronic Communication: Reinforcement and Change of Social Interaction. Organization Science 10, 83–103 (1999)
97. Poole, M.S., DeSanctis, G.: Understanding the Use of Group Decision Support Systems: The Theory of Adaptive Structuration. In: Fulk, J., Steinfield, C. (eds.) Organizations and Communication Technology, pp. 173–193. Sage, Thousand Oaks (1990)
98. Orlikowski, W., Yates, J.: Genre Repertoire: The of Structuring Communicative Practices in Organizations. Administrative Science Quarterly 39, 541–574 (1994)
99. Burton-Jones, A., Grange, C.: From Use to Effective Use: A Representation Theory Perspective. Information Systems Research 24, 632–658 (2013)

Reconfiguring Early Childhood Education and Care

A Sociomaterial Analysis of IT Appropriation

Melinda Plumb and Karlheinz Kautz

Faculty of Business, University of Wollongong, Wollongong, Australia
map016@uowmail.edu.au, kautz@uow.edu.au

Abstract. Existing studies of IT within early childhood education and care settings are scant, and those that do exist traditionally utilise a Cartesian worldview where humans and IT are separate self-sufficient entities with properties. In this worldview, change is attributed to either the technological or the human entity, leading to limited, either techno-centric or human-centred accounts of IT implementation and use. We reframe the activities in an early childhood organisation as a process of appropriation, and utilise a sociomaterial theory of technology appropriation alternative to the Cartesian worldview. We contribute a rich account of the changes that occur to the practices, the educators, and the technology itself during the appropriation process and demonstrate the theory's usefulness as an analytical tool for providing a deeper understanding of how early childhood educators appropriate a new technology into their practices in a sociomaterial, non-dualistic way.

Keywords: technology appropriation, early childhood, educators, sociomateriality.

1   Introduction

The number of early childhood education and care organisations who are innovating with information technology (IT) is increasing, with interest and support for IT to be integrated into policy, curriculum and practice [1]. To date there have been few empirical studies on IT in early childhood education and care organisations. Plumb et al. [2] found that the majority of existing research involves descriptive studies of use by the educators with the children and pedagogical benefits of the use of the IT as a teaching and learning tool with young children, interspersed with a few studies examining the acceptance of the IT by children and/or educators. These studies are useful for practitioners, but present a difficulty in that they can be classified as either: human-centred, which minimises the role of the technology and focuses primarily on the human or social side of the relationship; or techno-centric, which assumes the technology performs as intended and exists without historical or cultural contexts, leading to technology determinism [3]. Within the discipline of Information Systems (IS), studies of IT implementation and use traditionally utilise two core concepts: the IT artefact and the user. These studies are grounded in a dualistic worldview where

B. Doolin et al. (Eds.): IS&O 2014, IFIP AICT 446, pp. 30–47, 2014.
© IFIP International Federation for Information Processing 2014

humans and IT exist independently, and IT 'implementation' is a process of discrete stages where various decisions are made. The studies employ theories in a quantitative manner and provide useful information on factors and their contribution to the outcome of technology adoption, but neglect the "often messy process through which teachers struggle to negotiate a foreign and potentially disruptive innovation into their familiar environment" [4, p. 483].

Using a sociomaterial theory of technology appropriation that overcomes the traditional dualistic view, this research aims to understand the appropriation, "the way that users evaluate and adopt, adapt and integrate a technology into their everyday practices" [5, p. 6] of an innovative technology into the practices of an early childhood education and care organisation with particular focus on the changes that occur to the practices, the educators, and the technology itself during the appropriation process.

2 Theoretical Background: Sociomateriality and a Phenomenological Theory of Appropriation

Sociomateriality is an emerging worldview within the IS literature first introduced by Orlikowski [3, 6] together with Scott [7, 8] which reconceptualises the relationship between the social and the material. It rejects the concepts of discrete self-contained entities such as 'people', 'organisations' and 'technology' and instead accepts them as being inherently inseparable. As Orlikowski and Scott explain, it is "a move away from focusing on how technologies influence humans, to examining how materiality is intrinsic to everyday activities and relations" [7, p. 455].

Orlikowski's work has been influential in inspiring other sociomaterial conceptual contributions, such as those by Leonardi [9, 10] and with Barley [11, 12]. In turn, these influential conceptual contributions to sociomateriality have inspired scholars to adopt a sociomaterial perspective in IS/IT-related studies such as mobile IT usage [13], digital and physical visualisation boards in a hospital surgical emergency ward [14] software usability [15], and digital entrepreneurship [16]. The September 2014 special issue of Management Information Systems (MIS) Quarterly *Sociomateriality of Information Systems and Organizing* highlights the current mounting interest in "the relationship between the social and the material, in the context of our increasingly digital society" [17, p. 809], while also noting that debate exists around what constitutes the relational basis for the term sociomateriality [18, 19] although this is viewed as "quite healthy" for an emerging stream of research [17, p. 809].

Orlikowski [6] argues that sociomaterial approaches to studies of IS/IT can overcome the common dualist approach to studying technology and people (what she calls 'ontologies of separateness') and the Cartesian worldview, which is dominant in IS/IT literature and makes the distinction between subjects and objects and between individuals and the external world.

According to Poole and DeSanctis [20, p. 150], the concept of appropriation goes back to the 19th century philosophers Hegel and Marx who were concerned with "how humanity progressively learned to control and shape the natural world and how this, in turn, influenced and changed human society" and where to appropriate an object was "to use it constructively, to incorporate it into one's life, for better or worse" [20, p. 150]. Utilising this perspective in their study of group decision support systems (GDSSs), Poole and DeSanctis note "...GDSSs have no meaning apart from their use. Indeed, it is **use** [author's original emphasis] that makes GDSSs what they are in a given context and gives them reality" [20, p. 150]. Continuing with their work, DeSanctis and Poole [21] introduce the notion of technology appropriation as a time-extended process where mutual adaptation occurs; both the technology and the practices of an individual are changed through the attitudes, behaviours and intended and unintended uses of the technology.

IS/IT studies utilising a view of technology appropriation are often found in the computer supported collaborative work (CSCW) field of IS to understand the ways users give technology meaning and fit it into patterns of their every-day lives [see e.g., Silverstone and Haddon 1996, Dourish 2003, Pipel 2005, Balka and Wagner 2006, Stevens 2009; all cited in 22, p. 408]. In agreement with Poole and DeSanctis, Draxler and Stevens also note that during the appropriation process, "what a thing is depends therefore on how it is used, and how it appears into human activity" [22, p. 409].

However Riemer and Johnston [23, p. 4] contend that existing approaches in the technology appropriation literature draw on a dualist worldview, where technology and humans exist independently as things with properties. They state that a dualist understanding of technology appropriation is limiting in that:

> ...any changes occurring have to be attributed to changes in either the technology object (via changes to its properties or features) or in the user subject (via changes to internal representations, such as cognitive scripts)...such dualist accounts fail to capture: 1) changes to the technology as experienced by users (what technology becomes in practice, its meaning in the user world); 2) technological agency, as appropriation is typically attributed to the users as the causal agents of change; and 3) how appropriation of new technologies makes the world intelligible to users in new ways. [23, p. 4]

Riemer and Johnson's [23, 26] use of German philosopher Heidegger's ontological perspective in regards to overcoming these limitations in IT/IS appropriation studies is of particular interest for our research. Heidegger's [24, 25] sociomaterial alternative to the Cartesian worldview postulates that our basic mode of engagement with the world takes place through practices, which involve both social and material arrangements. A Heideggerian ontology posits the question: 'what are the kinds of ways that entities can be in the world?'; starting with humans, Heidegger calls the being of human *Dasein*, human existence is being-in-the-world and the way of being human is through 'engagement in practices' [26]. Dasein does not denote an individual; but rather the social being of humans, "whose mode of existence is distinct from that of other entities...engaged in social practices that at the same constitute what they do and who they are" [26, p. 5]. Heidegger also defines two other ways that entities can be in the world, in terms of how they are encountered by Dasein in the course of engagement in practices: *equipment*[1]; and *objects*.

When Dasein encounter an entity in the world for the first time, whether they are constructing the entity, or reflecting on it, it is encountered as an object of attention that is *present-at-hand*, but may still be *unready-to-hand*. The entity is encountered by Dasein in terms of its individual properties, rather than its use in practices [26]. When an entity is encountered as a means to perform a practice, it is encountered as equipment. Equipment as such is constituted through its relationship to other equipment, typical activities and purposes for which it is used, and lends itself to use without reflection; a craftsman has an embodied skill for using equipment in order to perform a task and equipment lends itself inconspicuously and naturally to this task [26]. When equipment fails or its fluent use is interrupted, or when an individual is acquiring the skill necessary to be involved with the equipment, the equipment becomes conspicuous and becomes an object unready-to-hand. In the Heideggerian ontology, equipment, practices and human identity are inseparably entangled and form one sociomaterial holism. Riemer and Johnston state:

> Constitutive of Dasein is to have practices. Practices depend on equipment for their performance. Therefore, Dasein as the human way of being depends on equipment. But the being of equipment depends on practices and therefore on Dasein. Hence, as much as equipment depends on Dasein for what it is, so Dasein is constituted through its engagement with equipment. [26, p. 9]

Riemer and Johnston [23] developed a phenomenological theory of IT appropriation based on concepts from Heidegger's relational ontology and it is their theory of IT appropriation which we chose to utilise for this research. They conceptualise the appropriation of technology as human engagement through a series of activities, during which the way of being of the technology moves from the foreground of being present-at-hand when first encountered, in the activity of inspecting the object to determine its suitability; to the background of ready-to-hand where it has assumed its place within the identity-practice-equipment holism and is in fluent, transparent use in the activity of performing, where the individual is performing their practices using the equipment in-order-to a achieve a purpose. A key element of Riemer and Johnston's theory is, in addition to Heidegger's concepts, a 'middle-ground' activity which they term 'place-making', involving "embodied activity that disrupts the existing equipment holism, changing socio-material practices as well as the being of the new and of existing technology" [23, p. 8]. In this activity the technology is considered as a tool which is unready-to-hand. Each activity can be analysed across three dimensions: the material, the practical and the social. An overview of the theory is presented in Table 1.

---

[1] We make note here that the term *equipment* is given a precise technical meaning by Heidegger and is not to be confused with its everyday connotation as merely physical implements or tools.

Table 1. A phenomenological theory of appropriation (based on Riemer and Johnston [23])

Dimension	Activities that unfold over time in appropriation		
Human engagement	Inspecting	Place-making	Performing
Way of being of technology	Present-at-hand	Unready-to-hand	Ready-to-hand In-order-to
Being of technology	Object	Tool	Equipment
Place in practice	Fore-ground	Middle-ground	Back-ground
Material dimension	Object properties are inspected using existing skills and expected affordances	Acquiring the skill to use the tool. Discovering what the tool affords	Equipment withdraws from attention and becomes a means
Practical dimension	Object is inspected against equipment and understandings of the existing practice	Placing the tool among other tools and within the logics of the practice	Equipment has a place among other equipment and practices
Social dimension	Object is inspected against existing projects and social norms	Making the tool proper in the practice. Placing the tool in social identity production	Equipment is normal and part of social identity

The use of Heidegger's relational ontology within this theory of technology appropriation holds to the fundamental tenant of a sociomaterial analysis that "the social and the material are inherently inseparable" [7, p. 456]. In particular the concept that the technology changes ontologically through the notion of 'ways of being' can provide new and valuable insights into the technology appropriation process. We thus utilise this theory to frame the sociomaterial analysis of the appropriation of an innovative IT within an early childhood education and care organisation.

3   Case Setting

This research involves an exploratory, interpretive case study within Big Fat Smile (BFS), an early childhood education and care organisation in metropolitan New South Wales, Australia. BFS is responsible for 23 early childhood centres within the region, providing education and care services for children aged zero to five. The IT under study is a software 'app' called Kinderloop that runs on tablets and mobile devices, in particular on Apple iPad tablets, but is also accessible on PCs via a web portal. It is promoted as a safe, secure and private way for early childhood educators to communicate with parents and families of children attending an early childhood centre, in addition to documenting information on child activity and development. This combination of technologies will be herein referred to as *iPadKinderloop*. Kinderloop began development in 2012 in response to the founder's concern about not having appropriate times and opportunities to communicate with the educators at his children's early childhood centre in regards to being informed about his child's activity through the day. iPadKinderloop aims to enhance early childhood centre-parent/family communications through the following process:

1. An early childhood centre installs the app onto their tablet or mobile devices, which are then made available to the educators during the day;
2. At appropriate times, the educator opens the app, takes a photo and writes a short description about what is occurring; the educator can link to learning outcomes, practices and principles, centre philosophy, national quality standards, policies and procedures, educational visions etc.;
3. The child/ren are 'tagged' in the photo;
4. The photo and annotation are then uploaded to the centre's secure Kinderloop;
5. Kinderloop automatically and securely posts update notifications to the tagged child's parents;
6. Parents can then login to the centre's Kinderloop using their own device with the app installed, or navigate to the online web portal using any Internet-accessible computer and see all of their child's updates and can 'like' or comment on the posts that are visible to them.

The motivation behind Kinderloop is an inherently social one: as a parent with children, the founder felt that communication between parents and families at the centre his child attended needed improving; parents are always rushed when picking up their children that they do not have time to stop and talk to the educators about how their child was through the day; and they also might feel guilty for leaving the child at a centre while going to work, wondering if they are okay.

4   Research Methodology

This research aims at obtaining a deeper understanding of the process of appropriating an innovative technology into the practices of an early childhood education and care organisation with particular focus on the changes that occur to the practices, the educators, and the technology itself during the appropriation process. We also aim to assess the applicability of the presented theory of technology appropriation as a sociomaterial lens into the appropriation process, and as such we have used the theoretical framework as background for our data collection, the coding of the data and the data analysis. Data collection occurred at four BFS centres that were appropriating iPadKinderloop between November 2013 and January 2014. Not all centres were at the same 'stage' or level of appropriation due to differences in the timing of the roll-out; although the BFS Head Office mandated the use of Kinderloop, it was left to centre directors to decide when they would start using it. The empirical data was collected via semi-structured interviews with two or three educators at each centre, each centre director, and the Chief Executive Officer (CEO) of the BFS organisation, resulting in a total of 13 interviews. The data was complimented by a collection of 12 short videos provided by the Kinderloop software founder which were comprised of short testimonials from current Kinderloop users, including educators, centre directors and parents/family members. These videos are available on the Vimeo website (http://vimeo.com/kinderloop). Data was also obtained via observations of current practices and the examination of secondary documents used by early childhood centres in Australia including the Early Years Learning Framework and National Quality Framework.

The transcriptions of the 13 interviews were thematically coded and analysed utilising the concepts from the theory of appropriation. First, the interviews were coded according to the dimension of human engagement (i.e. inspecting, place-making or performing). Second, we coded the data in relation to the material, practical or social dimension of the framework. The 12 short videos were first viewed by the first author who made notes on the vision, and these notes were subsequently coded and analysed in a similar manner to the interview transcripts. In the following we use pseudonyms for our interview participants when quoting original data.

5   Findings

5.1   Practices Prior to iPadKinderloop

To understand the reconfiguring of practices that occur with the appropriation of iPadKinderloop, it is useful to understand the practices of communicating with families and involving iPads within the BFS centres prior to iPadKinderloop.

Prior Methods of Communicating. Centre director Rochelle outlines how centres communicated with families of children attending their centre prior to the introduction of iPadKinderloop:

> In the old days, we used to put stuff in parent pockets, and parents would never check pockets. We put notes up on the door, parents wouldn't read them, and we were really frustrated that the communication wasn't getting through.

Prior Usage of iPads. Centres had begun to appropriate iPads before the arrival of Kinderloop and the establishment of iPadKinderloop. Educators initially encountered the iPads as objects with properties, featuring a practice-motivated perspective of the possibilities of use, they evaluated the suitability and applicability of the technology within an early childhood environment: the portability of the devices, allowing their use within all physical areas of the centre; the touch screen technology interface providing enhanced accessibility for young children; the ability to install a range of apps that provide both learning experiences and entertainment for young children. Educators compared the potential iPad use to other IT devices in the centre such as PCs, which was noted by Rochelle as not being ideal for use with the children due to: the fixed location, where "previously we would bring a group of children into the office to access the computer, to look stuff up, as part of research"; the limited fine motor skills of children impacting their ability to manipulate the mouse and making it "quite difficult" to use. Additionally the desire to provide a child-led responsive and emergent curriculum was a consideration, for example, as recounted in an incident by Cindy where the iPads allowed such an experience:

There was a conversation about a giraffe going, and I explained what colour was a giraffe's tongue, and they didn't believe me, so we used the iPad to YouTube a little video of a giraffe eating and they were amazed by the blue tongue, and we researched to find out why the giraffe's tongue is blue, all just happened so spontaneously and quickly within a space of five minutes.

The nature of the generation of children they are dealing with as early childhood educators, who routinely experience the technology in their day-to-day lives, and find the use of technology simply 'second-nature' was also a consideration, as Rochelle reflected: "[The iPad is] so much easier for the children to use...we noticed that a lot of the kids had iPads [at home] or were using their parent's phones...I think it is the way of the world and we have to embrace it". They recounted experiences with the iPads that indicated actively-performed place-making was occurring, a process whereby the educators were finding places to accommodate the technology within the existing practice-equipment-identity holism, as Anita explained:

We started off with just the iPads, and we used them mainly just for the kids to have a play with, we use them a lot for, like separation, in the morning. And then we moved on to using them more as an interest based thing, so we'll get some apps that focus on their interests, but it's more just free play that they use them for.

Prior Methods of Documenting Children's Learning and Development. Documentation of children's development is a critical aspect of the role of an early childhood educator, and the use of paper-based documentation occurs extensively within the early childhood sector [27]. Within the 'curriculum' for Australian early childhood education and care providers the process of documentation is noted as part of the assessment for learning and intentional teaching aspects of the role of an early childhood educator [28].

There were two key documents produced within the centres: the day book, known as a diary or reflection book, and child portfolios. The day book was observed at a centre and was a physical book which was placed at the entry to the centre and provided parents with the opportunity to see an overview of what their child and their peers have experienced during the day. It was comprised of printed photos and annotations either hand-written or typed which illustrated and described activities the children have participated in during the day.

Child portfolios were comprehensive hard-copy documents provided to parents at the end of the year which included photos, annotations and examples of their children's art or other artefacts which demonstrate the developmental and learning progress of the child. Portfolios were historically costly, hand-written documents with commercially-developed photos glued on the paper where required, but with more centres providing PCs for the educators to program learning plans and update children's portfolios, the presentation of the portfolios changed to word-processed printed documents which included printouts of photos taken with digital cameras.

5.2   First Encounters with iPadKinderloop: 'Inspecting'

The Present-At-Hand Way of Being. When iPadKinderloop is not in fluent use by a skilled individual, but is instead being inspected or reflected upon, its way of being is present-at-hand; that is, it is present as an object with features. iPadKinderloop therefore is an object not defined by its properties, but by its place within sociomaterial practices that make it intelligible in practical terms. However the properties of the iPadKinderloop object are not to be dismissed, as for technology to be appropriated, i.e. change its way of being from an object encountered as present-at-hand to equipment that is ready-to-hand, it will have certain material properties that enable it to do what it is supposed to do; what the developer designed it to do. Furthermore, the iPadKinderloop is evaluated as to its suitability and its appropriateness, as it has to "assume its place in the holism of equipment, shared practices, identities and social orthodoxies" [29, p. 10]. The following section first describes how the BFS CEO encountered iPadKinderloop, and then how centre directors and educators engaged in the activity of inspecting.

The Chief Executive Officer. The CEO of BFS was introduced to the Kinderloop founder at an industry conference in March 2012 and "made the decision that we would roll out Kinderloop to all of our centres, because we saw great value in it". This decision was shaped by the fact that BFS is in a crowded market of early childhood service providers and striving to differentiate them by providing high quality early childhood services with added values with Kinderloop being considered one such added value.

iPadKinderloop was present-at-hand as an object in the fore-ground of consideration by the CEO as he evaluated it against its expected affordances and against the existing practices and norms of the BFS early childhood education and care centres. In the social dimension, the CEO viewed the iPadKinderloop properties within the context of a number of social and cultural concepts, including parental guilt over leaving children at centres while they went to work and not knowing what they were doing through the day; time-poor parents; and the "need to provide as much information as possible to parents" and the "importance of strengthening family-centre communications".

It was also evident that that the properties of iPadKinderloop object were evaluated against existing considerations of the practical dimension that come with being the CEO of an organisation providing early childhood education and care services:

> When people are paying substantial money for the services we provide, you want to make sure that everything is available to them and you find ways in which the connections can be stronger. There's an onus on us, to ensure that the parents have as much information as possible, so they can feel good about their purchase decision! …[also] the ability for our educators in our centres to far more readily, and cost-effectively, deliver on their obligations, the documentation and reporting, and relationships with families is one major part of the seven assessment criteria against which we are all being rated, and everyone has a view about the 'My Schools' website, well there's now 'My Child'…

Against the context of an early childhood and care centre environment, particular iPadKinderloop properties were noted by the CEO within the material dimension: Kinderloop runs on mobile touch screen devices which allows educators to use iPad-Kinderloop while moving around; there is safe and secure access to the posts with photos and annotations on children in the centre; the provision of real-time notifications to parents; and the provision of a full digital history with search functionality which could be useful when educators are using the posts for documentation or reflection purposes.

Centre Directors and Educators. The activity of inspection of iPadKinderloop by centre directors and educators was distinctly influenced by the executive decision made by BFS Head Office in August 2013 that iPadKinderloop use would be mandatory for all BFS centres, although no strict time frame was enforced. Thus the iPad-Kinderloop object moved to the fore-ground of consideration first by centre directors and then educators, as they were now mandated to create iPadKinderloop by installing Kinderloop onto their iPad devices and begin appropriating it.

In the social dimension, centre director Judy recounts how at first she was reluctant to appropriate iPadKinderloop, but that changed once she inspected the Kinderloop component of iPadKinderloop:

> I was a bit reluctant at first, only because I was a new centre, and my focus is on settling these kids, and I don't want to complicate anything, and I need to make sure I'm establishing these relationships with children and families, and then when I actually had a look at it, I was like "oh my god what am I doing, this is going to help me with my families, and relationships!"

By observing the educators, in the practical and material dimension of the 'inspecting' activities of the appropriation process particular iPad properties came into view when consideration was given to their suitability for use in conjunction with Kinderloop: the real-time updating of children's activities was supported by the iPad's portability and ability to connect into the centre wireless networks; and the uploading of photos and text annotations was supported by the built-in camera and on-screen keyboard functionality. Because the educators were already using the iPad in their educator roles they felt comfortable with using them as part of iPadKinderloop, although some who used Android tablet devices noted that the Apple iOS interface on the iPads was unfamiliar.

5.3   Making Room for iPadKinderloop: 'Place-Making'

Once iPadKinderloop was established (i.e. the existing iPads installed with the Kinderloop software app within the four BFS centres) it presented as unready-to-hand. This meant that it was no longer an object in the fore-ground and centre of attention of the centre directors and educators, but similarly it had not become equipment and withdrawn from the focus of attention. Instead the centre educators and directors were now actively making sense of iPadKinderloop as a tool and looking for a place for it within the existing holism of their early childhood centre with its practices, equipment and human identity of the educators. This practice of negotiating, experimenting and conversing about iPadKinderloop is what Riemer and Johnston [23] call 'place-making' and is analysed within the three dimensions below.

Social Dimension – Involvement and Identity. Centre directors and educators spoke of negotiating norms or rules for 'proper' use of iPadKinderloop as they actively sought to make a place for it within their practices as early childhood educators. Centre director Rochelle spoke of formalised guidelines that included "a three sentence maximum for those individual posts; it's supposed to be something that's really easy and quick to put out, so it's not taking up a lot of our time". She also noted that her centre has "processes in place so that we're checking each other's posts" to ensure a certain level of quality. Educator Chris described an informally negotiated norm between himself and the other educator who teaches in his room at his centre, where they mutually negotiated to make "about 30 posts a day, we try our best to cover each child at least once".

Language changes can be considered evidence of taking ownership of new technologies as part of place-making in technology appropriation [23], and we found evidence of the use of new terminology for those centres recognised as fully participating in the Kinderloop experience: the term 'superlooper' was used by the CEO to refer to these centres, and by the Kinderloop organisation on their website to refer to two centre directors who are "key ambassadors".

Rochelle noted that "everyone was keen and motivated" when it came to iPadKinderloop, highlighting the social dimension of the iPadKinderloop place-making; there is a sense of involvement as educators at the centre associate themselves with the place-making practice.

Practical Dimension – Incorporating Into Existing Tools and Logics of the Practice. We found evidence that the main purpose or intention of the iPadKinderloop appropriation differed in a number of centres. At two centres in particular it was evident that the way iPadKinderloop was being used was directly influenced by the particular understandings that the directors had of the iPadKinderloop affordances and their evaluation of it as a tool amongst the existing practices of the centres.

At one centre, the centre director had inspected and evaluated the iPadKinderloop affordances and determined its suitability as a communication tool, but with a distinct focus on documenting learning that's happening, which is then useful for educators to 'cut-and-paste' when programming[2] to save time:

> We use it mainly as a communication tool, but we also try to show,
> in a quite condensed form, the learning that's actually happening as
> well...when we're programming, take bits and pieces off Kinderloop
> as well that we've seen, like little observations and we use it as part
> of the children's individual plans. (Rochelle)

---

[2] Programming here refers to the educators' activity of documenting an experience and activity sequence before and after observing the children within the early childhood centre.

In contrast, another centre director had developed strong views on not using it as a developmental documentation tool but more as a simple event-recording tool:

> We're not using it as a massive developmental tool for analysis of the learning that's occurring, because I don't think I'd like it to be used that way. The potential is there, you can do it, but I would never use it that way, because I think it's far more beneficial as a communication tool for families. When my staff are planning and programming, they use a different format, and they have a piece of paper, with a set of questions that they need to answer when they're observing a child's learning. (Judy)

This quote from Judy additionally illustrates the nature of the place-making activity as active sense-making occurs as iPadKinderloop is placed next to the existing tools used by the centre's educators to document, and decisions being made to keep the existing tools and practices for documentation rather than utilise the iPadKinderloop in that way. Active sense-making was also evident as educator Anita recalls that the annotations' content of the Kinderloop posts changed over time based on parental feedback:

> It used to be a formal observation of what the child was doing and how it links to the Early Years Learning Framework; we still do link the outcomes to the photos, but we'll just put 'LO 4.1' so that it means nothing to the parents, they can still see that but it's just for our use. So what we used to do is we would write something like 'Bella is using her right hand to draw a picture and from this we can see we she's got good fine motor skills', using that technical language whereas now we'd write 'Bella is having a great time drawing a picture for mum', it's really casual and more informal.

Centre directors and educators spoke of how the iPadKinderloop had changed the practices of providing the traditional day book and portfolios, to the point where these artefacts were discontinued and replaced by iPadKinderloop:

> In terms of programming, we don't have to do daily reflections anymore, which is good because Kinderloop puts out all the pictures we do, it lets people know what we're doing throughout the day. (Chris)

There was also evidence that the practices of communicating information to parents had changed substantially, not only in how the information was transmitted but also in the response from parents, indicating increased engagement:

> We've put a lot of things [on Kinderloop], like last year we did like a pet interest, and normally even if I were to email, we might get one or two photos of kids' pets…last year we put photos on a pet board, we talked about the pets, people brought pets in, and we had so much more engagement from families. (Rochelle)

As the iPadKinderloop appropriation continued for one centre, the changes in the practices of the centre changed the nature of the iPads as existing equipment as centre director Sharon explains:

> We haven't gone back and bought all those games again on to our iPads [after apps were erased to make way for Kinderloop]. And I suppose, because now the iPads are more used for people to record what's going on. So the iPads are not really used for the kids anymore.

Material Dimension – Acquiring Skill. iPadKinderloop was introduced initially into two centres identified as 'pilot' sites. Once it was given approval, it was rolled out into each centre by the centre director, who attended training with the Kinderloop developers before informally sharing knowledge with the centre educators. iPadKinderloop was quickly and easily grasped by the majority of educators, as the previous participant experiences with technology such as the iPad shaped their acceptance:

> It came to my notice that every employee at [a particular centre] was using it, including some people who were known to be less than enthusiastic, a bit frightened of technology, having a go, getting on board, and realising it wasn't this big frightening thing, it's quite simple to use for handheld devices, iPads and smart phones... (BFS CEO)

Every-Day, Meaningful Use: 'Performing'. Once an IT tool becomes fully accepted and is being used in a practical and meaningful way it becomes *equipment* and its way of being becomes ready-to-hand; in this state the equipment is encountered by Dasein in an 'invisible' way, in that the individual does not notice it or pay attention to it. Centre directors and educators spoke of iPadKinderloop as a normal part of their daily life within the centres in a natural and fluent way:

> In terms of the iPads, primarily for Kinderloop, either I'll walk around the room with that throughout the day, and basically just snap moments that are appealing to me, or that I think parents might like to see. And then I just type up about four sentences on the go and I post it straight away. We try our best to cover each child at least once... that's just a good way for us to keep in touch with the families. (Chris)

The educators spoke of how they used iPadKinderloop "every day", in real-time situations where they are "capturing the photo straight away, we're instantly recording the learning that's occurred, we're not missing a thing, and the parents aren't missing a thing either" (Judy). These iPadKinderloop accounts reflect on how humans deal with engagement in the world when everything is going well: "we just 'do' - we are absorbed with 'what' we are dealing with, without having to think or reflect on the 'how' of our doings" [30, p. 7].

As iPadKinderloop has found its place in the equipment-practice-identity holism, the educators and centre directors reflect on what impact iPadKinderloop has had on their role and identity as an educator and their associated practices: Rochelle reflected that "Kinderloop has made huge changes in the way we communicate with our families and has vastly improved the level of participation of families in the centre; we now have fun reporting while saving time!". Other educators spoke of the time-saving afforded by iPadKinderloop, and centre director Judy mused that it had the power to be transformative for the early childhood education and care industry:

> Well it could totally change our industry in so many ways…you know, just like these documents that we get from the government, things like that, that are very influential. Kinderloop can be that as well, yeah. It just saves so much time, you know! And those conversations that you start with the parents...

When iPadKinderloop has withdrawn into the background of the existing practices, it is evident that there is an assumed level of familiarity with the equipment, against which educators are then able to evaluate and suggest new features based upon the practices that have been transformed by iPadKinderloop:

> Initially you could only put one photo in, and then, working with the guys, they were like 'oh so you want to put more than one photo in?' and 'well yeah we'd like sometimes we want to show the progression of what a child's doing', so then they added the ability to include more photos. (Rochelle)

When something goes wrong with equipment, its way of being goes from *ready-to-hand* where its use is transparent, to being conspicuously visible and *unready-to-hand*, requiring action to resolve the problem [23]. Once the problem is resolved the equipment can move back into the background. We uncovered a problem with iPadKinderloop which resulted in a display of conspicuous visibility: two educators at one centre described issues with the Wi-Fi that the iPads were connecting to in order to use the Kinderloop software; when the Wi-Fi was down, educators were not able to post updates to the centre's Kinderloop, or posts were lost because the upload didn't complete. It caused one educator to become so frustrated she did not want to use iPadKinderloop anymore.

6   Discussion: Understanding the Entanglement within the Equipment-Practice-Identity Holism

6.1   iPadKinderloop and Centre Directors and Educators

According to Heidegger's ontological view of human existence, our mode of being is to be 'such-and-such' by doing 'such and such' [26]. Applied to our case study, we can see that our participants, the centre directors and educators, are concernfully engaged in the practices of early childhood education and care and in particular for the

focus of this case study, the practices of communicating with families and documenting children's learning and development, and being engaged in these practices, constitutes their identity as early childhood centre directors and educators.

These practices that the centre directors and educators are engaged in now depend
on iPadKinderloop as equipment, and we have shown how iPadKinderloop has ontologically changed through its 'ways of being' to become equipment within the world
of the participants through the process of appropriation:

- It was encountered firstly as present-to-hand, as an object constituted through its
  properties rather than a use-in-practice, where the centre directors and educators
  inspected it against their existing practices and equipment;
- Then secondly as a tool unready-to-hand, where the centre directors and educators
  are actively making a place for it within their equipment-practice-identity holism,
- And finally as equipment, ready-to-hand, where it assumed its place in normality
  among the other equipment and practices of the centres.

When iPadKinderloop is encountered as equipment by the centre directors and
educators, it is no longer encountered as a tablet device running a software application, but as an entanglement of and with those particular two pieces of IT, presenting
itself as a set of particular *in-order-to* entwined in a use practice which is context-
dependent, for example:

- In-order-to update parents on children's activity to inform them and/or alleviate
  concerns or guilt;
- In-order-to communicate centre news and activity information to parents;
- In-order-to document children's learning and development;
- In-order-to allow centres to save time and money on documentation obligations.

When the iPad as the platform for iPadKinderloop is extricated from iPadKinderloop, we can see that it also appears as a set of particular in-order-to entwined in a use
practice rather than as a given object: educators used the iPad in conjunction with
other software apps in-order-to facilitate children's learning, and in-order-to entertain
children, or in fact in-order-to calm children experiencing separation anxiety. This
concurs with Riemer and Johnston's musing that the design practices of the iPad intuitively follow an equipment perspective as it is "a music instrument, note-taking
device, personal organiser, inventory keeping unit, academic reviewing tool, light-
weight personal computer, video player, etc., depending on its place in a local practice" [29, p. 7], and also the findings from Riemer et al.'s study on the software
program Skype where they noted that the same technology object is often appropriated in entirely different ways [31].

In once again reflecting on the equipment-practice-identity holism, iPadKinderloop
as equipment can only be understood in terms of the situated context of other equipment and human practices, and in turn shapes the identity of these centre directors and
educators who are performing the practices that identify them. During the place-
making activities of iPadKinderloop appropriation, the existing practices of communicating with families and documenting children's learning and development
were transformed and thus transforming the identity of what it means to be an early
childhood educator. As Chris reflects:

It [iPadKinderloop] helped me save time which basically means less time off the floor mucking around with paper and typing it on computers, because I can do it all on the go and then because of that it means I get to spend more time with the children, and ideally that's what I want, and that's what the families want as well. And so if we do that then I'm getting the most out of the children and then I'm getting the most out of my role as a teacher.

6.2   iPadKinderloop and Parents and Families

Although we have focused on the changes to the practice-equipment-identity holism of the centre directors and educators and how their practices have been transformed, the data obtained from the video footage of short interviews with parents provided by the Kinderloop software founder allows us an insight into how iPadKinderloop has transformed the practice-equipment-identity holism of parents of children attending centres. In their familiarity with iPadKinderloop which has been shaped by their previous encounters with the tablet or mobile device that forms part of iPadKinderloop in other 'in-order-to' means, and in the context of their identity as parents and the practices that they engage in as being parents, they encounter iPadKinderloop as a series of means that are notably social in nature: in-order-to be reassured that their child is doing well ("Having two babies starting preschool at the same time, can be a bit nerve wracking at times so it's great to have that peace of mind that they're okay through the day, that they're enjoying their time at school" (Natalya)); in-order-to engage with their children ("[Kinderloop is] a really great conversation starter in the evening, because most young children can't remember what they did" (Megan)); and in-order-to include geographically distant family members in the lives of the children ("They [family in New York] miss out on those experiences so it's been a really great way to include them in our family life" (Megan)).

7   Conclusion

This study addresses recent calls to study the sociomateriality of IT [7] by providing a detailed, rich understanding of what happens during the appropriation of new IT within an early childhood education and care organisation. Rather than utilise a traditional dualist approach where the world (humans, IT) consists of independently existent things with properties, our study utilises a phenomenological theory of technology appropriation by Riemer and Johnston [23] built upon the non-dualist ontology articulated by Heidegger [24, 25].

We contribute to the IS literature a detailed sociomaterial account of how IT appropriation reconfigures organisations, in our case early childhood education and care centres as well as of how human identity, practices and IT are inescapably entwined, framed by the different understanding of our way of being in the world as humans engaged in practices co-constituted by equipment. Our study demonstrates that such a sociomaterial view of IT appropriation allows us to overcome the limitations of dualist accounts of IT appropriation and change, as we have shown that IT change is more than just reconfiguration of designed properties or features, rather the IT ontologically changes during the appropriation of the IT; and that changes to practices are more than just changes to cognitive beliefs and attitudes.

As we have provided a rich case study of a technology appropriation, we contribute to IS practice by exposing the activities within technology appropriation which provide a basis for managers to plan and prepare for technology appropriation. However further research is required to derive more detailed information to guide managers in facilitating the appropriation of technology.

We also acknowledge that there are implications to the appropriation of such technology including workplace privacy, employee performance monitoring, and the inadvertent recording of child misbehaviour and/or injury which have not been addressed in this study. The first author intends to conduct further research and interviews with participants in order to discuss such issues and consequences.

References

1. Bolstad, R.: The Role and Potential of ICT in Early Childhood Education – A Review of New Zealand and International Literature (2004), http://www.nzcer.org.nz/
2. Plumb, M., Kautz, K., Tootell, H.: Touch Screen Technology Adoption and Utilisation by Educators in Early Childhood Educational Institutions: A Review of the Literature. In: Proceedings of the 24th Australasian Conference on Information Systems, Melbourne (2013)
3. Orlikowski, W.J.: Sociomaterial Practices: Exploring Technology at Work. Organization Studies 28(9), 1435–1448 (2007)
4. Zhao, Y., Pugh, K., Sheldon, S., Byers, J.: Conditions for Classroom Technology Innovations. Teachers College Record 104(3), 482–515 (2002)
5. Mendoza, A., Carroll, J., Stern, L.: Software Appropriation over Time: From Adoption to Stabilization and Beyond. Australasian Journal of Information Systems 16(2), 5–23 (2010)
6. Orlikowski, W.J.: The Sociomateriality of Organisational Life: Considering Technology in Management Research. Cambridge Journal of Economics 34, 125-141 (2010)
7. Orlikowski, W.J., Scott, S.V.: Sociomateriality: Challenging the Separation of Technology, Work and Organization. Academy of Management Annals 2(1), 433–474 (2008)
8. Scott, S.V., Orlikowski, W.J.: Getting the Truth: Exploring the Material Grounds Of Institutional Dynamics in Social Media. Working Paper no. 177, London School of Economics and Political Science (2009)
9. Leonardi, P.M.: Digital Materiality? How Artifacts Without Matter, Matter. First Monday 15(6) (2010), http://firstmonday.org/htbin/cgiwrap/bin/ojs/index.php/fm/article/view/3036/2567
10. Leonardi, P.M.: When Flexible Routines Meet Flexible Technologies: Affordance, Constraint, and the Imbrication of Human and Material Agencies. MIS Quarterly 35(1), 147–167 (2011)
11. Leonardi, P.M., Barley, S.R.: Materiality and Change: Challenges To Building Better Theory about Technology and Organizing. Information and Organization 18, 159–176 (2008)
12. Leonardi, P.M., Barley, S.R.: What Is Under Construction Here? Social Action, Materiality, and Power in Constructivist Studies of Technology and Organizing. Academy of Management Annals 4(1), 1–51 (2010)
13. Leclerq, A., Carugati, A., Giangreco, A., Da Cunha, J.V., Blegnid Jensen, T.: A Sociomaterial View of the Scaffolding of Work Practices with Information Technology. In: ICIS 2009 Proceedings, Paper 197 (2009), http://aisel.aisnet.org/icis2009/197

14. Hultin, L., Mähring, M.: Visualizing Institutional Logics in Sociomaterial Practices. In: ICIS 2013 Proceedings (2013), `http://aisel.aisnet.org/icis2013/proceedings/OrganizationIS/4/`

15. Riemer, K., Vehring, N.: It's Not a Property! Exploring the Sociomateriality of Software Usability. In: ICIS 2010 Proceedings, Paper 215 (2010), `http://aisel.aisnet.org/icis2010_submissions/215`

16. Davidson, E., Vaast, E.: Digital Entrepreneurship and Its Sociomaterial Enactment. In: Proceedings of the 43rd Hawaii International Conference on System Science (HICSS), pp. 1–10. IEEE Computer Society, Los Alamitos (2010)

17. Cecez-Kecmanovic, D., Galliers, R.D., Henfridsson, O., Newell, S., Vidgen, R.: The Sociomateriality of Information Systems: Current Status, Future Directions. MIS Quarterly 38(3), 809–830 (2014)

18. Kautz, K., Blegind Jensen, T.: Debating Sociomateriality: Entanglements, Imbrications, Disentangling, and Agential Cuts. Scandinavian Journal of Information Systems 24(2), 89–96 (2012)

19. Kautz, K., Blegind Jensen, T.: Sociomateriality at the Royal Court of IS: A Jester's Monologue. Information and Organization 23(1), 15–27 (2013)

20. Poole, M.S., DeSanctis, G.: Use of Group Decision Support Systems as an Appropriation Process. In: Proceedings of the 22nd Hawaii International Conference on System Sciences (HICSS), vol. 4, pp. 149–157. IEEE (1989)

21. DeSanctis, G., Poole, M.S.: Capturing the Complexity in Advanced Technology Use: Adaptive Structuration Theory. Organization Science 5(2), 121-147 (1994)

22. Draxler, S., Stevens, G.: Supporting the Collaborative Appropriation of an Open Software Ecosystem. Computer Supported Cooperative Work 20 (4-5), 403-448 (2011)

23. Riemer, K., Johnston, R.B.: Place-Making: A Phenomenological Theory of Technology Appropriation. In: ICIS 2012 Proceedings (2012), `http://aisel.aisnet.org/icis2012/proceedings/SocialImpacts/5/`

24. Heidegger, M.: Sein Und Zeit. Neomarius Verlagg, Tübingen (1927)

25. Heidegger, M.: Being and Time. Macquarrie, J., Robinson, E. (trans.). SCM Press, London (1962)

26. Riemer, K., Johnston, R.B.: Artifact or Equipment? Rethinking the Core of IS Using Heidegger's Ways of Being. In: ICIS 2011 Proceedings, Paper 5 (2011), `http://aisel.aisnet.org/icis2011/proceedings/researchmethods/5`

27. Piper, A.M., D'Angelo, S., Hollan, J.: Going Digital: Understanding Paper and Photo Documentation Practices in Early Childhood Education. In: Proceedings of the ACM Conference on Computer-Supported Cooperative Work (CSCW), San Antonio, TX, pp. 1319–1328. ACM, New York (2013)

28. Department of Education: Belonging, Being & Becoming: The Early Years Learning Framework for Australia. Australian Government Department of Education, Employment and Workplace Relations (2009)

29. Riemer, K., Johnston, R.B.: What is IT in Use and Why Does It Matter for IS Design? Systems, Signs & Actions 7(1), 5–21 (2013)

30. Riemer, K., Johnston, R.B., Hovorka, D., Indulska, M.: Challenging the Philosophical Foundations of Modeling Organizational Reality: The Case of Process Modeling. In: ICIS 2013 Proceedings (2013), `http://aisel.aisnet.org/icis2013/proceedings/BreakthroughIdeas/4/`

31. Riemer, K., Frößler, F., Klein, S.: Real Time Communication – Modes of Use in Distributed Teams. In: ECIS 2007 Proceedings, Paper 56 (2007), `http://aisel.aisnet.org/ecis2007/56`

Technology and Sociomaterial Performation

Adrian Yeow[1] and Samer Faraj[2]

[1] SIM University, Singapore
adrianyeowyk@unisim.edu.sg
[2] Desautels Faculty of Management, McGill University, Montreal, Quebec, Canada
samer.faraj@mcgill.ca

Abstract. Organizational researchers have acknowledged that understanding the relationship between technology and organization is crucial to understanding modern organizing and organizational change [1]. There has been a significant amount of debate concerning the theoretical foundation of this relationship. Our research draws and extends Deleuze and DeLanda's work on assemblages and Callon's concept of performation to investigate how different sociomaterial practices are changed and stabilized after the implementation of new technology. Our findings from an in-depth study of two ambulatory clinics within a hospital system indicate that "perform-ing" of constituting, counter-performing, calibrating, and stratifying explained the process of sociomaterial change and that this process is governed by an overarching principle of "performative exigency". Future studies on sociomateriality and change may benefit from a deeper understanding of how sociomaterial assemblages are rendered performative.

Keywords: sociomateriality, assemblage, performation, healthcare IT.

1 Introduction

New ways of organizing are constantly emerging from different combinations of technology and organizational features and lead to renewed attention to the role of technology as a critical thread to the changing fabric of organizations. Thus, there is considerable interest among organizational researchers to understand and theorize the relationship between the social and the material whenever technology meets organizing [1-3]. Under the rubric of "Sociomateriality", an emerging research project within the fields of information systems and organizational studies has put forth a relational perspective between organizations and technology or the social and the material that challenges the privileged role of the human actor [3, 4].

One of the main contributions of sociomateriality is that it helps researchers recognize the importance of the mutual relationship between the social and the material. In fact, all contemporary organizational practices can be seen as constituted by an array of sociomaterial agencies [4]. It has also introduces a new vocabulary (e.g., affordance, entanglement, imbrication scaffold) as a way to express and discuss these mutuality relationships [5, 6]. However, this invitation to embrace a relational ontology is difficult to embrace given the traditional social science emphasis on objects rather

B. Doolin et al. (Eds.): IS&O 2014, IFIP AICT 446, pp. 48–65, 2014.

than relations, on describing object qualities rather than its evolution [2]. More importantly, this theoretical relationship of organization and technology has significant implications for our understanding of organizational change following the implementation of new technology.

Our research study contributes to this emerging stream of work by developing a performation lens based on Deleuze, DeLanda [7] as well as Callon [8] and his associates [9] work. We applied this lens in an empirical case to deepen our understanding of the perfomation process and to answer our research question: How are sociomaterial practices changed and stabilized after the implementation of new technologies? Our findings suggest that the change process of sociomaterial practices is characterized by four "perform-ing" of constituting, counter-performing, calibrating, and stratifying, and is governed by an overarching governing principle of "performative exigency". After developing our grounded findings, we join them with our new lens to propose a rich set of vocabulary to understand the evolving practices and provide new theoretical opportunity to deepen understanding of how sociomaterial assemblages are made performative as well as organizational consequences of the evolved assemblages.

2   Understanding Sociomaterial Change from a Performation Lens

The performation lens draws from work by Deleuze and Guattari [10], DeLanda [7] and Callon [8] and his associates [9]. We specifically consider two key concepts that underlie this lens – the concepts of assemblage and performation – and how they compare and contrast with existing work on sociomateriality.

Like existing views on sociomateriality [4, 11], this lens adopts a relational ontology and argues agency is produced by specific sociomaterial configuration or "assemblage". According to Deleuze and DeLanda, an "Assemblage" is an arrangement and combination of heterogeneous components, including discursive (e.g. techniques, logics, ways of working), social (e.g. relationships, structures) and material artifacts interrelated to one another in such a way that brings about evolving patterns of actions. This view has been incorporated in part within the writings of Michel Callon, Karen Barad, Lucy Suchman, Andrew Pickering and Wanda Orlikowski.

However, there are several important nuances of Deleuze and DeLanda's [7] notion of assemblage that have important implications for existing sociomateriality lenses. First, Deleuze and DeLanda proposed that the components that constitute assemblage have inherent properties apart from the assemblage. In that sense Deleuze and DeLanda proposed that assemblages are not ontologically one and its components are independent of the assemblage as per Barad's agential realism view. At the same time, Deleuze and DeLanda point out that each component has different relational capacities. The components' capacities, whilst based on its properties, depend in part on what other components and how they are related to each other. Using the notion of relational capacities, they argue that social realities exist not at the level of the component as proposed by others [12-14] but at the assemblage level, where individual components are interrelated to form the assemblage. At the level of the assemblage, the overall capacity of the assemblage is irreducible to its individual components and its properties; instead the assemblage's capacity is hard to determine a priori given that it depends on how each component's relational capacity is activated with other components and whether what other components are present. In other words, while the assemblage depends on its constituent components the properties of the components do not determine the whole assemblage, as it is partly dependent on how they are related together that activates different relational capacities. Thus as an example, a microcomputer has many properties by itself – it helps records, process, stores, etc. However, when put in a specific assemblage composed of different other components, different relational capacities (based on its inherent properties) may be exercised and activated, which in turn may lead the assemblage to perform differently. Thus a standalone computer related or installed with word processing program versus the same computer connected to a printer would lead to two different assemblages performing different practices – the former simply word processing while the latter the ability to process and print documents. Callon [8] referred to this principle in this way – assemblages are endowed with different capacities of acting depending on how heterogeneous components are adjusted and configured to one another.

In this way, Deleuze and DeLanda's assemblage synthesizes some different views held within existing sociomateriality research in that the relational ontology is important; it is important to consider the sociomaterial assemblage and its capacities and agency in specific time and place; yet at the same time, it is possible to understand assemblage by considering the assemblage's individual components and their attending relationships, but to consider that holistically and from a relational viewpoint as the assemblage's capacities are dependent on its relationships with other components within the assemblage.

Second, Deleuze and DeLanda's heterogeneous components are not limited to human actions or social structures and material artifacts. They were explicit in including other components that were typically not considered in sociomaterial studies – components that include symbols, expressions, rhetoric, discourse, logics, and ideas. This is important given that the motivations and reasons why actors and artifacts behave in certain ways and have specific properties are often found in these expressive components. This is especially highlighted in Callon [8] and associates' [9] work on economic sociology, which used Deleuze and DeLanda's assemblage to explicate how performances of economic realities are linked to economic theories via a host of actions and artifacts. Thus, Deleuze and DeLanda's assemblage complements the notion of affordance in sociomateriality by pointing to these discursive components as sources of perceptions of affordances and constraints.

Finally, Deleuze and DeLanda see the relations among the components within the assemblage as contingent and tenuous and that parts of the assemblage could easily be extracted from one assemblage to another creating different interactions, relationships and assemblages. This dynamism in their formulation of assemblages therefore aligns with the process of becoming that some sociomaterial research has focused on [15, 16]. Because assemblages are dynamic, it behooves us to understand the process by which assemblages emerge, change, and become stable. Yet at the same time, this formulation of assemblages does not just focus on the patterns and configuration of components, but rather, it is more concerned with how the new assemblage is rendered performative and its implications for organizing. This particular focus leads us to the second main concept – performance.

The notion of performance refers to the assembling process through which existing or new sociomaterial assemblages are rearranged and reconfigured so as to render it performative in the presence of preexisting social and material contexts [17, 18]. While Deleuze and DeLanda have broadly theorized on this processes (process of stabilizing and destabilizing assemblages), we turned to Callon [8], MacKenzie, and their associates' [9] empirical work within the field of economic sociology to develop the notion of performation.

Callon argued that while it is important to study the performativity of economic assemblages, it is more important to understand how these assemblages are rendered performative (made to perform) or the process "performation" (coined by Callon). This view is in line with research in science and technology studies that have looked at the work required to configure and make experiments work [e.g., 16]. Some of those studies have characterized the process as "mangling" – through which hybrid practices emerged with performances fixed neither wholly in the material or social entities [16]. Others point to the emergent configurations of expertise, skills, work procedures, practices and tools that serve to support the organization's performance [19]. This type of work as described in this stream of work tends to be "invisible" in that they are work that make and keep technologies and assemblages working [18, 20].

In general, Callon and associates' research agree with them in that performation is an emergent and dialectical process that typically takes place in the background. They tend to highlight the collective actions of not just actors but also material and discursive components in creating, changing, and stabilizing assemblages. In other words, performation is practical, performative as well as discursive [18, 21]. It attempts to describe the dynamic actions, fluid gatherings, and emergent interactions by which assemblages are incrementally linked and reconfigured so as to render them performative.

The performation process may go beyond a single sociomaterial assemblage to include other performances – that is, work that joins different assemblages' performances together seamlessly [18, 22, 23]. Thus another key point when considering the process of performation is the fact that sociomaterial assemblage is never performed in abstract or introduced tabula rasa in organizations. Instead, in a performation process, we have to explicitly recognize that sociomaterial assemblages perform with or as part of another set of sociomaterial assemblages in the same site of production [18]. The different preexisting assemblages serve as a "solid and obdurate" backdrop to new or changed assemblages as they may provide opportunities or limit and constrain the process by which new or changed assemblages evolve [18].

Finally, the performation process also leads us to evaluate and judge the outcomes of these actions from a performative exigency [8]. In other words, one would evaluate the "success" of the performation process given how well the new or changed assemblage performs, i.e., "performative exigency". The performative exigency provides the basis for the assemblage to either continue with the performation process such that additional work is required to be done (i.e., it is not performing well or as intended) or to begin stabilizing the changed assemblage. Thus the performation lens not only looks at the assemblage and how it changes, e.g., through the introduction and use of a new technology; it also considers the performative aspect or how the changed or new assemblage is performing.

Put together, the performation lens provides us with two important concepts to help better understand sociomateriality and change. The concept of assemblage – as an ontological-epistemological construct – helps to resolve some of the current tensions in sociomaterial research. While it focuses on organizational and social realities as assemblages, it does help us see that they are constituted by interrelated heterogeneous components. It also considers such assemblages as dynamic entities that could be changed as these components and relationships are reconfigured or even moved to other assemblages. Here the concept of performation helps to conceptualize this becoming process as one characterized by invisible work – work that involves pragmatic, collective actions enacted by the material, social and discursive components. Unlike current sociomateriality's focus on the patterns of interactions [15, 24], the performation lens considers the assemblage as well as its interior relations. Further the performation lens explicitly considers how the assemblage interacts within the context of other existing assemblages found within the site of productions. Finally, the performation process is in turn shaped by the performative exigency; in other words, the relative success of the assemblage performances determines the point at which the emergent assemblage begins to stabilize.

While the performation lens has provided us with a vocabulary to describe these issues, more work needs to be done to ground these concepts and deepen our understanding of the perfomation process by which new sociomaterial assemblage are made to work. Specifically, we still are unsure of the different "perform-ing" work that are required, the conditions leading to the "perform-ing" work, as well as the organizational implications of such sociomaterial changes. Our in-depth study of an EMR implementation across two different clinics attempts to provide insights into this process, specifically focusing on understanding the "perform-ing" and the conditions in which they are undertaken and how that consequently shape the final outcomes. We discuss the setting and our methods next.

3   Methods and Setting

3.1   Research Approach

We conducted an in-depth, longitudinal case study analysis of an EMR system implementation project [25]. We provide a brief overview of the setting and EMR project before describing the research methods in the following section.

3.2   Research Setting and Background

The two clinics belong to Centralsys, a pseudonym for a public state-wide hospital system on the East Coast of the United States. Centralsys owns and manages seven hospitals and health systems that together account for 1,800 beds. The EMR implementation process for Metro and Suburb took 14 months to complete. It involved over 65 full-time EMR project team members. All in all, the EMR system go-live was successfully launched with no major technical glitches.

3.3 Data Collection

The study took place between July 2007 and March 2009. During this 18 month-period, we spent a total 12 months of on-site observations, interviews and archival data collection at the two clinics and project management sites. Our involvement with the project covered three phases: the first phase lasted three months and included the EMR process design and implementation planning activities (July to September 2007), the second phase lasted eight months and was focused on implementation and initial use of the EMR system in both clinics (October 2007 to May 2008), and the third phase lasted two months and was focused on understanding how work practices had evolved after the clinics had used the EMR system for more than one year (February to March 2009).

We relied mainly on field observations of work practices in each clinic as well as observations of project meetings where designs of new practices were discussed. We also conducted in-depth interviews with the clinic staff and Centralsys project team to understand how the EMR practices are performing and to reflect on evolution of problems and their consequences in the EMR practices. In total, we were in the field for 91 days: 14 days at the EMR project management site, 47 days at Metro and 30 days at Suburb. We wrote up around 381 pages of field notes and conducted 95 formal interviews with EMR project team members, Centralsys management, and all the staff in the two clinics. We also collected nearly 2,000 archival documents including e.g., system requirements, standard operating procedures for the different clinic practices before and after the EMR.

3.4 Data Analysis

Our data analysis was focused on individual practice within each clinic. Practice is defined as actual patterns of activities and social interactions among organizational actors as they go about accomplishing specific organizational goals [26]. Using our observations of work as well as discussion during project meetings, we decided to focus on one practice (due to space constraints) – lab reporting – for our in-depth analysis. We chose this practice for three reasons. First, this practice was critical in its respective domain of work. Lab reporting form the bulk of follow-up patient care [27]. Secondly, it was significantly influenced by the new EMR system and therefore provided important data regarding its effects. Finally, based on our interviews with the clinic management and project staff, this practice had significant operational issues prior to the EMR implementations.

For our in-depth analysis, we first carefully compared the observed practices across clinics and then within clinics across time. This helped us determine how they were similar or different before the EMR implementation and how they had changed after the EMR implementation. Next, we compared the practice with those that were planned and documented in the EMR manuals and user requirements. This helped to surface how the post-EMR practice compared with the planned practice.

We used an inductive approach [28] to analyze how and why those differences in practices were observed. We coded the interviews, minutes, and observations that referred to implementations issues or problems related to the three practices that had surfaced during the implementation phase (the basis for "counter-performing"). Using these data, we constructed a composite narrative of the issues within the practice. With the issue narratives as conceptual anchors, we proceeded to first trace backward in time to understand the sources of these issues (the basis for "constituting") and later forward in time to understand the collective actions to solve and consolidate the new emergent practices (the basis for calibrating and stratifying). By iterating and comparing the practice's narratives with extant literature, we were able to identify the different categories of perform-ing and how they were related over time.

4   Findings

Our findings are presented in two sections. The first section provides detail of the existing issues surrounding the lab resulting practice at Metro and Suburb and how the implementation of a new EMR system led to different emergent new practice. The second section traces the sociomaterial change process from the performative assemblage perspective to explicate how and why this different emergent practice emerged.

4.1   Emergence of Different Metro and Suburb Practices with EMR

First, we briefly describe the site of production and the lab resulting practice. Metro clinic ("Metro") is a family practice clinic with six physicians, five medical assistants, nine support staff (front-desk, phone operators, referral coordinator and medical records) and one clinical manager serving 23,000 patient visits per year. Suburb clinic ("Suburb") provides family care services similar to Metro and has three full-time physicians, three medical assistants, four support staff, and one clinical manager, handling 8,600 patient visits per year.

Lab resulting practice incorporates all aspects of communication among physicians, support staff, laboratory and patient regarding the results of a patient's laboratory tests. A physician may order a lab test as a part of general assessment, to confirm a diagnosis, or to monitor drug therapy. The results of these tests must be appropriately communicated and followed up in order to ensure safe and effective care. As Metro had an on-site lab facility operated by an external lab provider, Metro's patients are sent directly to that lab for their lab works. Metro physicians therefore receive their lab results directly from the on-site lab office. In contrast, Suburb does not have an on-site lab. When a Suburb physician orders a lab test, the patient are given the lab test orders and find an external lab to conduct the tests. Patients usually choose one of the two larger laboratory test providers. The external lab will fax or mail the results to Suburb's physicians once the tests are conducted.

Overall, the goal of the physicians' lab resulting practice is to ensure that lab results are properly diagnosed by ordering physicians and communicated to patients in a timely and appropriate manner given the outcomes of the tests. But these practices were highly personal as they depended on each physician's preferred follow-up routine (Minutes from Physicians Advisory Group meetings). While some physicians attended to medically urgent lab results directly with the patient and delegated nonurgent cases to the medical assistants, other physicians would deal with all lab results personally. It also differed at the clinic level. At Metro clinic, they had implemented a policy that all covering physicians were notified of lab results even if they had not ordered them, while at Suburb clinic this was not so. Due to the large patient load, Metro physicians do not always follow up on reminders to advise patients of normal lab results, so they decided to inform all patients to call the clinic for results. At Suburb, the call back process is determined by the physician on a case-by-case basis. In some cases the medical assistant may be responsible for following up with the patient, while in other cases the patient may initiate the call.

The new EMR lab resulting practice performed well in Metro given that the link between its EMR and onsite lab provider's lab resulting system was properly interfaced. Suburb, however faced more problems with the new practice, as the lab providers were not onsite and the technical interfaces were not properly connected. Differing practices of Suburb's lab providers also contributed to ongoing contradictions of missing or lab results that are linked to existing lab orders in the system.

4.2   Process of Sociomaterial Change – Performativity Exigency on New Assemblage

In our analysis, we traced the sociomaterial change process and explicated four interrelated "perform-ing" surrounding the new assemblages: constituting, counterperforming, calibrating, and stratifying.

The first perform-ing was "constituting assemblage" – how the EMR artifact was constituted with components of the existing assemblages for the practice. Essentially, it focuses on the perform-ing of external actors i.e., the Centralsys and clinics' management, as they attempted to add a new technological component (in this case the EMR) in existing assemblages. In this "perform-ing", external actors had to consider how the new technological component is made a part of the whole, so as to combine it with other relevant components and to express that in a coherent way. In other words, to "constitute" the new component as part of the assemblage implies changes in the relations, components and boundaries of the assemblage, thereby creating new assemblages in the sites of production.

The expressive associated with the EMR lab resulting assemblage was one of "standardization" i.e., Lab resulting practice was redesigned so that the EMR integrated the clinics lab processes with the lab providers' systems. In the new EMR assemblage, work would be standardized so that all physicians would associate all lab orders with diagnosis and automatically send it electronically to the respective lab provider via the EMR system. All lab results would be electronically routed from the lab system back to the EMR inbasket following standardized routing rules set by Centralsys management. According to these rules, all normal lab results would be routed only to the ordering physician while abnormal results would be routed to all physicians in the clinic. This would allow for prompt follow up of abnormal results even if the ordering physician was off duty. In turn, the physician may choose to directly contact the patient concerning the results or may send this off to their medical assistants for other follow-up actions. This assemblage would be used in both clinics regardless whether they had an on-site lab or not.

This second "perform-ing" was "counter performing", which refers to how components and relations of the constituted assemblages breakdown leading to "counter-performances". Some counter-performances centered on contradictions *within* the assemblage, e.g., problematic relations or components. For lab resulting practice, the increased interactions between medical assistants and physicians for lab resulting created confusion among the Metro's physicians and medical assistants. Due to the rotation of medical assistants at Metro clinic, a mechanism had to be developed to ensure that lab results were followed up consistently. A "message pool" in the EMR system allowed inbasket requests to be sorted by physician's name. However, given the high volume of lab reports in the inbasket messages, the message pool soon proved to be highly unmanageable. Problems such as overlooking, or multiple medical assistants working on a single follow-up, frequently occurred.

Others counter performances centered on contradictions *between* assemblages. Some were contradictions between two new assemblages while others involved the new and existing assemblages. The lab resulting situation in Suburb was illustrative of contradictions between the new assemblage and existing assemblages. On the one hand, there were ongoing technical problems in the integration of the EMR system and the external lab systems. Unlike Metro who was interfaced with one system, i.e., the on-site lab provider system, Suburb had to be interfaced with two lab systems as their patients could choose from either lab provider. The Centralsys project team had stabilized the interface with the first lab provider system but had not anticipated the complications arising from integrating with the second lab provider. Part of the complications was that a lab order with two or more tests would have each test result sent back to the physician as separate reports in their in-basket. As one of the Suburb physician explained, the different lab test reports coming back separately (and on different timings) confused the ordering physician since they have to make diagnosis not only one test result but a set of test results.

On the other hand, how Suburb's patients interacted with the lab providers also created problems. Specifically, patients who go to an external lab provider (as in Suburb's case) are issued with a paper lab order slip while the electronic order is directly sent to the lab provider's system. When patients present themselves at the lab, sometimes the lab provider's staff unknowingly entered in a new lab order during registration. The lab technician who actually carries out the order would encounter two lab orders – one that was electronically transferred and one that was created during registration. This resulted in cases where the Suburb physician would receive two results or no results depending on whether the lab technician checked off on both the lab orders or checked off on the "wrong" lab order. In other cases, lab orders had time-related restrictions – some were activated only after a certain time frame (e.g., patients need to have the lab done one month after the visit) or in certain cases, the patient forgot to have the lab done within two months and the lab provider system automatically removed that order from its system. In these cases, patients may end up having the lab done – but as an unsolicited order. The results for unsolicited cases do not come back to the ordering physician as an electronic in-basket message but as a paper lab result. Thus it resulted in contradictions and counter-performances between the new EMR lab resulting assemblage and the existing lab order assemblages.

Calibrating perform-ing refers to how collective actions were enacted by different actors to repair and/or consolidate the new relations among different components within assemblages in reaction to counter-performances encountered. One series of calibrating "perform-ing" involved rearranging problematic relations or components within the assemblage in order to reduce or remove the counter-performances. Some of these calibrating "perform-ing" eventually led to changing these problematic parts.

For the lab resulting case in Metro, as discussed above, one of the initial design in view of the rotating medical assistant-physician policy was to utilize the message pool function in the EMR system. The counter-performances revealed that this new arrangement of a message pool did not work with the rotation policy. Centralsys ambulatory care operational leadership and Metro's management realized, however, that Suburb did not have such issues as they used a fixed physician-medical assistant arrangement. The calibration was to change the existing relationships among the medical assistants and physicians and Metro's own policies. This new arrangement assisted to reduce the confusion as medical assistants knew which in-basket instructions and messages to follow-up and also built up better coordination and communication between physicians and their medical assistants.

The other series of calibrating "perform-ing" was creating and re-establishing of new boundaries of the assemblages by adding or changing components and relationships across assemblages. This was mainly targeted at counter-performing contradictions between assemblages. We observed this mainly in Suburb's case. The first set of calibrating in Suburb was to re-establish the boundary of the lab resulting assemblage with the external lab provider systems that had been counter-performing due to technical interface problems. The Centralsys' project team spent nearly a year working closely with the lab providers' technical team to troubleshoot where the interfaces had problems in order to solve the multiple reporting interface issue.

This was however only part of the problem as discussed above. The next series of calibrating, which was done in parallel with the technical calibrating, involved clarifying and changing relations in work processes across the two assemblages. Specifically, the Centralsys team worked closely with the lab providers to clarify their work processes to deal with the issues of repeat and unsolicited lab results. However, Suburb continued to face problems when patients did not cooperate e.g., forgot their lab appointments and went after the lab order period etc. In such cases, Suburb physicians continued to rely on paper-based reports as part of the lab resulting practice.

Stratifying "perform-ing" refers to actions of human actors within the assemblages as well as actions enacted through the assemblages that occurred after the new assemblages are rendered performative again. However these new performances by the assemblage are not completely "optimal" or designed – there remained some minor issues here and there. Actors within the assemblages thus attempted to "smoothen" these issues through discourses that involved expressive components (e.g., efficiency concepts, patient-centricity) to codify and consolidate the new assemblages and their performances. At the same time, EMR assemblages performed a new form of accountability – a different form of "structure" – that the actors find themselves drawing upon as part of their practices. Together through intentional discursive actions that enrolled expressive components and emergent 'accounting' of the new assemblage on daily practices, the new EMR assemblages became stabilized.

Part of stratifying was to codify the assemblage by foregrounding the performances as one of the accepted practices via linking it to organizational expressive concepts like "efficiency" and "improvements" while shifting the new technological component to the background. For example the Director of Centralsys Ambulatory Care Operations pointed out that the new assemblage was working "more seamless" as earlier problems were no longer issues.

Similarly, physicians and other clinic staff made reference linking the new assemblages with patient-centric care and efficient workflows. For e.g., Metro's Dr. S tried explained in detail how the EMR-based lab resulting assemblage made his lab resulting performance "more efficient" by making information readily available.

Another part of stratifying was to discursively smooth over the minor issues that continued in the new assemblages' performance. For e.g., management and users admitted that some issues were distracting but expressed a need to compromise for the sake of how other parts of the assemblages were working. For example, in Suburb's lab resulting case, the practice manager agreed that things have improved albeit with specific issues for e.g., lab results not returning together or when new physicians joined the practice later.

> Things have gotten a little easier with the lab system as people are
> more familiar. [We had some] challenges with the two new providers,
> [they] threw us a [into a] loop. But now we have fallen into a routine
> with the systems. (Suburb Clinic Manager)

On the other hand, we noted that the ongoing performances of the new EMR assemblages as daily practices had introduced a new performance – a new form of accountability among those involved in the assemblages [29]. Part of the emergent accountability involved individual actors defining their identities and roles vis-à-vis other actors linked within the assemblage. The definition of identities and roles via the system so as to perform new accountability was especially salient in the case of medical assistants and physicians. In particular, the management claimed that the new lab resulting assemblage had aligned the medical assistants' actual work with the "ideal" medical assistant role and identity. Based on our data, we noted several key changes the EMR artifact brought to the new assemblages, which catalyzed the new accountability among different actors' and their roles. On the one hand, the new EMR system conferred new visibilities to the actions of individual actors and made it possible for other actors to compare their actions with other actors. On the other hand, the new EMR system enabled the focal actor and others to assess and evaluate their performances and react accordingly.

With regards to the latter point, we noted that nearly after a year into the system some of the medical assistants did get over the initial perception that EMR was "more work" to see the entire EMR as an important part of how they get their work done with the physicians. This brings us to the next aspect of stratifying, where actors now consciously or unconsciously drew upon the ongoing practices to perform new accountability. Thus, medical assistants and physicians have increased mutual accountability as a result of performing the new lab resulting assemblage. The assemblage's performance through the EMR system helped to better allocate responsibilities between the physicians and medical assistants.

The new accountability was drawn upon by the Centralsys' and clinics' management to measure, compare, and intervene with the assemblages' performance, in a very specific manner. For example, the clinic directors can get reports enumerating, summarizing and comparing the turnaround of lab resulting performances or scheduling output. Thus the different assemblages' performances are made accountable to management supervision and scrutiny. These reports through the EMR system enabled the management to drill-down to how each actor in the assemblage is contributing to the overall performance – e.g., particular physician or medical assistant's number of uncompleted inbasket messages and orders.

5   Discussion

Recently scholars under the rubric of sociomateriality have suggested that we need to take a relational perspective between social and material to understand organizations and change. Drawing upon Deluzian and DeLanda's [7] ontology, we sought to develop a potentially new lens and theoretical vocabulary – the performance lens – to understand how these sociomaterial assemblages perform within and across organizations. In particular, we used this performance lens to explore the dynamics of change when existing sociomaterial assemblages are faced with a new technology.

Principally, the performance lens contributes by making salient the role of collective actions by heterogeneous components – or "perform-ing" – in rendering the changed assemblages performative. From our findings, we identified four interrelated "perform-ing": constituting, counter-performing, calibrating, and stratifying. First, constituting explained how new assemblages emerged and are implemented i.e., actors draw on the expressive components such as new organizational goals and link them to the new IT artifact, which is then made part of the reconfigured assemblage. However, when these constituted EMR assemblages are implemented, counter-performing occurs as new relationships and new components breakdown within the new assemblages and between assemblages. Next, counter-performing becomes the targets for calibrating perform-ing, which involved rearranging problematic relations and/or components or adding relations and/or components across assemblages. Finally, as calibrating perform-ing renders the assemblages performative again, stratifying perform-ing emerged. Stratifying included discursive actions by human components that codified and consolidated the new assemblages as well as emergent performances of accountability that drew upon these assemblages.

Below, we elaborate on the contributions and significance of the performance lens in three different areas. First, we discuss how the performance process with its attending perform-ing helps us grasp more precisely the way assemblages are changed and rendered performative. These perform-ings builds on current sociomaterial research that has looked at how social and material are entangled together by expanding the scope and span of what and who are involved in this "invisible" work [18, 20]. Second, our analysis of counter-performing and calibrating revealed the process is not random but governed by an overarching pragmatism. We term this governing principle as "performative exigency" as the basis for determining the "success" of changed assemblages [8]. Third, we examine the organizational consequences of the evolved assemblages. Our findings show that beyond the obvious changes to each assemblage/practice across the two clinics, we noted that the new assemblages were associated with different performances of accountability [29, 30].

5.1   Performation and Perform-ing

Research on how social and material or human and artifacts become interwoven and entangled have often characterized it as a dialectical process involving tensions between single human actor (e.g., researcher or programmer) and a particular material artifact (e.g., laboratory apparatus or software program) [16, 31]. The process is driven by the resistance and accommodation experienced by the actors as they worked with the artifacts. Some of the recent studies have expanded this beyond human actions to include material agencies and how the two agencies become "imbricated" over time [15].

Our findings concerning the different perform-ing within the performation process extend this stream of research in several ways. First, unlike the current research that focuses on single user-artifact interactions, the perform-ing show that assemblages typically involved multiple groups of actors interacting with each other, sometimes directly and sometimes mediated by multiple material artifacts. Furthermore, the different actors are distributed across time and space. As shown in Callon and associates [8] study on the performativity of economics as well as in some recent work within the IS domain [31], this distributed multiplicity of actors means that it is not sufficient to consider individual user-artifact resistance and accommodation to understand how assemblages change and are stabilized. In fact, our study shows that perform-ing often involved resources and capabilities beyond that of individual components. Instead, our performation process shows the change process entails collective actions by different groups [8, 32]. These collective actions involved human actors with different capacities e.g., local users, project team members as well as hospital management working either in parallel or together to understand where the issues were and then putting in place strategic interventions. Further, some of these collective actions involved actors not directly using the system e.g., clinic management and project team. These actors enrolled material and discursive components as part of their managing, planning, and framing strategic interventions and material changes (e.g., policy change and interface development work) that were critical to rendering the assemblage performative. Thus unlike earlier studies of sociomaterial change, the performation lens enables us to take a wider analytical view beyond the immediate material and social interactions, so as to take into account the different types of collective work enacted by multiple groups of heterogeneous components.

Second, the perform-ing in the performation process provided a more nuanced appreciation for using a relational perspective to understand sociomaterial change. As shown in our findings as well as in recent sociomaterial work [5, 31], while each component may have their intrinsic properties, how "flexible" they are is are not based on those intrinsic properties alone but on how they are related with other components as well as on whether certain components are present or absent. For example, medical assistants are trained to use computer systems as part of their work and the EMR system supporting lab resulting was a piece of stable software. Yet when these two components were placed in the new lab resulting assemblage, the additional components such external lab systems changed the dynamics of the assemblage so that the medical assistant-EMR system link became problematic. In other words, the performation process is more than just failure of systems or user resistance. It is about understanding the emergent, situated dynamics among the multiple relations within and across assemblages.

Third, the performation process also bring to fore the role of other existing assemblages. Our performation and perform-ing argue that existing infrastructures plays a more active role than just acting as a "context" for current actions [33, 34]. Instead, we show that existing infrastructures are relational [35] and performative. In our constitutive and counter-performing perform-ing, we show that new assemblages are always linked to one or more assemblages [33, 34]. Furthermore, Callon and associates [8] mooted the idea that sometimes, in order for a focal assemblage to perform it has to ensure that other assemblages surrounding it co-performs. In other words, existing infrastructure or assemblages also shape how an assemblage is changed in terms of how it assists with or co-perform with the focal assemblage. This was well illustrated in our Suburb's lab resulting case where Suburb's new EMR lab resulting assemblage faced significant problems because their interfaces with the external lab system (an assemblage) were not performing correctly. The lab resulting assemblage also faced issues with how external lab providers' performed their lab tests and lab result data entry as the way they entered the data had important implications for how Suburb's physicians received the lab results. Thus, performance issues of sociomaterial assemblages may be due to how they are related with components from existing assemblages rather than issues emanating from the focal assemblage's own failings. Our performation view argues that we need to move one step beyond just taking into account existing structures and systems as those discussed in extant literature, but that we should include them into our analysis as active co-performing assemblages.

Finally, our performation process also speaks to a gap currently in most of sociomaterial research, i.e., how does changed sociomaterial assemblages become stable? Current studies of imbrication seem to imply an ongoing linear process of change without clearly explaining how and when imbrications end [12]. Other studies from Barad's [11] agential realism perspective tend to begin their analysis of a changed sociomaterial assemblage and focus on its consequences [5]. Our findings provide some insights into the perform-ing – Stratifying – that helped stabilize those changed assemblages. As discussed in our findings, stratifying involved actors enrolling discursive components to codify the assemblages as performative and actors consciously or unconsciously drawing upon the performed assemblages in enacting new accountability. Through the discourse and performances of new organizing structures, we found that the new assemblage in the two clinics became reified and taken-for-granted. The discursive aspect of stratifying attempts to make consolidate the new assemblages by linking it with a certain organizational logic or concepts (efficiency, patient-centric) while smoothing out "lumps" in the new assemblages [7]. In sense, the changed assemblage's ongoing ability to perform is highlighted by these discursive components thus suggesting a degree of rigidity of the new assemblages. This insight lends itself to future research that scholars within the domain of discourse research have also called attention [36]. With regards to new accountability performed as part of the reification of assemblages is discussed in the later section.

5.2   Performative Exigency

With regards to the idea of performative exigency, we argue that this principle extends current research on IT-enabled change. First, most IT-enabled change research has focused mainly on the "here and now" and do not provide more insights to the overarching change trajectory besides informing us that such changes tend to be ongoing [37, 38]. Second, some IS research that adhere to actor-network theory proposed that such changes are often emergent, random and subjected to "drift" as improvised uses and other unpredictable behaviors or interdependencies between human and material agencies emerge [39-41]. From our study, we argue against characterization of socimaterial change as random. We proposed that the performation process is governed by an overarching governing principle i.e., "performative exigency"; this pragmatic principle, which flows from the underlying performative approach, forms the basis for evaluating and driving the change process. The performative exigency therefore argues that the goal of any sociomaterial change is to cause the assemblage to perform better. Consequently, this performative exigency also sets the bounds to how the assemblage evolved. For example, in constituting the new assemblages, actors often enroll the efficiency principle, which is grounded on improvements of performances. Sometimes, actors may relate certain changes to current challenges to the performance of existing assemblages. More importantly, we see the performative exigency driving the calibrating perform-ing, where the overarching goal is to restore or change the assemblage's so as to render it performative again. This performative exigency therefore speaks to the guiding principle by which assemblages changed, evolved, and stabilized. We also point out that the performative exigency reflects a post-humanist perspective in that this guiding principle is not so much driven by heroic individuals or coalitions as it is determined and shaped by the network of relations among the different components [42].

5.3   Consequences of Sociomaterial Change – Transformed Accountability

Our findings on stratifying and how the different assemblages changed with the new EMR system also highlighted a surprising and important consequence of their new performances i.e., new forms of accountability. This finding resonates with emerging stream of research on discursive materiality [5]. Specifically, this stream of research argues that the inclusion of a technological artifact does not simply improve an assemblage's performance, it could potentially transform the performances of the assemblage as well. In the case of Scott and Orlikowski's [5] study of the TripAdvisor's ranking mechanism, they show that the mechanism did not just make travel information easier but actually actively performed new ways by which online travellers make sense of hotel information. Likewise, in our study, the EMR system did not just changed the way different practices were performed as we have described, it actually performed a new sense of accountability among the different groups of actors across the two clinics. In other words, as pointed out by Orlikowski and Scott [4] in their seminal piece on sociomateriality, we find that changes in sociomaterial assemblages have significant consequences on organizing and work. This adds to the extant literature that includes Barley's [43] seminal piece on how the use of CT scanners changed roles in radiology departments to a recent study by Barrett et al. [31] on the changes in work boundaries within pharmacies due to the use of a dispensing robot. The difference in our case was that the technology did not indirectly lead to those organizational changes; instead the fundamental change in how accountability was performed was the direct result of the technologies' performances.

As we have discussed above, the new accountability emerged given how the EMR system informates and make visible information across the assemblages [44]. The EMR system has also mediated and linked components that previously were not as "close". For example, in lab resulting, the medical assistants' work is much more closely linked to the physicians' work because of the new EMR lab resulting system. The tighter mediation of different parts of assemblages through the EMR system therefore catalyzed the performance of new accountability [45].

More importantly, and closer to the notion of "accountability" is that the new sociomaterial assemblage has created new ways of measuring performance to support evaluation and accountability, as well as, the allocation of responsibility [29, pp. 581-582]. The EMR in the new assemblages as discussed in the findings now renders each of the components as measurable, comparable and thus auditable (e.g. the output reports). Thus our findings show that medical assistants could track and see if the doctors have completed their in basket messages so that they can close their cases and vice versa for the physicians. In sum the performance of the EMR as part of the new assemblages led to a new configuration of relationships through its mediation and rendering of components measurable and comparable. These in turn helped to reconfigure new performances of accountability.

References

1. Zammuto, R., Griffith, T., Majchrzak, A., Dougherty, D., Faraj, S.: Information Technology and the Changing Fabric of Organization. Organization Science 18(5), 749–762 (2007)
2. Leonardi, P.M., Nardi, B.A., Kallinikos, J.: Materiality and Organizing Social Interaction in a Technological World. Oxford University Press, Oxford (2012)
3. Orlikowski, W.J.: The Sociomateriality of Organisational Life: Considering Technology on Management Research. Cambridge Journal of Economics 34(1), 125–141 (2010)
4. Orlikowski, W., Scott, S.: Sociomateriality: Challenging the Separation of Technology, Work and Organization. Academy of Management Annals 2(1), 433–474 (2008)
5. Scott, S., Orlikowski, W.: Reconfiguring Relations of Accountability: Materialization of Social Media in the Travel Sector. Accounting, Organizations and Society 37, 26–40 (2012)
6. Faraj, S., Azad, B.: The Materiality of Technology: An Affordance Perspective. In: Leonardi, P.M., Nardi, B., Kallinikos, J. (eds.) Materiality and Organizing: Social Interaction in a Technological World, pp. 237-258. University of Michigan Press (2012)
7. DeLanda, M.: A New Philosophy of Society: Assemblage Theory and Social Complexity. Continuum (2006)
8. Callon, M.: What Does It Mean to Say that Economics Is Performative? In: MacKenzie, D., Muniesa, F., Siu, L. (eds.) Do Economists Make Markets? On the Performativity of Economics, pp. 310–357. Princeton University Press (2007)
9. MacKenzie, D., Muniesa, F., Siu, L.: Do Economists Make Markets? On the Performativity of Economics. Princeton University Press (2007)
10. Deleuze, G., Guattari, F.: What Is Philosophy? Columbia University Press (1994)

11. Barad, K.: Posthumanist Performativity: Toward an Understanding of How Matter Comes to Matter. Signs 28(3), 801–831 (2003)
12. Kautz, K., Jensen, T.B.: Sociomateriality at the Royal Court of IS. Information and Organization 23(1), 15–27 (2013)
13. Leonardi, P.: Theoretical Foundations for the Study of Sociomateriality. Information and Organization 23(2), 59–76 (2013)
14. Leonardi, P., Barley, S.: Materiality and Change: Challenges to Building Better Theory about Technology and Organizing. Information and Organization 18(3), 159–176 (2008)
15. Leonardi, P.: When Flexible Routines Meet Flexible Technologies: Affordance, Constraint, and the Imbrication of Human and Material Agencies. MIS Quarterly 35(1), 147–167 (2011)
16. Pickering, A.: The Mangle of Practice: Agency and Emergence in the Sociology of Science. American Journal of Sociology 99(3), 559–589 (1993)
17. Callon, M., Muniesa, F.: Economic Markets as Calculative Collective Devices. Organization Studies 26(8), 1229–1250 (2005)
18. Law, J., Singleton, V.: Performing Technology's Stories: On Social Constructivism, Performance, and Performativity. Technology and Culture 41(4), 765–775 (2000)
19. Knorr-Cetina, K.: Tinkering toward Success: Prelude to a Theory of Scientific Practice. Theory and Society 8, 347–376 (1979)
20. Riemer, K., Johnston, R.S.: Place-Making: A Phenomenological Theory of Technology Appropriation. In: ICIS 2012 Proceedings (2012), http://aisel.aisnet.org/icis2012/proceedings/SocialImpacts/5/
21. Nicolini, D.: The Work to Make Telemedicine Work: A Social and Articulative View. Social Science & Medicine 62(11), 2754–2767 (2006)
22. Fujimura, J.: Crafting Science: A Sociohistory of the Quest for the Genetics of Cancer. Harvard University Press (1996)
23. Law, J.: On the Methods of Long-Distance Control: Vessels, Navigation and the Portuguese Route to India. In: Law, J. (ed.) Power, Action and Belief: A New Sociology of Knowledge, pp. 234–263. Routledge and Keegan, London (1986)
24. Oborn, E., Barrett, M., Davidson, E.: Unity in Diversity: Electronic Patient Record Use in Multidisciplinary Practice. Information Systems Research 22(3), 547–564 (2011)
25. Yin, R.: Case Study Research: Design and Methods. Sage (2003)
26. Schatzki, T.R.: Introduction: Practice Theory. In: Schatzki, T.R., Knorr-Cetina, K., von Savigny, E. (eds.) The Practice Turn in Contemporary Theory, pp. 10-23. Routledge (2001)
27. National Committee for Quality Assurance (NCQA): Standards and Guidelines for Physician Practice Connections – Patient-Centered Medical Home (PPC-PCMH). National Committee for Quality Assurance (NCQA), Washington, DC (2008)
28. Charmaz, K.: Constructing Grounded Theory: A Practical Guided Through Qualitative Analysis, 3rd edn. Sage (2006)
29. Miller, P., Power, M.: Accounting, Organizing, and Economizing. Academy of Management Annals 7(1), 555–603 (2013)
30. Scott, S., Orlikowski, W.: Sociomateriality – Taking the Wrong Turning? A Response to Mutch. Information and Organization 23(2), 77–80 (2013)
31. Barrett, M., Oborn, E., Orlikowski, W., Yates, J.: Reconfiguring Boundary Relations: Robotic Innovations in Pharmacy Work. Organization Science 23(5), 1448–1466 (2012)
32. Kjellberg, H.: The Death of a Salesman? Reconfiguring Economic Exchange in Swedish Post-War Food Distribution. In: Callon, M., Millo, Y., Muniesa, F. (eds.) Market Devices, pp. 65–91. Blackwell, Malden (2007)

33. Hanseth, O., Braa, K.: Hunting for the Treasure at the End of the Rainbow: Standardizing Corporate IT Infrastructure. Computer Supported Cooperative Work 10(3/4), 261–292 (2001)
34. Hanseth, O., Monteiro, E., Hatling, M.: Developing Information Infrastructure: The Tension between Standardization and Flexibility. Science, Technology, & Human Values 21(4), 407–426 (1996)
35. Star, S., Ruhleder, K.: Steps Toward an Ecology of Infrastructure: Design and Access for Large Information Spaces. Information Systems Research 7(1), 111–134 (1996)
36. Phillips, N., Oswick, C.: Organizational Discourse: Domains, Debates, and Directions. Academy of Management Annals 6(1), 435–481 (2012)
37. Leonardi, P., Barley, S.: What's Under Construction Here? Social Action, Materiality, and Power in Constructivist Studies of Technology and Organizing. Academy of Management Annals 4(1), 1–51 (2010)
38. Orlikowski, W.: Improvising Organizational Transformation over Time: A Situated Change Perspective. Information Systems Research 7(1), 63–92 (1996)
39. Ciborra, C.: From Control to Drift. Oxford Publishing Press (2000)
40. Latour, B.: Pandora's Hope: Essays on the Reality of Science Studies. Harvard University Press, Cambridge (1999)
41. Jones, M.: Information Systems and the Double Mangle: Steering a Course between the Scylla of Embedded Structure and the Charybdis of Strong Symmetry. In: Larsen, T.J., Levine, L., DeGross, J. (eds.) Information Systems: Current Issues and Future Changes, pp. 287–302. IFIP Press (1998)
42. Millo, Y.: Making Things Deliverable: The Origins of Index-Based Derivatives. In: Callon, M., Millo, Y., Muniesa, F. (eds.) Market Devices, pp. 196–214. Blackwell, Malden (2007)
43. Barley, S.: Technology as an Occasion for Structuring: Evidence from Observations of CT Scanners and the Social Order of Radiology Departments. Administrative Science Quarterly 31(1), 78–108 (1986)
44. Zuboff, S.: In the Age of the Smart Machine: The Future of Work and Power. Basic Books (1988)
45. D'Adderio, L.: The Performativity of Routines: Theorising the Influence of Artefacts and Distributed Agencies on Routines Dynamics. Research Policy 37(5), 769–789 (2008)

The Entwinement Logic of Practices

Insights from an Ethnography of Young IT Professionals

Hameed Chughtai and Michael D. Myers

University of Auckland Business School,
Private Bag 92019, Auckland, New Zealand
{h.chughtai,m.myers}@auckland.ac.nz

Abstract. This paper seeks to place the phenomenon of technology within the context of everyday practices using the logic of practical rationality. We draw some insights from our ethnography of young professionals and shed light on their everyday technological practices by invoking the concept of entwinement from hermeneutic phenomenology. Our findings reveal that the new generation users are becoming intimately entwined with information technologies in their everyday practices. Our study contributes toward the ongoing debate concerning the theorizing of technology and its relationship to practice.

Keywords: fieldwork, practical rationality, research methods, ethnography, Heidegger, entwinement.

1   Introduction

The question concerning the nature of one's interaction with technology remains open in information systems (IS) research [13, 21]. This question is further problematized by recent scholarship suggesting a rise of new generation of technology users [26, 27]. The young tech-savvy people, often labelled as Digital Natives, Generation Y, Millenials, or similar, are seen as absorbed in information technology (IT) in their everyday practices. Given that IS scholarship is concerned with the nature of people's interaction with technology, this contemporary phenomenon might shed some light on the key question regarding how to conceptualize IT in everyday practices. For example, if the new younger generation of users are indeed technologically savvy, then some of our IS theories which assume that people either resist technology or at least have some difficulty accepting it, such as technology acceptance model and its variants [17, p. 380], will be challenged and might need to be revised.

We find the shift in practices intriguing and begin by inquiring about the nature of one's technological immersion in everyday practices [15]. Accordingly, we take the view that in order to interpret practices it is important to see them through the logic of practical rationality; thus, we find an anchor in Heidegger's analysis of being-in-the-world which is grounded in the everyday practices from a practical perspective [9, 10]. Heidegger reminds us that we are 'always already' involved in the world in our mundane situations [5]; from this perspective, it is thus possible to interpret a phenomenon from *within* the practices in which people are already absorbed rather

B. Doolin et al. (Eds.): IS&O 2014, IFIP AICT 446, pp. 66–78, 2014.
© IFIP International Federation for Information Processing 2014

than conceptualizing practices externally, or taking an objective view. We find further support in the critical interpretation of being-in-the-world as *entwinement*, developed by Sandberg and Tsoukas [23]. They suggest that researchers need to study practices from an immersion perspective insofar as, following Heidegger, the people, too, are always already absorbed in their practices. They call this absorption our everyday entwinement in the world and provide a framework to study it. In this way, we find the interpretive concept of entwinement is appropriate for understanding everyday technological practices.

We draw on some of the insights from our critical ethnography of the everyday practices of young IT professionals in a large scale technology organization. The ethnographic method is suited to the study of the practices from an immersed point of view as it allows the field researchers to engage with the participants in their practice worlds [12, 23]. Our findings reveal that the entwinement logic of technological practices can be seen from three perspectives namely, purpose, skill and equipment. This multi perspective view sheds light on how young IT professionals are intricately entwined with technology in a holistic way in their everyday practices.

The paper is organized as follows. We first elaborate our theoretical perspective and highlight the significance of practical rationality. Next, we spell out the concept of entwinement from practical rationality, followed by interpreting the everyday practices as entwinement. We then present some evidence from the field regarding entwinement. The article concludes with a brief discussion and a few suggestions for further research.

2   Theoretical Perspective

We ground our inquiry in the everyday perspective on practices through Heidegger's analysis of being-in-the-world using practical rationality [10]. Heidegger's influence regarding the study of practices has been acknowledged in the parallel disciplines of organization [1, 8, 24, 28], management [22, 23], and computer science [4, 30]. Some IS researchers, too, have invoked Heidegger's hermeneutic phenomenology to criticize Cartesian trends in IS research [2, 3, 16]. According to this critique, IS research is dominated by theories that can be best described as espousing scientific rationality [e.g., 13, 21]. In this strand of research, everyday situations are often conceptualized through detached scientific worldviews. However, recent critical organizing scholarship redirects the attention of IS researchers to employ practical rationality, as developed within hermeneutic phenomenology, in order to understand the complex and mundane nature of everyday practices [22, 23]. In this way, it is possible to understand a practical phenomenon from *within* a practice in which one is usually absorbed rather than looking through an external objective lens.

In the practical immersion perspective, Sandberg and Tsoukas [23] suggest, building on the concept of being-in-the-world, that "we are first absorbed in practice before we start reflecting on it" (p. 345). Accordingly, they interpret one's everyday entwinement in practice as follows:

the notion of being-in-the-world stipulates that our most basic form of being is entwinement: we are never separated but always already entwined with others and things in [a holistic whole within] practice worlds. (p. 343)

Following Heidegger [10], they suggest that entwinement is the logic of everyday practices insofar as we can only understand a practice in relation to other practices, things and people in which it is entwined with [23, 24]. This argument finds further support in Dreyfus [5] who, too, suggests: "we can only describe the phenomena as they show themselves and show how they fit with the rest of human existence" (p. 162). From this perspective, a practice is seen as "noncontingent," Sandberg and Tsoukas [23] articulate, inasmuch as "it incorporates distinctions that provide its practitioners with a certain [spatiotemporal] orientation, without which the particular practice would not be what it is" (p. 343). We thus note that the entwinement perspective is found to be holistic as it suggests researchers should take note of a multi perspective 'nexus of practices' of participants within which they are usually absorbed in their everyday situations.

Insofar as the entwinement perspective puts forward an absorbed holistic view, we can then ask the question, how can one grasp the phenomenon if we are always already absorbed in our practices? The answer is found by interpreting instances of temporary breakdowns in established practices [14, 23, p. 344ff]. A temporary breakdown in practice temporarily brings the otherwise unreflective absorbed interaction to the fore and provides an opportunity to understand the practices. Prior IS research has shown that the temporary breakdowns in practice are a fruitful way to understand practices [4, 30]. There are two types of temporary breakdowns in practices which reveal the logic of entwinement [23, p. 347ff]: i) first order breakdowns and ii) second order breakdowns. While the former are unforeseen, the latter are caused by active intervention in an on-going practice; thus the latter are excluded from our research as it contradicts the ethnographic principle of non-intervention. Our inquiry, thus, deals with first order breakdowns in practice which are triggered by unexpected outcomes, deliberate reflection, as well as deviations or becoming aware of differences in an established practice (ibid). Given space limitations, a full scale discussion of breakdowns is not possible here, but for critical research on breakdowns in organizing practices, see Chia and Holt [1], Gibbs [8] and Sandberg and Dall'Alba [22]. Next, we develop entwinement as our main lens to understand technological practices.

3   Interpreting Technological Practices as Entwinement

Insofar as IT is increasingly becoming ubiquitous in everyday practice [26, 31], the new generation of users are often described as being deeply absorbed in their everyday technological practices. Consistent with the hermeneutic of entwinement, people are, thus generally seen as interacting transparently with IT [27], or simply entwined with it. Accordingly, as one engages with IT, mundane disruptions such as device failure temporarily bring the otherwise transparent practices to the fore. The technological practices, thus, becomes available for inquiry by the virtue of temporary breakdowns in practice. As shown earlier, an instance of breakdown might reveal the complex logic of entwinement in terms of our material interaction as well as the aspects of time and space within which the practice breakdown occurs.

In the entwinement perspective, a practice is both sociomaterial and spatiotemporal by the virtue of our being-in-the-world [22, 23]; here, a practice is interpreted as an "organized, open-ended spatial-temporal manifold of actions" and is always found to be in a holistic 'nexus of practice' [24, p. 471]. In this way, a practice is intelligible only when it is interpreted in the light of other entwined practices in a nexus. Accordingly, we take IT as holistic equipment which is entwined in our everyday practices through our being-in-the-world and thus dispersed over space time. A nexus of practice thus beckons to take a multi perspective view on the phenomena. According to Heidegger [10] the things that we relate to must be understood as part of the world that we also are part of, arguing thus: an instrument is what it does and this in a context of assignments. Accordingly, following Heidegger [10], and building on critical interpretations developed by Dreyfus [5] and Sandberg and Tsoukas [23], we note, IT when seen through the dialectic logic of entwinement is argued to be what it is in terms of,

1. Skills – in terms of actual usage of IT,
2. Equipment – as a holistic whole of IT in relation to one another, and
3. Purpose – within a situation and in relation to the holistic equipment and skills.

The concept of entwinement, hence, paints the dialectic as a circular relationship with no specific center (Figure 1): we can understand the purpose of technology that is referenced in the actual use; the purposeful use is, then, related to skills and yields meaning in a practice; and, similarly, the skills make sense through the purposeful use and also determines the use of a technology by assigning it to a task in order to achieve a goal. When one aspect is broken, or a perspective is not taken into account, the dialectic faces a practice breakdown.

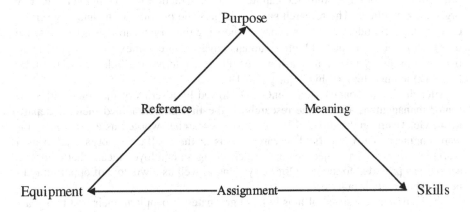

Fig. 1. Entwinement logic of technological practices

The conceptual understanding, as illustrated in our suggested entwinement model, stems from Heidegger's [10] being-in-the-world analysis, through the interpretations developed by Dreyfus [5] and Schatzki [24], to reveal the logic of everyday technological practices. Heidegger's insight concerning the entwined trinity of equipment, skills and purpose in everyday practices is already used in seminal studies of complex tool use in IS scholarship [30]. In this way, we support and extend the concept of entwinement which, too, builds on Heidegger's thesis, arguing thus: the entwinement logic of practices suggests taking the holistic being-in-the-world perspective in order to interpret the everyday use of technology. When taking the holistic understanding of technology, the entwinement perspective discloses that the cyclical triad logic of our everyday practices is perpetual, or trialectic in nature. Thus, the technological practices are seen as transparent as long as we fluidly interact with our surrounding world; only a breakdown in any of the relations will bring the dynamics of practices to the fore. Recent developments in critical scholarship have suggested that such breakdowns are not necessarily destructive since a moment of critical reflection may allow us to develop new skills [8, 14]. Subsequently, the newly acquired skills tend to move to the background of everyday practices as they persist in everyday use, the entwinement, too, becomes transparent once again.

Thus, we can say that the technology in everyday practices of younger generation can be seen as deeply entwined as holistic equipment always available (e.g., ubiquitous IT), which is then persistently used for various purposeful use leading to acquisition of new skills as well as everyday understandings. In this way, the entwinement logic can reveal how IT is conceptualized in the everyday practices of new generation users. We will now discuss the details of our ethnographic inquiry from which the entwinement lens stemmed, followed by some evidence from our fieldwork.

4   Research Method

We conducted a critical ethnography, spanning over eight months, amongst young IT professionals in order to study the nature of their interaction with IT in their everyday organizing practices. The research site is a large scale provider of technology services, GenOrg, a pseudonym. Our reason for choosing this organization was the presence of a high number of young IT professionals engaged in complex technological practices within an organization. Further, we followed interpretive field research guidelines [12] in our ethnographic inquiry [18, 19].

After the initial contact with GenOrg, followed by a series of meetings with their senior management, one of the researchers, the first author, joined their IT department, GenTeam, in August 2013. The onsite researcher worked as a part-time software engineer. Thus, the field researcher was at the coalface of organization as a working member of a project team. Further, being an employee meant that complete access was provided to the GenOrg IT systems as well as a window of opportunity to be absorbed in their practices.

The GenTeam consisted of mostly fresh graduates or people in their first two years of employment whereas the managers were more experienced. Interestingly, as we will reveal, in their technological practices, the actual use of IT is found to be blurred and any stereotypical generational references were absent. This is perhaps due to the highly technical nature of organizational work which further problematizes their absorption in IT. Thus, we find ourselves in a complex mesh of technological practices.

By the virtue of being an active member, as also suggested by Sandberg and Tsoukas [23, p. 350], the researcher's role was extended from a mere observer to "a temporary participant" thus acquiring the capacity to observe temporary breakdowns in the transparent practices of participants from their perspective on the field practice. In this way we were also able "to get practitioners to step back from what they routinely do" (Ibid) and reflect on their practices. We thus also found participants as "interpreters and analysts" of our ethnography as we immersed deeper in their field practices [12, p. 74].

Consistent with the ethnographic method, the data was collected primarily through participant observation. The field researcher being an active team member allowed us to document field notes containing "thick description[s]" [7, pp. 3-30] of weekly project's meetings and user groups' meetings, video-conferencing logs, informal chats, internal instant messaging service logs, internal communications using organization's e-mail service, photographs, audio notes and working with organization's internal knowledgebase. All our field notes were documented either on the spot, where the situation permitted, or soon afterwards. By the virtue of an active team member, it was often possible to document events while being absorbed in the field practices, or often as an event unfolded. Further, on many occasions the participants were aware as the field researcher switched between the ongoing practices to documenting the field notes. The field notes were almost always taken digitally, usually on a workstation or using a mobile device where possible.

We also conducted 10 semi-structured qualitative interviews with select participants [20]. The interviews ranged from an hour to two hours. While most interviews were semi-structured, some participants were quite candid during the interview and thus tended towards being more unstructured insofar as we followed the narrative painted by the participants. Further, we adhered to the guidelines suggested by Myers and Newman [20] regarding qualitative interviews. Finally, all of our data was captured and coded using NVivo. Given the massive amount of data collected over eight months, we draw on just a fragment of this evidence for this paper.

5   Evidence from the Fieldwork

Here we present our interpretation of a single significant issue from three different perspectives in an attempt to shed some light on the intricacies of the entwinement. All examples are written from the field researcher's point of view.

5.1   Entwinement Perspective – Purpose

We begin with a seemingly mundane event from the fieldwork when I was asked to join an expert user group meeting. Although the meeting was routine for GenOrg, we documented an instance of a temporary breakdown in practice during the discussion of the GenWeb architecture. The meeting was quite informal and steered by a young technical analyst, Tom. During the course of the meeting, it became quite clear that some of the users were struggling to grasp the latest infrastructural level changes in their flagship software product. Many of such people were longtime users and considered themselves confident in the use of the GenWeb software tools. However, we observed that the new changes, although subtle, were significant as they threatened and thus revealed the otherwise transparent practices of the users. Tom listened to the many critical conversations, regarding the proposed change in established technological practices, and then demonstrated, on a large screen, how intuitive the new changes were. Contrary to the claim of some users, his point was that many people are simply sticking to 'the decade old technological practices'. This is what he said:

> We are in the future, people... And have you ever noticed [that with] the technology... you can do some amazing things, like stream in real time [etc.] but people don't get excited because they are used to it and they just expect it to work so if anything [referring to GebWeb software] stop working, people [complain]: 'ah, typical technology, not working anymore' (smiles). (Excerpt from the usergroup meeting)

He went on to reflect that instead of attributing the failure to the technologies, the organization users need to find more clever ways to interact with the new tools. Later on, he brought back the question of intuitive purposeful use of technology in everyday organizing practices and emphasized that most of the users face difficulty because they take IT with an inherent purpose either as a 'fixed' solution or something 'special' which needs to be used only in a set way. Consider the following remarks as Tom discusses with the user group how they can use the GenWeb technologies as a tool and encourage them to modify it up to their purpose and needs:

> When you are using [GenWeb], it is a *tool*, and as a tool it can be used well, it can be used badly. And, I think, the number one thing that you can always do to create success is [by]... *being intuitive with it*. (Excerpt from the usergroup meeting)

He then listed several technical examples of complex use of organizational tools. Elsewhere in the field, we observed the use of GenWeb as a tool within the GenTeam everyday practices as well. Many people used the organizational software services for more than one purpose, sometimes entwining personal and organizational lives. For instance, the IT platform that hosted GenWeb knowledgebase was also found to be used for personal notes, work notes, as well as a communication medium within the organization. Many participants casually told me that such uses were not intentional but increasingly became part of their practices. Further, the purposeful use of organizational equipment, driven by the skills of users, revealed that the practical purposeful use of technology mattered to these participants quite a lot. As Tom said:

> [IT] is all about your personal choice, and it is driven by your personal interest, all you have to do it then just use it as you like it. (Excerpt from the interview)

Here, we observe the participant puts emphasis on the use of IT through personal involvement (rather than having a fixed use or a static purpose). We can, then, say that through entwinement logic of practices the purpose is disclosed as a plastic concept. Tom, and many others, linked the unintentional but purposeful use of IT to their acquisition of skills. This is discussed next.

5.2   Entwinement Perspective – Skills

After a few months in the field, we observed that some young participants were quite often *playing* with new technologies on their own accord. Same participants were also working on the latest software solutions. While there were others who were not participating in such endeavors, they were at least aware of their skill level. As one young participant, Amy, (who was not working in a pure technical role), gasped after praising a programming solution, as developed by a colleague, "I wish I could do that, but this is not for me." When I inquired casually, why the programming skill is 'not for her?' she explained that she is curious and finds it as an interesting skill but she had 'no purpose' to do so. She was somewhat doubtful about simply gaining the skill without engaging in a purposeful use. She recalled that once a colleague tried to teach her programming skills, "I just didn't know what to do with it; there was no real task anyway," she giggled timidly.

The question concerning technological skills was further problematized by a young developer, Tom. Despite being a keen programmer, Tom painted a mundane picture of technological practices and says the young people, as he discussed and mirrored his own perspective, 'seem to have better skills' but they are simply using it intuitively rather than 'thinking about it'. In an interview, Tom reflected on this very phenomenon regarding new generation's practices as something banal:

> [We are] the people who can naturally pick up new technologies, and are intuitive... [for example] learning a new smartphone is so simple, it's easy [because] it makes sense... people [like me] who are at least grown up with enough technologies to know, how it happens, how it generally works, you know. They are not double-clicking the thing that needs single clicking and so forth (laughs). (Excerpt from the interview)

Astonishingly, his confessional insight became a prophecy as we witnessed a similar breakdown event in a project meeting soon afterwards. The meeting involved a demo for GenWeb mobile features on a touch screen tablet device. In this demo, the users were required to perform 'right-click' functionality. However, insofar as the touch screens usually do not have right-click due to absence of mouse like interfaces, it caused some confusion among some team members; thus, a breakdown in ongoing practice, as documented in this excerpt from the field notes:

> The [touch screen tablet] is passed around to see a specific touch functionality, [a senior manager] wonders: "but how do you right-click on this thing,"... [a young participant] then teaches her how right click works [on the tablet] and [the manager] looks genuinely surprised on this discovery, but asks: "but why do you need to right click on a tablet, it doesn't make sense," and [the younger participant] reply is affirmative: "I think it's for the people who are *stuck* in the old design. (Excerpt from the field notes)

The breakdown incident further reveals two interrelated concepts; first, the technological skills actualized differently for different people. For instance, the manager who didn't know how to interact intuitively, thus a breakdown occurred in technological practices. However, as the breakdown brought forth the practices for inspection by becoming aware of a phenomenon, the manager correctly recognizes the flaw is in the design not his or her own practice. Thus, the senior manager's skills converge toward new generations' practices. Second, a conflict in practice actualization triggers another subtle temporary breakdown via unexpected outcome i.e., click functionality. Thus, it brought the entwinement to the fore again as the young participant reflected on the nature of design which, again, usually remains hidden. We thus observe how skills are subtly entwined with purpose and equipment.

5.3   Entwinement Perspective – Equipment

Perhaps the entwinement of technology in everyday practice is best seen from the equipment perspective. We observed in the field how fluidly members of GenTeam interacted with IT in their practices. We also acknowledge that, from the periphery, it might appear as an 'organizational norm' to be amidst many technologies; however, the case in point is to precisely open up the said taken for granted practices for scrutiny especially as technology is increasing becoming ubiquitous in everyday life (as well as at work). For instance, Tom, like many other participants, worked on multiple technologies simultaneously, often including virtual IT solutions where a physical machine was not present; further, he revealed that he was also an avid gamer in his spare time. In this perspective, he compared the ubiquity of IT in his mundane affairs to the complex organizing technological practices and found a failure is equally 'annoying' insofar as certain technologies are seen as essential as 'a feature of life':

> [a technological tool] breaking down [is frustrating after] it becomes accepted technology [as] *a feature of your life*, and [because] you come to accept that it is there [whether at work or home], and you come to accept that it is working, and so, you are used to that and start to forget about it. (Excerpt from the interview)

We thus began to observe an obvious characteristic of participants' practices that technologies are seen entwined as integral and ubiquitous parts which are deemed to be working all the time. Further, a breakdown is seen as a breakdown in the life of individuals where entwinement is usually transparent and fluid. Interestingly, other participants shared this significance but their interpretations varied. For instance, Julie, a young developer, found the ubiquitous IT as an opportunity to switch to other equipment in case of a failure. Her perspective, too, brings us closer to entwinement as Heidegger [10, p. 97] points out "there 'is' no such thing as *an* equipment." Similarly, IT is not a thing on its own but always seen from one practical perspective to other things. In this way, we note the ubiquitous IT, as Tom finds, hides with persisted use in practice in that it becomes taken for granted.

The entwinement logic of practice thus begins to reveal IT as transparent holistic equipment in everyday practice. Further, IT is understood vis-à-vis the actual involved use in practices, as Julie once described how technological work practices transparently entwine with her everyday practices. Within this absorbed involvement with technology, when asked if she thinks a technology *qua* technology, she replied:

What is there to think about? Honestly. If something is new … like a new game … do you think about it when you play it? No, you don't. You just play it. Same thing is for technologies, like [social networks], it's just there. I give it a try, see if I like it or not. Most of things, well, you don't know whether you like it or not unless you try. So, just use it. (Excerpt from the interview)

Her insight remains unanimous among all the participants at GenOrg as most of them readily endorse the holistic view of IT as equipment. For instance, Tom, too, said, for him, interacting with IT is akin to an invisible tool which he transparently uses whereas others find it is holistically pervasive everywhere. Thus, it is not surprising, in this instance, the use of technology is found to be analogous to playing an invisible game, arguing thus: insofar as interacting fluidly with ubiquitous IT, as if being immersed in a game, is seen as intuitive, transparently purposeful, it requires absorbing oneself in the practice, and thus influences (and is itself conditiond by) practical skills. We thus suggest that the entwinement logic of practices uncovers a multi perspective view which could help IS researchers to conceptualize IT in everyday practices.

6   Discussion

Our study is concerned with one of the central questions in IS scholarship: how do people engage with technology in their everyday organizing practices? We provide a partial solution by looking at the new generation of users from their absorbed perspective. Our solution takes the form of interpreting the interaction with technology using entwinement logic of practice. Following Dreyfus' [6] critical approach, we reinstate to "begin with practices" in order to make sense of our complex interaction with technology.

Numerous calls have been made to pay attention to the ubiquity of technology in everyday practice [26, 31]. We respond and show that researchers and organizations can learn a lot from the everyday practices of younger generations' use of ubiquitous technology. The new generation users are found to be intuitively comfortable with technology, contrary to the traditional view which holds that people generally resist new technologies. As IT becomes ubiquitous in the everyday practices, the new users develop a rather complex automatic relationship with technology. This insight is significant for organizations to manage the younger workforce which are shown to be entwined with technology. A disruption in a fluid technological practice is seen as a disruption in everyday life. We further extend this insight to invite IS researchers to examine design practices to develop tools in a way that are 'invisible' and transparent in practice. Here, Heidegger's [10] insight has begun to manifest itself in contemporary software practices of solution designing which are, as demonstrated, intimately entwined in our everyday practices. Stroustrup [25, p. 19] remarks concerning the design of innovative technological solutions: "[g]ood software is invisible…[yet] [we] can be annoyed or hurt if it doesn't do what it is supposed to do. We can be annoyed or hurt if what it is supposed to do doesn't suit our needs." Accordingly, we have witnessed the same phenomenon in the field; thus, we can say a new conceptualization of design practices might be required in the light of the entwinement logic of practices.

We suggest the concept of entwinement might also be significant for IS research methods as it might help us review our theoretical and practical approaches in the light of contemporary technological practices. For instance, a key finding from our fieldwork is that entwinement is quite strong in young people's practices: insofar as technology is ubiquitously available, the technological practices tend to be more transparent. As one participant succinctly puts, 'it just makes sense'. Taking a cue from field evidence, we can, then, suggest taking a practical approach using practical rationality toward conceptualizing information technology. In this way, it might be helpful for researchers to understand how a technological phenomenon manifests in practice and, then, interpret it according to and from *within* the very practice which envelops it [5, 10, 23]. Taken together with the preceding insight concerning transparency of technology, we note that the entwinement perspective can further bring the design and practice aspects within IS scholarship closer to develop better tools and systems.

We have also shown the significance of an absorbed perspective on practices to grasp IT in everyday situations. In our ethnography of young professionals, who are found to be absorbed in their technological practices, we have uncovered that for the new generation users, IT is increasingly seen as a hidden tool interwoven in their transparent practices. Further, our fieldwork reveals that new generation users find using the technological tools as intuitively engaging in an invisible *play* like dialectic. This evidence strongly relates to the entwinement's underlying roots of absorption in practices [5, p. 66], and within such absorption, "not only is equipment transparent; so is the user." As shown earlier, only a breakdown in practices brings our attention to technology with which we are invisibly engaged in, our entwinement otherwise remains hidden. In this perspective, this is exactly what we have observed and interpreted as the entwinement logic in the field practices.

Our field evidence thus endorses the view that information technology can be seen as holistic 'invisible' equipment which not only remains hidden in practice but in fact should remain in the background for one to work smoothly [29]. Although practice breakdowns are critical to inquire about the practices, the researchers and organizations need to ensure the breakdowns are minimal. To sum it up, the ubiquitous IT is becoming increasingly transparent, it is only when it breaks down that we find how deeply entwined we are with it in our everyday practices [10, p. 188ff, 15, p. 282, 303].

7 Conclusion

We have suggested the entwinement lens as a significant theoretical and practical tool to study the shifting ways of engaging with technology. Contrary to the prevailing perspectives grounded in scientific rationality of practices, we offer an absorbed perspective to interpret the practical phenomena from within contemporary everyday practices using the practical rationality of entwinement. In this way, IS researchers can critically examine the everyday practices by stepping in rather than stepping out of the practices. The entwinement perspective thus invites field researchers to be closer to field practices. Some researchers in parallel disciplines of organizing and management studies have begun to investigate entwinement in more depth, specifically in terms of practice breakdowns [14] and sense making within organizations [11, 22]. A fruitful avenue for IS researchers is to inquire the said strands in the context of technological practices. For instance, insofar as the practical rationality of entwinement discloses a play like dialectic, how can we further understand the complex spatiotemporal dynamics of such dialectic in organizing practices? Another possible way is to shed light on the significance of entwinement in skill acquisition vis-à-vis engagement with equipment through practical rationality. Thus, we find the entwinement logic of practices potentially opens up new avenues for IS scholars and practitioners alike and creates possibilities to conconceptualize and theorize complex everyday practices in a coherent manner.

References

1. Chia, R., Holt, R.: Strategy as Practical Coping: A Heideggerian Perspective. Organization Studies 27, 635–655 (2006)
2. Ciborra, C.: Situatedness Revisited: The Role of Cognition and Emotion. In: Bagnara, S., Smith, G.C. (eds.) Theories and Practice in Interaction Design, pp. 107–116. Lawrence Erlbaum, London (2006)
3. Ciborra, C., Hanseth, O.: From Tool to Gestell: Agendas for Managing the Information Infrastructure. Information Technology & People 11, 305–327 (1998)
4. Dourish, P.: Where the Action Is: The Foundations of Embodied Interaction. MIT Press, Cambridge (2004)
5. Dreyfus, H.L.: Being-in-the-World: A Commentary on Heidegger's Being and Time. MIT Press (1991)
6. Dreyfus, H.L.: Reflections on the Workshop on "The Self". Anthropology and Humanism Quarterly 16, 27–31 (1991)
7. Geertz, C.: The Interpretation of Cultures. Basic Books, New York (1973)
8. Gibbs, P.: Heidegger's Contribution to the Understanding of Work Based Studies. Springer, London (2011)
9. Heidegger, M.: History of the Concept of Time: Prolegomena. Indiana University Press, Bloomington (1985)
10. Heidegger, M.: Being and Time. HarperPerennial/Modern Thought, New York (2008)
11. Holt, R., Sandberg, J.: Phenomenology and Organization Theory. In: Tsoukas, H., Chia, R. (eds.) Philosophy and Organization Theory, vol. 32, pp. 215–249. Emerald, Bingley (2011)
12. Klein, H.K., Myers, M.D.: A Set of Principles for Conducting and Evaluating Interpretive Field Studies in Information Systems. MIS Quarterly 23, 67–94 (1999)
13. Leonardi, P.M.: When Flexible Routines Meet Flexible Technologies: Affordance, Constraint, and the Imbrication Of Human And Material Agencies. MIS Quarterly 35, 147–168 (2011)
14. Lok, J., de Rond, M.: On the Plasticity of Institutions: Containing and Restoring Practice Breakdowns at the Cambridge University Boat Club. Academy of Management Journal 56, 185–207 (2013)
15. Mannheim, K.: The Problem of Generations. In: Kecskemeti, P. (ed.) Essays on the Sociology of Knowledge, pp. 276–320. Routledge and Kegan Paul, London (1952)
16. Mingers, J.: Embodying Information Systems: The Contribution of Phenomenology. Information and Organization 11, 103–128 (2001)
17. Morris, M.G., Venkatesh, V.: Age Differences in Technology Adoption Decisions: Implications for a Changing Work Force. Personnel Psychology 53, 375–403 (2000)

18. Myers, M.D.: Qualitative Research in Information Systems. MIS Quarterly 21, 241–242 (1997)
19. Myers, M.D.: Investigating Information Systems with Ethnographic Research. Communications of the AIS 2, Article 23 (1999)
20. Myers, M.D., Newman, M.: The Qualitative Interview in IS Research: Examining the Craft. Information and Organization 17, 2–26 (2007)
21. Orlikowski, W.J.: Sociomaterial Practices: Exploring Technology at Work. Organization Studies 28, 1435–1448 (2007)
22. Sandberg, J., Dall'Alba, G.: Returning to Practice Anew: A Life-World Perspective. Organization Studies 30, 1349–1368 (2009)
23. Sandberg, J., Tsoukas, H.: Grasping the Logic of Practice: Theorizing Through Practical Rationality. Academy of Management Review 36, 338–360 (2011)
24. Schatzki, T.R.: The Sites of Organizations. Organization Studies 26, 465–484 (2005)
25. Stroustrup, B.: Programming: Principles and Practice Using C++. Addison Wesley Professional, Crawfordsville (2014)
26. Vodanovich, S., Sundaram, D., Myers, M.D.: Research Commentary: Digital Natives and Ubiquitous Information Systems. Information Systems Research 21, 711–723 (2010)
27. Wang, Q., Myers, M.D., Sundaram, D.: Digital Natives and Digital Immigrants. Business & Information Systems Engineering 5, 409–419 (2013)
28. Weick, K.E.: Designing for Thrownness. In: Boland, R.J., Collopy, F. (eds.) Managing as Designing, pp. 74–78. Stanford Business Books, Stanford (2004)
29. Weiser, M., Brown, J.S.: The Coming Age of Calm Technology. In: Denning, P.J., Metcalfe, R.M. (eds.) Beyond Calculation, pp. 75–85. Springer, New York (1997)
30. Winograd, T., Flores, F.: Understanding Computers and Cognition: A New Foundation for Design. Ablex, Norwood (1986)
31. Yoo, Y.: Computing in Everyday Life: A Call for Research on Experiential Computing. MIS Quarterly 34, 213–231 (2010)

Counter-Mapping as Assemblage

Reconfiguring Indigeneity

Gwilym Eades[1] and Yingqin Zheng[2]

[1] Department of Geography, Royal Holloway University of London, Surrey, UK
Gwilym.Eades@rhul.ac.uk
[2] School of Management, Royal Holloway University of London, Surrey, UK
Yingqin.Zheng@rhul.ac.uk

Abstract. This paper explores the utility of assemblage theory for intergenerational counter-mapping and, through this, for reconfigurations of indigeneity. Counter-mapping is theorised as a kind of assemblage that, through intergenerational learning, is fundamentally memetic (composed of evolving units of information) in nature. Assemblage is theorised as having three aspects (relations of exteriority, meshworks and memes) for reconfiguring indigeneity in line with spatio-temporal aspects of memes. Counter-mapping assemblages are explored with examples of First Nations' (indigenous peoples residing in Canada) political and commemorative activity. *Kaachewaapechuu*, a long commemorative walk in the northern Quebec Cree village of Wemindji, acts as a case study for exploring how assemblages-as-memes can be used to theorise new kinds of counter-mapping that reconfigure indigenous commemoration precisely as political, and therefore as not separate from more media-driven aspects of Canadian politics, including those concerning its First Nations. Global positioning systems and Google Earth mapping platforms were used during the primary author's participation in *kaachewaapechuu*, providing for the exploration of new media platforms upon which such a re-theorised politics might be envisioned.

Keywords: counter-mapping, assemblage, meme, indigeneity, Cree, Canada.

1   Introduction

This paper about mapping and counter-mapping builds upon the current discourse on sociomateriality which centres on the relationship between information technology and organizational practices, where the social and the material are perceived as deeply imbricated [33, 40-42]. The material agency, or performativity, of artefacts have been long recognized and extensively theorized in the literature under the umbrella of actor-network theory [7, 30, 31] which is inherent to the sociomaterial approach. The sociomaterial perspective encourages us to resist "preoccupations of separation" and pay attention to "notions of distributed agencies, sociomaterial practices, and performative relations as these play out in organizational realities" [42, p. 466]. Drawing on Actor-Network Theory [32, 51], Orlikowski and Scott [42] call for a relational ontology of

B. Doolin et al. (Eds.): IS&O 2014, IFIP AICT 446, pp. 79–94, 2014.
© IFIP International Federation for Information Processing 2014

materiality in organizational life, and use the term "sociomaterial assemblages" as opposed to a perception of "discrete entities of mutually dependent ensembles" [42, p. 467]. While the term has been taken up in various studies [e.g. 21, 53, 54], the concept of "assemblage" has often been taken as a given and rarely unpacked. Emphasis is often on the entanglement of human and material agency. Less examined are elements of temporality, spatiality, becoming, inherent tension and power contestation.

"Agencement" in French, the concept of assemblage originates from Deleuze and Guattari [18] and depicts a heterogeneous collectivity with multiple connects that is constantly in flux and becoming. The Deleuzian concept is then developed by various theorists across different fields, most notably by DeLanda [15, 17] into a social theory. An assemblage is not reducible to the properties of its component parts but emergent from the actual exercise of their capacities. In other words, an assemblage is *"both the provisional holding together of a group of entities across differences and a continuous pro-cess of movement and transformation as relations and terms change"* [1, p.178]. The concept of assemblage thus lends itself to explore "open ended collectives" [3] and how they achieve stabilisation and transformation. If we move beyond the locus of technical systems within organisations, which is often the topic of information systems research, we could consider the performativity of sociomaterial assemblages in broader, trans-local contexts [37].

In this paper, we mainly draw upon concepts from DeLanda's [15-17] assemblage theory to explore the performativity of mapping and counter-mapping. We examine counter-mapping in the context of an indigenous ritual, specifically in the northern Quebec village of Wemindji. Power and resistance lie at the heart of commemorative counter-mapping rituals such as the long walk in Wemindji. We conceptualize the long walk which involves creating a trail on Google Earth as an assemblage that produces alternative spatial-temporal relations to those which have become hegemonic through temporal sedimentation or powerful imposition. The aim of this article is to explore and apply concepts from Deleuzian assemblage thinking in order to advance previously underexplored perspectives of sociomaterial assemblage in relation to temporality, spatiality, identity, hegemony, contestation and transmission between knowledge regimes.

2   Mapping and Counter-Mapping

Maps are defined broadly as "graphic representations that facilitate a spatial understanding of things, concepts, conditions, processes or events in the human world" [25, p. xvi; quotation from 57, p. 1]. Mapping can be defined as the process of mapmaking, one that involves planning, data collection, production, and critique [52, p. 12]. The final product of mapping is a map, inscribed (written or printed) on paper or image file; stored in the brain as a mental map; performed as a journey; or scratched into the sand [5]. Cosgrove [11, p. 1] offers a theoretically sophisticated definition of mapping as "visualizing, conceptualizing, recording, representing, and creating spaces graphically...a graphic register of correspondence between two spaces, whose explicit outcome is a space of representation." This definition is both broad enough to encompass a range of media and mapping activities while avoiding limiting mapping activities to those associated with the state, at the same time as confining itself to the graphical register.

Mapping is thus the process of producing and reproducing "a spatial understanding" of a part of the world. The political nature and performativity of maps and mapping have long been noted. For example, Wood [56, p. 7] characterises mapping as that which serves state interests (such as statistical profiles and territorial extents) through the production of maps. In relation, counter-mapping, classically defined, is always performed against state mapping. State mapping, since its advent in the 15th century (in Europe), has evolved to include multi-national corporations and global power with an interest in controlling territory through the production and deployment of maps [5]. Peluso [45] has examined this 'classic' kind of counter-mapping by looking at indigenous mapping efforts conducted in response to state and multi-national industrial-scale logging in Indonesia. These efforts resulted in graphical depictions (i.e. maps) of indigenous territories that countered state and industrial maps by showing indigenous interests in the land, including resource areas. To use another example, the Gitksan (a northwest coast Canadian indigenous group) used counter-mapping to produce an alternative view of territory from that of a neighbouring First Nation, the Nisga'a. Ultimately this case went to the Canadian courts [50] and proceeded according to mapped (and counter-mapped) oral and inscribed evidentiary material.

We are concerned here, however, with a much broader conception of the idea of counter-mapping as that which produces, through mapping, an alternate space of representation to one which has become hegemonic for reasons that may include state power, but might also simply include inertia and stasis through time. Counter-mapping so defined would [cf. 55, p. 272] seek to challenge existing hegemony through the creation of an alternate space of representation instantiated by the counter-mapping. Many kinds of counter-mapping will suffice as examples here, including those not only from Indonesia [34, 45], but also from British Columbia [50] and Australia [9], to take two examples from countries whose indigenous inhabitants continue to try to counteract ongoing legacies of colonisation and resource extraction from outside.

The linear path of *kaachewaapechuu*, or going offshore, repeatedly (i.e. every year during an event called Cultural Awareness Week) cuts across territorial trapline blocks historically defined by both state and market (hierarchical) interests operating in Wemindji Cree territories over the course of three centuries [8, 38]. Because the resistance to state territorial blocks involves a kind of counter-work that uses maps and mapmaking, we theorise the Cree commemorative walk as a kind of counter-mapping [45, 55].

3   Counter-Mapping as Assemblage

Below, we explore two key concepts from assemblage using key texts form DeLanda [15-17] to analyse the case study of cultural awareness week in Wemindji, with special focus on *kaachewaapechuu*. We then argue that counter-mapping assemblages are memes of intergenerational knowledge transmission which reconfigures indigenous identities.

3.1   Meshwork, Relation of Exteriority, and Memes

Meshworks are non-hierarchical sets of connections. They resemble the networks common in information technologies, but reflect less linear movement between nodes and more non-linear wayfaring tracks, paths, and affordances closer to Cree and other indigenous worldviews [27, p. 80]. Delanda [15] notes that, while states often favour hierarchies, non-state actors favour meshworks, though in reality some kind of hybrid between meshwork and hierarchy results from interplays of power and resistance.

Counter-mapping, as a political activity caught up in global networks of counter-power, is necessarily outward-looking, engaged, and practical, resonating with similar struggles around the globe. This is referred to here as *relations of exteriority* [17]. DeLanda mentions that assemblages "should never be considered more than component parts entering into relations of exteriority with other component parts" [17, pp. 44-45). For example, Escobar's [23] work examines indigenous strategies of what he calls counter-work, or sub-altern strategies for producing alternate hegemonies. These strategies operate at several levels simultaneously, in non-hierarchical networks that increasingly make, re-make, or strengthen local-global, region-nation, and region-region connections and resonances. This is to say that counter-mapping often operates in opposition to national, multi-national, or global circuits of power, such as when indigenous peoples in Indonesia produce resource maps in the face of large scale logging operations and state power [34, 45].

First Nations, native, and aboriginal groups (to use three alternate ways of describing indigenous groups in Canada and elsewhere, with 'First Nations' exclusive to Canada) undertake commemorative counter-mapping activity in heterogeneous ways that nonetheless echo and resonate with each other. Part of the reason for this is an underlying similarity in indigenous conceptions of space [22], but in large part it is also mutual awareness across large distances of commonalities of concern in the face of homogenising tendencies of global capital and state forces [23]. Thus, different movements across the globe relate to each other in ways external to individual needs (relations of exteriority), and they do so precisely because the underlying spatial structures, philosophies, and topologies mesh at a very fundamental level (meshworks). Escobar [23, p. 286], paraphrasing DeLanda [16, p. 161], notes that "differences in intensity drive fluxes of matter and energy; individuals possess an openness and capacity to affect and be affected and to form assemblages with other individuals (organic or not), further differentiating differences through meshing."

Memes refer to evolving units of cultural information [15, p. 185]. Meshworks are meme-like structures. Memes evolve across statistically varying sets of probabilities that change in non-directional ways towards new tendencies based upon cultural (as opposed to natural) selection. The meme that is the long walk in Wemindji will evolve based upon environmental and cultural pressures that cause it to vary over time while retaining, for the time being, its identity as the long walk offshore, or *kaachewaapechuu*.

3.2   Indigenous Resistance and Counter-Mapping Assemblages

There are two options for resistance to inscriptions of power and to assertions of the controlling grids, lines, and frontiers of economic, cultural, and political change. First, by adopting the tools of the dominant culture, the subaltern may inscribe resistance from the peripheries and margins in the form of maps, diagrams, and art that challenge and counter messages from centres. Second, resisting practices might help ensure cultural continuity through the preservation and use of local and indigenous languages, life-worlds, and named places.

Indigenous resistance embodies *relations of exteriority*, namely, as self-organising, heterogeneous assemblage-memes [23, p. 286]. Wholes emerge from parts that remain differentiated, open, and fluid, maintaining the capacity to change the shape of the whole after its emergence. In Canada, a pan-indigenous movement and system of blockades emerged late in 2012 after Attawapiskat Chief Theresa Spence began a liquid hunger strike in reaction to the policies of Stephen Harper, Canada's Prime Minister. Sympathetic First Nations in areas of resource exploitation (primarily logging and mining) began undertaking symbolic shutdowns of access roads and coalesced into a movement called Idle No More. The concept of individual in Idle No More highlights what is meant by relations of exteriority and part/whole relationships. Chief Theresa Spence, an individual person, became part of a larger set of movements that, in large part, retained their individuality despite placing themselves firmly under the banner of Idle No More.

Relations of exteriority mean that parts do not de-differentiate themselves or homogenise with the emergence of a whole. Individuals (persons, collectives, or movements) do not lose their identities or become subsumed or subjugated to the power of the whole. Instead, these individuals maintain coherence and fluidity in time of political crisis and action. In Canada, earlier moments of blockade have played out in similar ways (i.e. before Idle No More). Blomley [6] describes how blockades became commonplace in British Columbia, Canada in the 1980s and 1990s, in response to lack of action around treaty rights by provincial governments, who were seen to be in the pockets of large multi-national resource extraction corporations. Individual First Nations in BC (of which there are nearly 200) began taking action in order to bring their grievances to the attention of BC leaders and politicians. News and word of blockades have the ability to move quickly across space, and to be replicated efficiently, in a way that could be described as a meme. These are memes that are long lasting in the sense of providing real knowledge of sets of conditions and locations for creating and maintaining effective blockades against powers destructive of indigenous interests.

To use another example, from the northwest coast of British Columbia, the Nisga'a were part of an historic land claims settlement achieved in large part through negotiation at several levels simultaneously, with severe modifications of their territorial claims by the neighbouring Gitksan, in part through an act of counter-mapping on the part of the latter. One of the first actions the Nisga'a took after the settlement of their land claim was the establishment of a set of trails and routes, which we would characterise here as assemblage-memes, commemorating their Tseax lava bed and volcanic cone. These two physical features are prominent in Nisga'a landscape, narrative, myth, and everyday contemporary life and their commemoration through signposting and trail maintenance are part of a larger strategy to bring tourists and other interested parties to the area.

The case of *kaachewaapechuu*, and similar commemorative activities, is a much less political affair, though various aspects of media play a large part in relaying important information about challenges brought about by histories of colonisation in Canada. The commemorative route is a primary way of pointing out how First Nations cultures survive, adapt, and thrive despite state and market pressures to conform to dominant (southern) society. We argue below that the activities of Cultural Awareness Week in Wemindji, including both *kaachewaapechuu* and an art contest, form an assemblage-meme with relations of exteriority linking up to wider concerns in indigenous communities in Canada and elsewhere through non-hierarchical meshworks. While on the surface less political in content than court- and state-driven counter-mapping efforts described above, cultural awareness week is part of larger indigenous efforts to maintain the integrity and continuity of local and traditional knowledge systems including language, history, and culture.

4   The Long Walk: An Assemblage through Time and Space

Methodologically, the case of Wemindji presented here is based on notes and data collected during the lead author's ethnographic research in Wemindji over two visits in 2008 and 2010. These visits, part of ongoing collaborations between Colin Scott's [49] team of McGill researchers and the Cree Nation of Wemindji, offered a chance for the primary author to write about Cree culture (i.e. ethnographically) and conduct participatory action research [29] by using global positioning system (GPS) as a drawing and narrative device in conjunction with the digital earth platform Google Earth [10, 35] as part of the counter-mapping endeavor. More information will be provided in section 4.2.

4.1   The Long Walk as an Assemblage

The long walk in Wemindji is called *kaachewaapechuu* in Cree, which means 'going offshore'. It is a performance that includes participants of all ages from young children to elders walking to an old dwelling site approximately 40 kilometres south of the current town site of Wemindji. The walkers roughly follow the shoreline during the course of this three-day journey, which takes place in winter, allowing them to cut across frozen expanses of bay, and to stay on top of what in summertime would be very soft muddy bog, swamp, and marsh lands. Kaachewaapechuu is part of cultural awareness week, a yearly set of events organised by the community centre staff in Wemindji, Quebec, Canada.

The assemblage of *kaachewaapechuu* is heterogeneous and complex, consisting of a wide range of representations of the communities and their history, e.g. books, maps, mass media, and multiple knowledge systems, indigenous people and white participants, the natural environment, and various technologies. The publication of the book *Wemindji Turns 50* [12] was part of a larger communication strategy for disseminating information to Wemindji and surrounding Cree communities in the region of eastern James Bay. This important publication includes a map and three oblique or top-down aerial photo or satellite images of Wemindji and the surrounding region. These views from above provide context for and introduction to the bulk of non-map material that makes up *Wemindji Turns 50*. These maps serve as kinds of memes for drawing the reader into the story of Wemindji, and they serve to demonstrate how Wemindji is both evolving and growing. The overall story of Wemindji consists in turn of sets of stories told, for the most part, by elders. Thus, the book as a whole is a kind of intergenerational knowledge transmission effort and it is a commemorative journey of its own, an assemblage-meme for mapping Wemindji's past.

In addition to the single-run publication just described, the local radio station remains a powerful hub in Wemindji not only for advertising the various activities of Cultural Awareness Week, but also for coordinating unrelated social functions, from hockey games to bingo to organising search and rescue missions for lost hunters or explorers. *Kaachewaapechuu* itself, and Cultural Awareness Week as a whole, are very well advertised (and supervised) activities, well-known and with high participation rates showing a good turnout from year to year due in no small part to feasting and gaming activities that form part of the week. This is relevant because it demonstrates that assemblage-memes do not exist in isolation but are always implicated and imbricated, at various scales or levels, with other evolving assemblage-memes that variously form part or wholes as assemblages shift and adapt. Radio, paper publications and, as we will see below, digital earth platforms combine and re-combine, assembling elements for the memetic transmission of knowledge about Wemindji, its region, and the place of these in both Quebec and Canada.

As an exterior, outward-looking, relation between interacting individuals at multiple scales, counter-mappings such as *kaachewaapechuu* represent not introspective events, but performances seeking (literally) outsides. The long walk journey takes participants out onto the land in order to dispel any easy notions of what life on the land must have entailed for ancestors of the distant and near past. Past times were not all of hardship, and relations between traders and Cree were most often both prosperous and amicable, generally speaking, for many decades and even centuries after initial contact between indigenous peoples and the outside world. This narrative of prosperity and peace does not always mesh with elders' stories found in the locally produced book *Wemindji Turns 50* [12] when forces playing out at multiple levels from the global down through the regional and local translated into hard times for Cree people in Canada in the early and middle parts of the 20th century. This, in turn, is due in large part to colonial and governmental legacies of residential schooling and transformation of the market relationship into one dominated by multi-national capital, hydroelectric development, and mining activities [8, 20, 26, 46, 48].

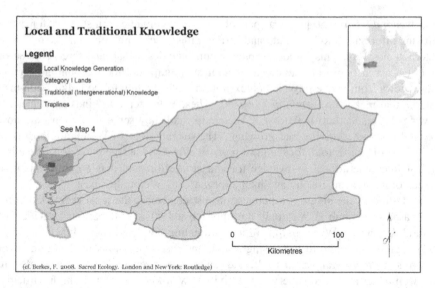

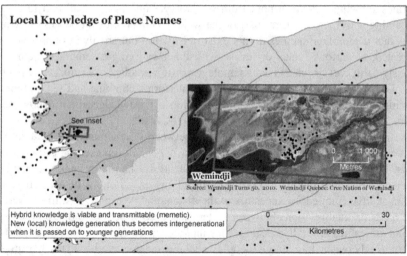

Fig. 1. Trapline territories and knowledge systems in Wemindji (Category I lands are those in which the Cree have exclusive hunting and trapping rights, as defined under the James Bay and Northern Quebec Agreement of 1975)

Figure 1 shows clearly two aspects of life in Wemindji, knowledge of which tends quite easily to become partitioned between town- and land-based systems. Local knowledge is thus not easily conflatable with traditional knowledge [4]: the former tends to be concentrated while the latter is more dispersed across the trapline territories. All of this makes for a very complex assemblage indeed, one involving tools and maps; elders, youth, and their parents; local and traditional knowledge systems; and the complex and entwined histories of commercial, colonial, and governmental interests.

4.2   Participatory Mapping in the Cultural Awareness Week

Participatory mapping, part of a larger suite of qualitative methods called participatory action research [29], was used during cultural awareness week in order to generate a line drawing of *kaachewaapechuu*. This line was draped upon a Google Earth base map (Figure 2), printed as a strip map on paper, and entered into the art contest, which was also part of cultural awareness week. Visual and textual ethnographic methods (i.e. methods for writing about culture [cf. 47, 13]) were then used to document the reception of the map during the contest, the judging of which took place during a feast at the end of cultural awareness week. Mapping and ethnographic components blurred together and cannot be analytically separated, since during *kaachewaapechuu* while the GPS line was being generated, there was an ongoing ethnographic component, a writing of culture undertaken by the lead author in the form of notes, observations, and ongoing conversations with participants in the walk. The GPS line is considered to be an inscription or recording of a meme that is in turn part of an assemblage for performing the long walk.

Participatory mapping generated not just a line and a map, but a story/meme about how the walk went, how it was going (during the walk), sprinkled with references to how elders and ancestors would have walked the path in the past. For example it was mentioned many times within earshot of children that in the past a hunter or a trapper would make the 40 kilometre journey in one day, while pulling their own supplies (including food, cooking implements, clothing, and hunting gear) behind on a sled [8]. Thus, mapping blended into ethnography and vice-versa. During the final feast at which time judging of art entries took place, many participants in the feast (but not the art contest) approached the Google Earth strip map/meme inscription to make comments, offer observations, or check the route taken (out of interest in the choice of route, or to verify its fidelity to a mental map or previously performed route). The assembly of people was literally another assemblage that could scrutinise and comment upon the meme produced by the prior interlocking assemblage-meme that had performed the mapping on the land itself.

During both the long walk and the art contest/feast, many asked questions about either the GPS unit (with its own self-contained miniature map) or about the Google Earth map, less out of interest in technical points, than from a concern with the information contained in the maps. When an adjustment was made by the primary author to the GPS unit (for example, marking or verifying a place-name), it became a standing joke to ask 'how far?' But the joke was, of course, a serious question revolving around anxious concern about the distance both covered and remaining. It usually led to environmental observations about the state of the weather, snow conditions, different kinds of vegetation, or the quality of food to be had in the vicinity (in terms of species presence, or what we had for lunch). When feast participants asked about the Google Earth map in the art contest it was usually to point out an area where we had deviated from an expected route at a specific place, and this was tied to concern for well-being. To be lost on the territories belied inexperience, danger, and potential loss. Thus the exact replication of the meme *kaachewaapechuu* is performed by the self-similarity and checking capabilities of the assemblage of which it is formed and is a part.

Fig. 2. Google Earth with kaachewaapechuu GPS line (Community Centre, Wemindji)

4.3   Counter-Mapping, Materiality, and Memes: Travelling across Time and Space

One of the aspects of counter-mapping assemblages is that they could be memetic; that is, consisting of units of cultural information transmitted intergenerationally. The aspect of counter-mapping we theorise here is neither subversive nor upsetting of local traditions or expectations. Instead, the return to the old living site south of present day Wemindji represents a counter-mapping of the past. It is a chance to re-trace, in reverse, the path followed by elders and ancestors; to revisit the original site of the village they abandoned when they moved to higher ground in 1960. But it is not simply an act of looking back. It is a way of looking ahead, to the horizon of things to come, best represented by the physical presence of youth during the long walk.

As the group moves away from town and plenty into the vastness of the surround-ing land and its traplines it becomes focused on particularities of the journey encoun-tered in sequence. Traplines in Canada have a complex history whose development is entangled with both internal and overseas markets for furs. The trapline system is based upon discrete blocks of non-overlapping territorial units that to some extent map onto pre-contact structures. Extents were formalised with the onset of market relations between Cree and representatives from the Hudson's Bay Company (HBC) which dominated the fur trade in Quebec in the early 1900s [8, 24, 28, 38]. The rela-tionship between the Cree and the HBC was long lasting and, for the most part, consisted in mutually beneficial interactions [24, 38, 39]. After the decline of HBC by the mid-1900s, for a number of years in the early to middle parts of the 20th century, starvation occurred amongst some Cree families. It was due to a very complex set of factors, including, but not limited to, fluctuations in the prices of furs, variability in species numbers from year to year, and the decline of HBC itself. There were periods of hardship, often alluded to or mentioned outright in elder stories and in *Wemindji Turns 50.*

Concern for well-being and healing can be identified as primary motivations for commemoration in Wemindji, as noted by the many stories of starvation, abuse, and hard-times weathered in the community during the past. Part of the impetus for the change of dwelling site, from the old village habitation 40 kilometres south to the new town site, was a desire for younger generations not to have to experience those hard times. There is a sense of improving life conditions concurrent with cultural loss and cultural colonisation that at times seems to offset the improvement. Cross-generational concerns about loss of traditional values are not confined to Cree alone, however, as the generational critique comes with the territory, going hand-in-hand with technological advancement and change beyond what older generations are able to incorporate into their worldview.

Elders in Wemindji are keen to tell stories about the land and about past times both of plenty and of the times when game and food were scarce. *Kaachewaapechuu* is a chance for elders to demonstrate to the younger generations what life was like in the old days, with a captive audience tied together by the track followed each year to the old village site. Its purpose is not to shock but to contextualise through the perfor-mance of the long walk what life on the land is like. An intergenerational assemblage of individuals of different ages and experiences and styles of learning come together to make the journey using various tools such as sleds, snowshoes, moccasins, walking sticks, hats, coats, and wide range of other objects and implements. Each object and individual becomes, in the performance of *kaachewaapechuu*, a part of the assemblage for the production and enactment of powerful and long-lasting spatial memes.

Furthermore, indigenous individuals, in the DeLandean [17] sense of individual as multiplicity, use mapping platforms, devices, and tools to build trans-local resonances concurrent to the performance of local rituals of commemoration [23, 55]. This has potentially profound implications for re-configuring indigeneity in light of emerging and evolving mapping technologies such as Google Earth and GPS. The experience of using Google Earth, a free (but not open source) geo-browser for exploring, querying, and mapping the surface of the earth, provides an illustration of how *kaachewaapechuu* can be visualised in new ways that upset easy notions of scale and spatial hierarchy. The fluidity with which the user of this digital earth platform is able to zoom in and out to visit and examine high resolution images of locales, regions, countries, and continents, with rapid on-the-fly changes in direction, is quite different from using a paper map or aerial photograph. The abilities of contemporary digital earth platforms to perform such computationally demanding operations was in the realm of science fiction only a few years before Google's unveiling of the platform in 2005 [2]. The fluid nature of re-scaling using digital earth pan, zoom, and flight functions is posited as part of the ease with which counter-mappings as relations of exteriority may be both enacted and visualised, using interfaces that allow for spontaneous, branching, and non-hierarchical methods of interaction with depictions of (customary and traditional) meshwork spaces.

Scale is both an important, and a very fluid, conceptual tool for examining how the memetic nature of counter-mapping that is *kaachewaapechuu* works, from the level of intergenerational transmission of spatial knowledge performed on the land as elders and youth interact and learn from each other; to the level of the line traced by the walked path itself, generated by a GPS device and draped across a digital earth platform.. The GPS further focuses on the fact that this movement is sequential and thus ordered in a particular way. The ordering of the journey is achieved through rituals of preparation involving securing enough nourishment to provide the physical energy to make it at least to the first day's stopping point. As part of the assemblage for counter-mapping, the GPS played a somewhat literal part in the sense that it acted like a 'pencil' for drawing a line or trajectory that mapped the group [43]. In other words the GPS used its tracking function to sample points with a frequency such that the points formed a smooth line corresponding to the trajectory of the journey.

This line can be seen as part of a meshwork of already existing and previously performed routes and spatial narratives draped across the surface of the land. These previous performances can be re-lived through the telling of stories about previous journeys, linking up to the present at joining points, nodes or, more properly, meshpoints at junctions and named places [27]. The telling of such spatial stories often involves children and elders and is therefore posited to be *memetic* (with evolving units of place-based information) in nature [14, 19].

4.4   Counter-Mapping and Reconfiguring Indigeneity

Systematic and historical forces shape considerations of indigeneity in Canada, going back to a time well before contact between white and indigenous peoples in the

New World. Communication between Europeans and the original inhabitants of North America consisted, at first, of devastating smallpox and perhaps influenza epidemics. The colonizers' diseases got there before they did. The representation of a portion of space and colonial power structure inscribed on paper spread very quickly after colonial interests established themselves in North America [22].

Today, satellite TV, cellular telephones, the internet, and GPS (among other technologies) are reconfiguring the lives and aspirations of youth through rapidly evolving memes that often have nothing to do with life on the land. The passing of just two generations has been enough to see a move from hunting and gathering through seasonal movements to a sedentary pattern characterized by insecure affluence. Youth, often driven by boredom, run towards southern attractions against the advice of elders, who now place a great deal of stress upon education. There is a perceived lack of relevance of educational content among youth to elder despair over cultural directions in which mainstream media is taking the community, especially the younger people. Wemindji has a regional school-board structure that is, in many ways, a model of what indigenous-led educational systems can achieve. But according to youth at a public-speaking event held yearly in Wemindji, the curriculum doesn't include enough about the traditional ways of the Cree such as building dwellings, travelling, and developing a relationship with local landscapes [22].

In distinction to and often in rebellion against expectations of older generations, many northern and indigenous youth are (re)claiming their identities by making renewed efforts to interact with traditional territories. Local efforts in Wemindji have resulted in youth-driven efforts to foster heightened awareness of local space and traditional activities. Sometimes aboriginal youth despair of connecting to their culture and to the land around them. Some even kill themselves and suicide clusters are widely, if sporadically, known in northern Aboriginal communities. There is some evidence that changes in the brain resulting from lack of interaction with place can lead to depressive states. There is also evidence that suicidal ideation among teenagers can become contagious. This etiology suggests that a richer connection to the land might be especially important for the health and happiness of young people in the north. Wemindji is seen as an example of a community that has often successfully evaded negative repercussions of colonization, due in no small part to activities exemplified in the commemoration of *kaachewaapechuu* [22].

There is no better way to achieve engagement than by interacting with the land itself, noting first that for indigenous peoples, sometimes the territory precedes the map. The territory is in turn preceded by the land before cartographic inscription. This is potentially no better appreciated than by intelligent and energetic but often deeply ironic youth seeking meaning in a rapidly changing world. In the case of *Kaachewaapechuu*, the Google Earth map was entered into the Wemindji art contest and was incorporated into that larger performance, enveloped by local artists and community members whose individual and collective gazes consumed maps and map-like objects spread out against the walls of Wemindji's community hall. Therapeutic use of maps leads, then, from inscription to performance. Performance and embodied activity lead to strengthened identity in and through participation in community life in interaction with the territories inscribed on maps or drawings. Seeing such full circles, youth can regain a sense of wholeness [22].

5   Concluding Remarks

This paper uses the concept of assemblage to explore the heterogeneous, situated and contested nature of mapping. This move serves to politicise and open up the previous thinking in mapping and counter-mapping, allowing for cross-scale linkages across multiple levels and landscapes [36]. The study echoes and extends the call of the so-ciomaterial discourse to consider materiality as relational, entangled and performed in sociomaterial assemblages. Moreover, it is an attempt to broaden the scope of soci-omaterial research as represented in the IS literature which often investigate informa-tion systems in a business context. Counter-mapping of indigenous groups is a response to global assemblages of post-colonial legacy and discourse, capital power of multi-national corporations and marketization, as well as dis-embedding modernity engrained with trans-local technologies. Conceptualised as sociomaterial assemblag-es, the long walk of *kaachewaapechuu* embodies aspects of meshwork, relation of exteriority and memes, mapping routes and junctions of the past and present. Moving across time and space, counter-mapping assemblages form dynamic connections among trans-local knowledge systems as well as older and younger generations, re-connecting the lifeworlds of modernized indigenous groups and their history, tradition and natural territories, thereby reconfiguring their identities [22]. This is significant not only to indigenous populations, but to all societies experiencing the tension, dis-juncture and replacement between tradition and modernity, local and global, and those between individual and collective.

The materiality in the counter-mapping assemblage of the long walk are not only enacted in the drawing on Google Earth, featuring accessible and detailed satellite imagery of customary lands [cf. 44], tools used in the journey such as sleds, snow-shoes, moccasins, walking sticks, etc., weather conditions such as rain and snow, but also in reconnecting with the land, old village sites and territories which embody memories and knowledge of the tribe that older generations are keen to pass on the younger ones. While this version of the narrative does not go into great detail to show how mapping technologies, tools and other material elements are "performed", we try to stick to the Deleuzian notion of assemblage as heterogeneous and "open-ended collectives" [3] in which artefacts form an integral part. Moreover, we argue that it is the *becoming* of the assemblage, namely, the ritual practice of the long walk across time and space, which constitutes a resistance to the post-colonial legacy, often stabi-lised and represented in the artifact of maps, and a reconfiguration of the indigenous identity of the Cree people.

References

1. Anderson, B., Kearnes, M., McFarlane, C., Swanton, D.: On Assemblages and Geography. Dialogues in Human Geography 2(2), 171–189 (2012)
2. Bar-Zeev, A.: Keyhole, Google Earth, and 3D Worlds: An Interview with Avi Bar-Zeev. Cartographica 43(2), 85–93 (2008)
3. Bennett, J.: Vibrant Matter: A Political Ecology of Things. Duke University Press (2010)
4. Berkes, F.: Sacred Ecology, 2nd edn. Routledge, London (2008)

5. Black, J.: The Power of Knowledge: How Information and Technology Made the Modern World. Yale University Press, New Haven (2014)
6. Blomley, N.: "Shut The Province Down": First Nations Blockades in British Columbia. 1984-1995. BC Studies 111, 5–35 (1996)
7. Callon, M.: Some Elements of a Sociology of Translation: Domestication of the Scallops and the Fisherman of St Brieuc Bay. In: Law, J. (ed.) Power, Action and Belief: A New Sociology of Knowledge, pp. 196–223. Routledge and Keegan, London (1986)
8. Carlson, H.: Home is the Hunter: The James Bay Cree and Their Land. UBC Press, Vancouver (2008)
9. Chatwin, B.: The Songlines. Vintage, London (1986)
10. Clifford, J., Marcus, G. (eds.): Writing Culture: The Poetics and Politics of Ethnography. University of California Press, Los Angeles (1986)
11. Cosgrove, D. (ed.): Mappings. Reaktion, London and New York (1999)
12. Cree Nation of Wemindji: Wemindji Turns 50. Farrington Media Milton, Ontario (2010)
13. Davies, C.A.: Reflexive Ethnography: A Guide to Researching Selves and Others. Routledge, Milton Park (2008)
14. Dawkins, R.: The Selfish Gene. Oxford University Press, Oxford (1976)
15. DeLanda, M.: A Thousand Years of Non-Linear History. Zone, Cambridge (1997)
16. DeLanda, M.: Intensive Science and Virtual Philosophy. Continuum, London (2002)
17. DeLanda, M.: A New Philosophy of Society: Assemblage Theory and Social Complexity. Bloomsbury, London (2006)
18. Deleuze, G., Guattari, F.: A Thousand Plateaus: Capitalism and Schizophrenia. University of Minnesota Press, Minneapolis (1987)
19. Distin, K.: The Selfish Meme. Cambridge University Press, Cambridge (2005)
20. Desbiens, C.: Power From the North: Territory, Identity, and the Culture of Hydroelectricity in Quebec. UBC Press, Vancouver (2014)
21. Doolin, B., McLeod, L.: Sociomateriality and Boundary Objects in Information Systems Development. European Journal of Information Systems 21(5), 570–586 (2012)
22. Eades, G.: Maps and Memes: Redrawing Culture, Place, and Identity in Indigenous Communities. McGill-Queen's University Press, Montreal and Kingston (2014)
23. Escobar, A.: Territories of Difference: Place, Movements, Life, Redes. Duke University Press, Durham (2008)
24. Francis, D., Morantz, T.: Partners in Furs: A History of the Fur Trade in Eastern James Bay 1600-1870. McGill-Queen's University Press, Montreal and Kingston (1983)
25. Harley, J.B., Woodward, D.: Preface. In: Harley, J.B., Woodward, D. (eds.) Cartography in Prehistoric, Ancient, and Medieval Europe and the Mediterranean (The History of Cartography, vol. 1), p. xvi. University of Chicago Press, Chicago (1987)
26. Hornig, J. (ed.): Social and Environmental Impacts of the James Bay Hydroelectric Project. McGill-Queen's University Press, Montreal and Kingston (1999)
27. Ingold, T.: Lines. Routledge, London (2007)
28. Innis, H.: The Fur Trade in Canada (Revised). University of Toronto Press (1956)
29. Kindon, S., Pain, R., Kesby, M.: Participatory Action Research Approaches and Methods: Connecting People, Participation, and Place. Routledge, London and New York (2007)
30. Latour, B.: Science in Action: How to Follow Scientists and Engineers Through Society. Harvard University Press, Cambridge (1987)
31. Latour, B.: Technology is Society Made Durable. In: Law, J. (ed.) A Sociology of Monsters: Essays on Power, Technology and Domination, pp. 103–131. Routledge, London (1991)

32. Latour, B.: Nonhumans. In: Harrison, S., Pile, S., Thrift, N.J. (eds.) Patterned Ground: Entanglements of Nature and Culture, pp. 224–227. Reaktion Books (2004)

33. Leonardi, P.M.: Theoretical Foundations for the Study of Sociomateriality. Information and Organization 23(2), 59–76 (2013)

34. Li, T.M.: The Will to Improve: Governmentality, Development, and the Practice of Politics. Duke University Press, Durham and London (2007)

35. Marcus, G., Saka, S.: Assemblage. Theory, Culture and Society 23(2-3), 101–106 (2006)

36. Marston, S., Jones III, J.P., Woodward, K.: Human Geography Without Scale. Transactions of the Institute of British Geographers 30(4), 416–432 (2005)

37. McFarlane, C.: Translocal Assemblages: Space, Power and Social Movements. Geoforum 40(4), 561–567 (2009)

38. Morantz, T.: White Man's Gonna Getcha. McGill-Queen's University Press, Montreal and Kingston (2002)

39. Morantz, T.: Relations on Southeastern Hudson Bay. Avataq Cultural Institute, Montreal (2012)

40. Orlikowski, W.J.: Sociomaterial Practices: Exploring Technology at Work. Organization Studies 28(9), 1435–1448 (2007)

41. Orlikowski, W.J.: The Sociomateriality of Organisational Life: Considering Technology in Management Research. Cambridge Journal of Economics 34(1), 125–141 (2009)

42. Orlikowski, W.J., Scott, S.V.: Sociomateriality: Challenging the Separation of Technology, Work and Organization. Academy of Management Annals 2, 433–474 (2008)

43. O'Rourke, K.: Walking and Mapping. MIT Press, Cambridge (2013)

44. Parks, L.: Cultures in Orbit: Satellites and the Tele-visual. Duke University Press, Durham and London (2005)

45. Peluso, N.: Whose Woods Are These? Counter-mapping Forest Territories in Kalimantan, Indonesia. Antipode 27(4), 383–406 (1995)

46. Piper, L.: The Industrial Transformation of Subarctic Canada. UBC Press, Vancouver (2009)

47. Pink, S.: Doing Visual Ethnography. Sage, London (2007)

48. Richardson, B.: Strangers Devour the Land. Chelsea Green, White River Junction (1991)

49. Scott, C. (ed.): Aboriginal Autonomy and Development in Northern Quebec and Labrador. UBC Press, Vancouver (2001)

50. Sterritt, N., Marsden, S., Grant, P., Galois, R., Overstall, R.: Tribal Boundaries in the Nass Watershed. UBC Press, Vancouver (1998)

51. Suchman, L.: Human-Machine Reconfigurations: Plans and Situated Actions. Cambridge University Press (2007)

52. Tyner, J.: Principles of Map Design. Guilford, New York (2010)

53. Wagner, E.L., Moll, J., Newell, S.: Accounting Logics, Reconfiguration of ERP Systems and the Emergence of New Accounting Practices: A Sociomaterial Perspective. Management Accounting Research 22(3), 181–197 (2011)

54. Wagner, E.L., Newell, S., Piccoli, G.: Understanding Project Survival in an ES Environment: A Sociomaterial Practice Perspective. Journal of the Association for Information Systems 11(5), 276–297 (2010)

55. Wainwright, J.: Decolonizing Development: Colonial Power and the Maya. Blackwell, Malden (2008)

56. Wood, D.: Rethinking the Power of Maps. Guilford, New York (2010)

57. Woodward, D., Lewis, G.M.: Introduction. In: Woodward, D., Lewis, G.M. (eds.) Cartography in the Traditional African, American, Arctic, Australian, and Pacific Societies (The History of Cartography), vol. 2(3), p. 1. University of Chicago Press, Chicago (1998)

Understanding the Emergent Structure of Competency Centers in Post-implementation Enterprise Systems

An Assemblage Theory Approach

Arun Aryal[1], Redouane El Amrani[2], and Duane P. Truex[1]

[1] Georgia State University, Atlanta, USA
aaryal1@mygsu.onmicrosoft.com, dtruex@gsu.edu
[2] NEOMA Business School, Reims, France
redouane.elamrani@neoma-bs.fr

Abstract. Prior research provides conflicting insights about the link between investment in enterprise systems and firm value and in the ES governance mechanisms. The literature generally suggests that management should cultivate its technical and organizational expertise to derive value from currently deployed Enterprise Systems (ES) [8]. In the realm of practice, ERP vendors and configuration/integration partners strongly recommend the creation of an organizational structure to govern the ERP implementation and post-implementation process to improve project success and extract greater value from the ES investment. The ES literature, while unclear on the formation, and functioning of ES governance units, suggests the need for formal and fixed governance structures. This research utilizes Deleuze's assemblage theory and emergence theory to explain the genesis and evolution of the governing 'structure' known as the Competency Center (CC). Our results illustrate the business needs driving the structuring processes behind the CC, are also those that lead to unintended and destabilizing outcomes. Whether the CC 'assemblage' survives to provide value depends on how the emergent issues are handled and how the assemblages are "positioned". This research suggests effective ES governance is not derived from a prescribed step-wise process yielding formal structures, but rather form an organic process of assemblage.

Keywords: assemblage theory, competency centers, enterprise systems, post-implementation.

1 Introduction

Leveraging Enterprise System (ES), to achieve true long-term business value is problematic because direct causal links between ERP implementation and firm value have never been clearly established [3]. In traditional ERP implementations, these systems are essentially well integrated transactional systems whose potential is never fully realized [21]. Making the next step, wherein firms relying on integrated systems can capitalize on current and context-rich organizational competency, requires two things. First, continual development of the knowledge and governance frameworks born of

B. Doolin et al. (Eds.): IS&O 2014, IFIP AICT 446, pp. 95–114, 2014.
© IFIP International Federation for Information Processing 2014

the ERP implementation process. Second, linking the transactional data arising from successful ERP implementation to Business Intelligence (BI).

The task of governance enabling the linkage between ERP data and BI requires far more than simply upgrading to new versions, implementing new modules, or customizing the existing system. Prior research suggests cultivating technical and organizational expertise to leverage and derive increased value from currently deployed ES [8]. In practice, both ERP vendors and implementation partners strongly recommend the creation of an organizational structure to guide and govern the ERP implementation process. Often this requirement is built into the service level agreements and contracts. These structures are typically called 'competency centers'[1].

Unfortunately the IS literature offers no generally agreed definition for the term Competency Center [11, 13, 14, 17]. Accordingly, for the purposes of this research, we define the Competency Center (CC) as:

> *the governance structures and processes that are responsible for implementation as well as the ongoing training, support, use, upgrades to ESs.*

IS research literature also offers little practical understanding of how these structures work, how they are maintained and how they evolve over time. For instance, few IS studies deal with the notion of the competence center at all and none consider the post-implementation evolution of a CC, specifically their role in optimizing the ERP Implementation and the convergence with BI capabilities. Nor are there studies comparing the post-implementation experience comparing different organizational logics and contexts across firms. ES implementation has been the focus of many research, but, the interaction between IT expertise and organizational competencies during the post-implementation phase continues to perplex the IS management community and challenges IS researchers.

Extant IS literature suggests that successful ES implementations and utilizations achieve both tactical and strategic goals [16]. The literature is also replete with stories of how flawed ES may bring organizations to their knees [2, 22, 30]; but some firms have had spectacular success in implementing ERP systems and using these systems to fuel the analytical and decision making capabilities e.g. Business Intelligence (BI). We look to such firms to learn how they have managed to achieve these successes. In contrast, other firms have struggled and sometimes abandoned the goal by either decommissioning the ERP or simply using these resources as powerful transaction processing systems, never realizing their full potential. We also look to some of these firms to understand why and learn what factors led to abandonment or selecting alternative paths. Our research questions are: What are the roles and responsibilities for different stakeholders in CC? How do CC's form and evolve? As the CCs evolve, how do they form and maintain relationships between various business units? Are these relationships formal or informal? Are there organizational factors that suggest one path vs. another?

---

[1] Competency Center is a SAP specific term to describe a 'structure' that is responsible for implementation, stabilization and post implementation support of applications and business processes in organizations. 'Center of Excellence' is also used as a synonym to the term 'competency center'.

This research is grounded in assemblage theory and brings a complementary view from 'emergent theory' [18] to support our theoretical background. Assemblage is a more recent social theory that examines the phenomenon more holistically, i.e. analyzes a 'whole' as well as the 'parts' that make the 'whole'. This ability to analyze different levels makes assemblage theory useful in its application to examine Information Systems more thoroughly. To date, there have been only a limited number papers published that explicitly engage with this lens. Research phenomenon that is emergent, more recursive than dialectical, and characterize more by interactions among the "constructs" and the systems as a whole, are particularly suited to investigate through assemblage theory [25]. Assemblage theory offers a particularly evocative way of examining the emergent properties and evolution about CCs for the following three reasons. First, CC as a 'system' is comprised of many heterogeneous 'subsystems' such as 'subject matter experts', 'business users', 'IT experts', and various managers. Second, emergence of CC is the result of interaction between and among these sub-systems. Assemblage theory helps to conceptualize the contingent interactions of different components (ERP, BI, structure, process, business unites, parameters, customization, etc.) in a more continuity dynamic perspective. Third, the constant dynamic interaction continuously shapes and re-shapes the CC structure. Assemblage theory allows for the possibility of open configuration, continuous connections, not in an inextricable combination of interrelated parts, incessantly transforming organization and its IS.

The paper is organized as follows. We begin with an explanation of our theoretical background and a review of literature on ES post-implementation. Although the literature does not deal directly with competency center, this literature provides background for our investigation. We then outline the research method adopted for the empirical part of this study and summarize the key findings. In the Discussion section, we will analyze results from the cross-case analysis. In the conclusion section, we offer implications of our findings for research and practice.

2   Theoretical Background and Literature Review

An innate property of an assemblage is its heterogeneous character. Assemblage, first proposed by Gilles Deleuze and Felix Guattari [10], is derived from the French word *agencement* referring to the ongoing processes of arranging, organizing, and congealing of heterogeneous bodies of concepts in connecting to each other. Assemblage emphasizes that "parts" that make the "whole" are fluid, exchangeable, and can have multiple functions. These components can be "pulled" out of one system, "plugged" into another. As DeLanda [9, pp. 10-11] describes,

> these relations imply, first of all, that a component part of an assemblage may be detached from it and plugged into a different assemblage in which its interactions are different. In other words, the exteriority of relations implies certain autonomy for the terms they relate.

In Deleuzian ontology, a priori fixed notion of structures is not possible. Deleuze, in his later (post-Guattari collaborative) work, equates being as univocally, difference, and thus rejects any possible 'fixed' structures. We interpret this as meaning, purpose and its realization in 'structuring' forms (to borrow from Paul Hopper's [19] theory of Emergent Grammars) is always not fully determined and always in process. It is an emergent regularity [19] vs. a fixed structure. The 'structure' we describe are various snapshots of 'organizational forms' captured in moments in time. In that way, it gives us the possibility of analyzing contingent interactions between IT (supported here by ERP and BI systems), organization and actors as well as the emergent properties of the complex whole. ERP and BI applications were implemented in interaction with processes and actors, and developed during many phases. This position take us away from a static way of managing those interactions and emphasis fundamentally the idea of formation of complex configurations that eliminate the idea of a fixed and stable ontology for the organization evolution (or transformation).

An assemblage arises from the interplay of five primary constructs, four of which are members of two continua. The first is the material–expressive continuum, and the second is the territorialization– deterritorialization continuum (c.f., Figure 1).

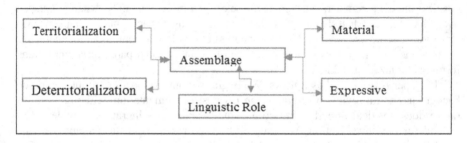

Fig. 1. Different components of assemblage

The material-expressive continuum. Material constructs are physical objects or logical constructs, things with which people interact, such as information system (ERP modules, e-business platform, Supply Chain Management (SCM) applications, BI analytics), a department (Marketing, Finance, IT department), a legal system and the like. Expressive constructs are the responses that people have to material constructs. A driver sees a stop light and stops, sees a police car when driving and reduces speed. In an ES scenario, if an ERP software displays an error message, an expert user might be able to interpret it and take an appropriate action, whereas if a novice user might exit out the current screen or click 'buttons' at random. Closing out the current screen or interpreting an error message is a reaction to a material (error message in the system). Both the material constructs and many of the expressive behaviors are described in formal and informal linguistics artifacts, e.g., laws, employment manuals, and social norms transmitted by word of mouth.

The territorializing–deterritorializing continuum. Territorializing refers to actions that are oriented towards maintaining and reifying existing structures; making structures more rigid and concrete. In the realm of IS, the term 'electronic concrete' refers to how some systems lock users into one way of doing things. De-territorializing references forces and actions that are oriented to maintaining flexibility and fluidity in extant structures. They are transactional dynamic forces that take place in everyday activity and sensemaking. Alter's "Theory of Workarounds" deals with precisely this concept [1]. In the ERP governance, formation of a core team can be an example of territorialization. However, if that team is not given any 'real' authority, the team could not function very well and could dissolve, thus deterritorializing. Deterritorialization should not automatically be equated to a negative element. In many cases, deterritorialization is helpful to the transform the use of an ERP system from a local specialization to a cross-functional integration. For example, an organization may employ some key 'core groups' to manage ERP integration issues, but, if the group structure (territorialization component) is too rigid or unsupportive from the perspective of the different stakeholders, these key users might by-pass the established core-group and seek assistance from their coworkers or other sources. This is an example of deterritorialization since it destabilizes the 'assemblage' of the core groups. But, this deterritorialization, a kind of 'workaround', is not an 'undesired' outcome.

Linguistic elements. It is through linguistic mechanisms, speech and writing, that the interplay of these continua is expressed and the way social negotiation occurs. Linguistic elements can be sales report, requests for proposals, employee handbooks, and stories told within a shared organizational context. It is through language that assemblages are manifest. They are realizations of the interplay among the constructs. For example, the announcement of a sales competition (linguistic element) wherein only the top sales person will win the prize, will have an effect on how a sales team organizes itself and influences how members treat each other. "The Assemblage", as an emergent property, formed by interactions among the components. Once formed, assemblages have the reciprocal ability to affect and alter their own organizing constructs. However, the "consistency" or the "coherence" of its different components doesn't necessarily predetermine the form of the assemblage. In Deleuze's approach, consistency and coherence are not qualities that precede assemblages, rather they are emergent properties that do or do not arise from assemblage. In assemblage theory, the concept of emergence is referenced but is not a well-developed construct. So we turn to other sources for help in making this construct clear.

A fuller Theory of Emergence was initially proposed by Paul Hopper [18, 20] and has been further developed in the domain of IS by Truex et al. [32], Truex & Baskeville [31], Chae & Poole [6]. In this body of work, the notion of emergence takes the adjective 'emergent' seriously as a continual movement towards structure, a postponement or 'deferral' of structure, a view of structure as always provisional, always negotiable, and as epiphenomenal, that is, at least as much an effect as a cause.

Structure that is emergent is not an overarching set of abstract principles, but more a question of a spreading of systematicity, never fully formed always 'in-process', hence 'emergent'. An emergent structure or emergent system is like a story that is in the process of being told, being embellished and reinterpreted with each telling. It is a living artifact, never finished and never full structured, hence in emergence theory 'structures' are referred to as emergent regularities vs. finished structures.

Emergent systems are not abstract entities, but structuring in process taking place in real time, encountering and solving real life interactive problems. They are products of transactional interaction, sensemaking and negotiation of the meanings of other assemblages. Emergent theory tries to describe this process in terms that reflect its transitoriness and lack of intrinsic stability. A priori views of structure often go hand in hand in with exclusively cognitive perspectives that attribute structure to individual mental faculties without reference to the social and pragmatic conditions that enable these faculties in the first place. In other words, the world as it is encountered must fit these pre-existent models, in contrast to emergent perspectives according to which the model is adjusted constantly in real time.

The emergence theoretical perspective does not actively seek fixed units of analysis rather it seeks recurrent patterns that create movement toward structure. Emergence seeks to offer a fuller exploration of the role of materiality and contextual constraints within the organizing process.

Emergence theory does not view organizational emergence as a primarily rational and consensual process but as occasions of discourse understood to be power laden, disputed and subject to unpredictable outcomes. With these essential properties, an emergence theoretic perspective can be useful in describing how two axes, the territorialization and deterritorialization, and material and expressive. Carter et al. [5] further classify emergence into discourse emergence and materiality emergence.

Materiality emergence. Information systems and organizations are continually adapting and responding to perceived changes in material conditions. Moreover, in their discussion of emergence and information systems, Truex and Klein [33] suggested a mutually constitutive relationship between information systems and social systems that is both power laden and disputed. The ability to better address material conditions of organizing in the information systems arena is an important strength of emergence theory.

Dispute negotiation emergence. The discourse is always self-referential and in process. Systematicity (i.e., organizing) spreads through loose coupling of organizational conversations that result in a host of complex intra- and inter-relationships. Each conversation is laden with material and contextual constraints, power/knowledge issues, and temporal irregularities and precludes the notion of organizations evolving either rationally, or meaningfully. Conflict need not be resolved rationally for organizations to work.

When synthesizing the concepts from dispute negotiation (discourse) emergence and materiality emergence, we propose a research model as described in Figure 2.

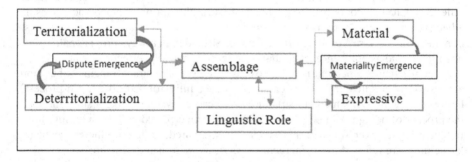

Fig. 2. Research framework

Applying assemblage and emergence theories to our research helps us understand how a CC configuration is the outcome of interaction among the constructs of the two continua. In the current ES literature [11, 14, 17]; the manner and processes by which CCs acquire their emergent structure is unclear. The way organizations adjust to the ES and the way the ES is adapted to improve organizational fit, a critical condition to realizing benefits from firm's ES investment, is also unclear [34]. Large firms having already finished their ERP implementation [16] typically find themselves dealing with usage and evolution issues. The uncertainties associated with ES use often relate to the way firms try to exploit the convergence of ERP and Business Intelligence (BI). There is considerable disagreement as to how post-implementation support should be structured and the roles that the business community and IT should play in this struc-ture [35].

Taking an assemblage approach helps explain the existence the many adoption contexts and their dynamics and helps identify the shifting boundary conditions for the creation of the CC between business and IT units.

Turning once again to the literature we find general agreement that exploiting the significant investment in ERP and BI applications requires developing organizational capabilities to enhance fit between system functionality and business needs [12]. There is also general agreement in the literature that achieving organizational capabil-ity is predicated on effectively leveraging multiple knowledge and expertise sources throughout the organization [4]. The key resource is organizational knowledge and how this knowledge is distributed throughout the organization. Newell et al. [27] have noted the primary challenge for project teams is how to coordinate and integrate such distributed knowledge in dynamically changing environments. During the post-implementation phase, the challenges are even more pronounced because the support mechanisms established for the project implementation phase (consultants, leadership, project managers, project teams, subject matter specialists, etc.) has typically dis-persed. Then, how should the organizational knowledge and competencies assets brought to bear during the ERP implementation be coordinated and integrated during the post-implementation phase?

Practitioner and academic literature propose the creation of a structure often called "competency center" manage and leverage organizational knowledge and expertise. The positioning and organization of this structure are decisive as to its ability to energize the ES and ensure consistency. Centralizing a firm's know-how around a duality of professional and technical expertise and plays a key role in keeping experts in a firm and in increasing their functional and technical skills which significantly reduces the need of external consultants. However, it is yet unclear under which con-ditions, decentralized or centralized, formal or informal, virtual or traditional ap-proach a CC is more efficient.

3   Methodology

This paper reports findings from the first stage of an ongoing project in which the unit of analysis is the organization. These data were captured from three, in-depth case studies conducted at three different large organizations in three different industries. To understand how the CCs are formed and evolved, we sought to understand the viewpoint of the key stakeholders that are important decision makers in forming and shaping CC. Since case studies allow the researcher to become familiar with the data in its natural setting and the context [23] and allows for a deeper understanding of a particular phenomenon [24], we chose this research approach to maximize the rich-ness and accuracy of data, transferability of the findings and to identify candidate constructs and variables for follow on study.

3.1   Sample Selection and Data Collection

Our sample selection began with the requirement that the study sites needed to include firms that were relatively mature in their use of ERP systems and were not ones just completing or recovering from the implementation of a new ERP. Accordingly we limited the sample to firms having had active ERPs for more than five years and which were dealing with post-implementation and BI integrations issues or firms that had made a transition to more comprehensive use of these systems. The sample has been opportunistic in the sense that we reached out to firms in France, the US Southeastern region, and Korea where we have close business contacts and where we were connected to ERP user support groups. As we made connections with ERP manager-users many of whom are in ERP user groups and industry related associations, other potential sites were suggested by those interviewed, hence the 'snowballing' aspect of the sampling approach. For this paper, we selected three large distinct institutions in South East USA to explore and investigate the emergent conditions and evolution of governance structure. Interviewing, snowball sampling and coding were done simultaneously as is the practice in qualitative research where data collection and analysis is intertwined [26]. Our data collection has involved on-site observation, structured and semi-structured interviews, document collection, and follows up interviews after initial data coding. We conducted semi-structured interviews based on an interview template developed beforehand and approved by our university's Institutional Review Board (IRB) human subjects research protocols by the study team and pre-reviewed with key informants who were experienced project leaders for ERP and BI implementations projects as well as ongoing support efforts.

In selected instances we reviewed the transcribed interviews and our interview notes with the informants to probe, check accuracy and extend our understanding of observations. These interviews were held with stakeholders involved in managing ERP and BI CC as well as managers holding different levels of responsibility and roles within the firm.

The organizations we chose to collect data all had at least four modules of SAP installed for at least five years. Data collection began in April 2012 and ended in May 2014. Interviews were conducted with multiple members of the CC team in each organization as well as people involved for year but who were working elsewhere. This gave us a solid multi-perspective historical view of the ES setting. The people we interviewed can be classified into two broad categories, the first, key decision makers in CC such as director of IT, and second, team members who were middle managers or team leaders. Interviews were recorded and transcribed. During coding fields notes and other data were compared to the transcriptions.

The semi-structured interview questions were designed to solicit the participant's recollection of the formation of CC and evolution of CC in their own words without "guiding" them through it. In each instance at least two of the study investigators were present. The protocol involved having one of the researchers responsible for capturing field notes and monitoring the trajectory of the interview. When offered additional evidence in the form of diagrams, policy documents, organograms and the like were also collected. Where possible these data were augmented by publicly available documents. The transcriptions have been annotated and enriched by reference to these additional data. The annotated notes and transcripts are being refined through the further discussions with study informants.

Table 1. Study firms and informants

Organization	Informants	1st round	2nd round
Case 1 Home Goods (HG): Global Producer and marketer of consumer and commercial portfolio of products. HG has successfully implemented SAP modules and performing BI and Analytics functions via SAP HANA. HG was established more than 75 years ago. Through many acquisitions, HG has seen significant growth in the last 25 years.	Director of IT, Division Finance VP	April 2012	April 2013
Case 2 Regional Southern University (RSU): Major southeastern university with student population of more than 24,000. While established more than 100 years ago, student population has increased from 18000 to 24,000 in the last 20 years.	CIO, Director of ES	April 2012	March 2013
Case 3 Material Supply (MS): Established in 1970s, MS started out as a small store. Now MS has more than 2,500 locations in North America and is larger still with its international operations. It was an SAP 'Lighthouse Partner' and its implementation project was one of the largest and celebrated successful SAP projects worldwide in this business sector, having implemented SAP in more than 300 stores in one non-US setting.	Director of IT Senior Project Manager	April 2012	April 2013

As is typical in intensive qualitative studies, the researchers are immersed in the data. Analysis and sensemaking is a continuous versus a discrete process that arises from the continuing engagement with the data. Two formal approaches are being used to further interrogate the textual data. Researchers used independent methods for coding the transcripts and later exchanged notes with one another and the informants to check for face validity and consistency. One of them used NVivo and the other MS Word. In both instances open coding techniques described by Strauss and Corbin [29] were applied, where textual data were converted into codes that expressed or described specific categories, sub categories, or concepts. A third approach has been to use latent semantic analysis, and the tool Leximancer, to identify common themes and idioms arising in the respondent's narratives.

3.2   Data Analysis

The interview data were transcribed and data processing was divided into three sections, coding procedures (sorting), data reduction techniques (categorizing), and drawing conclusions (mapping).

Coding procedures deal with strategies to handle the semi structured interview data, as well as the document analysis. The intent of "Open Coding" refers to an encoding method developed by Glaser and Strauss [15], which enables the examination, comparison, conceptualization and categorization of data. Analysis was done in parallel using latent semantic text analyzer, Leximancer, and NVivo. Leximancer provides further insights into the content analysis: "Leximancer provided a means for generating and recognising themes, including themes which might otherwise have been missed" [7, p. 188]. Our findings are derived from the analysis of third level of coding.

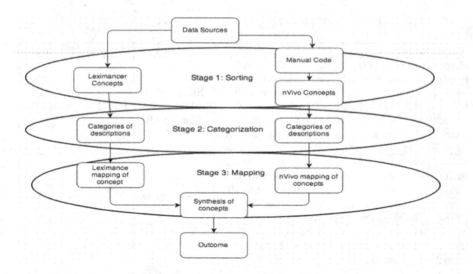

Fig. 3. Overall data analysis process utilizing Leximancer and NVivo (Adapted from Penn-Edwards [28])

Stage 1: Our Starting Point – Leximancer Analysis. Leximancer, a latent semantic analysis software tool, converts text to bit patterns and then presents a complete concordance of terms in the text(s) under study. Researchers can choose to remove, exclude and combine terms for further analysis. The tool then conducts various analyses on these patterns identifying measures such as frequency of occurrence, frequency of co-occurrence with other words (bit patterns) thus identifying idioms that are also coded for frequency of occurrence and co-occurrence and other measures of interconnectedness. These are presented in tables, including frequencies and linking concepts to the actual underlying text and as concept maps displaying the relative strength of its existence and relationship measures along different thresholds. The map illustrates the concepts present in the texts and certain aspects of relationships among concepts.

This approach provides an unbiased and transparent conceptual analysis of the text. However that does not mean the researcher accepts these raw concepts as a final result. Rather they provide beginning point and foundation for further analysis. When synthesized with other forms of coding (e.g, NVivo and manual coding) the technique provides a more complete view of the data and its meaning. Just like with other traditional Content Analysis tools, using Leximancer the researcher can modify settings to reduce the noise in the data. For example, one can remove 'filler' terms, identify synonyms and combine similar concepts as part of a data refinement and filtering process [7].

Stage 2 and 3: Open Coding in NVivo and Synthesis with Leximancer Concepts. As is typical in intensive qualitative studies, the researchers are immersed in the data. Analysis and sensemaking is a continuous versus a discrete process that arises from the continuing engagement with the data. Two formal approaches are being used to further interrogate the textual data. Researchers used independent methods for coding the transcripts and later exchanged notes to check for intercoder reliability with NVi-vo and the other MS Word as organizing and coding tools. In both instances open coding techniques described by Strauss and Corbin [29] were applied, where textual data were converted into codes that expressed or described specific categories, sub categories, or concepts. This allow us to further explore and develop the concepts initially identifies in the Leximancer analysis.

4 Case Analyses, Findings and Discussion

In this section we proceed in a linear case-by-case basis. We first describe the CC structure for each of our cases, paying attention to how they are situated ('becoming') within in each organization as well as the links the CC has to various business units. We then apply our assemblage framework to each case in order to analyze the inter-play of four constructs, the material–expressive continuum, and the territorialization–deterritorialization continuum.

Table 2. Organization and CC structure

Organization	ERP and BI systems	CC Structure
RSU	Banner, Oracle-PeopleSoft, ADP SAS business analysis Executive Management have no direct ERP to BI analytics	Informal structure
MS	SAP R/3 to ECC 6; exploring for CRM SAP BI throughout the organization	Formal "Center of Excellence" reporting to the CIO
HG	All SAP modules SAP BW throughout the organization	Formal Structure "Business Process Champions" Under the authority of CIO

4.1 Case 1 HG

HG operates in a formal CC environment where CC has clear vision and there are established positions and career path within CC for employees. The CC was created through formal chartering process initiated by the CIO and CEO. The founding prin-ciple behind the CC was that CC would govern deployment, development and sup-port. The clears goal for HG's CC is to consolidate to a single instance of SAP throughout organization and achieve a team composition within the CC including more business people than IT. In this organization membership in the CC is seen to be career enhancer and is a sought-over posting. In choosing CC members there exists a formal application and interviews process aimed at recruiting talented people having business savvy.

> While some department or even countries are in development mode, others are in post-implementation use mode, CC manages both environments. Our goal from the get goes was to get business on SAP. Get people into one common platform. (KR – Director of IT)

Once the people are recruited into CC, they are referred to as "business process champions" and these employees go back to their respective departments and carry out the agenda for CC and represent their unit to the CC. It is like being in dual Ambassadorial roles.

> Prospective members are nominated from the departments, interviewed and selected based on the fit. There are separate career paths for the employees. These employees are crucial to the success of CC, essentially they are the "bridge" between the department and CC. In our CC, we have mostly business and some IT people in CC: between 300-500 members." (KR – Director of IT)

The CC established clear guidelines for applications integration as well. Once the decision was made to have single instance of SAP running across the organizations, employees were encouraged to not to deviate from SAP.

> KR (director of CC) has some very good disciplines and his Boss and the organization says we are going SAP and anything which deviates from SAP is not necessarily a rogue application, but needs to be very well vetted. (MM – Finance VP)

Even in this formal structure where goals of the CC were clear, there are established roles and responsibilities for employees. The successes of the CC were not merely from the structure but the interaction between different BU and informal relationship employees' form. For example according to MM, the Finance VP, "We rely on relationship these business process champions have within their department to promote the cause for CC, which is one of the reasons, we insisted on having more business people in CC than IT people." "For the big job, we do have to go through formal process. However RJ has established enough credential to get many things done just by having gentleman's agreement."

4.2   Case 2 RSU

RSU operates in a semi-formal CC environment where there are established positions within CC; however, the interactions among different actors are not clearly defined or regulated. The governance body was intentionally created and is based on upper management's philosophy that a too formalized process stifles creativity and innovation.

> Because when we were looking at trying to get a formal governance structure, we got a pushback from all over the campus. That's exactly the reason we had those informal structures are in place and people felt threatened because we were trying to formalize. (DW – Director of ES)

Each of the IT departments in the organization is entrusted to collaborate and form partnerships as needed to facilitate effective and efficient operations and find appropriate resolutions as issues arise. These relationships are recognized, even called 'committees' locally but are temporal coming and going, as circumstances demand. As the CIO of RSU explains this phenomenon:

> Because we built informal relationships one to another within the organization, I don't feel like I need an SLA with DW (Director of ES) to get the things done and I hope DW feels the same way about me. (DE – CIO)

This semi-formal environment permits dynamic CCs to be created, evolve, and/or disbanded as necessary. An example is the relationship established between Enterprise Systems & Services (ESS) and Enterprise Information Management (EIM). ESS is the IT department responsible for supporting the ERP and other administrative systems within the organization. EIM is responsible for BI system and fulfilling the reporting requirements from the various systems. As technology emerged within the organization, a need to collaborate was recognized which afforded the opportunity for ESS and EIM to engage the management teams from both areas in an open forum to discuss ideas, upcoming changes, and new initiatives. Meetings are tentatively scheduled each month but the decision to meet depends upon the current situation or projects underway.

> Beginning of each year we call a meeting called Management by Objectives for all our employees and one of the things that I wanted to implement is that all assistant directors regularly meet and exchange ideas. (DE – CIO)

While this initiative is an example of a formal approach arising from a high level meeting, but how initiative is finally implemented is not formal at all.

> One of the assistant directors, Assistant Director of the Web group reaches out to all the different people that are involved in the web development across the campus and pull out those people together as a group. He has taken a pretty unique approach, he calls it is Donuts and Development. Quite simply, it is a meeting to discuss issues while eating donuts. He pulls those people together on a regular basis and gets into a collaborative project or....pull together or works with us (CC). (DW – Director of ES)

Another example of a semi-formal CC is the establishment of a Project Management (PM) office within ESS. There are three other IT groups within the organization in addition to ESS. Each of these IT groups has differing responsibilities ranging from supporting the campus network and infrastructure to assisting with the research computing needs of the academic departments. This semi-formal CC was formed to provide project management planning and services across the IT division through the ESS department.

This center functions in lieu of a formal Project Management Office (PMO) for the organization and provides support for major IT division projects. This center also facilitates project manager meetings across departments to aid in sharing IT project-related information throughout the organization.

> The advantage of having the flexibility to have informal CC without having to seek formal governance approval greatly enhances the organization's ability to distribute information more readily and respond to issues more rapidly. The semi-formal competency center structure is well suited to our organizational culture and works well in our environment. (DW– Director of ES)

4.3   Case 3: MS

This project was slated to be SAP's single biggest retailing implementation in the world in domain in which SAP was not dominant. Hence SAP had a vested interest in making this a clear success. In fact they named this firm a 'Lighthouse Partner" and provided unprecedented support form SAP AG and SAP US. This relationship and the vendor contract virtually required that MS operated in a formal and canonical CC environment.

> SAP led the initial structure and ideas were how to move beyond project team and be sustainable as a support structure. In that structure we had few people from SAP and we also had consultants. (DT – Director of IT)

Given the sheer scope of the project MS did not have enough internal expertise, thus it relied on SAP and consultants to fill many roles within the CC, numbering over 600 people during the height of the implementation. While project team implemented the ERP, during post-implementations, most of the CC employees went back to their previous positions and the CC team shrunk to fewer than 50 people responsible for all ERP support, bug fixes, updates and new initiatives.

Once MS was familiar with the governing concept of the CC, MS tried to recruit more people from within the organizations and reduce the reliance on consultants. The size and composition of the CC kept fluctuating for other reasons as well. At the same time some consultants were offered jobs and brought into the firm, which created very dynamic environment, in some measure because these hires did not know the business form the inside out. Not only was the structure of the CC emerging, the relationship between players was quite dynamic as well.

When the implementation project was complete, employees went back to their business units or left to work on other ERP implementation projects. The result was a breaking of the desired "link" between the CC and the business units.

> Key individuals were taken out of the business verticals. These people were well trained, usually came from consultancies and knew how to work with finance and end users. When this project moved into post production and they (cc employees) disseminated back out to their verticals and reported in. (HC – Senior PM)

4.4   Discussion—A Synthesis Understanding in Light of Assemblage and Emergence Theories

The territorialization–deterritorialization continuum. HG falls in the middle of the continuum; it reflects a more balanced relationship between rigidity and fluidity. For instance, roles and responsibilities are clear, people are vetted for CC membership and IS applications are also carefully vetted as to how they will interact with extant enterprise systems yet, Such tight boundary conditions would suggest rigidity. But business process champions / dual ambassadors serve a bridging function and create strong CC to BU bi-lateral linkages.

When CC first introduces the initial configuration plan for the ERP and BI, these plan and framework are an example of territorialization process. These configuration have specific requirements and management procedures. These procedures solidify assemblage. However, as the organizations start the process of re-configuration and customization, the initial assemblage is destabilized. In response, CC initiate territorialization process by helping to create new culture and re-stabilizing the identity of the assemblage. For example, in RSU, the CC has connected the entire business units and, in a sense, created a cross-functional culture that assistance and collaboration to everyone who has access to ERP and BI applications. CC provides mechanism for enabling dialogue among people, groups, functions and business units to easily collaborate, thus, helping managers to organize their post-implementation use. This collaborative optimization of ERP and BI becomes a catalyst of the process of territorialization.

In the three cases, CC is acting as hub between IT and business sides. The linking of IT and business is the result of recognizing that technical integration and organizational integration are the faces of the same piece and need to be me managed as an assemblage. This assemblage process allows certain flexibility and   preparing and rendering ES and organization process for more cross-functional integration.

The material–expressive continuum. The material aspects in all three cases are represented by the people, roles and their evolving relationships. The expressive aspect is represented differently in each case. In HG the expressive is manifest as the direct interaction with the material. For instance people identified for or promoted to the CC are rewarded by recognition or other tangible benefits. RSU is closer to the expressive end of the continuum because relies more on symbolic gestures vs. formal recognitions and rewards. At MS, the expressive is not an outcome of the material. Being in a CC at MS does not garner recognition or direct career enhancement. As such the expressive is less tangible than in HG, and is closer to the material end of the continuum.

We are confident that the 'Big Picture' model (Figure 4 below) sufficiently coveys the social-interactive aspects of the governing structuring process. It is important to note that in all settings the primary focus is on Business, processes, and people followed by upgrades and projects. The technical aspects of ERP systems, such as modules, reference models, data bases and models, configuration plans and the like, are not nearly as prominent and do not take the same weight as the business function oriented concepts. The CC ensures the robustness and reliability of the information infrastructure but, at the same time, enables heterogeneous groups of information consumers to use information in a coordinated way to achieve organizational goals.

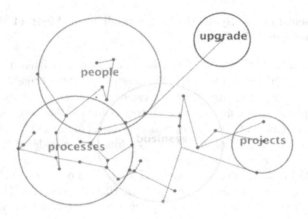

Fig. 4. Big picture concepts

Even within the major concepts the ERP system itself is not a major component. For instance examining the underlying sub-components we find that 'data', 'load', 'systems', and' solutions' are all related to concept of 'processes'. The concept 'business' is comprised of sub-components' 'management', 'project', 'organizations' and 'veterans'. Veterans refer to experienced employees in the organization. Tools and sales are related to people. While upgrade and projects are part of CC, they are not as important as people, processes, and business.

Emergence: CC Structuring Elements in the Cases. Table 3 presents instances of emergence observed in the case data. In MS, candidate members were sought out from different BU into the CC to devote time in dealing with development and deployment issues. This newly created structure forced the new members to quickly acclimate and assimilate into this new environment. Since there were no formal recognitions or rewards, some people simply went back to their BU. This turnover rate prevented from creating a strong link between the CC and BU. People either identified with their CC role or BU role, but not the dual role they were expected to play. Thus, the CC was always structuring and never achieved the status of an emergent regularity.

When RSU wanted to implement a formal structure, it got pushback from the organization and had to abandon the idea of forming a permanent clear structure. However, RSU adapted and employed a different approach from which an informal governing structure emerged. For example, a "Project Management informal group" meets regularly with other groups to discuss important issues. This informal approach which emerged as response to the opposition of formal structure, gave inspiration to other groups to organize the informal meetings as well.

Table 3. Elements of assemblage

Assemblage Concepts	HG	RSU	MS
Territorialization Elements that make assemblage rigid	Boundaries are formed. Formal roles and responsibilities. Even the IS applications were "vetted".	Fluid boundaries, key people invited to CC but no permanent residency in CC, relied on informal relationship	Clear boundaries. People were nominated from the BUs to be in the CC. People were either in CC or BU. Not enough strong "links" between the CC and BU.
Deterritorialization Elements that make assemblages fluid	Dual ambassador role: even in the CC, people maintain their BU roles (and vice versa) creating strong and flexible links between the CC and BU	"Overlapping interactions"	Established relationship in the department
Materials (e.g., ERP, BI, Resources, proximity relationships among resources)	Nominated from department, then interviewed to be in CC CIO, CEO	People who were "Overlap in interaction" CIO, CEO, CTO	Key individuals from different BU and Outsourced partner – SAP, Latin America Group, Canada Group
Expressions (e.g., Symbolic and non-symbolic, agendas, goals, mission)	A single instance of SAP, provide common platform, clear career incentives	Manage competencies in different BU, camaraderie	Original intent of ERP financial system replacement

In HG, recruitment process, employee's roles and employee rewards were planned and clearly structured. Even in this structured settings, HG realized that informal links were emerging where people interacting with their old BUs. Responding to this emergent issue, the CC established a policy that people will not be "taken out" of BU rather they will act as "business process champions" creating a de-facto dual ambassador role wherein the CC members still resided in their respective BU.

This instance of emergence exerts a "positioning" force that keeps the newly formed assemblage in play never being fixed in a relative position in either the material-expressive or territorialization–deterritorialization continua. In the case of MS, emergent issues kept the assemblage from achieving its deterritorialization properties. As a result, the CC in MS was not able to establish a clear "link" between the CC and BU.

While MS did not deal with the emerging issue which was preventing MS from achieving a balance positioning in territorialization–de-territorialization continuum, HG quickly realized that along with clear structure and employee roles and reward structure, the informal links and collaborations are important for establishing a successful CC.

5   Contributions and Limitations

This study was motivated to fill a void in the literature regarding the existence and the configuration of the CC unit during post-implementation phase. Given the growing importance of ES software and the ubiquity ERP in Fortune 500, Fortune 100 and most mid-size firms worldwide and the inevitability of maintaining these systems and trying to extract increasing value from the investment in them, it is increasingly necessary to understand the role of post-implementation governance structures on the improvement of these ES investments. For instance, the findings in RSU suggest that informal liaison mechanisms are more critical to knowledge integration than are formal structural arrangements such as those deployed at MS. In all three cases the business need was found to be one of the key internal requirements driving the structuring processes behind the CC that led to unintended and destabilizing outcomes. It appears that organizational reliance on ES creates dependence on those systems that in turn gives the CCs more apparent power over the organization. But this power has impact of destabilizing the former more permanent system. Thus CCs are an example not of structure but rather assemblages.

Whether this assemblage survives to provide value to an organization or not depends on how the emergent issues are handled and how the assemblages are "positioned". IT applications serve business users, as such it is understandable that demands from business unit can motivate the creation of a CC along a particular trajectory intended to support the integration and the use of the ES. However, we found that not all business needs are equally influential and often do not traverse the intended path.

6   Conclusion

The research reported in this paper is one of few empirical studies focused on ES competency center during post-implementation phase. It offers evidence of emergent processes shaping CC organizational structuring and it is a step examining the role of this new structure. As such it helps gain a better understanding of the CC unit, how it is configured and structured and the role and mechanisms mitigating the relationship between business units and IT departments.

The assemblage theory and emergence approach provide a strong background to study how the organizational and IT resources and competencies supported the key actions within different ES CC configuration. It also provides a theoretical framework to understand why and how the actions and decisions were executed in each specific context. It highlights to focus research attention on dynamic and emergent issues rather than structures and rigid frameworks that are the focal point of much of the ES literature and canonical consulting wisdom.

References

1. Alter, S.: Theory of Workarounds. Communications of the Association for Information Systems 34, 1041–1066 (2014)
2. Barker, T., Frolick, M.N.: ERP Implementation Failure: A Case Study. Information Systems Management 20(4), 43–49 (2003)

3. Benitez-Amado, J., Walczuch, R.M.: Information Technology, the Organizational Capability of Proactive Corporate Environmental Strategy and Firm Performance: A Resource-Based Analysis. European Journal of Information Systems 21(6), 664–679 (2012)
4. Bhatt, G.D., Grover, V.: Types of Information Technology Capabilities and Their Role in Competitive Advantage: An Empirical Study. Journal of Management Information Systems 22(2), 253–277 (2005)
5. Carter, M., Takeda, H., Truex, D.: An Epistemology of Organizational Emergence: The Tripartite Domains of Organizational Discourse and the Servitization of IBM. In: Barrett, M., Davidson, E., Middleton, C., DeGross, J.I. (eds.) Information Technology in the Service Economy: Challenges and Possibilities for the 21st Century. IFIP, vol. 267, pp. 367–370. Springer, Heidelberg (2008)
6. Chae, B., Poole, M.S.: The Surface of Emergence in Systems Development: Agency, Institutions, and Large-Scale Information Systems. European Journal of Information Systems 14(1), 19–36 (2005)
7. Crofts, K., Bisman, J.: Interrogating Accountability: An Illustration of the Use of Leximancer Software for Qualitative Data Analysis. Qualitative Research in Accounting & Management 7(2), 180–207 (2010)
8. Davis, J.M., Kettinger, W.J., Kunev, D.: When Users Are IT Experts Too: The Effects of Joint IT Competence and Partnership On Satisfaction With Enterprise-Level Systems Implementation. European Journal of Information Systems 18, 26–37 (2009)
9. DeLanda, M.: A New Philosophy of Society: Assemblage Theory and Social Complexity. Continuum (2006)
10. Deleuze, G., Guattari, F.: A Thousand Plateaus: Capitalism and Schizophrenia. University of Minneapolis Press, Minneapolis (1987)
11. EL Amrani, R., Aryal, A., Sarkar, S., Truex, D.: The Key Determinants of a Successful Competency Center: It Depends! In: Proceedings of the SIG-Enterprise Systems Pre-ICIS Conference (2012)
12. Elbashir, M.Z., Collier, P.A., Davern, M.J.: Measuring the Effects of Business Intelligence Systems: The Relationship Between Business Process and Organizational Performance. International Journal of Accounting Information Systems 9(3), 135–153 (2008)
13. Eriksen, L.-B., Axline, S., Markus, M.L., Drucker, P.: What Happens After "Going Live" With ERP Systems? In: Competence Centers Can Support Effective Institutionalization. AMCIS 1999 Proceedings, Paper 268, vol. 268 (1999), http://aisel.aisnet.org/amcis1999/268
14. Gallagher, K.P., Worrell, J.L., Mason, R.M.: The Negotiation and Selection of Horizontal Mechanisms to Support Post-Implementation ERP Organizations. Information Technology & People 25(1), 4–30 (2012)
15. Glaser, B.G., Strauss, A.L.: The Discovery of Grounded Theory; Strategies for Qualitative Research. Aldine, Chicago (1967)
16. Grabski, S.V., Leech, S.A., Schmidt, P.J.: A Review of ERP Research: A Future Agenda for Accounting Information Systems. Journal of Information Systems 25(1), 37–78 (2011)
17. Granebring, A., Révay, P.: Enterprise Resource Planning Competence Centres: A Case Study. Kybernetes 34(9/10), 1551–1562 (2005)
18. Hopper, P.J.: Emergent Grammar. Berkeley Linguistics Society 13, 139–157 (1987)
19. Hopper, P.J.: Some Recent Trends in Grammaticalization. Annual Review of Anthropology 25, 217–236 (1996)
20. Hopper, P.J.: Emergent Grammar. In: Tomasello, M. (ed.) The New Psychology of Language: Cognitive and Functional Approaches to Language Structure, vol. 1, pp. 155-75. Lawrence Erlbaum, Mahwah, NJ and London (1998)

21. Kallinikos, J.: Deconstructing Information Packages: Organizational and Behavioural Implications of ERP Systems. Information Technology and People 17(1), 8–30 (2004)
22. Kholeif, A.O., Abdel-Kader, M., Sherer, M.: ERP Customization Failure: Institutionalized Accounting Practices, Power Relations and Market Forces. Journal of Accounting & Organizational Change 3(3), 250–269 (2007)
23. Lee, A.S.: A Scientific Methodology for MIS Case Studies. MIS Quarterly 13(1), 33–50 (1989)
24. Lee, A.S., Baskerville, R.L.: Generalizing Generalizability in Information Systems Research. Information Systems Research 14(3), 221–243 (2003)
25. Marcus, G.E., Saka, E.: Assemblage. Theory, Culture & Society 23, 101–106 (2006)
26. Miles, M.B., Huberman, A.M.: Qualitative Data Analysis: An Expanded Sourcebook. Sage (1994)
27. Newell, S., Tansley, C., Huang, J.: Social Capital and Knowledge Integration in an ERP Project Team: The Importance of Bridging and Bonding. British Journal of Management 15(S1), S43-S57 (2004)
28. Penn-Edwards, S.: Computer Aided Phenomenography: The Role of Leximancer Computer Software in Phenomenographic Investigation. Qualitative Report 15(2), 252–267 (2010)
29. Strauss, A., Corbin, J.: Basics of Qualitative Research. Sage, Thousand Oaks, CA (1998)
30. Truex, D.: ERP Systems as Facilitating and Confounding Factors in Corporate Mergers: The Case of Two Canadian Telecommunications Companies. Systemes d'Information et Managemen 1(6), 7–21 (2001)
31. Truex, D.P., Baskerville, R.: Deep Structure or Emergence Theory: Contrasting Theoretical Foundations for Information Systems Development. Information Systems Journal 8(2), 99–118 (1998)
32. Truex, D.P., Baskerville, R., Klein, H.: Growing Systems in Emergent Organizations. Communications of the ACM 42(8), 117–123 (1999)
33. Truex, D.P., Klein, H.K.: A Rejection of Structure as a Basis for Information Systems Development. In: Stamper, R.K., Kerola, P., Lee, R., Lyytinen, K. (eds.) Collaborative Work, Social Communications and Information Systems, pp. 213–236. Elsevier, Amsterdam (1991)
34. Volkoff, O., Elmes, M.B., Strong, D.M.: Enterprise Systems, Knowledge Transfer and Power Users. Journal of Strategic Information Systems 13(4), 279–304 (2004)
35. Worrell, J., Gallagher, K., Mason, R.: Understanding the Structure of Post-Implementation ERP Teams. In: AMCIS 2006 Proceedings, Paper 307 (2006), http://aisel.aisnet.org/amcis2006/307

Activities to Address Challenges in Digital Innovation

Jesper Lund

Halmstad University, Halmstad, Sweden
Jesper.lund@hh.se

Abstract. Based on a literature review, this paper identifies four socio-technical challenges relating to innovation actor's interactions in digital innovation. Furthermore, the paper explores how these challenges can be addressed. The challenges are investigated in a case study of digital innovation. The study is based on a two year long research and development project where an e-newspaper concept and a demonstrator based on e-paper technology was developed. Based on empirical findings, the paper presents eight activities which address the identified socio-technical challenges with digital innovation. The activities are: 1) support transparent digital ecosystem relationships, 2) facilitate cross-organizational communication, 3) create digital value blueprints, 4) translate heterogeneous knowledge, 5) involve all relevant user groups, 6) identify, design for, and authenticate digital user values, 7) design for multiple contexts of use, and 8) prototype iteratively.

Keywords: digital innovation challenges, innovation activities, digital technology, e-newspaper, e-paper.

1 Introduction

Digitization of analogue products is currently changing our society [1, 2]. As an example, digital services based on digitization of music, TV, and voice calls have led to digital innovations such as Spotify, Netflix, and Skype. These services are widely adopted and have changed the ways users consume media and communicate via voice over IP. Digitization in this case creates value adding services for consumers who can use these digital services on multiple devices anytime and anywhere. However, digital innovation is not only providing added value to consumers. The mentioned digital innovations are also examples of how digitization creates new markets and rearranges device manufactures and content provider's roles in digital ecosystems. As such, digital innovation has a high impact on firms and entire industries. In the mentioned examples, there have been rapid and profound changes in the music and broadcasting industry, as well as for phone operators.

Digital innovation as a notion refers to the embedding of digital computer and communication technology into a traditionally non-digital product [3]. The notion also refers to the process of creating new combinations of digital and physical components that produce novel products or services [4]. Digital innovation is based on digital technology. Digital technology can be categorized by layers consisting of devices, networks, services and content [4]. As different layers of digital technology

B. Doolin et al. (Eds.): IS&O 2014, IFIP AICT 446, pp. 115–131, 2014.

requires different competencies, knowledge, and resources, innovation actors often need to either setup or join innovation networks to be able to succeed with digital innovation [5, 6, 7]. Given the characteristics of digital technology, digital innovation becomes networked and complex with a need for involving heterogeneous actors and resources [1, 8]. The layered modular characteristic, and the generativity of digital technology, pose two specific challenges for digital innovation. Firstly, it requires actors to cooperate over organizational boundaries and demands knowledge exchanges between actors with different backgrounds, competences and knowledge. In other words, digital innovations require multiple actors with knowledge and resources in the different layers of the technology to cooperate [1, 9, 10]. Secondly, the generativity of the digital technology creates large and varied audiences with heterogeneous requirements on digital innovations [1, 11, 12]. The combination of this added complexity, heterogeneity, and networked features of digital innovation, are challenging how we innovate successful digital technology [1, 13, 14].

The mentioned challenges primarily relate to the interaction, i.e. the relationships and exchanges between actors in innovation networks working with digital innovation. Several calls for research on socio-technical challenges in digital innovation can be found [see e.g. 1, 8, 15]. Much of prior research within digital innovation has been dominated by a conceptual nature [see e.g. 4, 13, 14]. There are few examples of empirical research on how digital innovation plays out in practice [1]. This paper aims to address these calls for research, by firstly investigating the specific challenges relating to actor's interactions in digital innovation, and secondly, by empirically investigating activities to address these challenges. The paper is therefore structured around the following research question: *What are the challenges with actors' interactions in digital innovation, and how can these be addressed?* By identifying challenges with digital innovation in related literature, and presenting suggestions of activities to address these based on empirical findings, this paper primarily contributes with actionable insights to the emerging field of digital innovation.

In this paper, an example of digital innovation from the newspaper industry is used to investigate how these challenges can be addressed. E-paper technology captured the interest of the newspaper industry through revealing the possibility of a newspaper service via an e-paper device with high readability and low power consumption. The digitization of the newspaper presented several opportunities for the industry to reach new markets, and cut production and distribution costs. However, newspapers needed to team up with other actors to be able to explore the digital innovation at hand. The case of the e-newspaper, a newspaper service specifically designed for an e-paper device, illustrates the challenges with heterogeneous actors interacting in an innovation network. Several previously unconnected actors such as newspaper organizations, network providers, software companies, hardware device manufacturers, and advertising companies, had to intertwine their perspectives, business models and technological frames to realize the e-newspaper concept.

2   Related Literature

Digital innovations as artifacts are based on layered digital technology which can be divided into four different layers: device layer, network layer, service layer, and content layer [4]. These layers lay the foundation for two important separations: the separation between service and device due to re-programmability, and the separation between content and network due to homogenization of data [4]. Designers can combine components from different layers to create new digital innovations due to standardized interfaces. In every layer there has been an emergence of technical and practical capabilities for using that layer on a nonproprietary model that would make access easier, cheaper, and less controllable by any single actor [16]. One effect for digital innovation as a process is that when more actors have access, they also need to collaborate in order to be able to develop digital innovations spanning across all four layers.

Layered digital technology is an example of a modular industry structure that enables independent firms to introduce innovations into established markets. Furthermore, the modularity allows the best players in each of the layers to be involved and innovate, due to users wanting innovations that mix and match components from the different layers [17]. Hence, digital innovation built on layered digital technology often requires different actors from different fields to cooperate in innovation networks. This knowledge heterogeneity is challenging digital innovation [10]. Digital technology is also described to have a generative characteristic [1, 4].

Digital technology becomes more and more malleable and dynamic. This generativity enables new functionality and capabilities which can be added after a product is out on the market [1, 4, 11]. This can once again be exemplified with smart phones acting as platforms for apps or the PC as a powerful adaptable machine. Apps turn smart phones and PCs into adaptable and changeable digital tools, supporting large and varied target groups and many different aspects of use. Digital innovation targeted against everyday use also leads to a change in the view of the user. The notion of a user needs to be expanded beyond users as organizational members [18]. With today's digitalization, users do not solely use computing capabilities for work or organizational purposes, but they also interact with computing technologies in much broader social contexts [2]. As a result, user needs and requirements are often highly heterogeneous in these contexts of use [2, 12, 18].

Concurring with the ideas of heterogeneous digital technology and users, there is a growing acknowledgment that digital innovation is a collective achievement by many actors and stakeholders, often with different meanings and conflicting interests [5, 6]. As digital innovation becomes more networked, it drives a need for collaboration which spans over organizational realms [4]. During the last two decades there has been a shift in how innovation networks are formed and viewed by organizations. This is especially evident within technology development fields such as digital innovation [9].

Digital innovations that are created and driven by increased heterogeneity of knowledge are redefining services and products. Digital innovation is re-organizing industries, generating new business logics, and changing business models [19]. Within fields of rapid technological development, such as digital innovation, there is a great diversity of actors. In the innovation networks formed around digital innovation, firms and universities are critical features to enable innovation capacity. One enabler of this capacity is knowledge dispersion between heterogeneous actors [20, 9]. Innovation networks provide access to diverse sources of capabilities and information, and the interaction between the actors increases the innovativeness at the individual firms. Successful interorganizational relationships therefore fuel firm innovation and growth [9].

Innovating in a network can be viewed as a Socio-technical process [13]. Innovation is a social given that, "obtaining, transforming and sharing knowledge is a negotiation and sense-making process, through which an actor's identity and relationships to others are negotiated and re-defined" [19, p. 10]. Innovation processes within heterogeneous networks that involve multiple actors are complex. The complexity becomes even more evident whilst working with digitization of products and services [19]. Even so, the strategy to involve several actors in an innovation network is based on the possibilities of resource sharing and therefor, also sharing the risks. This is especially evident in fields of technological uncertainty [9]. Social aspects, such as trust, commitment and power, needs to be facilitated in heterogeneous innovation networks as they influence the relationships between actors in innovation networks [21]. Table 1 presents a summary which highlights how characteristics of digital technology challenge socio-technical aspects of digital innovation according to related literature.

Table 1. Socio-technical challenges with digital innovation

Challenge	Description	Reference
1. Modular co-operation	Modular layers of digital technology enable digital innovation. Different layers require actors with diverse knowledge bases to co-operate in innovation networks. As a result, digital innovation processes become complex and networked.	2, 4, 5, 6, 16, 17
1.1 Knowledge exchanges	Knowledge between heterogeneous actors needs to be dispersed to enable innovation capacity. The translation and exchange of knowledge between heterogeneous actors is challenging.	9, 10, 19, 20
2. Diverse consumer groups	Generativity of digital technology enables adaptability of a digital innovation after it is implemented. This generativity leads to large, diverse, and uncoordinated user groups and markets.	1, 2, 4, 11
2.1 Heterogeneous user requirements	Large, diverse, and uncoordinated audiences of digital innovations lead to multiple use contexts and heterogeneous user requirements.	2, 12, 18

3   Research Approach

To enable the exploration of the research question a multi-method approach was chosen [22, 23]. Exploratory studies are appropriate in new fields of study where little is known about a phenomenon [24]. The use of multiple research methods is especially suitable in exploratory and explanatory studies where there is limited or crude knowledge [25]. Furthermore, a multi-method approach has the possibility to provide a wide and complete understanding of a phenomenon studied. As different research methods focus on different aspects, combining multiple methods provides a possibility for a richer understanding of a research topic [23]. A case study approach was selected in which a digital innovation case was studied from the perspective of challenges and activities that addressed them.

This paper is built on a two-step process. First, it summarizes socio-technical challenges in digital innovation based on a review of related literature. Secondly, it investigates a case of digital innovation to identify activities which addressed the challenges. A two year research and development project called DigiNews [ITEA 03015] was chosen. The project was active between 2004 and 2006 and included partners from Belgium, Spain, Netherlands, France and Sweden. Data concerning the project was also gathered in 2008 and 2010. The research and development consortium formed in the project consisted of several major technology firms, media houses and universities. The DigiNews project aimed at defining, architecting and demonstrating a solution for a digital newspaper (i.e. the e-newspaper). The solution included all parts needed to produce, distribute and consume digital news, i.e. all steps from publisher to reader. The project also explored ways to maximize the chances of a successful introduction to the market; this included the creation of different business plans and strategies. In this paper the project partners in DigiNews are viewed as actors in an innovation network formed around the e-newspaper.

Even though the data was not collected specifically with the intention to identify activities which addressed challenges within digital innovation, the DigiNews project was deemed suitable to do a retrospective analysis of a case of digital innovation. DigiNews was selected for this purpose due to a) the e-newspaper being an example of a digital innovation as it concerns the embedding of digital computer and communication technology into a traditionally non-digital product, and b) DigiNews enables an analysis of the process of creating new combinations of digital and physical components that produce novel products or services.

The actors involved in the innovation network are coming from several different organizations and industries incorporating a highly heterogeneous knowledge base in the network. Also, the technology used to create the e-newspaper is a valid example of layered digital technology which incorporates components on all four layers with different actors engaging in each of the layers. Also, the consumers of an e-newspaper are an example of a large, varied, and uncoordinated audience. Readers, advertisers, and newspaper staff provide a good example of heterogeneous users of digital innovation. Finally, the e-newspaper case is a contemporary and interesting example of a traditional industry in need of finding new digital innovations in order to have the ability to compete with new actors on the market, such as e.g. Google.

The data collection conducted in DigiNews is based on three different sets of data which are primarily generated from design and business model studies (see Table 2). The data from the first set concerning needs and requirements was gathered from eight workshops and ten focus group meetings. To ensure the involvement of the users and to receive the publishers domain knowledge, three different focus groups were initiated; one with users, one with advertisers, and one with newspaper designers. In the focus group sessions, concepts and prototypes of the e-newspaper were developed and evaluated iteratively.

The second data set was initiated with prototype testing during the autumn of 2005. The prototype test was designed to test different design solutions as well as to investigate user attitudes towards the e-newspaper concept. Data set 2 concluded with a real life test of the e-newspaper. Ten families were involved who tested an early version of an e-newspaper, published on an actual e-paper device (in this case the iRex iLiad) during a two week period in autumn of 2006. The real life test was designed to specifically explore pros and cons with an early version of an e-newspaper, as well as the users' preferences and intentions to adopt.

The final set of data involves seven interviews with eight respondents. The interviewees represented five newspaper actors, and two technology actors in the project. The interviews, ranging between approximately 30 and 160 minutes, were recorded and later transcribed. The interviews were built around themes such as background, learning outcomes, value networks, business models, technical and design aspects of the e-newspaper, internet and other media channels, and the influence of different technologies on the organization and management. This data set also contained documentation which mirrored the whole DigiNews project. The documentation includes project meeting minutes, agendas, preliminary and final reports, and deliverables from the project. The data also consisted of the project application, as well as some external technical reports.

Table 2. Overview of data collection

	Data collection	No. of respondents	Type of data
Data set 1	*Needs and requirements*	54	8 future workshops and 10 focus group meetings
Data set 2	*Prototype testing*	36	Observation, interview, questionnaire
	Real life evaluation	12	Online diary, questionnaires, interviews
Data set 3	*Interviews*	8	Interviews with newspaper and technology actors
	Documentation	-	Reports, agendas, minutes from meetings

In this paper, data from all datasets are used to enable a retrospective analysis based on the summary of socio-technical challenges with digital innovation. However, it is primarily the interview data from dataset two and three and the documentation from dataset three, that are used to provide the foundation for the empirical case.

The transcribed interview data, as well as the documentation was analyzed as follows. A coding technique [26] was used to thematically categorize the data based on the four identified socio-technical challenges with digital innovation. In order to categorize the data, patterns were sought after and identified in the data [26]. Excerpts in the transcribed material, as well as in the documentation, were marked with assigned colors. This facilitated data categorization according to the corresponding themes. These themes were then summarized and used in the paper to illuminate empirical aspects of the four socio-technical challenges.

4   The Case of the E-Newspaper

In late 2003, an innovation network was formed in relation to a research and development project called DigiNews. At the core of the project was the e-paper technology, a new display technology with promising features.

The main advantage with e-paper technology was that it could provide users with the same reading experience as traditional paper. Compared to traditional displays such as LCD and LED displays, e-paper has a reflective display technology without back light. Most e-paper technologies have a high resolution that is comparable with the resolution used in traditional newspapers. Compared to traditional displays it was also very power efficient, as power is only required when updating the display. All in all, e-paper technology was (and still is) a promising technology for industries such as newspapers or book publishers.

Based on e-paper technology, the e-newspaper concept was a possible digital innovation that could address some of the problems the newspaper industry was facing. At the time, newspapers were forced to think in new ways as most of them faced declining subscription and advertising revenues. The e-newspaper concept included two parts: the e-paper device and the e-newspaper as a service, e.g. the content published on the device. The e-newspaper supported mobility in the sense of allowing updated news anytime and anywhere, and could be seen as a digital news service published on an e-paper device. A wide diffusion of this digital innovation would dramatically reduce production and distribution costs. Therefore, the e-newspaper was an interesting prospect for the newspaper industry. Moreover, there was a belief that the e-newspaper could reach new audiences, e.g. young people. The challenge for a successful launch lied within finding enough additional value for the users to choose an e-newspaper before a printed one. Another challenge with the e-newspaper innovation was that a successful launch concerned both the adoption of a device, the e-paper device, and new services [27].

The innovation network initially formed around DigiNews consisted of 24 actors from nine European countries representing industry, SME, research labs, and academia. The five industry actors initially involved included Philips Applied Technologies, who was responsible for developing the e-paper technology. A technology based on E-ink, one of the dominant designs of e-paper technology available. Within this group of actors several newspapers were either indirectly (via The Swedish Newspaper Publishers' Association) or directly involved. Furthermore, a large R&D unit from the British Broadcasting Corporation (BBC) was involved. The 12 SMEs that were initially involved included actors developing supporting technologies for the e-newspaper such as text-to-speak, cryptographic communication, secure and mobile payment solutions, wireless communication, display and device developers, audio and video streaming and decoding, and mobile applications. Seven academic or research lab actors were initially involved with expertise ranging from publishing systems, network communication, software and hardware development, collaborative design, interaction design, usability studies, and field studies.

Worth noting is that two perspectives were used when designing the e-newspaper concept. One perspective was more futuristic and disregarded some technical restrictions. The other perspective was used for the design of the demonstrator used in the final evaluations of the e-newspaper. Both perspectives focused on the potential of e-paper technology. However, as this technology was not fully developed when the project was initiated, there was a technological uncertainty regarding the potential of e-paper. To make a distinction between the two perspectives in the case description, the "e-newspaper concept" and the "e-newspaper demonstrator" is used when applicable. If only the "e-newspaper" is referred to, the text is including both perspectives.

4.1   Modular Cooperation

The e-newspaper, based on layered digital technology, exemplifies the need to involve multiple actors to enable this particular digital innovation. Newspapers had to be involved in the content layer to produce news and stories. Also, advertisers had to be involved in this layer. Research labs, newspapers, and SMEs had to be involved in the service layer of the e-newspaper. A multitude of services were involved in the e-newspaper, ranging from secure and mobile payment solutions to location based systems and text to speak. In the e-newspaper, the device layer consisted of the e-paper device. This device included a display of e-paper and communication interfaces to distribute content to the device. Furthermore, it had memory capabilities to store content. Finally, several actors had to be involved in the network layer, both from academia and research labs as well as SMEs to investigate suitable future communication networks to be used. The e-newspaper concept was initially planned to be distributed via different media with different characteristics.

The actors came from four different levels; industry, SME, research labs, and academia. Within every level there were quite different interests, goals, perspectives, and knowledge bases that meshed up in the innovation network. For example, the interests of the research labs differed somewhat from the academic partners who had a more open agenda to what was possible to focus on in the project. There were similar differences in interests and goals when comparing industry actors with SME actors. The SMEs had quite narrow interests mapping towards their profiles and competences while the industry actors had a wider room for movement within the innovation and design process of the e-newspaper.

The different goals, and in some cases opposing interests, of the heterogeneous actors led to conflicts that had to be handled. The most apparent conflicts were between Philips, who developed the main prototype of the e-paper device, and the newspaper actors. Early on in the project, Philips presented ideas on how the e-newspaper could be produced and distributed. In these ideas they viewed themselves as a central hub where content (both ads and news) were stored in a database owned by them. Philips then planned to package the content and deliver the e-newspaper themselves out to the readers. In this scenario, newspapers were transformed to content deliverers, losing both their distribution channels and their relations to the readers as well as to the advertisers as customers. The first schematics of this e-newspaper concept made it clear that there were very different goals and interests, but also perspectives, that had to be handled in the innovation process.

The management of the project was responsible for handling the conflicting interests of the heterogeneous actors involved in the innovation network. Reviewing minutes of meeting, revealed conflicts of interest during the whole project. These conflicts challenged the collaboration and the commitment of different actors in the project. This became apparent when actors started developing solutions that were not compatible.

Reviewing the documentation, one problem with conflicting interests and collaboration issues was determined to be rooted in the power balances within the network. As the project was managed by Philips, their views and interests were dominant when deciding the focus of the innovation process of the e-newspaper demonstrator. This created problems in some of the meetings and led to commitment issues from some of the other actors. For example, newspapers did not agree on the business model proposed by Philips as it embodied a conflict of business interests. Philips did also disregard findings in the user studies which led to several identified issues during the evaluations of the e-newspaper demonstrator.

Knowledge Exchanges. Another challenge concerning heterogeneous actors is knowledge distribution. Trying to share and distribute knowledge over organizational boundaries about technical aspects, as well as business and design aspects relating to newspaper domain knowledge, were sometimes challenging. These difficulties could be seen in the discussions concerning the needs and requirements of the e-newspaper, as well as business models and value chains (for more details, see [28]). Due to a difference in work culture and tradition, the newspaper industry and the consumer electronic industry had a hard time communicating, sharing knowledge, and overall fully understanding each other's perspectives.

The example of researchers disseminating users' needs and requirements as design and usability guidelines could also be used to explain challenges in relation to knowledge distribution. When researchers provided input to the design of both the e-paper device, as well as the e-newspaper service, much of it was disregarded or not deemed as important by the developers. Based on these examples, it appeared that it was indeed challenging to share knowledge and learn from each other in a network with heterogeneous actors. Finally, the last challenges identified concerned alignment of interests between the actors involved. It seemed as if it was hard for the involved industries to sometimes move away from existing paths and to think in new ways. To enable the realization of the digital innovation at hand, an alignment of interests between actors involved in the different layers of the technology seemed to be necessary. This could be seen in the occasionally rigid ways that both the consumer electronic and the newspaper actors looked at their products and services. This can be traced in both interviews and minutes where existing business models were most often discussed as role models for the e-newspaper. This lack of alignment in interest between technology developers and the newspapers were in retrospect hindering the development of the e-newspaper concept.

4.2   Diverse Consumer Groups

Viewing the e-newspaper from the challenges related to diverse consumer groups, the following empirical observations can be made.

The e-newspaper is an example of a digital innovation that is targeted towards everyday use. As such, it is a mundane artifact targeted towards a wide group of users. The newspaper industry did not want to limit their target group to the people that already read traditional newspapers on a daily basis. They wanted to also reach new target groups and offer a digital innovation that could be widely adapted and possibly replace the traditional newspaper. As such, the digitization of the newspaper led to that a more heterogeneous user group of readers was targeted.

It was not only the market aspect of the e-newspaper that led to heterogeneous user groups. The context of use for the e-newspaper was also wide. Something that led to this was that new needs and requirements were identified compared to the traditional newspaper. Mobility was identified as an important value of the e-newspaper concept during workshops that were conducted with readers and newspaper staff, as well as in the testing and evaluation of the e-newspaper. This value included portability, e.g. the possibility to bring the e-newspaper with you while commuting or traveling. Accessibility and updates were other identified aspects important for the e-newspaper concept, e.g. to be able to always access and get updated content. Localization was also identified as an aspect of mobility which included contextualized content (e.g. ads and news). Even if portability is something that relates to a traditional newspaper as well, localization together with accessibility and updates are not (for more details, see [27, 29]).

Finally, a challenge for the e-newspaper realization was the willingness to change within the different user groups. In the design, test and evaluation of the e-newspaper it became evident that all three user groups had to have their needs and requirements met in order to be willing to adopt an e-newspaper. For some readers, an e-newspaper would in most cases lead to new reading habits. This was appreciated in some cases, in others not (for more details, see [27]). Again, the heterogeneity of the readers meant that the design had to be very flexible and adaptable. At the same time, the newspaper staff and advertisers heterogeneity challenged the design process to incorporate a very wide set of needs and requirements.

Heterogeneous User Requirements. These aspects of the e-newspaper, together with a heterogeneous user group, did challenge the design process of this particular digital innovation. From a user perspective, the heterogeneous needs and requirements led to several design challenges. These concerned, for example, creating a design that retained the traditional newspaper feel (to satisfy existing readers habits) while simultaneously having features that would attract a young target group (for more details, see [29]). In addition to this, the different contexts of use meant that a flexible and adaptable service had to be designed. A service that not only included delivering updated and context aware news, but also ads that were targeted to the right group of users, as well as to the right time and location.

As the e-newspaper had to meet heterogeneous requirements and needs, both the device and the service had to be flexible and adaptable. Even so, the e-newspaper was not designed to be generative and malleable, it was deemed to have to provide tangible user values for the readers. Not only the readers of the e-newspaper were heterogeneous, but also the advertisers as well as newspaper staff could be classified as heterogeneous users. These users all had very different purposes of using an e-newspaper (and the backbone publishing system). The design of the e-newspaper had to be able to handle a wide set of different types of ads supporting needs and requirements of advertisers ranging from small businesses to large national businesses. From a newspaper staff perspective, the e-newspaper had to provide an interface to existing publishing systems which were quite diverse. Furthermore, the editing of an article was restricted based on the technical properties of the e-newspaper demonstrator. The design therefore had to handle the different type of journalists' and newspaper designers' requirements.

To be able to handle the heterogeneous user needs and requirements, a user centered design process was planned and carried out in DigiNews. By including all identified user groups in the design of the e-newspaper concept, a complex set of needs and requirements were identified. To be able to handle these, focus groups were created to both design and evaluate the evolving e-newspaper concept. However, as one of the industry actors of the network did not prioritize the findings, the e-newspaper demonstrator used to test the e-newspaper was not fully aligned with the identified user needs and requirements. Several issues influencing adoption became evident and were identified in the final evaluation of the e-newspaper demonstrator (for more details, see [27]).

5   Discussion and Conclusion

The DigiNews case illustrates all four identified challenges and also illuminates some activities which can address these challenges. These suggested activities are discussed below and summarized in Table 3.

5.1   Modular Cooperation

As shown in this case, different layers of the modular technology required actors with diverse knowledge bases and interests to cooperate in DigiNews. As a result, the digital innovation process became complex and networked. This is similarly described in the related literature [16, 17, 4, 2, 5, 6].

In the e-newspaper case, there were several instances of conflicting interests between different levels of actors. It was rather hard for the involved actors to move away from existing paths of innovation, and align their interests with each other in order to find new value chains and business models. In hindsight, it seems like problems relating to alignment of interest, e.g. to find new ways of collaborating and being flexible by meeting half way in order to be able to act on identified user values, might be one of the reasons behind the initial problems with the e-newspaper innovation.

Another challenge in the modular cooperation was related to the conflicts that arose during the case. Some of the conflicts could be traced to the different cultures and backgrounds of the actors. The different backgrounds and cultures, as well as different knowledge basis, challenged the collaboration on several occasions in Digi-News. Some of the reasons for these challenges probably relate back to conflicting interests.

A way to address these challenges could be to create more transparent processes. If the innovation actors are explicit regarding their goals, interests, and agendas during the initiation of a network, some of the problems identified in the case would have been solved. Based on the DigiNews case, it becomes apparent that there needs to be activities which can facilitate the communication and collaboration between the heterogeneous actors involved in digital ecosystems. The activities need to create relationships and involve relevant actors to enable both the development and implementation of digital innovations. One way to handle conflicting interests, conflicts and power balances could be to conduct activities which create and communicate a blueprint for the value network in a digital ecosystem. Such a blueprint would illuminate different actors' roles in both the development as well as the implementation of a digital innovation and could therefore be used to explicitly address actors' interests and roles in an ecosystem.

Based on these insights, the following three activities are suggested to meet the challenge of modular cooperation in digital innovation: a) *support transparent digital ecosystem relationships*, b) *facilitate cross-organizational communication*, and c) *create digital value blueprints*.

Knowledge Exchanges. Knowledge needs to be shared and dispersed between heterogeneous actors in order to support a digital innovation process [20, 19, 9, 10]. The literature highlights some challenges, e.g. how to manage the heterogeneity of IT-knowledge resources when working with digital innovation [2]. Scholars also write about how innovation capacity is enabled by knowledge dispersion [9]. In DigiNews, different knowledge bases challenged communication and knowledge sharing within the network. There seemed to be a need for facilitating knowledge sharing between actors, and finding objects that could be used to communicate over knowledge boundaries.

In digital innovation, there needs to be knowledge transfer activities which are organized in way that support exchanges between actors with different knowledge, agendas and innovation trajectories [8]. In DigiNews, this was done by setting up workshops with different actors to ideate and transfer knowledge and perspectives between the involved actors. These knowledge transfers were primarily done from users to researchers, and from researchers to the developers. The researchers translated findings from the user studies into personas, user scenarios, mock-ups, prototypes, and requirement documents to enable a knowledge transfer between user groups and technology developing actors. As such, these translations of knowledge activities helped disperse and exchange knowledge between the heterogeneous actors involved in the innovation network.

Based on these findings, the following activity is suggested to meet the challenge of knowledge exchanges in digital innovation: *translate heterogeneous knowledge*.

5.2   Diverse Consumer Groups

Generativity of digital technology makes digital innovations malleable and adaptable. This generativity leads to large, diverse, and uncoordinated user groups and markets [1, 2, 4, 11].

Diverse consumer groups have several implications for digital innovation processes, one of these is the variety of contexts of use. Having a variety of contexts of use requires flexible and adaptable digital devices and services that are malleable. This is both a design and a technical challenge that needs to be addressed when working with digital innovations targeted towards everyday use. The generativity of digital technology needs to be incorporated in the design of both devices and services to support large and varied user groups. In DigiNews, the e-paper device and its technical backbone did not open up for third party apps like e.g. today's smartphones. As the e-newspaper bundled hardware and service, technical and usability limitations in the e-paper device might have inhibited the adoption of the first versions of the e-newspaper. Today, numerous newspaper services exist for different tablets and these services are in most cases not coupled with hardware devices.

Besides different contexts of use, the e-newspaper presented the diverse user groups with different values. In DigiNews, readers, newspaper staff and advertisers all had different purposes and the e-newspaper provided different kinds of user value depending on use group. The added value for the different groups of users had to be acknowledged and designed for. Again, this was handled in DigiNews by actively involving all of the users in the design and innovation process. However, the diverse user groups also required activities that investigated user value, designed for this value, and authenticated the value in real life evaluations.

Based on these insights, the following three activities are suggested to meet the challenge of diverse consumer groups in digital innovation: a) *involve all relevant user groups*, b) *identify, design for, and authenticate digital user values*, and c) *design for multiple contexts of use*. These activities also relate to the last identified socio-technical challenge with digital innovation, heterogeneous user requirements.

Heterogeneous User Requirements. Large, diverse, and uncoordinated audiences of digital innovations lead to heterogeneous user requirements [2, 12, 18]. In the case of

DigiNews, the e-newspaper product with accompanying services aimed to replace the traditional newspaper. However, when digitizing a mundane product as the newspaper, there was a need to involve a very wide and heterogeneous base of users. Examples of users involved were readers, advertisers, and newspaper staff.

Heterogeneous user requirements and needs resulted in difficulties in the design and innovation process of the e-newspaper. The digital innovation process of the e-newspaper included a user centered approach to handle the challenge of heterogeneous needs and requirements. The process aimed at involving all the different user perspectives and therefore readers, newspaper staff and advertisers were all included. However, this approach was time consuming and expensive. Therefore, there still seems to be a need to find methods and techniques that can identify heterogeneous users' needs and requirements, and package these in communicable ways. In Digi-News this was done by prototyping and iterative testing, which led to guidelines for the design of the e-newspaper complemented with the rationale for every guideline.

Based on these findings, the following activity is suggested to meet the challenge of heterogeneous user requirements in digital innovation: *prototype iteratively*.

In conclusion, Table 3 summarizes a set of activities, originating from the empirical findings, which aim to address the identified challenges in digital innovation. Based on these findings, future studies are suggested to further investigate how digital innovation can be orchestrated to address socio-technical challenges in digital ecosystems. This paper could then be regarded as a first stepping stone for these investigations.

Table 3. Activities to address socio-technical challenges in digital innovation

Challenge	Suggested activity	Description
1. Modular co-operation	*Support transparent digital ecosystem relationships*	Create transparent relationships to illuminate actors' initial goals, interests, and agendas in digital ecosystems.
	Facilitate cross-organizational communication	Facilitate the communication and collaboration between the heterogeneous actors involved in innovation networks.
	Create digital value blueprints	Create and communicate a blueprint for the value network in a digital ecosystem illuminating different actors' role in a digital innovation.

Table 3. (*continued*)

1.1 Knowledge exchanges	*Translate heterogeneous knowledge*	Conduct knowledge translating activities such as workshops with different actors to ideate and transfer knowledge and perspectives between involved actors.
2. Diverse consumer groups	*Involve all relevant user groups*	Involve all relevant users in the ideation, development and implementation of a digital innovation.
	Identify, design for, and authenticate digital user values	Identify added digital value for different groups of users and address this in the design and evaluation of a digital innovation. Authenticate the digital values in real life evaluations.
	Design for multiple contexts of use	Design flexible and adaptable digital devices and services that are malleable.
2.1 Heterogeneous user requirements	*Prototype iteratively*	Iterative prototyping can be efficient to identify and evaluate heterogeneous user requirements.

References

1. Yoo, Y., Boland, R.J., Lyytinen, K., Majchrzak, A.: Organizing for Innovation in the Digitized World. Organization Science 23(5), 1398–1408 (2012)
2. Yoo, Y.: Computing in Everyday Life: A Call for Research on Experiential Computing. MIS Quarterly 34(2), 213–231 (2010)
3. Henfridsson, O., Yoo, Y., Svahn, F.: Path Creation in Digital Innovation: A Multi-Layered Dialectics Perspective. Sprouts: Working Papers on Information Systems 9(20) (2009), http://sprouts.aisnet.org/9-20
4. Yoo, Y., Henfridsson, O., Lyytinen, K.: Research Commentary – The New Organizing Logic Of Digital Innovation: An Agenda For Information Systems Research. Information Systems Research 21(4), 724–735 (2010)
5. Van de Ven, A.H.: Running in Packs to Develop Knowledge-Intensive Technologies. MIS Quarterly 29(2), 365–378 (2005)

6. Yoo, Y., Lyytinen, K., Yang, H.: The Role of Standards in Innovation and Diffusion of Broadband Mobile Services: The case of South Korea. Journal of Strategic Information Systems 14(3), 323–353 (2005)
7. Vanhaverbeke, W., Cloodt, M.: Open Innovation in Value Networks. In: Chesbrough, H., Vanhaverbeke, W., West, J. (eds.) Open Innovation: Researching a New Paradigm, pp. 258–281. Oxford University Press, Oxford (2006)
8. Boland, R.J., Lyytinen, K., Yoo, Y.: Wakes of Innovation in Project Networks: The Case of Digital 3-D Representations in Architecture, Engineering and Construction. Organization Science 18(4), 631–647 (2007)
9. Powell, W., Grodal, S.: Networks of Innovators. In: Fagerberg, J., Mowery, D., Nelson, R. (eds.) The Oxford Handbook of Innovation, pp. 56–86. Oxford University Press, Oxford (2005)
10. Yoo, Y., Lyytinen, K., Thummadi, V., Weiss, A.: Unbounded Innovation With Digitalization: A Case of Digital Camera. In: Annual Meeting of the Academy of Management (2010)
11. Zittrain, J.L.: The Generative Internet. Harvard Law Review 119, 1974–2040 (2006)
12. Henfridsson, O., Lindgren, R.: User Involvement in Developing Mobile and Temporarily Interconnected Systems. Information Systems Journal 20, 119–135 (2010)
13. Yoo, Y., Lyytinen, K., Boland, R.J., Berente, N.: The New Wave of Digital Innovation: Opportunities and Challenges: A Report on the Research Workshop 'Digital Challenges in Innovation Research' (2010), http://ssrn.com/abstract=1622170
14. Svahn, F., Henfridsson, O.: The Dual Regimes of Digital Innovation Management. In: Proceedings of the 45th Hawaii International Conference on System Science (HICSS), pp. 3347–3356. IEEE Computer Society, Los Alamitos (2012)
15. Thomsen, M., Åkesson, M.: Understanding ISD and Innovation through the Lens of Fragmentation. In: Dwivedi, Y.K., Henriksen, H.Z., Wastell, D., De', R. (eds.) TDIT 2013. IFIP AICT, vol. 402, pp. 467–480. Springer, Heidelberg (2013)
16. Benkler, Y.: The Wealth of Networks: How Social Production Transforms Markets and Freedom. Yale University Press, New Haven (2006)
17. Farell, J., Weiser, P.J.: Modularity, Vertical Integration, and Open Access Policies: Toward a Convergence of Antitrust and Regulation in the Internet Age. Harvard Journal of Law and Technology 17(1), 86–134 (2003)
18. Svensson, J., Ihlström Eriksson, C., Ebbesson, E.: User Contribution in Innovation Processes – Reflections from a Living Lab Perspective. In: Proceedings of the 43rd Hawaii International Conference on System Science (HICSS), pp. 1–10. IEEE Computer Society, Los Alamitos (2010)
19. Yoo, Y., Lyytinen, K., Boland, R.J.: Innovation in the Digital Era: Digitization and Four Classes of Innovation Networks. Working Paper. Temple University (2009)
20. Van de Ven, A.H., Polley, D.E., Garud, R., Venkataraman, S.: The Innovation Journey. Oxford University Press, Oxford (1999)
21. Svensson, J., Ihlström Eriksson, C.: Exploring Social Aspects Influence on Change in Network Relationships – A Case Study of Digital Innovation. International Journal of Social and Organizational Dynamics in IT 2(4), 14–33 (2012)
22. Mingers, J., Gill, A.: Multimethodology: Theory and Practice of Combining Management Science Methodologies. Wiley, Chichester (1997)
23. Mingers, J.: Combining IS Research Methods: Towards a Pluralist Methodology. Information Systems Research 12(3), 240–259 (2001)
24. Patton, M.Q.: Qualitative Research and Evaluation Methods, 3rd edn. Sage, Thousand Oaks (2002)

25. Pinsonneault, A., Kraemer, K.L.: Survey Research Methodology in Management Information Systems: An Assessment. Journal of Management Information Systems 10(2), 75–105 (1993)
26. Miles, M.B., Huberman, A.M.: Qualitative Data Analysis, 2nd edn. Sage, Thousand Oaks (1994)
27. Ihlström Eriksson, C., Svensson, J.: A User Centered Innovation Approach Identifying Key User Values for the E-Newspaper. International Journal of E-Services and Mobile Applications 1(3), 38–78 (2009)
28. Ihlström Eriksson, C., Åkesson, M., Bergqvist, M., Ljungberg, J.: Forming a Value Network – Analyzing the Negotiations between Actors in the E-Newspaper Case. In: Proceedings of the 42nd Hawaii International Conference on System Science (HICSS), pp. 1–10. IEEE Computer Society, Los Alamitos (2009)
29. Åkesson, M., Ihlström, C.: Designing and Evaluating the Calm Electronic Newspaper. In: ECIS 2006 Proceedings, Paper 161 (2006), http://aisel.aisnet.org/ecis2006/161

Materiality, Health Informatics
and the Limits of Knowledge Production

Hamish Robertson[1], Nick Nicholas[2], Tuly Rosenfeld[1], and Joanne F. Travaglia[1]

[1] Faculty of Medicine, University of New South Wales, Sydney, Australia
h.robertson@neura.edu.au, tuly@rosenfeldconsulting.com.au,
j.travaglia@unsw.edu.au
[2] The Demographer's Workshop, Sydney, Australia
tthedemo@bigpond.net.au

Abstract. Contemporary societies increasingly rely on complex and sophisticated information systems for a wide variety of tasks and, ultimately, knowledge about the world in which we live. Those systems are central to the kinds of problems our systems and sub-systems face such as health and medical diagnosis, treatment and care. While health information systems represent a continuously expanding field of knowledge production, we suggest that they carry forward significant limitations, particularly in their claims to represent human beings as living creatures and in their capacity to critically reflect on the social, cultural and political origins of many forms of data 'representation'. In this paper we take these ideas and explore them in relation to the way we see healthcare information systems currently functioning. We offer some examples from our own experience in healthcare settings to illustrate how unexamined ideas about individuals, groups and social categories of people continue to influence health information systems and practices as well as their resulting knowledge production. We suggest some ideas for better understanding how and why this still happens and look to a future where the reflexivity of healthcare administration, the healthcare professions and the information sciences might better engage with these issues. There is no denying the role of health informatics in contemporary healthcare systems but their capacity to represent people in those datascapes has a long way to go if the categories they use to describe and analyse human beings are to produce meaningful knowledge about the social world and not simply to replicate past ideologies of those same categories.

Keywords: knowledge production, health informatics, critical analysis, materiality.

1 Introduction

In this paper we argue that while the conceptual distinction data-information-knowledge (and wisdom) [1] is ubiquitous in the information sciences, it remains poorly understood and actualized in some informatics sub-fields, and in particular in health informatics. We then consider how the political economy of new technology can be taken for granted or unexamined in ways which serve to naturalise the

B. Doolin et al. (Eds.): IS&O 2014, IFIP AICT 446, pp. 132–148, 2014.
© IFIP International Federation for Information Processing 2014

'inevitability' of technological innovations [2]. We show how the teleological orienta-tion of the health sciences, as a seemingly dominant secular mythology of progress and virtue is in actuality compromised by the carrying forward of some questionable intellectual constructions (including concepts, ideas and ideologies) and the failure to integrate other emergent information science constructions that are prevalent outside of health informatics.

We go on to explore number of specific examples of a problematic aspect of health informatics as a site of skewed knowledge(s) about human beings as individuals and as social beings as well as loci of illness and disease. These examples demonstrate the persistence of deeply ideological social constructions reproduced through the: tax-onomies of database structures applied in health informatics (with an absence of sus-tained critical inquiry on the same); highly reductive nature of what passes for patient information in many of these systems and: data exclusions that can occur in establish-ing and maintaining such systems.

Leaving aside important questions of political and organizational motivations in particular, we focus primarily on the structuration of data inputs to information systems and especially health information systems with their materialist consequences for knowledge production, in general, utilizing case studies such as the 'hot spotting' of vulnerable groups. Taxonomic structures and classificatory systems about human beings are deeply implicated in the support and reproduction of historical social hie-rarchies and inequalities, by creating the illusio of 'objective scientific' (that is, em-pirical and therefore by implication or assertion ideological neutral) discussions of social divisions such as class, socio-economic status, 'race' and the like [3, 4]. We discuss some examples of why and how this happens as well as the ways in which this limits (and delimits) the boundaries of scientific practice in the health informatics domain. The central relationship between theory and practice is also a key aspect of this discussion. The issue of not asking certain types of questions or failing to analyze particular kinds of data we leave for a later discussion.

Lastly, we propose that to make claims to the production of scientific knowledge, including medical scientific knowledge, requires that practitioners meet certain stan-dards of practice in their work. We question whether a technical domain making claims to scientific status and scientific knowledge production should exhibit a greater reflexivity in relation to its implications and application to social issues than is cur-rently exhibited in health informatics. Disciplinary integrity requires a science to do more than simply produce the established knowledge architectures and to inquire more actively on the inclusions and exclusions practiced within the sub-disciplines that the discipline supports. The information sciences have shown significant activity in this area as their methods and theories have expanded in recent decades but, we maintain, this remains a poorly developed aspect of health informatics which remain largely subordinate to, particularly, medicine as the dominant knowledge production and authorizing paradigm in the health sciences generally.

2   Informatics as Social Scientific Practice

The pervasiveness of information systems and their role in complex scientific and social policy and practice often begs the question of how they are constituted and used in relation to their objects of study. This is especially relevant in the context of the collection of data and information *about* human beings where the study of humans is, usually by omission, assumed to be as developed as those which are applied to the collection of physical phenomena.

Information systems are designed and developed to collect, structure and analyze data and information to produce domain-specific knowledge, through the application of sets of formal methods and processes including ontologies, classificatory schemata and information taxonomies [5]. Their essential purpose is not simply or solely the neutral collection of administrative or research data but rather the production of knowledge (that is actionable, meaningful data and information) [6] about some aspect of the world.

Information systems are designed to produce a relatively discrete epistemic domain which informs their audience about some selective aspects of the human and/or natural worlds (meaning philosophical ontology not information ontology in this context). Yet many such systems default to the collection aspect, some to the analysis aspect, and a far lesser proportion to the explicit production of knowledge, in spite of claims to the contrary.

These collection processes range widely from project briefs and business cases on through to interoperability criteria and data sharing protocols. This is a continuously expanding field because the technology, its applications and its users are all in a seemingly un-ending state of development, production and innovation. Growth and diversification are central features of the information sciences in the digital information age [7]. Recent developments have led to the 'big data' construct in which the growth in data is characterized by volume, variety, velocity, veracity, variability and value [8, 9]. The big data construct currently emphasizes the process or processes associated with the acquisition of data, rarely exposing information structures themselves or the processes associated with the collection or classification of such data. This acts we argue, to create what Bourdieu calls an *illusio* [4], that is an implicit belief in the value of the data collection process, and at the same time, to hide (through the creation of 'doxa' or taken for granted-ness)[4] the socially influenced development of the methods themselves: including how data and information are collected; how terms and terminologies are defined; the choice to include or exclude particular information; which individuals, groups or populations are included or excluded in any given collection; and even how data are 'cleaned' [10-14].

Key to any collection process are the decisions made to exclude or include certain kinds of data. This can be seen in some cases, as a mechanism through which there is an acceptance or rejection of the prima facie legitimacy of certain kinds of information. Even the generic claim in the research and information sciences to collecting 'raw' data can be seen as highly problematic and contestable. As Gitelman argues in the aptly titled *Raw Data is an Oxymoron* [14, p. 3], "Data need to be imagined *as* data, to exist and function as such, and the imagination of data entails an interpretive base". All data collection processes are predicated on specific disciplinary and institutional reasoning and constraints, including two of the most common - cost (How much can we afford to collect? Whom can we afford to include in the collection) and belief (What data are important to collect?). This is usually represented as an objective, rationalistic process that produces data uncontaminated by the collectors' and their commissioning institutions practices and beliefs. Yet such processes necessitate an explicit or implicit rationale for the inclusion and exclusion of certain data or information from the initial development of design through to the final analysis processes.

The other side of this equation, as noted above, is the large amounts of data and information that are not collected at all. No information system, or its producers, is so naïve as to suggest they collect everything. The capacity to collect data is finite even if the potential data domain or sub-domain is seemingly infinite. Exclusions are necessary and even data collected via remote or mediated technical systems automatically exclude the majority of the available information, as information systems are themselves finite [15] and as indeed are human perceptual and analytical capacities [16]. The point here is not that *some* data or information will need to be excluded, but that the way in which this exclusion is consistent with the historical and persistent exclusion of minority groups, including women, in research studies [17, 18] and from big data environments, such as national censuses, all the way down to the level of the inclusion or exclusion of specific "non-human" participants [19, 20] and the researchers themselves [19].

The largely unproblematized illusio that big data does or will somehow by-pass this social, systematic and systemic flaw by the sheer amount of data collected, remains a dominant feature of its value, and virtue, claims. Big data analysis relies on the same systems that systematically exclude certain types of data or individuals, for example census data, where definitions of ethnicity, have been shaped, accepted or rejected according to the power relations within and across countries at any given point in time [21-23]. In this sense, the production of data can be understood as a form of practice, in the Bourdesian sense, that is a dialectic between the social structures and systems within which data are generated and collected and the human and organizational agency which determines what should be deemed data, and which data are worthy of capturing and preserving [24, 25].

Many data collection systems have been limited by the state of technology available at any specific point in time, this is understandable. But more problematic has been the tendency to ignore aspects of the wider ontological domain in order to validate existing technologies. This can have the effect of constraining epistemic frameworks to what can be physically captured and analyzed. Thus broad physical and social science questions can be delimited by the physical and conceptual tools currently available. In this sense, technical systems (in both the ontological and epistemological sense) can constrain or narrow the growth of knowledge because the investment in their explanatory power requires that their very real limitations are minimized in discourse about them [26].

3   Problematizing Health Informatics

Health information systems tend to support two major knowledge production domains. The first is clinical practice and its associated sub-domains including pathology, pharmacology, radiography and so on. The second is characterized by the administrative data required by funders, including governments and insurers, usually central to administrative practices such as financial reporting and, in association with classification systems, some data about patients (often summary demographics) and their conditions utilizing the International Classification of Disease and a variety of related taxonomies [27].

However, it is reasonable to suggest that *patients* are not the primary focus of either of these systems and that this might be one reason why the reform of patient information systems, including the development of electronic health records and portable patient records, have proven so problematic in practice. On one side, clinicians may feel that they 'own' their data systems and the information in them while on the other, funders and regulators feel that they own their side of the informatics equation [28: see both article and correspondence]. Since neither party sees *patient* information as especially central, the idea of divesting any aspect of that ownership (and its attendant organizational authority) is viewed poorly by both parties.

In health informatics this problem is compounded by a number of factors. Health informatics focuses on the applied aspects of clinical and administrative information work, at times shying away from the theoretical as though tacitly accepting the idea that knowledge production does not necessarily, implicitly or explicitly, involve theory [29]. As a result, such work can be presented as though the researchers have or take no position on the social and political issues that any health system produces and reproduces in its work [30, 31].

At the same time, health systems take social categories to be as materially real and concrete as the categories used for biological and physiological phenomena, pathological indicators, diagnoses and so on. In other words, there is a deep commitment to the materiality of data that supports existing knowledge structures and ideological positions on the nature of knowledge and its importance in the clinical and administrative aspects of health systems and health informatics.

This commitment to counting and collecting is partly a result of the deeply social role of medicine and nursing since their development as central activities in healthcare, mostly developing in the nineteenth century during the emergence of the modern territorial nation state [32, 33]. Public health systems and health insurance schemes were built in part to support the concept of the nation as a healthy body and this conceptualization of the nation as a singular entity, containing a structured arrangement of multiples, emerged at the same time as scientific racism and eugenics, producing an interlinking of these concepts that persist down to the present day [34, 35]. The result can be a blurring of the significance of the embodiment of difference between the cytokine count in a biopsy as an indicator of the presence of cancer or the formal and informal use of socio-historical categories of "personhood", and the status of such persons, and the lived experience of the individuals involved [36].

4   Missing the Meaningful: Place, Space and the Current Limits of Health Informatics

If, as argued here, health information systems tend to be controlled by the dominant medical perspective then it seems fair to suggest that the knowledge such systems can (be permitted to) produce is likely to be 'approved of', that is accepted as doxa, by medicine. Thus there is already a central aspect to the way in which health information systems are involved in a process of co-production. They legitimate and reinforce the kind of data, information and knowledge that medicine as a discipline finds acceptable. Knowledge that falls outside of these established and often conservative parameters is much less likely to impinge on this dominant paradigm [37].

There is already an awareness that the focus of many health information systems is not about people as individual human beings. Indeed as Simpson and Novak have observed even Electronic Health Records (EHRs) collect comparatively little data about the broader social and economic context of patent's lives, much of which would be relevant to their potential illnesses, treatment and possible cure [38].

The micro focus of clinical medicine is poor at integrating the broader social epidemiological context of patients' lives that often impacts directly on their health status. The recent work of Jeffrey Brenner in Camden, New Jersey is an example of how complex systems can collect patient data, such as address, and fail to use it in any clinically meaningful way. Brenner, an emergency department doctor, spent his evenings developing a spreadsheet of his department's 'superutilizers'. He was able to show very quickly that a very high proportion of people with chronic health conditions, low incomes and limited health insurance were all co-located in one public housing building in Camden. Their emergency department visits were far above the average, costing the health system itself considerable amounts of money and leading to a cycle of ill-health for the patients who always sought treatment late in their acute episodes. As a result of identifying this single, ubiquitous fact – the patients' address – he was able to target local interventions which limited or even prevented the need for and use of expensive emergency services and which have resulted in significant reductions in utilization [39] and improvements in morbidity.[1]

While the idea that location is important to health has most recently been packaged around the idea of 'hot spotting', it is well known and understood across many disciplines, including medicine, public health and geography. John Snow's famous 1854 cholera map is, in effect, an exercise in medical and public health 'hot spotting' [40]. Yet what the hot spotting study (and the media coverage and funding attention it has attracted) shows is that while the general importance of location may be understood, and locational data routinely and systematically collected from patients, the analysis and application of even the most basic quotidian data was dependent not on information systems but on curious and committed individuals who went beyond the information system as it stood.

The failure to integrate and act on broader contextual information about a patient's (or class of patients) social environment is clearly still an issue for health systems and many of the health professions. Even those health professionals who have the opportunity to observe the lived environments of patients such as occupational therapists and community geriatricians, have a limited capacity to collect and apply social information to the bigger picture. The information systems used for acute care systems and community health systems, for example, do not always interact well or even at all. Data collected about medical errors (including errors of omission where patients do not obtain the care required in a timely and appropriate fashion) do not routinely include fields for patients' identity or language spoken. The various emphases of these information silo systems are only rarely what could be called a 'system' in the usual formal sense of the idea. Rather, the complex historical development of such systems,

---

[1] See http://www.rwjf.org/en/about-rwjf/newsroom/
features-and-articles/Brenner11.html

often disconnected and serving the very different needs of very different users, can have little at all to do with lived experience of patients.

One final aspect emerges in the information science domain from this lack of understanding of and capacity to apply locational or place inference in the clinical and administrative domains. The many sciences that currently work with locational information and analysis as central to their activities all emerged at about the same time as medical informatics. They are all largely a result of advances in computational information science that took place during and shortly after the Second World War. The combination of computational science, aerial surveillance and navigational telemetry required for military rockets to travel from one place to another all developed in the same window as medical informatics.

The potential knowledge development associated with the spatial and locational aspects of health that could have occurred did not take emerge, and health and medical geography remain entirely marginal to work conducted in mainstream healthcare and health information systems. Despite these silos the development of geographic information science, including both theory and computer-software approaches, emerged in the 1960's and has gained momentum in recent years as digital technologies have developed and expanded. Goodchild felt that the field had developed sufficiently well to warrant the term 'geographical information *science*' which took the field beyond the hardware-software computer system nexus to one of specific types of knowledge production [41]. In the last decade or so, the emergence of 'virtual earth' software environments such as Google Earth have made the integration of spatial coordinates, of varying levels of precision, a much more viable possibility that at any time previously. Soon we are likely to see the expansion of the concept of 'place-based' knowledge in a variety of sciences and yet the question remains as to what extent this will reflected in healthcare where place has, for so long, had no place [42].

In the previous sections we have alluded to the way in which the processes of collecting, categorizing and utilizing data is directly influenced by the limits within, placed on, and utilized by, the field of health informatics. One of the issues with current knowledge production is the way in which the field has recently emerged from the basic forms of linking up and bundling together of a variety of clinical and administrative information systems within medicine and healthcare management [43]. Yet, the very definition of the broader (not just medicine) field of health informatics often defaults to a form of medical informatics due to dominance clinically, and more specifically medically, trained personnel in health information management in this field [44, 45]. The convergence of medicine and information technology has a long history of problematic results with many systems experiencing failures in both the development and implementation phases with a variety of clinical and other consequences [46, 47].

An example of how health informatics can lag behind external developments can be seen in the (to date) limited incorporation of the dimension (and theory) of space within health information systems in particular and health information analysis more generally. Geographic information science and technology have developed rapidly since their emergence in the 1960's. Many sciences make active use of GIS and related software and methods in their work as can be seen from archaeology and anthropology to climate science [48].

The material world that scientific practices aim to understand and explain is multi-dimensional including three-dimensional (x, y, z) space, temporality (t) and scalar issues as a fifth dimension as can be seen with any map or time series map [49]. The two-dimensional file requires a huge range of reductionist processes to make that material world conform to traditional information architectures but this process of reducing or even deleting complexity to fit current technologies means that some changes in the field are passing some disciplines by. Indeed, we would argue, reduction *as* representation is integral to much of what passes for knowledge production across a variety of disciplines.

In the health information sciences the spatial dimension is a fringe area of interest. Many health information systems do not collect useful spatial data or index patient information in analytically useful ways. The developments of spatial sciences are poorly incorporated into health informatics and yet health information systems are increasingly extending outside their traditional domain of the acute care hospital, through the emergence of tele-health, m-health and e-health. These new fields reflect the controlled extension of health informatics via the acceptance and incorporation of certain, selective, aspects of rapidly developing technologies associated with increasing bandwidths, mobile devices and remotely accessible database environments via the cloud. Most of these technologies are highly enabled spatially (e.g. GPS, RFID etc) and many uses have been found in other industries for these spatial capabilities. The potential of space and place factors are on the rise in health informatics but the a-spatial construction of health informatics around the hospital environment means that the incorporation of spatial thinking remains limited.

5   The Power of Taxonomies and Categories in Knowledge Production

The creation and collection of data, information and knowledge occurs, as we have previously discussed, through the use of material and conceptual technologies. One such technology is the use of taxonomies and categories. Bowker and Star have argued that taxonomic systems can have a deep and abiding influence on how we produce accepted knowledge about the world and that the values we attach to concepts constructed and represented through such taxonomic processes [5]. The application of taxonomic processes to human beings can have both a reductive and productive aspect, in that self-definition can be deeply influenced by the social definitions that are supported by the purportedly objective taxonomies of the sciences.

Classification is clearly part of how humans function cognitively as human beings. But classification also has its own consequences in that, especially since the 19th century, the elision between scientific and social taxonomies has become difficult to separate and people have become used to, and some would argue indoctrinated in, accepting the authority of science being applied to complex social phenomena without clearly distinguishing between the social and scientific domains [50, 51]. The pervasive nature of classification systems and taxonomies often possess an implicit moral hierarchy (poor health behaviours, bad lifestyle decisions, low health literacy, non-compliance) add scientific weight to socially ordered systems of surveillance and control [52, 53].

Hacking offers an explanatory process for how this knowledge production process operates [54]. First, specific processes permit the production of certain kinds of knowledge through 'engines of knowledge' which are, in order: count; quantify; norm; correlate; medicalize; biologize; geneticize; normalize; bureaucratize; and resist. The last of these is perhaps more indicative of efforts at countervailing knowledge production but, we would suggest, relies on the individual's capacity to recognize the application and power of these other engines in shaping not only how individuals are taught to think as individuals and as social creatures but also their ability to shape and delimit our environments, in Bourdieu's terms, their habitus [55]. To identify a 'false consciousness' that requires resistance an individual or group needs to have an awareness that these are generated engines of knowledge and not objective data, information and knowledge about the material world.

Systems such as the International Classification of Diseases (ICD) [27] and the Diagnostic and Statistical Manual of Mental Disorders (DSM) [56] are two of the more highly recognised classificatory systems in use in the health sciences generally. Both of these experience considerable internal contestation and debate but this is often unclear to external observers who are used to accepting knowledge taxonomies as 'given' [57-59]. The power of a successful classification process and taxonomic edifice can be seen in its unquestioned acceptance outside of the field of its production. This power has, as Hacking observed, the ability to produce new types of people, as well as to shape the way such people are permitted to exist. There is a strongly normative dimension to the taxonomic process because it is a powerful form of knowledge production that has, once authorized, the capacity to reproduce, defend and extend itself.

Perhaps more important than this is the capacity for such systems to delimit the scope of further developments in their fields and to regulate and even police the boundaries of knowledge production. Hacking's first engine – that of counting, as we have shown, is neither automatic nor neutral, and the progression of data through subsequent engines, and their conversion from packets of 'facts', through contextualized information and actionable knowledge, to the point where they 'warrant' bureaucratization reflect wider social and power relations, and cannot be seen simply as a neutral or positive process of information gathering. By omission or commission, the transformation of data in health as in every other sector, has real and significant implications for those whom the data is meant ultimately to represent.

6   Digital Materiality and the Production of Knowledge

One of the central identifying aspects of contemporary health informatics practice is the gradual expansion of digitally collected data within system that were historically wedded to the written document. Resistance to digitization has been strong is some parts of healthcare and data control is a central aspect of the shift to digitization in medical practice.

Patient safety information can be seen as another example of how information systems can be compromised by disciplinary politics and utilised to protect the interests of practitioners at the expense of those they were established to assist. The introduction of systems designed to collect information about mistakes, errors and failures in health systems has long been in development [60]. Even now, many of these systems are problematic because the definitions of harmful practice and harmful outcomes are still largely administered by those within the healthcare system and public involvement, while increasing, remains limited [61]. While they may encourage reporting, studies have found that small scale direct record review – rather than large scale reporting – is more accurate in identifying major errors [62]. In addition, as previously mentioned, many of these systems take a technical perspective that minimizes the collection of data about the patient as a person and instead defaults to an emphasis on the collection of information about 'critical incidents' and the application of an associated terminology of risk. These systems can inadvertently minimize the materiality of the patient (and the clinicians) to whom errors occur and increase, preferentially, the nature and location of the 'incident' in a terminology that defines these events as failures of abstracted and over-arching systems rather than as the direct experiences of humans, and of particular groups.

This inward focus on the collection, classification and review of errors rather than of patients has led to a situation where ever more sophisticated technological systems continue to be based on simplistic conceptual schemata. By not including elements such as ethnicity or disability, these taxonomies ignore the social patterning of errors, which the scant evidence that is available shows, most closely resemble the social determinants of health [63, 64].

In part then we can see how the 'realness' or materiality of information is a strategic device in the activities where information systems are situated. The data is both 'raw' and 'real' – this validates the information system and the processes as well as the actual outcomes and their applications. The information experts position themselves as objective because this is a central strategy for professional legitimacy in the modern state and economy – professionals produce legitimate and authorizing knowledge. Consequently, it is a strategic process to ensure that the data supports the power of the system within which it is implemented and that it does not provide power, either by accident or purposively, to those outside of that system.

6.1   Making the Immaterial Real

The process of digitally producing, instantiating and regulating database taxonomies, categories and fields that rely on social constructs for their deployment has the effect of reifying these constructs. That is the process itself tends to make ephemeral phenomena that are stored in binary coding as real as the events the data claims to capture. In some cases, as we have seen with patient safety information systems, this process can make the data more real to the system than the person to whom the event happened. This has the effect of reducing the individual to the status of data and even, in some cases, less than the data, because so much of their materiality is left out of these digital systems. The reductive processes of classification and data capture leave so little of the individual left digitally speaking that their physical existence can easily be seen as less than that of the system in which their delimited details are held, in essence the digital ghost in these digital machines.

Even the claims made for digitizing individual genetic code still potentially reduce us to the quantified, numericised versions of the biological reality of genes and the bodies that those genes 'inhabit' [65]. Thus, except in the most deterministic sense possible, those representations are not us or ourselves but an instrumental and even preferable form of 'us'. Current debates and legal cases about data sharing, with or without consent [66], in a variety of jurisdictions make this point very clearly – individuals don't own data about or from about themselves because political and economic systems have priority-making claims to both a higher moral purpose (usually couched as potential future benefits – teleology and transcendence in the one ambit claim) and to the benevolent representation of all of us over any single one of us who might choose to object [67].

Health care systems also make claims to expertise and that expertise supports their authority to act in various ways, often without the possibility of an engaged or informed (or any) response from those whose data is collected, categorised and indexed within these information systems. If we consider that expertise is at least partly informational (medical knowledge, risk knowledge, how the system works, available choices and the lack of them) then it is clear that healthcare information systems primarily support the existing power and authority of health care providers. Information is representational and, as noted above, refined and practiced forms of representation, however problematic on close inspection, can acquire a social life of their own. The equation of expertise authorizing specific systems of representation is an instrument of power in its own right. This links health information systems to Foucault's key concepts of governmentality and biopower through the regulatory frameworks and self-regulation that 'expertise' manufactures and which experts manage [68, 69]. In other words, health information systems are a central enactment of this regulatory process which discursively enables self-regulation by manufacturing the limited number of legitimate categories a person and their identity can be permitted to have within such information systems.

Foucault also discussed very early in his writing the importance of space as an avenue for governmentality including the shifting role of the hospital and its organisation of space [70]. Elden has taken this idea and developed it in relation to the concept of *territory*. He suggests that territory need not be physical but instead can be entirely conceptual so long as it is understood as existing in the minds of those who believe in its existence [71]. This can be seen in the nature of maps representing different claims to the same physical space, expressed as territory. In this sense, the hospital can be seen as a territorial space claimed by medical and nursing personnel on the one side and political, managerial and administrative personnel on the other. The development of the hospital as a physical architecture of knowledge can be seen not only in Foucault's analysis but in the geographical work of Livingstone [72].

Based on this contruction we can begin to think of health information systems as virtual spaces, even territories, of governmentality. The obsession with governments in tracking all forms of electronic communication in their efforts to ensure a 'secure' state illustrates how easily an information domain becomes an exercise in total governance through the constitution of a digital territory or set of territories.

7   Informational Biopolitics

Biomedical informatics has been an 'emerging field' for decades [73]. The concept of biopolitics has a history going back at least to the 1920s and the work of Rudolf Kjellén, with some suggestion that it can be effectively situated in the work of Schopenhauer, Nietzsche and Bergson [74]. Its current formulation emerged mainly from Michel Foucault's work in the mid-1970s [75]. Illich's *Medical Nemesis* emerged at about the same time indicating that philosophy and sociology were beginning to take a serious interest in knowledge production within medicine in particular [37]. Even McKeown's somewhat older argument about the role played by medicine in human health improvements can be seen as sitting within a cultural discussion about what claims can be made by a discipline to self-represent and actively promote its contribution to societal improvements and the knowledge that supports those claims [76, 77].

More recently the notion of 'incidentalomas' has entered the health environment. The term refers to tumors located incidentally through the application of highly detailed scanning technologies. This is part of a broader field of incidental findings understood to exist in medical research and practice, one which research projects have had to accommodate by including provisions for them in various clinical screening activities and the like [78, 79]. The procedures identify these 'incidental' tumors while looking for other, suspected, diagnostic features. These tumors often have no clinical symptoms or suspicious characteristics and, as a consequence, there is a growing awareness that new technologies identify phenomena not currently implicated in the pathology of an existing or suspected disease state. Acting surgically on some of these, such as aneurisms, can be almost or even as risky as the potential clinical threat that their presence might lead to at some future point. Advances in scientific and medical technologies, invariably information-based, can produce their own clinical sequelae. They are assumed to be risks because they are imaged as such and our systems and people have been conditioned to act on observable risks even when the consequences are distant in time and potential effect.

8   Social Hegemony and Information

Information theory is generally accepted as having social and political implications in most if not all of its implementational aspects [80]. There is therefore an understanding that information systems produce particular types of knowledge that are then acted on in specific ways, both good and bad, in societal contexts. Even if the knowledge produced through information science were entirely 'objective', the uses to which that knowledge is often put cannot be seen in the same light. Discussions about data security and access rights are one aspect of this discussion but representational issues are another under-explored aspect of the information sciences.

Information collection about society and the groups and individuals who constitute society benefited enormously from the development of demography and statistics. The kind of conceptual and taxonomic abstraction required to understand complex social processes only began to take on our 'modern' idea of a scientific activity in the Victorian era. It was then that statistical surveys of the people within nation states began to gain momentum. Prior to this a major difficulty had been to actually map the state cartographically but now with statistical survey instruments, the whole population could be 'captured' as data even in contexts where the definition of what a population actually is have not been resolved [31]. This required the development of categories and implicitly social taxonomic systems to analyze the information in those categories.

The problem with these categories is that they move beyond mere representation to *become* the populations they are used to represent in information systems that cannot by their very nature cope with the complexity of individual human beings. Hacking's people-producing processes also find any kind of nuanced difference difficult to deal with and the categories represented by field names in databases take on a normative character of their own [11]. There is, across the many disciplines that produce these kinds of knowledge, a cultural dimension that reflects the specific preferences and imbedded understandings of how data is collected, what information is produced and analyzed, and lastly the acceptable representations of those knowledge production processes [81].

Information collection has moved far beyond this analogical and descriptive approach to a digitally enabled environment in which there are claims that it will be possible to understand the whole of the material world [2]. One of those claims is that 'data' will ultimately explain both 'society' in the abstract sense and also the actual societies in which we live.

Allied to this is a level of digital surveillance never previously possible and which operates across the entire field of human engagements from government and commerce, through to data collection about individuals' behaviors, habits and beliefs. Marketing and managerial practice are data-informed and those same practices are being gradually incorporated into healthcare including medical practice and health administration. In all these activities there is a claim that 'patients' and 'consumers' (yet again abstract categories claiming to represent real people) will benefit both directly and indirectly from this information collection and analysis. The language of risk, quality, value and choice is pervasive as a rationale for continuous change even in systems where we may not have, as citizen consumers, indicated any specific dissatisfaction with the status quo. Consequently, discourses of risk and quality are employed as strategies for systemic change by corporations and governments whose intention is change regardless of consumer and citizen opinion. The manufacture of informational concepts, which risk and quality have become regardless of their historical origins, makes them instruments for the manipulation of systems claimed to be representative and collaborative. Being able to reposition the meaning of terms and use those same terms as justifications for policy changes within societies makes them highly useful as political strategies. Coole has discussed how these processes work in relation to the shift in aged care policy and political discourse. The increase in data capture *about* older people may contribute very little to the betterment *of* older people [82].

9   Conclusion

In this paper we have sought to explore in a brief and general way how information systems are instruments of biopolitical practice and that they influence the social environment by legitimizing some aspects of our material reality and de-legitimizing or even deleting other possibilities for human identity. The nature of information, its collection, analysis and representation within society is not an abstract and objective process but a deeply politically engaged activity. Indeed, the various knowledge claims associated with information including 'raw' data, data objectivity and analytical neutrality as being an ideological representation and a claim for authority which has significant social effects.

As a result, we suggest, information systems and their associated practices which purport to be doing 'objectivity work', are engaged in an often a-theoretical form of political practice. The failure to acknowledge or understand the way data is constituted and becomes information within and across a variety of scientific and social scientific sub-cultures is an epistemic failure in its own right. To make claims about producing legitimate knowledge requires of the producer an informed understanding of what knowledge is, how it is produced and where it comes from. The deeper history of the conceptual primitives apparent in health informatics and the information sciences more broadly need to be subject to scrutiny of this type. The moralizing discourse so prevalent in healthcare and health policy (the selfish 'bed blocking' elderly, the lazy obese, the uncaring mothers, the willful smokers, the ungrateful disabled etc) is so assuredly political in its conception and deployment that there is a risk of intellectual dishonesty in ignoring these links.

The information sciences need to be critically informed and engaged. Some already are, including library science and geographic information science. There needs to be a move from a utilitarian viewpoint which claims to be driven by practical aims serving practical outcomes to a more nuanced inquiry on its own practices, underpinnings and assumptions. The nature of health information science must engage with the power of its political positioning and the influence it has on knowledge and understanding once it is produced and acted on as evidential and true.

References

1. Rowley, J.: The Wisdom Hierarchy: Representations Of the DIKW Hierarchy. Journal of Information Science 33, 163–180 (2007)
2. Breen, M.: Information Does Not Equal Knowledge: Theorizing the Political Economy of Virtuality. Journal of Computer Mediated Communication 3(3) (1997)
3. Bourdieu, P.: Distinction: A Social Critique of the Judgement of Taste. Harvard University Press (1984)
4. Bourdieu, P., Wacquant, L.J.: An Invitation to Reflexive Sociology. University of Chicago Press, Chicago (1992)
5. Bowker, G., Starr, S.: Sorting Things Out: Classification and Its Consequences. MIT Press, New Baskerville (2000)
6. Bhatt, G.D.: Knowledge Management in Organizations: Examining the Interaction between Technologies, Techniques, and People. Journal of Knowledge Management 5, 68–75 (2001)
7. Negroponte, N.: Being Digital. Hodder and Stoughton, London (1995)
8. Ahalt, S.C.: Data Science and the NCDS: Putting North Carolina First in Data through the National Consortium for Data Science. Presentation at the University of North Carolina, Chapel Hill (2013)
9. Bellini, P., di Claudio, M., Nesi, P., Rauch, N.: Tassonomy and Review of Big Data Solutions Navigation. In: Akerkar, R. (ed.) Big Data Computing, pp. 57–101. CRC Press, Boca Raton (2013)

10. Nagel, T.: The View from Nowhere. Oxford University Press, Oxford (1989)

11. Haraway, D.: Situated Knowledges: The Science Question in Feminism and the Privilege of Partial Perspective. Feminist Studies 14, 575–599 (1988)

12. Galison, P., Daston, L.: Objectivity. Zone Books, London (2008)

13. Boyd, D., Crawford, K.: Critical Questions for Big Data. Information, Communication & Society 15, 662–679 (2012)

14. Gitelman, L.: Raw Data Is an Oxymoron. MIT Press, Cambridge (2013)

15. Gleick, J.: The Information: A History. Fourth Estate (2011)

16. Duncan, S., Barrett, L.F.: Affect is a Form of Cognition: A Neurobiological Analysis. Cognition and Emotion 21, 1184–1211 (2007)

17. Nature: Putting Gender on the Agenda. Nature 465, 665 (2010)

18. Cherubini, A., Oristrell, J., Pla, X., Ruggiero, C., Ferretti, R., Diestre, G., Lesauskaite, V.: The Persistent Exclusion of Older Patients from Ongoing Clinical Trials Regarding Heart Failure. Archives of Internal Medicine 171, 550–556 (2011)

19. Guthrie, R.V.: Even the Rat Was White: A Historical View of Psychology. Pearson Education, Upper Saddle River (2004)

20. Beery, A.K., Zucker, I.: Sex Bias in Neuroscience and Biomedical Research. Neuroscience & Biobehavioral Reviews 35, 565–572 (2011)

21. Saperstein, A.: Capturing Complexity in the United States: Which Aspects of Race Matter and When? Ethnic and Racial Studies 35, 1484–1502 (2011)

22. Simon, P.: Collecting Ethnic Statistics in Europe: A Review. Ethnic and Racial Studies 35, 1366–1391 (2011)

23. Simon, P., Piché, V.: Accounting for Ethnic and Racial Diversity: The Challenge of Enumeration. Ethnic and Racial Studies 35, 1357–1365 (2011)

24. Bourdieu, P.: Outline of a Theory of Practice. Cambridge University Press, Cambridge (1977)

25. Bourdieu, P.: The Logic of Practice. Stanford University Press, Stanford (1990)

26. Bourdieu, P.: Is a Disinterested Act Possible? In: Bourdieu, P. (ed.) Practical Reason: On the Theory of Action, pp. 75–91. Stanford University Press, Stanford (1998)

27. Centers for Disease Control and Prevention: International Classification of Diseases, Tenth Revision, Clinical Modification (ICD-10-CM). Centers for Disease Control and Prevention, Hyattsville, MD (2014), http://www.cdc.gov/nchs/icd/icd10cm.htm

28. Blumenthal, D., Tavenner, M.: The "Meaningful Use" Regulation for Electronic Health Records. New England Journal of Medicine 363, 501–504 (2010)

29. Barnes, B.: Scientific Knowledge and Sociological Theory. Routledge, London (2013)

30. Anderson, W.: Teaching 'Race' at Medical School Social Scientists on the Margin. Social Studies of Science 38, 785–800 (2008)

31. Krieger, N.: Who and What Is a "Population"? Historical Debates, Current Controversies, and Implications for Understanding "Population Health" and Rectifying Health Inequities. Milbank Quarterly 90, 634–681 (2012)

32. Carroll, P.E.: Medical Police and the History of Public Health. Medical History 46, 461–494 (2002)

33. Elden, S.: The Birth of Territory. University of Chicago Press, Chicago (2013)

34. Anderson, Z.: One 'Body/Nation': Pathology and Cultural Citizenship in Australia. Cultural Studies Review 15, 110–129 (2009)

35. Weiss, K.M., Long, J.C.: Non-Darwinian Estimation: My Ancestors, My Genes' Ancestors. Genome Research 19, 703–710 (2009)

36. Skloot, R., Turpin, B.: The Immortal Life of Henrietta Lacks. Crown Publishers, New York (2010)

37. Illich, I.: Medical Nemesis: The Expropriation of Health. Random House, New York (1976)

38. Simpson, C.L., Novak, L.L.: Place Matters: The Problems and Possibilities of Spatial Data in Electronic Health Records. In: AMIA Annual Symposium Proceedings 2013, pp. 1303–1311. American Medical Informatics Association (2013)
39. Gawande, A.: The Hot Spotters: Can We Lower Medical Costs by Giving the Neediest Patients Better Care? The New Yorker, 40–51 (January 24, 2011)
40. Snow, J.: On the Mode of Communication of Cholera. John Churchill, London (1855)
41. Goodchild, M.F.: Geographical Information Science. International Journal of Geographical Information Systems 6, 31–45 (1992)
42. Fisher, T.: Place-Based Knowledge in the Digital Age. ArcNews 34(3), 1-6 (2012)
43. Vest, J.R., Gamm, L.D.: Health Information Exchange: Persistent Challenges and New Strategies. Journal of the American Medical Informatics Association 17, 288–294 (2010)
44. Flynn, R.: Clinical Governance and Governmentality. Health, Risk and Society 4, 155–173 (2002)
45. Flynn, R.: Structures of Control in Health Management. Routledge, London (2012)
46. Joint Commission on Accreditation of Healthcare Organizations (JCAHO): Safely Implementing Health Information and Converging Technologies. Sentinel Event Alert 42,1-4 (2008)
47. Goodman, K.W., Berner, E.S., Dente, M.A., Kaplan, B., Koppel, R., Rucker, D., Winkelstein, P.: Challenges in Ethics, Safety, Best Practices, and Oversight Regarding HIT Vendors, their Customers, and Patients: A Report of an AMIA Special Task Force. Journal of the American Medical Informatics Association 18(1), 77–81 (2011)
48. Kosiba, S., Bauer, A.M.: Mapping the Political Landscape: Toward a GIS Analysis of Environmental and Social Difference. Journal of Archaeological Method and Theory 20, 61–101 (2013)
49. Goodchild, M.F.: Twenty Years of Progress: GIScience in 2010. Journal of Spatial Information Science 1, 3–20 (2014)
50. Cohn, B.S.: Colonialism and Its Forms Of Knowledge: The British in India. Princeton University Press, Princeton (1996)
51. Richards, T.: The Imperial Archive: Knowledge and the Fantasy of Empire. Verso, London (1993)
52. Mayes, C., Thompson, D.B.: Is Nutritional Advocacy Morally Indigestible? A Critical Analysis of the Scientific and Ethical Implications of 'Healthy' Food Choice Discourse in Liberal Societies. Public Health Ethics 7, 158–169 (2014)
53. Bacon, L., Aphramor, L.: Weight Science: Evaluating the Evidence for a Paradigm Shift. Nutrition Journal 10, 9 (2011)
54. Hacking, I.: Kinds of People: Moving Targets. Proceedings of the British Academy 151, 285–318 (2007)
55. Swartz, D.: Culture and Power: The Sociology of Pierre Bourdieu. University of Chicago Press (2012)
56. American Psychiatric Association: Diagnostic and Statistical Manual of Mental Disorders: DSM-5. American Psychiatric Publishing, Washington, DC (2013)
57. Cooper, R.: What is Wrong with the DSM? Historical Psychiatry 15, 5–25 (2004)
58. Sadler, J.Z., Fulford, B.: Should Patients and Their Families Contribute to the DSM-V Process? Psychiatric Services 55(2), 133–138 (2004)
59. James, J.: Health Policy Brief: Transitioning to ICD-10. Health Affairs (March 20, 2014)
60. Beckmann, U., West, L., Groombridge, G., Baldwin, I., Hart, G.K., Clayton, D.G., Runciman, W.B.: The Australian Incident Monitoring Study in Intensive Care: AIMS-ICU. The Development and Evaluation of an Incident Reporting System in Intensive Care. Anaesthesia and Intensive Care 24, 314–319 (1996)

61. Vincent, C., Coulter, A.: Patient Safety: What About the Patient? Quality and Safety in Health Care 11, 76–80 (2002)
62. Sari, A.B.-A., Sheldon, T.A., Cracknell, A., Turnbull, A.: Sensitivity of Routine System for Reporting Patient Safety Incidents in an NHS Hospital: Retrospective Patient Case Note Review. BMJ 334, 79 (2007)
63. Davis, P., Lay-Yee, R., Dyall, L., Briant, R., Sporle, A., Brunt, D., Scott, A.: Quality of Hospital Care For Maori Patients in New Zealand: Retrospective Cross-Sectional Assessment. The Lancet 367, 1920–1925 (2006)
64. Lawthers, A.G., Pransky, G.S., Peterson, L.E., Himmelstein, J.H.: Rethinking Quality in the Context of Persons with Disability. International Journal for Quality in Health Care 15, 287–299 (2003)
65. Barnes, B., Dupré, J.: Genomes and What to Make of Them. University of Chicago Press (2009)
66. Boyd, D., Crawford, K.: Critical Questions for Big Data: Provocations for a Cultural, Technological, and Scholarly Phenomenon. Information, Communication & Society 15, 662–679 (2012)
67. Rouvroy, A.: Human Genes and Neoliberal Governance: A Foucauldian Critique. Routledge (2007)
68. Foucault, M.: The Birth of the Clinic: An Archeology of Medical Perception. Vintage, New York (1975)
69. Foucault, M.: The Birth of Biopolitics: Lectures at the Collège de France, 1978-1979. Picador, New York, NY (2010)
70. Foucault, M.: Security, Territory, Population: Lectures at the Collège de France, 1977-1978. Burchell, G. (trans.). Palgrave Macmillan, Basingstoke (2008)
71. Elden, S.: Plague, Panopticon, Police. Surveillance & Society 1, 240–253 (2002)
72. Livingstone, D.N.: Putting Science in Its Place: Geographies of Scientific Knowledge. University of Chicago Press, Chicago (2010)
73. Bernstam, E.V., Smith, J.W., Johnson, T.R.: What Is Biomedical Informatics? Journal of Biomedical Informatics 43, 104–110 (2010)
74. Lemke, T., Casper, M.J., Moore, L.J.: Biopolitics: An Advanced Introduction. NYU Press, New York (2011)
75. Foucault, M.: Society Must Be Defended: Lectures at the Collège de France, 1975-1976. Ewald, F. (trans.). Macmillan, London (2003)
76. McKeown, T.: The Role of Medicine: Dream, Mirage or Nemesis. Nuffield Provincials Hospital Trust, London (1976)
77. Colgrove, J.: The McKeown Thesis: A Historical Controversy and Its Enduring Influence. American Journal of Public Health 92, 725–729 (2002)
78. Ballantyne, C.: To Know or Not to Know. Nature Medicine 14, 797–797 (2008)
79. Wolf, S.M., Paradise, J., Caga-anan, C.: The Law of Incidental Findings in Human Subjects Research: Establishing Researchers' Duties. Journal of Law, Medicine & Ethics 36(2), 361–383 (2008)
80. Laudon, K., Laudon, J.: Management Information Systems: International Edition, 11th edn. Pearson Higher Education, New Jersey (2009)
81. Knorr Cetina, K.: Epistemic Cultures: How the Sciences Make Knowledge. Harvard University Press, Cambridge, MA (1999)
82. Coole, D.: Reconstructing the Elderly: A Critical Analysis of Pensions and Population Policies in an Era of Demographic Ageing. Contemporary Political Theory 11, 41–67 (2012)

Digital Drugs

An Anatomy of New Medicines

Tony Cornford[1] and Valentina Lichtner[2]

[1] Department of Management, London School of Economics and Political Science,
London, UK
t.cornford@lse.ac.uk

[2] Decision Making Research Group, School of Healthcare, University of Leeds, Leeds, UK
v.lichtner@leeds.ac.uk

Abstract. Medicines are digitalized as aspects of their regulation and use are embodied in or draw from interlinked computerized systems and databases. This paper considers how this development changes the delivery of health care, the pharma industry, and regulatory and professional structures, as it reconfigures the material character of drugs themselves. It draws on the concept of assemblage in presenting a theory-based analysis that explores digital drugs' ontological status including how they embody benefit and value. The paper addresses three interconnected domains – that of use of drugs (practice), of research (epistemology) and of regulation (structures).

Keywords: pharmaceutical preparations, individualized medicine, digital drugs, healthcare, assemblage.

1 Introduction

> *Anatomy: 1. The art of studying the different parts of any organized*
> *body, to discover their situation, structure, and economy; dissection.*
> *[...] 4. The act of dividing anything, corporeal or intellectual, for*
> *the purpose of examining its parts; analysis; as, the anatomy of a*
> *discourse.* (http://en.wiktionary.org/wiki/anatomy)

Medicines[1] and the ways we use and regulate them are changing, transformed by digitalization [1]. This reconfiguration is associated with visions of scientific,

---

[1]   In this paper we use the word medicines and drugs almost as synonyms. We recognise however that they offer slight but significant shifts of emphasis. 'Medicine' evokes the practice of medicine and hence the practices of medicines, while drug evokes the manufactured product and its chemical character/materiality. Thus in this most basic sense the thing we address has an inherent multiplicity. The US National Library of Medicine thesaurus (MeSH – Medical Subject Heading) avoids this tension in its own way using the term Pharmaceutical Preparations – "Drugs intended for human or veterinary use, presented in their finished dosage form" (NLM - Medical Subject Headings - 2014 - Unique ID D004364 - http://www.nlm.nih.gov/cgi/mesh/2014/MB_cgi?mode=&term=Pharma ceutical+Preparations&field=entry – Accessed 15 Sept 2014).

B. Doolin et al. (Eds.): IS&O 2014, IFIP AICT 446, pp. 149–162, 2014.

therapeutic, managerial and financial breakthroughs from 'better' medicines and in particular 'better' digitally mediated medicine use practices. Expectations include: help in meeting the needs of aging populations with multiple chronic diseases, the targeting of medicines to individuals (personalization) to significantly increase efficacy and reduce overall cost, and computerized clinical decision support that can reduce the burden of harm caused by adverse drug events (ADEs). The pharma industry too is reconfiguring as it faces increasing competition from 'generics', reductions in the pipeline of new medicines entering the market and the 'patent cliff' off which large pharma companies fear to fall [2, 3]. Such pressures spur changes in how current drugs are marketed, distributed and paid for [4]. Pharmaceutical business models are realigned to build new relations between patients, health care institutions and the pharma industry, with drug products enmeshed in or recast as a set of services, and with payment (pricing/reimbursement) shifting from the 'product' to outcomes.

The digitalization of medicines is reflected in a number of overlapping areas of contemporary research and development including *electronic prescribing, stratified medicine, personalized medicine, smart drug platforms, medical profiling, pharmacovigilance, value based pricing* and *pharmacogenomics* (Table 1). The specifics of the 'breakthrough' vision vary, as do the digital mechanisms and resources that are imagined or deployed, but taken overall these initiatives seem to offer new possibilities for therapeutic improvement and innovation through digitally mediated ways of using drugs. We believe they also foreshadow multiple possible changes in broader medical practices, institutional structures, value chains and business models.

This paper presents a theory-based view of what we term *digital drugs*, including how they embody benefit or value. The work is part of the scoping of a RCUK funded project addressing how, why and with what consequence medicines are digitalized. In contrast to the established view of medicines as artefacts located in a stage-based model of linear progression from drug development, through innovation and testing to approval and clinical use [5] this work sees drugs as constituted 'in-use'[6], as performed, and with their agency located and expressed within and as connections among sociotechnical and economic contexts. In the wider project we ask three primary questions: 1) what is a digital drug – exploring the conceptual and analytical shift from physical/chemical artefacts towards some digital sociomateriality; 2) how use-practices, markets and business models evolve for semi-configured and servitized kinds of medicines; 3) consequences for/changes in the 'wider whole' and the relations between the parts/players (pharma and health industries, payers, research, regulatory practices, patient-doctor relations, etc.). Cutting across these areas are multiple questions of *value*: therapeutic value, clinical value, health enhancement, value as management of risk or reduction of harm, market value, value in exchange, value in use, value for money, and ethical values.

Table 1. A sample of contemporary digital hybrids in medicines use

Concept	Definitions	Digital mechanisms
Electronic prescribing (EP)	"The utilisation of electronic systems to facilitate and enhance the communication of a prescription or medicine order, aiding the choice, administration and supply of a medicine through knowledge and decision support and providing a robust audit trail for the entire medicines use process." (Connecting for Health, quoted in [7]) On DSS, see also: [8]. For an example of the application of DSS and EP in personalized medicine see: [9]	Decision support; error reduction; contributing to electronic patient record and Big Data repositories.
Stratified medicine (SM)	"Refers to the targeting of treatments (including pharmacological and non-pharmacological interventions) according to the biological or risk characteristics shared by subgroups of patients." [10] See also: [11] Often combined with, or used as synonym for Personalized medicine (PM)	"Targeting therapy and making the best decisions for groups of similar patients"; finding those who benefit most (or face greater risk), finding those who respond to this treatment.
Personalized medicine (PM)	"An emerging practice of medicine that uses an individual's genetic profile to guide decisions made in regard to the prevention, diagnosis, and treatment of disease. Knowledge of a patient's genetic profile can help doctors select the proper medication or therapy and administer it using the proper dose or regime" (National Human Genome Research Institute, cited in [8]). See also: [12]	Targeting therapy and making the best decisions for a specific patient, on the basis of how the body will respond to treatment; selecting the right/best therapy on the basis of the patient's 'omics' and expected response to active ingredient(s).
Smart Drug Platforms (SDP)	"The same pharmaceuticals you take today, with one small change: each pill [contains] a tiny sensor that can communicate, via a digital health feedback system, vital information about medication-taking behaviors and body's response" (paraphrased from [13]). Also seen in wearable devices often linked to mobile phone e.g. Apple HealthKit.	Smart pills, smart patches (e.g. [14]). Devices and platforms for data acquisition and analysis. Tight feedback on medicines as released in the body.
Medical profiling (MP)	The process of determining a patient's 'omics' (a person's characteristics in terms of molecular components and biological pathways, such as genes, transcriptomic, proteomic, metabolomic, and autoantibody) for purposes of PM or SM [15]. See also: [16]	Informing SM categorizations and PM therapeutic decisions.

Table 1. (*continued*)

Value based pricing (VBP)	Payment to drug suppliers on the basis of the therapeutic benefit achieved. [35, 36]	Linking outcome data at patient level to payment; rebalance risk/reward
Pharmaco-vigilance (PV)	The assessment of the public health importance of potential new signals found in medicines-use data (e.g. adverse drug reactions) and the confirmation and quantification of risks identified and risk minimization measures (paraphrased from [17]). For an example of use of digital sources (e.g. social media) for this purpose, see [18]	Adverse event reporting systems, population scale outcomes data via EHR; prospective analysis.
Pharmaco-genetics (PG)	"Examines inherited or acquired variations in genes that dictate drug response, disposition, or toxicity and explores how these variations can be used to optimize medication therapy." [19] Similar to PM and MP, but specific to genetic profile and pharmaceutical therapy.	Genomics and genomic profiling; epidemiological resources.
Anti-counter-feiting (AC)	Falsified medicines are fake medicines that pass themselves off as real, authorized medicines. Falsified medicines may: contain ingredients of low quality or in the wrong doses; be deliberately and fraudulently mislabeled with respect to their identity or source; have fake packaging, the wrong ingredients, or low levels of the active ingredients (paraphrased from European Medicines Agency web site). See also: [20]	Supply chain integration (bar codes, security codes; tamper proof packaging); consumer services (website seals/logos) and digital services.

2   Origins and Character of Digital Drugs

Medicines have always been hybrids (actor networks) - in part biochemical actor (active molecule(s)), in part material delivery system (pill, infusion, suppository, box, leaflet, cold chain), in part informational resources (representations and scripts to validate therapeutics and designate safe and appropriate use). And all bound up with complex and diverse social, scientific and economic interests and practices. However, the examples in Table 1 suggest that contemporary medicines in use become more materially, informationally and algorithmically complex, e.g. more digitally potent. We identify these as *digital drugs*[2] – that is:

---

[2] There is a possibility that something like a clinical medicine might emerge and be administered in a form that is essentially a pure digital phenomenon, e.g. an abstract 'program' of biochemical action to be compiled, 'downloaded' and 'run' in the body. More simply, a therapy such as a gym routine might be seen this way. For example the UK NHS 'Couch to 5K' is a therapy embodied in podcast downloads for achieving basic fitness through running [21]. A Google search of 'digital drugs' will also give information on possible audio-based psychotropic recreational drugs – so called 'digital highs'. In the sense that music can change your mood, perhaps even suppress pain, this is plausible. However, the general professional opinion is that the technology of 'binaural beats' is an interesting sensory phenomenon but psychotropically ineffective and that those who do get high are experiencing at best a placebo effect [22].

drugs that are both dependent on and substantially constituted by multiple digital representations and connections, and whose use and effectiveness is strongly mediated through digital means.

The lens we use to study digital drugs is assemblage [23] – drugs as performed bundles of artefacts, interests and practices that connect and interact with wider wholes, including clinical work (use), research practices that validate utility/value and mitigate/metricate risk (clinical trials, systematic reviews, pharmacovigilance) and regulatory frameworks to guide practice (regulations, protocols and guidelines).

In using the concept of assemblage we follow the broadly Deleuzian approach [23, 24]. Assemblage signifies digital drugs as events and conjunctions in time and sources of qualitative difference (something happening, some things entangled, something noticed, something different, a process or processes at work, an enactment). In the Deleuzian vocabulary an assemblage is rhizomic, a question of emergence (emergent properties, generativity) in open systems – "the always-emergent conditions of the present" [23]. An assemblage is not then a 'thing' (as in a network), with specific life-span or essence. Rather, assemblage is understood in a metaphysics in which "the concept of multiplicity replaces that of substance, event replaces essence and virtuality replaces possibility" [25]. This implies actions and performance of complex and multiple causality/functional interdependencies (e.g. as a medicine is found in a body or bodies, modeled in a genomic profile, supplied, or prescribed), and is not tied to a fixed format or a single unambiguous event or outcome. This is in contrast to the term *hybrid* used here to refer to the (digital) drug as artefact and actor, including its mix of material/digital resources and its evolved sociomaterial agency. We might say that *assemblage* is a concept applied to the 'instantiation' of the drug hybrid in use – the 'here and now' in a context (including in virtual contexts and in simulations).

We approach digital drugs by opposing the concept to its non-digital or pre-digital i.e. analogue version. The generations of medicines within our established regulatory structures, including the post-Thalidomide medicines, are essentially *analogue drugs* –seen as organic artefacts operating in an organic world of the body. Norbert Wiener, commenting on the probabilistic world of quantum mechanics, notes "the recognition of a fundamental element of chance in the texture of the universe" [26, p. 11]. In this sense anything analogue/organic is incomplete and uncertain ("...this random element, this organic incompleteness" [26, p. 11]). This 'incompleteness' certainly applies to medicines and their use. We are used to (or resigned to) the 'quantum' effect in medicines even as we strive for a stronger and stronger evidence base and thus certainty. Indeed the quantum is rather large given that most drugs prescribed to people do not work as desired most of the time[3]. Contemporary moves to digitize medicines may be seen as an attempt at closing down 'this organic incompleteness' within a digital certainty – e.g. through stratified medicine, genomics etc. as well as anti-counterfeiting systems or pharmacovigilance. It is tempting to imagine, as some proponents of these

---

[3] The average NNT (Number Needed to Treat) for a licensed drug used in secondary care is well over 5, and for a prophylactic drug (e.g. aspirin for prevention of stroke) it may be well over 1000; that is over 1000 persons need to receive the drug, including paying for it and suffering possible side effects, for one to obtain a therapeutic benefit [27]. As a point of contrast everyday paracetamol (acetaminophen) which a dentist may give you after an extraction has an NNT of around 4.5 for post-operative pain [28].

approaches do, that the shift to digital will drive down the quantum effect as it opens access to mechanisms that can validate actions and reduce error terms by orders of magnitude. This is not our position. Through the concept of assemblage, we argue, the quantum of the digital is made apparent, seen for example, in the simulated or more generally in the multiplicities that digital ontology accommodates.

Yoo's definition of digitalization recognizes this transition from analog to digital as fundamental: "the encoding of analog information into a digital format and the possible subsequent reconfigurations of the socio-technical context of production and consumption of [the associated] products and services" [29, p. 137]. He proposes that such digitalization occurs in various ways: at the level of a physical object (e.g. a digital infusion pump in place of an analog gravity infusion roller clamp; a 3D tamper proof bar code on a package), at the level of digital/digitally mediated routines (a digital algorithm for prescribing; a smart phone app to raise adherence to therapy), or as new representations (a genomic account of personalized efficacy; a digital information resource on drug-drug interactions driven by massive electronic health records databases).

Any division between a digital drug (and digital quantum) and an analogue drug (and organic quantum) is not of course clear cut. Transitions occur over years as existing resources are reconfigured in digital forms and new resources added or retrofitted. Our argument is, however, that as more of the active work we expect medicines to do (their agency) is (co)located in the digital, as digital resources and mechanisms are added and combined, and as this agency (re-)aligns to specific interests and goals, be they therapeutic, social or economic, then the nature of what a drug is, and how a medicine of medicines is practiced, 'tips' and something distinct and new emerges – a different kind of drug, a different set of practices, different assemblages. This in turn implies, we argue, new social, organizational and market structures.

Thus, as Yoo's definition of digitalization suggests and as assemblage requires, our interest is not focused ultimately on the digitizing of the information/object or the new digital routines or new representations, significant though these are – and of course we do need to consider the specific characteristics of digital products and services (as products/artefacts and as representations/services) and the 'bit string' economics that they obey [30]. But it is the 'subsequent reconfigurations' that are foreshadowed as seen in events and actions that we explore.

3   Three Domains: (In-)Use, Research, Governance

We approach digital drugs as assemblage from the perspective of three traditional domains in which they are by convention 'assembled' and within which issues of their value are addressed. These are the domain of clinical and therapeutic use, the domain of reflexive enquiry and research (gathering of 'evidence', knowing), and the domain of regulation and governance. These three domains are well established, each with its own practices and an established role/narrative as how we benefit (or not) from medicines. We do not consider here the biochemical domain, important though it is. These domains are of course interlinked, and one of the characteristics of medicines digitization is that these domains connect more and more e.g. events/assemblages are larger, stronger, richer, and more dynamic.

3.1   In-Use

As suggested above, digital drugs emerge in part out of efforts to computerize existing medicines use practices (prescribing, supply, administration, adherence, etc.) and in this way 'digitalize the object' with consequential ontological changes. Since the turn of the millennium it has been a key ambition of developed country health care policies to computerize prescribing in both primary care and secondary care and specifically to exploit the benefits of clinical decision support systems (CDSS) in helping prescribers select the right medicine for the patient, and to do so on the basis of a (digital) medical record (e.g. providing clinical data including in areas such as allergies), and data on recommended therapeutic strategies, available medicines, cost/cost effectiveness, and the effects of interaction among them (e.g. [31]). Similarly in the administration of medicines to or by patients, technological systems and devices such as smart pill boxes or text alerts are deployed to encourage or enforce adherence and record actual use [32]. Much of this work has necessarily been piecemeal (perhaps better described as 'targeted') as specific clinical practices and operational needs have been given computer 'support' (prescribing, dispensing, supply, administration, audit, 'academic detailing', phamacovigilance, etc.). CDSS are also understood as a necessary technological infrastructure, a necessary representation, without which a widespread application of personalized medicine cannot be contemplated [33], e.g. to enable the use in clinical practice of the 2500 genetic tests now already available [8, 34].

The potential *therapeutic value* and/or *service value* that motivate such projects include improved safety and reduction in errors and harm, more consistency of (good) practice, more efficient operations with less waste, and better documented therapy. In this way initiatives to computerize medicines-use are by convention set against the familiar litany of contemporary existential health care problems: rising health care costs, unacceptable error rates and the harm they cause, demographic change, managing a growing burden of treatable chronic disease. Ambitions of progress in these areas are predicated on the existence of good informational infrastructures that represent valid forms of data (e.g. [35]). Many of these ambitions have not yet been fully met but the quality, coverage and scale of data infrastructures improves over time.

More system-focused policy motives reflect a desire for more *net value* (i.e. more health benefit and less harm) and *value for money* out of budgets for medicines. In the English NHS about 50 million population generate a yearly drugs bill of about £12bn. This leads to a perceived need to exploit digital technologies both to help control this significant line of expenditure and to increase the effectiveness of what is spent in improving health outcomes.

Models of the use of digital drugs and their regulation are founded on ideas of digital systems for establishing efficacy, expressing protocols and in the realization of individual patient's care pathways. This approach to medicines and their use is portrayed as offering a 'personalized' (or stratified) service (or services) wrapped around the medicine. Perhaps most significantly, the personalization process – the process to match your genetics and medical history, test results and other 'omics'[4] to what is

---

[4]   Omics: a neologism used to describe a range of scientific fields (proteomics, genomics etc.) studying important biomedical aspects about a patient or patient group for subsequent use in personalised or stratified medicine; used also to refer to a person's characteristics in terms of molecular components and biological pathways (e.g. transcriptomic, proteomic, metabolomic).

known about medicines and therapy - becomes a separate institutional endeavor. Thus a new industry of 'diagnostics' has emerged (with *economic value*) which serves through devices, tests, data analysis and protocols to control and target therapy choice and therapy delivery – generating a trajectory of events. This is an arena of practice in which the balance of business interests and clinical or public health interests is today unclear. More generally the development of an industry and services for diagnostics can be seen as an example of a 'service-dominant logic' (servitisation) [36] as a drug becomes less a standard product, and is more performed by a complex set of *value generating services* (*value* here being taken in multiple senses of the word; see above). The clinical utility of the therapeutic intervention (its relevance and usefulness in patient care [37]) "becomes a moving target" as information on its benefits and risks increases for groups or for individual patients [37]. As part of this, 'patients', their bodies and their carers may (but it is in no way inevitable) become more active participants in therapy, with their involvement too digitally mediated – a possible reconfiguration of the patient and their role as actor and information source (e.g. in consultations) to a data source (e.g. through wireless monitors or smart pills).

The health value a medicine generates, and the ability to identify this, becomes an open and multiple question – how to find a *value-in-use* (e.g. the model of a market in services, and in particular digital services). This moves away from traditional ideas of a *value-in-exchange* (the model of a market for products). This change in perspective is directly seen in contemporary policy debates as national systems and payers consider 'value based pricing'– e.g. paying (or not paying) for the therapeutic service (or outcome), not for the molecule, and using a multi criteria algorithm and feedback to identify those that pass the value test and those that fail it [38, 39].

3.2   Research – Evidence in the Doing

A large armory of methods and techniques are today available to support scientific enquiry into medicines biochemical efficacy and other consequences and side effects (e.g. their validation as safe and effective) including statistical measures of outcomes as in a controlled trial, and synthetic metrics such as Number Needed to Treat (NNT) and Number Needed to Harm (NNH). These methods, refined in the past 70 or so years, underpin the established processes through which a new medicine is developed, tested and then licensed for specific uses. It is also the basis for the primary means by which a healthcare professional is given guidance on what medicines to use, when and how. Research findings are synthesized into protocols or guidelines for practitioners based on clinical data with or without some element of health economics (*value for money*).

In the UK for example, a national body - the *National Institute for Health and Care Excellence* (NICE) - prepares guidance on drug treatments which balances clinical and therapeutic benefits against cost[5]. Fundamental to this is the use of randomized control trials (RCT) and the types of knowledge that can be derived from trials, both individually and through meta-analysis (e.g. Cochrane reviews). It is in this way that we confidently (i.e. within confidence intervals, given the 'random element and

---

[5] http://www.nice.org.uk/guidance/index.jsp?action=bytreatment& TREATMENTS=Drug+treatments Last accessed 15 September 2014.

organic incompleteness' of life) assert the therapeutic value and risks of a new medicine for specific conditions and/or subpopulations, or recompute them for older drugs. However clinical trials in their traditional form are increasingly considered unsuitable to obtain the evidence on benefits and risks of medicines tailored to specific individuals – for example a trial now has to assess both the efficacy of the treatment and the efficacy of the diagnostic that underpins the stratification, the co-dependent development of drugs and molecular diagnostics [40]. As Lewis et al. suggest of personalized medicine "[It] forces us to question contemporary biomedical views of evidence, including its generation and use in decision making" [40]. There is thus a new focus on a set of complementary approaches to metricate value generated by medicines as they are to be used and as they are revealed through intensive digitization in the domain of use. Individual patient data collected/entered by clinicians at the point of care, or provided by the patient (now a data source), are aggregated into 'Big Data' as a potential basis for a new knowledge. A range of new analytic tools analyze or 'mine' these often non-standardized data and sift through the 'data turmoil' [41]. Among these analytic resources, for example, are new data-driven approaches to test the relationship between biomarkers and clinical outcomes [42] or for standardizing function instead of components in RCTs of complex interventions [43]. Alternatively, "real-time surveillance of individual patient outcomes" [37] may complement trials and improve evidence and support personalization. Drawing on digital resources, trials and experiments can be set up as "randomized studies embedded in routine care" through the use of electronic patient record databases [41]. Through such means the duration of trials and evidence gathering will shorten, some hope. For example, with an active distributed surveillance system in place "a full-scale observational study to evaluate the association between angioedema and drugs targeting the renin–angiotensin system was designed, conducted, and completed in 11 months" [44]. The perception of the need for such methods and the sense of urgency to exploit new research opportunities can be traced in part to the case of the pain killer and anti-inflammatory drug Vioxx. This medicine was licensed in 1999 and withdrawn in 2004. It took over 3 years and a number of patient deaths (disputed but probably in 6 digits [45]) before the negative side effects were acknowledged by the makers and the drug withdrawn from the US market [46]. The proposition is that, with digitalized patient records, and an effective and proactive pharmacovigliance system, such a case could be identified earlier with overall less harm [44].

3.3   Governance and Regulation

Research designs reflecting digitization, as described above, imply significant modifications to regulatory regimes. Regulators have been among the most active in adapting to the new world of digital drugs. The FDA, the US regulator, has made many changes in its processes to accommodate a perceived new urgency in drug approval processes including a fast-track process for 'breakthrough therapies' [47]. There is a somewhat similar designation of 'orphan drugs' in medical areas where patient numbers are small and investments are unlikely to be made on the usual commercial basis. If and when medicines are fast tracked (a concept with a history traced back to the early period of HIV/AIDS), and are expected to have a weaker research provenance at the time of licensing, they rely more on digital resources for monitoring of "post marketing safety and effectiveness" [44]. In such circumstances medicines-in-use data can serve to "raise or lower the level of concern about the overall risk–benefit profile of particular drugs", a capability that is described by the FDA as being transformational for the licensing process [44]. More generally they acknowledge the ability of these new resources of data to help fulfil the FDA's role. In the words of the FDA, it has "evolved its regulatory processes in response to – and in anticipation of – scientific developments" [48], noting how it has responded to personalized medicines and the associated growth of diagnostic products by, "collaborating in key research, defining and streamlining regulatory pathways and policies, and applying new knowledge in product reviews" [48]. Meanwhile, Australia has, arguably, the first national framework to assess personalized medicine for coverage or reimbursement decisions [49].

As suggested above, digitization and the availability of data generated in clinical care practices (in-use) and held in national registries, migrate from a pure research (trial) status to embody more directly various interests including of health care system managers and the payers, patients and patient groups, and the pharmaceutical industry [50, 51]. That is, research in both new and old formats, and digitalized and synthesized prospective data sets become engaged in the systems of governance and regulation that surround medicines use. Research data thus will directly feed the development of detailed and comprehensive protocols of use (and non-use) for powerful and expensive drugs, described as frameworks for 'appropriate medicines use' [50]. Niezen et al. report research in The Netherlands on registries (national databases of medicines use for a specific class of patient) as digital artifacts that are both an object to be managed, and an instrument to manage with. In this way clinical work (using medicines with patients and feeding the registry) and regulatory work (setting the protocol guidelines and reimbursement rules) become closely co-constitutive and co-evolving. In their analysis they question the desirability of a regulatory system that pursues a new 'digital objectivity' where available data embodies truth – as seen in many Big Data endorsements, and captured in the idea of the 'death of the denominator' when n=All (see also [52]). They contrast such digital objectivity with the more established 'regulatory objectivity', the kind of knowledge that is based on multiple evidential resources and embodies conventions and trade offs and collective expertise [53, 54].

4   Conclusion

In this paper we introduce the new concept of *digital drugs* as the intensified integration of digital services, data resources and algorithms into the practices of medicines. We anatomize it to reveal some of the main components (use, regulation, research) and mechanisms and relations using the lens of assemblage. The digitalization efforts that characterize the movement towards digital drugs are for the most part undertaken in the name of understanding, best practice, precision, and certainty. The individual initiatives and innovations described here can be seen individually as the expression of some regular and rational plan or policy to enhance the efficacy and efficiency of health care. Our view, our conceptual repertoire, and our chosen lens of assemblage, however, suggest something else or at least a different account of motivations and mechanism. As proposed here, digitization (digital mediation of drugs) is pursued as a means to address the organic quantum of chemicals in the body. However, the complexity and multiplicity of elements that converge in or constitute a digital drug and its 'use/reuse' suggest that it need not, and perhaps should not, be seen as a pursuit of a certain or specific outcomes. Digital drugs are manifest as diverse, distributed, cumulated and dissected events and incidents across and between domains. They also permit multiple outcomes as data resources grow, algorithms learn and reconfigure, and virtual phenomena take new roles. Such multiplicity and instability is a price paid for the desired outcomes, for example in the case of in-use experimental designs or big data driven protocols (digital objectivity).

Markus and Saka introduce assemblage as a technique of collage and "something that generates enduring puzzles about 'process' and 'relationship'" and "[offers] an odd, irregular and time-limited object for contemplation" [23]. Applying it in these terms to medicines, this paper raises issues that might be assessed against a wider understanding of digitalization.

First, is the idea of digital drugs themselves, or more generally of movement (re-configurations) towards a digital materiality that attaches to and 'takes over' classes of artifacts. In this it recasts them ontologically away from an artefactual existence to one of assemblage - found in a complex ecosystem of data, algorithm and temporally unstable conjunctions, actual, real, virtual or simulated.

Second, and embedded within this perspective, is the question of the 'mechanisms' of the digital as rational processes of improvement, as (digital) controllers, as sense-making, and as generative forces. Our case, and the examples in Table 1, suggests that there is opportunity here for useful fundamental categorizations of this digital agency through artefactual and assemblage conceptualizations.

Third and finally, is the question of knowledge processes (research designs) as embedded in these phenomena. The methodological arsenal of the evidence based community (that of innovators, regulators and evidence-based practice) is changing and adapting. Event and transaction are at the core, able to be inspected, accumulated and animated in ways that were not possible in earlier eras. This reconfiguration is core to the phenomena of interest. But can the IS community reconfigure its research agendas and methods to meet this challenge?

Acknowledgements. We would like to thank the colleagues with whom we have discussed various ideas and aspects of this work and the anonymous reviewers who offered insightful comments on a previous version of this paper. We also acknowledge the research grant EP/L021188/1 (2014-2016) awarded by the Research Councils UK Digital Economy Theme to support this work.

References

1. Yoo, Y.: Computing in Everyday Life: A Call for Research on Experiential Computing. MIS Quarterly 34, 213–231 (2010)
2. PricewaterhouseCoopers: Pharma 2020: The Vision – Which Path Will You Take. PricewaterhouseCoopers, London (2007)
3. Goozner, M.: The $800 Million Pill – The Truth behind the Cost of New Drugs. University of California Press, Berkley and Los Angeles (2004)

4. OFT: Medicines Distribution: An OFT Market Study. Office of Fair Trading, London (2007)
5. FDA: The Drug Development Process. U.S. Food and Drug Administration, http://patientnetwork.fda.gov/learn-how-drugs-devices-get-approved/drug-development-process
6. Orlikowski, W.J.: Using Technology and Constituting Structures: A Practice Lens for Studying Technology in Organizations. Organization Science 11(4), 404–428 (2000)
7. Cornford, T., Savage, I., Jani, Y., Franklin, B.D., Barber, N., Slee, A., Jacklin, A.: Learning Lessons from Electronic Prescribing Implementations in Secondary Care. Studies in Health Technology and Informatics 160, 233–237 (2009)
8. Shoenbill, K., Fost, N., Tachinardi, U., Mendonca, E.A.: Genetic Data and Electronic Health Records: A Discussion of Ethical, Logistical and Technological Considerations. Journal of the American Medical Informatics Association 21, 171–180 (2014)
9. Bell, G.C., Crews, K.R., Wilkinson, M.R., Haidar, C.E., Hicks, J.K., Baker, D., ... Hoffman, J.M.: Development and Use of Active Clinical Decision Support for Preemptive Pharmacogenomics. Journal of the American Medical Informatics Association 21, e93-e99 (2014)
10. Hingorani, A.D., van der Windt, D.A., Riley, R.D., Abrams, K., Moons, K.G.M., Steyerberg, E.W., ... Hemingway, H.: Prognosis Research Strategy (PROGRESS) 4: Stratified Medicine Research. BMJ 346, e5793 (2013)
11. Hamburg, M.A., Collins, F.S.: The Path to Personalized Medicine. N England J. M. 363, 301–304 (2010)
12. Schleidgen, S., Klingler, C., Bertram, T., Rogowski, W., Marckmann, G.: What Is Personalized Medicine: Sharpening a Vague Term Based on a Systematic Literature Review. BMC Medical Ethics 14, 55 (2013)
13. Proteus Digital Health: Digital Medicines – Shifting the Care Paradigm, http://www.proteus.com/future-products/digital-medicines/
14. Proteus Digital Health: Digital Health Feedback System, http://www.proteus.com/technology/digital-health-feedback-system/
15. Chen, R., Mias, G.I., Li-Pook-Than, J., Jiang, L., Lam, H.Y.K., Chen, R., ... Snyder, M.: Personal Omics Profiling Reveals Dynamic Molecular and Medical Phenotypes. Cell 148, 1293–1307 (2012)
16. Nuffield Council on Bioethics: Medical Profiling and Online Medicine: The Ethics of 'Personalised Healthcare' in a Consumer Age. Nuffield Council on Bioethics, London (2010)
17. Medicines and Healthcare Products Regulatory Agency: Pharmacovigilance – How We Monitor the Safety of Medicines, http://www.mhra.gov.uk/Safetyinformation/Howwemonitorthesafetyofproducts/Medicines/Pharmacovigilance/index.htm
18. Freifeld, C., Brownstein, J., Menone, C., Bao, W., Filice, R., Kass-Hout, T., Dasgupta, N.: Digital Drug Safety Surveillance: Monitoring Pharmaceutical Products in Twitter. Drug Safety 37, 343–350 (2014)
19. Goldspiel, B.R., Flegel, W.A., DiPatrizio, G., Sissung, T., Adams, S.D., Penzak, S.R., McKeeby, J.W.: Integrating Pharmacogenetic Information and Clinical Decision Support into the Electronic Health Record. Journal of the American Medical Informatics Association 21, 522–528 (2014)
20. Almuzaini, T., Choonara, I., Sammons, H.: Substandard and Counterfeit Medicines: A Systematic Review of the Literature. BMJ Open 3, e002923 (2013)

21. NHS Choices: Couch to 5K,
    `http://www.nhs.uk/Livewell/c25k/Pages/couch-to-5k.aspx`
22. Connolly, K.: Can 'Digital Drugs' Get You High? BBC News (July 22, 2010),
    `http://www.bbc.co.uk/news/world-us-canada-10668480`
23. Marcus, G.E., Saka, E.: Assemblage. Theory, Culture & Society 23, 101–106 (2006)
24. De Landa, M.: Intensive Science and Virtual Philosophy. Continuum Press, London (2002)
25. Smith, D., Protevi, J.: Gilles Deleuze. In: Zalta, E.N. (ed.) The Stanford Encyclopedia of
    Philosophy (Spring edn. 2013),
    `http://plato.stanford.edu/archives/spr2013/entries/deleuze`
26. Wiener, N.: The Human Use of Human Beings. Houghton Mifflin, Boston (1954)
27. Chatellier, G., Zapletal, E., Lemaitre, D., Menard, J., Degoulet, P.: The Number Needed to
    Treat: A Clinically Useful Nomogram in Its Proper Context. BMJ 312, 426–429 (1996)
28. Toms, L., Derry, S., Moore, R.A., McQuay, H.J.: Single Dose Oral Paracetamol
    (Acetaminophen) with Codeine for Postoperative Pain in Adults. Cochrane Database of
    Systematic Reviews 1, Article CD001547 (2009)
29. Yoo, Y.: Digital Materiality and the Emergence of an Evolutionary Science of the
    Artificial. In: Leonardi, P., Nardi, B., Kallinikos, J. (eds.) Materiality and Organizing:
    Social Interaction in a Technological World, pp. 134-154. Oxford University Press, Oxford
    (2012)
30. Quah, D.: Digital Goods and the New Economy. CEP Discussion Paper CEPDP0563.
    Centre for Economic Performance. London School of Economics and Political Science
    (2003),
    `http://eprints.lse.ac.uk/2236/1/Digital_Goods_and_the_New_Ec`
    `onomy.pdf`
31. Blumenthal, D., Tavenner, M.: The "Meaningful Use" Regulation for Electronic Health
    Records. New England Journal of Medicine 363, 501–504 (2010)
32. Dixon, B.E., Jabour, A.M., Phillips, E.O.K., Marrero, D.G.: An Informatics Approach to
    Medication Adherence Assessment and Improvement Using Clinical, Billing, and Patient-
    Entered Data. Journal of the American Medical Informatics Association 21, 517–521
    (2014)
33. Kawamoto, K., Lobach, D., Willard, H., Ginsburg, G.: A National Clinical Decision
    Support Infrastructure to Enable the Widespread and Consistent Practice of Genomic and
    Personalized Medicine. BMC Medical Informatics and Decision Making 9, 17 (2009)
34. Welch, B.M., Kawamoto, K.: Clinical Decision Support for Genetically Guided
    Personalized Medicine: A Systematic Review. Journal of the American Medical
    Informatics Association 20, 388–400 (2013)
35. Buntin, M.B., Jain, S.H., Blumenthal, D.: Health Information Technology: Laying The
    Infrastructure For National Health Reform. Health Affairs 29, 1214–1219 (2010)
36. Vargo, S.L., Lusch, R.F.: Evolving to a New Dominant Logic for Marketing. Journal of
    Marketing 68, 1–17 (2004)
37. Lesko, L.J., Zineh, I., Huang, S.M.: What Is Clinical Utility and Why Should We Care?
    American Society of Clinical Pharmacology and Therapeutics 88, 729–733 (2010)
38. Claxton, K., Briggs, A., Buxton, M.J., Culyer, A.J., McCabe, C., Walker, S., Sculpher,
    M.J.: Value Based Pricing for NHS Drugs: An Opportunity Not to Be Missed? BMJ 336,
    251–254 (2008)
39. Claxton, K., Sculpher, M., Carroll, S.: Value-Based Pricing For Pharmaceuticals: Its Role,
    Specification and Prospects in a Newly Devolved NHS. CHE Research Paper 60. Centre
    for Health Economics, University of York (2011)

40. Lewis, J., Lipworth, W., Kerridge, I.: Ethics, Evidence and Economics in the Pursuit of "Personalized Medicine". J. Pers. Med. 4,137-146 (2014)

41. Schneeweiss, S.: Learning from Big Health Care Data. New England Journal of Medicine 370, 2161–2163 (2014)

42. Ren, Z., Davidian, M., George, S.L., Goldberg, R.M., Wright, F.A., Tsiatis, A., Kosorok, M.R.: Research Methods for Clinical Trials in Personalized Medicine: A Systematic Review. In: Srivastava, R. Maksymowicz, W. Lopaczynski,W. (eds.) Los. In: Translation: Barriers to Incentives for Translational Research in Medical Sciences, pp. 659-684. World Scientific, Singapore (2014)

43. Hawe, P., Shiell, A., Riley, T.: Complex Interventions: How "Out of Control" Can a Randomised Controlled Trial Be? BMJ 328, 1561–1563 (2004)

44. Psaty, B.M., Breckenridge, A.M.: Mini-Sentinel and Regulatory Science – Big Data Rendered Fit and Functional. New England Journal of Medicine 370, 2165–2167 (2014)

45. Bhattacharya, S.: Up to 140,000 Heart Attacks Linked to Vioxx. New Scientist (January 25, 2005), http://www.newscientist.com/article/dn6918-up-to-140000-heart-attacks-linked-to-vioxx.html#.VBGLgGMvDTd

46. Singh, D.: Merck Withdraws Arthritis Drug Worldwide. BMJ 329, 816 (2004)

47. Brewer, G.J.: Drug Development for Orphan Diseases in the Context of Personalized Medicine. Translational Research 154, 314–322 (2009)

48. FDA: Paving the Way for Personalized Medicine – FDA's Role in a New Era of Medical Product Development. U.S. Food and Drug Administration (2013), http://www.fda.gov/downloads/scienceresearch/specialtopics/personalizedmedicine/ucm372421.pdf

49. Merlin, T., Farah, C., Schubert, C., Mitchell, A., Hiller, J.E., Ryan, P.: Assessing Personalized Medicines in Australia: A National Framework for Reviewing Codependent Technologies. Medical Decision Making 33, 333–342 (2013)

50. Niezen, M.G., Bal, R., De Bont, A.: Reconfiguring Policy and Clinical Practice How Databases Have Transformed the Regulation of Pharmaceutical Care? Science, Technology & Human Values 38, 44–66 (2013)

51. Burstin, H.: The Journey to Electronic Performance Measurement. Annals of Internal Medicine 158, 131–132 (2013)

52. Gitelman, L. (ed.): Raw Data Is an Oxymoron. MIT Press (2013)

53. Beaulieu, A.: Voxels in the Brain Neuroscience, Informatics and Changing Notions of Objectivity. Social Studies of Science 31, 635–680 (2001)

54. Beaulieu, A.: From Brainbank to Database: The Informational Turn in the Study of the Brain. Studies in History and Philosophy of Biological and Biomedical Sciences 35, 367–390 (2004)

Exploring the Role of Social Media
in Chronic Care Management
A Sociomaterial Approach

Hamid Pousti[1], Cathy Urquhart[2], and Henry Linger[1]

[1] Faculty of Information Technology, Monash University, Melbourne, Australia
{hamid.pousti,henry.linger}@monash.edu
[2] Business School, Manchester Metropolitan University, Manchester, UK
c.urquhart@mmu.ac.uk

Abstract. This paper examines how social media can support communities of patients with chronic illness and their care givers. This study is a qualitative case study and is informed by grounded theory. Sociomateriality is adopted as a theoretical lens to understand and explain the key findings. Our findings suggest that there is a dynamic relation between the contrary roles that social media in chronic care management and this is not only attributed to the functionalities of these technologies but to the attributes of patients and their states of health. We were also able to observe how these technologies are bounded up with human activities in the ways that separating them is not possible. What we learnt from our findings is that the ways patients and carers use of social media can change their perceptions about their conditions, and influence how they understand and approach the management process.

Keywords: social media, community, sociomateriality.

1   Introduction

This paper examines how social media can support communities of patients with chronic illness and their care givers. Chronic disease are long term universal disorders, characterized as complex and non-curable conditions with prolonged impacts on individuals and communities [51]. It is argued that the complex process of chronic care management is challenging the wealth and functionalities of many individuals and communities by putting extra demands and pressure on the scarce healthcare and other communal resources [35]. However, studies suggest that information and communication technology can alleviate the adverse impact of chronic disease by supporting many aspects of the management process and potentially improve its outcomes [34, 42].

Recent studies show that there is a growing trend of using social media in the process of chronic care management [49], to the extent that some researchers believe this trend is transforming the process from a clinical-based activities to a more self-managed and community dependent process [25, 73].

B. Doolin et al. (Eds.): IS&O 2014, IFIP AICT 446, pp. 163–185, 2014.
© IFIP International Federation for Information Processing 2014

While more empirical evidence is being reported regarding the different aspects of such a transformation [e.g. 66, 76], there is still little known on how these new technologies can influence or support the communities of patients and carers that form around chronic care management. This is because social media afford new types of behaviors that were previously difficult or even impossible to achieve before these new technologies being adopted by patients and carers [53, 58].

The lack of solid scholarly knowledge to explain the empirical patterns of use of social media in healthcare activities, calls for a deeper understanding of how social media can support patients and carers who take parts of the management process online. Further, there is a need to explore how the online activities that occur through social media can influence the offline process of the chronic care management and its outcomes.

In light of these motivations, the purpose of this study is to explore and unpack the potential role of social media in supporting community of patients and carers involved in chronic care management. It also aims to deepen our understanding of how such roles may arise from users' perceptions about the affordances and constraints of social media. As such, the question this study aims to answer is:

> *What roles can social media play in supporting chronic care management, and how the characteristics of social media influence such supporting roles?*

This study is a qualitative case study [27, 86], and is informed by grounded theory as its method of exploration and analysis [32]. Sociomateriality is adopted as a theoretical lens to understand and explain the key findings of this study [70]. By offering a relational perspective, this theoretical lens enables this study to highlight the unique and distinctive roles and capabilities of social media in chronic care management that exist beyond the material features of these technologies and the agency of their users, alone.

The paper proceeds as follows. The next section gives an overview of the wide range of literature on the use of social media in healthcare settings. We then discuss the sociomaterial lens used for this study in section 3. In section 4, we explain our methodology, including the grounded theory approach used in the study. Section 5 contains our findings about the role of social media in chronic care management. In Section 6, we engage our findings with the existing literature and our theoretical lens for the purposes of a discussion. Our final section comes to some conclusions about the role of social media in chronic healthcare management.

2   Literature Review

Literature about the application of social media in healthcare highlights the significance of these technologies in creating new opportunities for interactions and conversations between people who are involved in healthcare activities [56]. In particular, the literature points to the promising potential of social media in chronic care management, as well as the ways these technologies may challenges the process [52].

Recently, there has been also a growing body of literature that highlights the means by which social media is transforming the process of chronic care management from a more clinical practice to a more community-based activity [25, 66].

In identifying the influence of social media in chronic care management, some researchers [e.g. 17] focus on social networking sites to highlight how these type of social media platforms can assist patients and caregivers to make better informed decisions and improve the quality of their lives. Wicks et al. [88] also highlight how Facebook, and other social networking communities can be built around data-sharing platforms, where patients share different types of information about their medical and social conditions.

The role of social media in facilitating the interaction between practitioners and patients is also highlighted in some of the studies that are concerned with chronic care management. For example a study by Jain [41] highlights how social networking sites are used by general practitioners who deliberately decided to become friends or connect with their patients to engage patients and also become more approachable. However, Keckley and Hoffmann [44] suggest that there is a complexity around this type of interaction and they cast doubts on the effectiveness of such approaches.

Stellefson et al. [76] present an analytical comparison between the traditional methods of providing health related information to patients with chronic disease, and the new trend of using social media. They argue that in the traditional methods of information provision, public health experts were providing chronic disease information in static form through Web 1.0, which primarily make written and audio materials available online. However, the rapid growth in adoption of social media has provided opportunities for participatory Internet interventions, to help individuals with chronic diseases become actively engaged in their own health care and become both the producers and consumers of information they need [61, 74].

More studies also highlight other aspects of chronic care management that could be influenced by the use of social media. For instance, Mo and Coulson [59] shows how social media can empower patients to become more active participants in the management of their conditions. Setoyama et al. [75] highlight the supporting role of social media facilitating the formation of online support groups, and Hara and Hew [38] shows how these technologies support information and knowledge sharing process.

Most of these studies examine or measure the influence of social media on the outcome of chronic care management [64]. Their approach is mostly to measure some medical or psychological parameter against certain features and functionalities that are designed into social media platforms [15]. One area that these studies leave almost untouched is how the use of social media by patients and carers can change the perception of these groups about their health conditions and how that in turn would influence the ways they use social media. This calls for further investigation on the relation between technological aspects of social media and the social and human aspects chronic care management.

In the field of IS, in the recent years, IS scholars have shown an increasing interest in studying social media [82]. The importance of social media, and the significance of studying them as new technological innovations, have been widely discussed by IS scholars. The topic has been approached from variety of perspectives, including affordances of social media [e.g. 53, 79], their implications for virtual teams and communities [e.g. 89], their operational implications for organisations [e.g. 20], and their implications for social change [e.g. 5].

However, as Fichman et al. [26] argue, there is a need for more research from the IS community into the opportunities and challenges that social media can offer in the area of health IT issues. Agarwal et al. [3] contend that the importance of technologies such as social media in healthcare is increasing, as these technologies are playing more influential roles in making healthcare services more affordable and more reachable. They argue that the significant role of IT in modern healthcare warrants more attention from IS researchers, especially in the areas that pertain to the expansion of online health communities.

3   Theoretical Lens

Sociomateriality is a theoretical framework that conceptualizes the social world through the relations between material agency of artifacts and the social agency of human [70]. The sociomaterial perspective attempts to explain the social world as the enactment of meanings and materiality in everyday practices [69]. In doing so, this perspective focuses on the performativity of a 'social object' – the term that what was initially coined by Berger and Luckmann [13] – and its relation to its material features [90]; rather than representing this object through language and numbers [8].

Agency is at the heart of sociomateriality. However, this view makes a distinctive move away from seeing agencies of both people and artifacts, as primarily independent and self-contained entities that influence each other, either through impacts (deterministic approach) or interactions (constructivist approach) [10]. Instead, the focus is on agencies that have so thoroughly saturated each other in a way that boundaries between them are dissolved.

In this perspective materiality refers to the constituent features of a technological artifact that are available to all users in the same way [48]. However, as Majchrzak and Markus [54] put, because people come to materiality with diverse goals and perceptions, an artifact can afford distinct possibilities or limitations for particular actions. This because the material out of which an object is made can provide multiple affordances and it is possible that one object can produce multiple outcomes [79]. Therefore, although materiality exists independent of people, but affordances do not.

From the sociomaterial perspective, the affordances of a technology are a set of potential possibilities that emerges through interactions between people and technology in practice, rather than as properties of either people or technology [40]. In other words, affordances depend not only on the material and functionalities that characterize an artifact, also on the expertise, processes, and people's understandings of what the artifact can afford.

Looking at social media artifacts through the lens of affordances provides several advantages. The main advantage, according to Treem and Leonardi [79], is that focusing on the entangled relationship between users and the material features of social media enables researchers to avoid privileging social determinism in explaining the patterns of social media use by users and ignoring the properties of the technology itself. The implication of this perspective for research is that the researchers need to base their analysis on the entangled and symbiotic relationships between the actions to be taken in a specific context and the capabilities of these technologies [53].

4   Methodology

This study takes a qualitative case study approach [27]. Taking a qualitative approach was essential, as gaining an understanding of the role of social media in chronic care management and how these technologies can influence the dynamics of this process are deeply embedded in the actors' subjective understanding of the applications and roles of these technologies in chronic care management [62].

Data collection and data analysis of the study was informed by grounded theory [32, 80]. The choice of grounded theory approach was entirely appropriate because very limited theoretical studies exist in this area and further exploration was essential [68]. The use of grounded theory as powerful exploratory approach was fruitful. Its flexible coding process enabled the investigation to focus on the contextual elements of the use of social media and unpack the underlying assumptions that would inform the actions and decisions of the key players in using these technologies for the management purposes.

While grounded theory provided this study with unique capabilities, we acknowledge that the findings of studies that are based on grounded theory can be very detailed and context bounded [47, 81]. To address this concern, we concur with Orlikowski [68] and Walsham [86] and argue that the detailed findings of this study can be scaled up to generate more abstract and general explanations through the process of 'analytic generalization'. This means that the findings will be explained with insights from the extant literature, and in the light of the existing formal theory [81], in our case, sociomateriality.

4.1   Data Collection

Informed by the grounded theory method, the data collection of the study was designed in three stages of exploration of the subject matter, conceptualization of the phenomenon, and theorization [32]. Each stage was informed by the analysis of data from previous stages.

At the exploratory stage, a focus group was conducted to explore the preliminary dimensions of the research problem, as well as the initial constructs that could inform the processes of constant comparison and theoretical sampling. The focus group was comprised of 10 participants, and all the participants were patients with arthritis and their carers. The session took two and half hours and was mediated by a professional mediator. The choice of arthritis was well justified as it is the most prevalent chronic disease in many developed countries [71], and it is one of the most widespread chronic conditions around the world [6].

This stage revealed a number of key findings. First, it revealed the preliminary concepts related to role of social media in chronic care management. Second, it showed that although social media have promising potential for supporting chronic care management, there are a number of areas that were marked by significant uncertainties around social media use. Third, it suggested that many of the characteristics and applications of social media mentioned by the participants were related to or influenced by the material aspects of social media. The latter findings suggested, in Strauss's [77] language, that sociomateriality is a proper theoretical lens 'to grapple' with in order to explain the phenomenon under investigation.

Followed by the focus group, data was collected from social media sources, and complemented with semi-structured interviews. The initial concepts that emerged through the analysis of the focus group guided the process of collection, coding, and analysis of the data that came from social media resources. Major data came from variety of online patient forums and other social media platforms such as Facebook and Twitter. Forums used for this study were open to the public and researchers and were sponsored and maintained by health authorities, support organizations, and universities. The stories posted on the forums came from participants with different backgrounds and were generally from patients and carers, however, patients' family members, doctors, and other health professionals were also active members in those forums.

Forums were categorized into 17 categories based on the disease type they were representing. From the 17 different categories, the top five categories that represented the most prevalent chronic disease [71] were chosen and forums with the highest volumes of posts were selected for the study. We observed that there was a correlation between the prevalence of a disease and the volume of interactions in forums. The collected data were examined through the process of constant comparison. This process enabled us to sharpen our thinking about the emerging concepts by writing theoretical memos, and enrich our understandings of their complexities.

For the purpose of theoretical sampling, a set of keywords (e.g. Facebook, forum, or online) that could help to identify messages and stories that were pointing to the use of social media were used. The result returned with 633 stories, mainly from people who were involved in the management of arthritis, diabetes, autism, asthma, and breast cancer. The 633 stories/messages were reviewed and 223 of them identified as relevant items based on the activity they represented (i.e. use of social media), the purpose of the activities (i.e. chronic care management), and the relevancy of the stories to the research question.

This stage of data collection spanned over a three months period, followed by interviews with some of the key participants in the forums. In total, nine semi-structured interviews were conducted for the deeper investigation of the emerging themes and for the purpose of reaching more theoretical saturation. The complementary sources of data provided valuable insight into the practices of social media by patients and carers, and also assisted in reaching theoretical saturation. In general, the iterative process of coding and analysis through constant comparison enabled the study to search out for contrasts and negative evidence while becoming sensitive to any new emerging concepts with possible alternative explanations [22]. Table 1 presents detailed information about the data sources used in this study.

It is noteworthy that the use of social media resources provided this study with unique possibilities. For example, with regard to the analytical processes of coding, social media resources provided interesting benefits to this study by making it more convenient to collect new data, deeper exploration of the dimensions of the phenomenon, and to better contrast the findings with the previous observations within the study.

Table 1. An overview of the data collection and data sources

Data source	Number of items/ participants	Type of stories/participants	Stage
Focus group	10 participants	10 arthritis patients	Exploration
Arthritis forum	68 stories	31 patients, 25 carers, 9 nurses, 2 physiotherapists, 1 rheumatologist	Conceptualisation
Diabetics forum	64 stories	36 patients, 13 carers, 9 nurses, 1 GP, 4 social workers, 1 allied health	
Depression forum	29 stories	21 patients, 8 carers	
Asthma forum	28 stories	21 patients, 5 carers, 2 nurses	
Breast cancer forum	34 stories	23 patients, 5 family members, 4 nurses, 2 allied health	
Interviews	9 participants	5 practitioners, 2 patients, 2 carers	Theorising/ corroboration

4.2 Data Analysis

Informed by the grounded theory, a rigorous Glaserian [31] approach to coding was taken in this study. Therefore, coding took place through three stages of open, selective, and theoretical coding. The approach enabled to explore the major constructs and their dimensions pertaining to the use of social media in chronic care management. The coding approach also helped the researcher to ensure that theoretical saturation of the emergent categories was reached.

The data analysis proceeded with close reading and coding of the stories and messages extracted from the online forums, as well as the transcripts of the focus group and interviews. Particular attention was given to the perspectives of the patients and carers, as the major actors, in order to understand how and why they would use, or avoid using, forums or other social media platforms for managing their conditions. Figure 1 presents an overview of the analytical development of the emerged concepts.

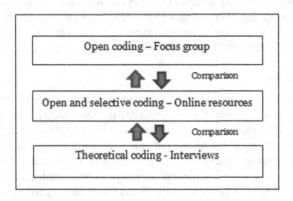

Fig. 1. Overview of the coding process

5   Findings

This section presents the findings as they were built up in the coding process. We present five categories that contribute to the theme of Role of Social Media: Building sense of community, Emotional support, Empowerment, Use of information, and Barriers. The composition of the theme is shown in the Figure 2. We also provide a chain of evidence for each category, so readers can see sample quotes for each category and the basis of that category in open coding.

5.1   Building Sense of Community

This selective code illustrates the means that social media can supports the creation of a sense of community as the patients and carers interact with each other. It shows how social media can help to bridge some of the social gaps that may result from issues such as differences in age, gender, or health conditions. This category shows social media supports the creation of *a sense of community* in chronic care management by *building rapport* among patients and carers (e.g. connecting people with different languages, or connecting people with different life experiences), supporting *diversity* (e.g. connecting people with different cultural backgrounds or in different age groups), facilitating peer and *social support* (e.g. supports social networks), facilitating *learning* (e.g. sharing experiences), and supporting *communication* (e.g. supporting multiple channels and methods of communication)

5.2   Emotional Support

This selective code represents how the use of social media can assist patients and carers to get *emotional support* as they engage in the process of chronic care management. Management of chronic disease is usually with many uncertainties and surprises, creating many emotional difficulties for patients and care givers and therefore, in long term, getting *emotional support* becomes an important aspect of chronic care management [37]. In the light of this important aspect of the management process, the findings of this study revealed that social media can provide *emotional support* to the patients, carers, and their families by being a source of *emotional comfort* (e.g. helps to show sympathy or showing patients that they are not the only ones who have health problems), and by giving them access to the resources or interactions that can help them *to raise their hopes* for a better future (e.g. supports sharing positive experiences, or spreading encouraging words).

5.3   Empowerment

Traditionally chronic care management is a paternalistic process where the power of decision making and directing the management process mainly rest in the hands of practitioners [12, 28]. The finding of this study disclosed that social media can change this balance of power by enabling the patients and carers to *gain new capabilities* to support the management process (e.g. overcoming communication barriers), giving them more *control* over the management affairs (e.g. helps patients to become proactive), and equip them with *resources* (e.g. knowledge about existing local facilities) that enables them to *negotiate* healthcare and issues related to the management of their conditions (e.g. asking for better resources or alternative treatments).

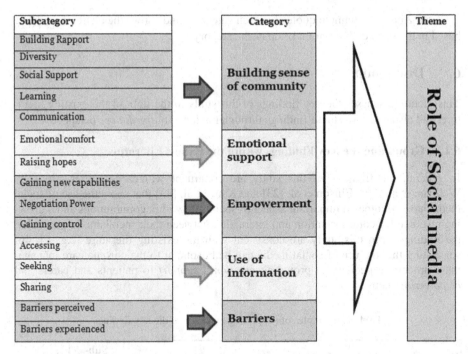

Fig. 2. An overview of the development of the Role of Social Media theme

5.4 Information Use

Chronic care management is an information intensive process [24]. This selective code represents how social media can support different information processes pertaining to chronic care management. The category of information use highlights the role that social media can play in facilitating the processes of information seeking (e.g. looking for information about their diseases or seeking information about the implications of the treatments they receive), information accessing (e.g. talking to people with similar condition), and information sharing (e.g. sharing their experiences with healthcare systems).

5.5 Barriers

The category of *barriers* illustrates the major uncertainties, concerns, and *barriers* against the adoption and use of social media in the management of chronic disease. While many studies suggest that social media have the potential to transcend the social and spatial *barriers* of chronic care management [9, 83]; the findings of this study suggests that this is not always the case. Therefore, it is important to understand what the *barriers* of using social media in chronic care management are and how they can debilitate the potential of social media for supporting chronic care management. Such an understanding can also assist to obviate these *barriers* or alleviate their impacts. Evidence indicated that there are two major groups of 'experienced' (e.g. source of bad news, or information quality can be poor) and 'perceived' (e.g. lack of confidence in using technology, or uncertainties around the legal issues of using social media) *barriers* to the use of social media in chronic care management.

Table 2 provides sample quotes for each category, and shows the chain of evidence based in the open codes that make up each category.

6   Discussion

This section discusses the key findings of this study in the light of the existing literature, and also discusses these findings through the lens of *affordances* perspective.

6.1   Grounding the Key Findings within the Extant Literature

In general, the findings of this study are congruent with earlier observations by Wellman et al. [87], Ellison et al. [23] and Kane et al. [43] that show the use of social media have become an important aspect of social life within communities and a growing resource for communication and interaction between their members. In particular, the findings from this study are consistent with the existing literature [e.g. 15, 46] suggesting that the use of social media can be beneficial to the chronic care management process, especially in providing *emotional support* to patients and carers and *empowering* them.

Table 2. Examples of supporting evidence of the key findings

Open code	Sample quote	Sub-category	Category
Source of comfort	*It's been more of a source of comfort actually than a lot of the other resources which I found on the Internet*	Emotional comfort	Emotional support
Sympathy	*When I feel I want some sympathy and want to talk to somebody, I will be very tempted to go on the forum and talk to people there*		
Giving vent to feelings	*Thanks for allowing me to vent. Today has been tough and very depressing*		
Sharing positive experiences	*One of the best moments was when someone wrote how the person who couldn't get from the kitchen to the bathroom without a cane finally overcame it*		
Encouragement	*There was a lot of patting on the back trying*		
Accessing new resources	*Social media have opened up a whole lot of different avenues and new resources for us*	Gaining new capabilities	Empowerment
Overcoming communication barriers	*He is not able to speak anymore but still he can communicates with our children and friends through Facebook*		
Understanding of the conditions	*I think I'm learning gradually that the OA symptoms deteriorate in the cold*	Negotiation power	

Table 2. (*continued*)

Negotiation for resources	*You know, having to learn about the healthcare system, they develop some sense of what it is about and how to negotiate it*		
Knowledge acquisition	*Knowledge is power really.*		
Being proactive	*I often look up for information there to find out what services are available in my area and where I need to go and ask for them*	Gaining control	
Prevent surprises	*Nothing was anymore going to be a surprise or a shock for me about the procedure.*		
Choice	*I think when you have the right information you will feel easier with any decision that you make*		
Seeking information about diseases	*Patients these days go online or use social media mainly for information seeking*	Seek	
Seeking information for implications of treatments	*I did talk about the possible drugs that I could use*		Use of Information
Accessing relevant information	*Some information that is not actually relevant to them*		
Accessing information for decision making	*It is a very compelling sort of way of using technology to help and support patients to make decision about what they want to do*	Access	
Accessing to information for education	*They can actually educate you by offering you relevant information*		
Sharing contents	*Only took me 8 weeks and 2 days to get this [photo of a drug]*	Sharing	
Sharing experiences	*He blogs about his experiences of living with RA*		
Common language	*So, we kind of dumped it down with spoons and made up our own way of talking about it.*	Building rapport	
Same age group	*I have been looking for support groups for younger people like myself (30).*		
Same gender	*We encourages young women with arthritis*		
Individuality	*It's such an individual thing*	Diversity	Building a sense of community
Difference of geographical location	*When you talk to different people, somebody in far north or in America*		
Spectrum of a disease type	*We are all different because it is a spectrum*		
Social inclusion	*For some isolated and lonely people, that it opens up a new world to them*	Social support	
Social interaction	*It is really good that he is able to stay in touch with other people*		

Table 2. (*continued*)

Social network	*You can have a network of people to support you*	Learning	
Sharing experiences	*People are talking about their own experiences*		
Sharing knowledge	*I think most people that go on the forum are extremely knowledgeable and well prepared to teach you*		
Learning from feelings	*I know exactly how your husband feels and I can actually tell you why*		
Communication with individuals	*It gives you the opportunity to actually communicate with other patients*	Communication	
Communication with the community	*There's Facebook, there's Twitter and there are other amazing stuff out there have made it much easier for us to communicate with other people*		
Source of bad news	*You don't hear the good news on there. You just hear the bad news*	Barrier experienced	Barrier
Depressive	*I stopped using the forum as it made me feel depressed*		
Information relevancy	*The biggest challenge for us is the information we have on our Facebook are relevant*		
Lack of control over the content	*The risk is that we will have little or no control over the content of Facebook*		
Reliability of sources	*The forum will give you a lot, but again I find, you're better off talking to somebody who is expert rather than getting it from unreliable sources*		
Social isolation	*My friends only communicate with me on Facebook*		
Social gap	*People who use social media are in different social state from those who don't use technology*		
Confidentiality concerns	*We are bound by laws that say we cannot talk to other people about our patients*	Barrier Perceived	
Lack of regulations	*In terms of Facebook, there is no regulation for doing social media-based consultations*		
Age dependency	*Because arthritis patient are all older we couldn't communicate with them through Facebook*		
Computer literacy deficit	*I don't understand what any of that is because I was a swimming instructor*		
Language barriers	*Something that we haven't done well at all in the past with our ethnics groups with none English background*		

Our findings show that an important aspect of using social media for chronic care management is that it can provide valuable emotional support to the patients and care givers. This finding is consistent with Frost and Massagli [29], Nakayama et al. [63],

Setoyama et al. [75], suggesting that the use of different social media platforms can create positive emotional feelings for the patients and carers.

Emotional comfort found as a major dimension of *emotional support*. This finding is supported by Chung and Kim [18] study of social media that shows the use of social media technologies such as blogs can generate a sense of emotional gratification and satisfaction among patients with chronic care. Vilhauer [85] also highlights instillation of hope, and catharsis, as two major benefits of social media mediated support groups. This is in accordant with the finding of this study suggesting *raising hope* as a major aspect of *emotional support* attainable through the use of social media.

The *empowering* role of social media has been widely discussed within the literature [59, 91]. In the context of healthcare and especially chronic care management, the role of social media in *empowering* patients and carers is also highlighted frequently [e.g. 25, 52]. In our findings we showed that one of the aspects of *empowerment* is the patients' feelings that they have more *control* over the management process. This finding is consistent with Van Uden-Kraan et al. [84] as their study of online support groups for patients with chronic illness reveal that sharing experiences through social media can *empower* patients by leading them to a feeling of regaining *control* over their personal lives and their future.

In our findings we also highlighted how social media can contribute into patients' and carers' *empowerment* through provisions of *new capabilities* such as accessing to new resources and expanding the scope and range of *communication*. These findings tally with the earlier research by Bartlett and Coulson [11] that shows the significant role of social media in expanding *communication capabilities*; also a study by O'Connor [65] highlights how social media technologies provides *access to new resources* that are beneficial to chronic care management.

We also explored social media support patients' and carers' *empowerment* by giving them more *negotiation power*. This aspect is not explicitly identified in the literature, but Van Uden-Kraan et al. [84] implicitly point to this aspect, by showing how the use of social media can help patients to feel confident in their relationships with their physicians. So, we believe our finding with regard to *negotiation power* extends the current literature about the *empowering* role of social media in healthcare.

The extant literature also supports the findings from this study that highlights the *barriers* of using social media for chronic care management. Studies by O'Keeffe and Clarke-Pearson [67] show that the use of social media can create distress and *emotional discomfort* for patients as they frequently read unpleasant news about their friends or other patients with similar conditions. Issues related to poor *information quality* and the *reliability of information* accessible through social media are also widely discussed by researchers [1, 57]. Also, the different aspects of the social concerns related to the use of using social media by patients and carers are highlighted by Dutta-Bergman [21].

Although not all the identified concerns about the *legal dimensions* of the *barriers* are discussed within the literature, *confidentiality* and *privacy* have been highlighted strongly within the literature [1, 7]. Evidence from literature also supports our findings regarding the *lack of self-efficacy* as a *barrier* of using social media for chronic care management. For example, findings from Nakayama et al. [63] show that *age* and *lack of confidence* contributes in patients' avoidance to the use of social media. However, we suggest that our findings about *the lack of computer literacy* and *language barriers* can extend the literature in this area by adding new dimensions to these constructs (e.g. how the technological features of social media such as user interfaces couple up with users' health conditions and enact as a barrier) that were previously unexplored .

6.2   Viewing Our Findings through the Lens of Sociomateriality

One way to explain the increasingly symbiotic relationship between social media and healthcare activities is through the lens of affordances. We adopt Majchrzak et al. [53] definition of affordance and define technology affordances as the mutuality of actors' intentions and technology capabilities that provide the potential for particular actions.

In the light of this definition, a preliminary exploration of the use social media in chronic care management, shows that the ways the capabilities and limitations of these technologies are perceived by the patients and carers are highly influenced by the material aspects of social media platforms [72]. Also, findings from other studies [e.g. 58] show that many of the actors involved in chronic care management, specially patients and carers, often could enact new practices or achieve outcomes such as mobilizing social resources or fast and timely dissemination of sensitive information, that would not be possible without the use of social media and engaging with material features of these technologies. As such, informed by Gibson [30] and Hutchby [40], we contend that our empirical findings lend themselves to analysis from an affordance perspective.

The relational concept of technology affordances suggests that social media have no inherent properties, boundaries or meaning but, as Barad [8] suggests, these technologies are bound up with the specific material-discursive practice that constitute their characteristics and affordances. As Zammuto et al. [90] point out, based on the affordances perspective, technological possibilities of action are not given but they depend on the intent and perception of the actors enacting them.

Using an affordance lens suggests that although social media and the social features of chronic care management may exist independently of each other, their value for explaining the role of social media in the management process comes from how their agencies enact together.

This means, although social media and chronic care management process may have their own potentials and constraints, but as Zammuto et al. [90] argue, an affordance perspective recognizes that a technological object has some recognized functionality but needs to be recognized as a social object. In other words, the influence of social media, as social objects – a term first coined by Barley [10] – on the management process cannot be separated from, for example, patients' status of health, their technology literacy, their communities, or any other social features pertaining to the management process. We therefore suggest a number of key affordances of social media in the context of chronic care management.

Emotional Support Affordance. The emotional support affordance is defined as a potential of social media to provide patients and carers with emotional support through emotional comfort and instillation of hopes. This affordance is enacted by the assemblage of material features of social media (e.g. hardware, software, or interfaces) and social features of chronic care management (e.g. friendship, or peer support).

Technologically, interactive environments such as online forums that enable synchronous and asynchronous interactions are needed to have the basic capabilities and elements of emotional support in place [2]. In addition, databases, usually supplied through a service provider coupled with physical storage environments and other hardware are needed to store the history of interaction and give the capability of retrieving data to patients and carers [34]. Further, algorithms are generally essential for authentication and protection of users' privacy and confidentiality [14] as many of the online participants seek support while staying anonymous [63] or only interested to communicate with certain people [34].

These technological features of social media need to be coupled with important social features of the management process to enact the affordance. These social features can include the type of the medium [36], the chronic disease types [58], the participants' demographics [19], the culture of the online forum [55], and the participants' attitudes and communication skills [60].

The emotional support affordance assists to understand and explain the role of social media in the outcome of chronic care management in ways that examining either social media or the management process separately does not. By investigating how social media can be used by different actors to provide emotional support to patients and carers, interdependencies and potential sources of support can be more easily identified. Also, features of social media that are more useful to the provision of such support and those that are less attractive can be more accurately pinpointed.

Empowerment Affordance. We define this affordance as the potential of social media in empowering patients and carers. The empowerment affordance is enacted through the relationship between the material features of social media (e.g. information representation, multiple format support, and information sharing spaces) and social features of chronic care management (e.g. knowledge acquisition, interaction with service providers, or decision making).

Technologically, several technological features are needed to enable this affordance. Technologies such as wikis, blogs, and online forums that enable users to produce, share, and access information are needed to support capabilities lead to patients and carers empowerment [74, 83]. In addition, technologies that support the representation of information in different formats such as text, video, and audio are needed to help the patients and carers understand the different dimensions of an issue and acquire knowledge with more depth about the issues related to the management of their disease [91]. These technical and material features of social media need to be conjoined with some of the significant aspects of chronic care management to make the empowerment affordance possible.

Several chronic care management features are needed as well to enable empowerment affordance. Features such as making decisions about different aspects of treatments [15], negotiating work place related issue [45], educating friends and families [56], and taking part in social activities [33], are just a few to name.

The affordance of empowerment assists to explain the role of social media in identifying the roles and relation between the actors involved in chronic care management. By examining how social media can give patients and carers a stronger voice and enable them playing a more central role in the management process, we can get a clearer understanding of how social media can support them to become more independent from healthcare services and engage in a more effective and fruitful self-management process. Also, by examining the empowerment affordance across different actors, it is possible to identify inter-power-relationships and inter-power-dependencies, which in turn could assist to get a deeper understanding of the technological and social features that, could more effectively support empowerment capabilities.

Barriers Constraint. While the concept of affordance mainly represents potential capabilities for actions, as Hutchby [40] explains, an artifact's affordances and constraints are similar in nature. The notion of constraints emerges from an artifact's affordances and how people perceive an artifact can put constraints on their possibilities for action based on its affordances [54]. Accordingly it is useful to consider how constraints might play out in using social media in chronic care management. Participants did independently identify constraints, which underlines why the theoretical lens is so helpful when considering this research problem.

The barriers constraint in our study is defined as the potential harm of using social media in chronic care management. This constraint is enacted through the dynamic relationship between the material agency of social media (e.g. security, confidentiality, and meta-information) and social agency (e.g. regulations, online relationships, information reliability) of chronic care management.

Several technological features of social media contribute in enactment of this constraint. Features like accessibility of depressive or concerning information [63], poor filtering features [4], complex interfaces and process [39], lack of methods or algorithms to evaluate the quality of imparted information [57], and insufficient level of confidentiality [4] are a number of material features of social media that contribute in the barriers constraints.

These technological features need to be coupled with some important social aspects of chronic care management to enact as barriers. Social features such as legal issues [78], health literacy [16], and age [19] can influence users' perceptions about the capabilities of social media, and the ways they could assist or harm patients and carers during the management process.

The barriers constraint helps to explain the potential harm that the use of social media can cause of patients and carers. By examining this constraint(s) across diverse actors, it should be possible to identify features or functionalities of social media that are potentially insignificant or damaging to patients and carers and may adversely impact chronic care management. Also, it helps to understand the social concerns that the causes that improvises or diminishes the potential values of applications of social media in chronic care management.

It is noteworthy that these barriers and affordances are not permanent, but they are dynamic as the relations between the material agency of social media, and the social agency of the patients and carers can change [8]. In fact these affordances (constraints) that enact through such a relationship can also be a factor in changing the perceptions of users about the affordances of social media and therefore, the nature of users' perception about the affordances and constraints of social media can change over time. This change of perception, however, is yet influenced by users' new understandings of the material aspects of social media and how they can enact in a dynamic relationship with the social aspects chronic care management.

7   Conclusion

The question we aimed to answer in this study was: *How can social media support communities of patients and carers that form around the complex process of chronic care management?* Our investigation revealed that social media can play a supporting role in a number of ways including enabling patients and carers to *build a sense of community*, provide *emotional support* to each other, *empower* one another, and also assist each other to *access, share, and search for the information* they need. We also observed that social media did not always play a supporting role, and could create concerns around their potential harm to patients and carers.

By focusing on its key findings of *emotional support, empowerment,* and *barriers*, this study also highlighted how these three aspects of social media use can influence the process of chronic care management. In explaining these key findings, we adopted an affordance perspective. This approach furnished us with a set of analytical concepts that put stress on inseparability of technological and social aspects of social media. The affordance perspective also allowed us to base our understandings on our participants' perceptions about the potentials of social media, emancipated us from framing and packaging their views within pre-defined concepts and constructs that attempt to establish superiority of either technology or social over the other. Our finding show that social media does not always play supporting roles to chronic care management but they may sometimes act as obstacles and barriers to the management process. These roles, however, are not permanent and fixed but can change as patients and carers learn more about themselves and the capabilities of social media. Our findings suggest that there is a dynamic relation between the contrary roles that social media can play in chronic care management and this is not only attributed to the functionalities of these technologies but to the attributes of patients and their states of health. This sociomaterial characteristic of social media can have implications for the design of these technologies as well as for their applications in healthcare communities.

By focusing on the role of social media in the context of chronic care management, we were able to observe how these technologies are bounded up with human activities in the ways that separating them is not possible. What we learnt from our findings (for example, how empowerment or barriers are perceived) is that the ways patients and carers use of social media can change their perceptions about their conditions, and also influence how they understand and approach the management process. In other words, social media is not seen just as technological artifacts, but as an aspect of the management process that constructs the every experiences of having chronic disease for patients and carers. At the same time, these experiences identify how social media can support or prevent the outcomes of the management process to be achieved.

We believe this study makes two major contributions. First, it expands our analysis and knowledge of the role of social media in supporting healthcare communities in ways that investigating either social media or healthcare communities alone does not. Second, this study provides insights into how social media can assists the future design of possible toolkits aim to help the patients and carers to build their own self-managed communities. For instance, our identification of certain barriers would imply that any self-managed community would have to be prepared to help and support patients to minimize the possible emotional discomforts or the social pressures that may occur by the use of social media. As another instance, considerations have taken into account by the community to make sure that patients felt comfortable with legal issues. We also argue that the findings of this study are transformable to communities within similar social context [50].

Communities are dynamic social entities. So, we believe the findings of this study can be used to conduct further research on how the use of social media can influence the dynamics and attributes of communities (e.g. resilience, sustainability, or adaptability), especially those that exist or form in complex and uncertain environments.

References

1. Adams, S.A.: Revisiting the Online Health Information Reliability Debate in the Wake of "Web 2.0": An Inter-Disciplinary Literature and Website Review. International Journal of Medical Informatics 79(6), 391–400 (2010)
2. Adlassnig, K.: Web-Based Resources for Peer Support – Opportunities and Challenges. In: Medical Informatics in a United and Healthy Europe: Proceedings of MIE 2009, the XXII International Congress of the European Federation for Medical Informatics (2009)
3. Agarwal, R., Gao, G., DesRoches, C., Jha, A.: Research Commentary – The Digital Transformation of Healthcare: Current Status and the Road Ahead. Information Systems Research 21(4), 796–809 (2010)
4. Agichtein, E., Castillo, C., Donato, D., Gionis, A., Mishne, G.: Finding high-quality content in social media. Paper presented at the Proceedings of the 2008 International Conference on Web Search and Data Mining (2008)
5. Ali, S.R., Fahmy, S.: Gatekeeping and Citizen Journalism: The Use of Social Media during the Recent Uprisings in Iran, Egypt, and Libya. Media, War & Conflict 6(1), 55–69 (2013), doi:10.1177/1750635212469906
6. Alwan, A., Armstrong, T., Cowan, M., Riley, L.: Noncommunicable Diseases Country Profiles 2011. World Health Organization, France (2011)
7. Antheunis, M.L., Tates, K., Nieboer, T.E.: Patients' and Health Professionals' Use Of Social Media in Health Care: Motives, Barriers and Expectations. Patient Education and Counseling 92(3), 426–431 (2013)
8. Barad, K.: Posthumanist Performativity: Toward an Understanding of How Matter Comes to Matter. Signs 28(3), 801–831 (2003)
9. Barak, A., Boniel-Nissim, M., Suler, J.: Fostering Empowerment in Online Support Groups. Computers in Human Behavior 24(5), 1867–1883 (2008)
10. Barley, S.: What Can We Learn from the History of Technology? Journal of Engineering and Technology Management 15(4), 237–255 (1998)
11. Bartlett, Y.K., Coulson, N.S.: An Investigation into the Empowerment Effects of Using Online Support Groups and How This Affects Health Professional/Patient Communication. Patient Education and Counseling 83(1), 113–119 (2011)
12. Beisecker, A.E.: Patient Power in Doctor-Patient Communication: What Do We Know? Health Communication 2(2), 105–105 (1990)
13. Berger, P., Luckmann, T.: The Social Construction of Reality: A Treatise in the Sociology of Knowledge. Doubleday, New York (1967)
14. Campisi, P., Maiorana, E., Neri, A.: Privacy Protection in Social Media Networks a Dream That Can Come True? In: Proceedings of the 16th International Conference on Digital Signal Processing (DSP). IEEE (2009)

15. Catherine, H.Y., Parsons, J., Mamdani, M., Lebovic, G., Shah, B.R., Bhattacharyya, O., ... Straus, S.E.: Designing and Evaluating a Web-Based Self-Management Site for Patients with Type 2 Diabetes – Systematic Website Development and Study Protocol. BMC Medical Informatics and Decision Making 12(1), 57 (2012)
16. Chiarella, D.: Using Web 2.0 to Create an Autism Resource. Journal of Consumer Health on the Internet 13(3), 281–286 (2009)
17. Christodoulou, M.: Networking: The New Social Revolution in Health Care. The Lancet Oncology 12(2), 125 (2011)
18. Chung, D.S., Kim, S.: Blogging Activity Among Cancer Patients and Their Companions: Uses, Gratifications, and Predictors of Outcomes. Journal of the American Society for Information Science and Technology 59(2), 297–306 (2008)
19. Correa, T., Hinsley, A.W., De Zuniga, H.G.: Who interacts on the Web?: The intersection of Users' Personality and Social Media Use. Computers in Human Behavior 26(2), 247–253 (2010)
20. Da Cunha, J., Orlikowski, W.: Performing Catharsis: The Use of Online Discussion Forums in Organizational Change. Information and Organization 18(2), 132–156 (2008)
21. Dutta-Bergman, M.: Trusted Online Sources of Health Information: Differences in Demographics, Health Beliefs, and Health-Information Orientation. Journal of Medical Internet Research 5(3), e21 (2003)
22. Eisenhardt, K.M.: Building Theories from Case Study Research. Academy of Management Review 14(4), 532–550 (1989)
23. Ellison, N.B., Steinfield, C., Lampe, C.: The Benefits of Facebook "Friends:" Social Capital and College Students' Use of Online Social Network Sites. Journal of Computer-Mediated Communication 12(4), 1143–1168 (2007)
24. Eysenbach, G.: From Intermediation to Disintermediation and Apomediation: New Models for Consumers to Access and Assess the Credibility of Health Information in the Age of Web 2.0. Studies in Health Technology and Informatics 129(1), 162–166 (2007)
25. Eysenbach, G.: Medicine 2.0: Social Networking, Collaboration, Participation, Apomediation, and Openness. Journal of Medical Internet Research 10(3), e22 (2008)
26. Fichman, R.G., Kohli, R., Krishnan, R.: The Role of Information Systems in Healthcare: Current Research and Future Trends. Information Systems Research 22(3), 419–428 (2011)
27. Flyvbjerg, B.: Case Study. In: Denzin, N.K., Lincoln, Y.S. (eds.) The Sage Handbook of Qualitative Research, 4th edn., pp. 301–316. Sage, Thousand Oaks (2011)
28. Forster, R., Gabe, J.: Voice or Choice? Patient and Public Involvement in the National Health Service in England under New Labour. International Journal of Health Services 38(2), 333–356 (2008)
29. Frost, J.H., Massagli, M.P.: Social Uses Of Personal Health Information within PatientsLikeMe, an Online Patient Community: What Can Happen When Patients Have Access to One Another's Data. Journal of Medical Internet Research 10(3), e15 (2008)
30. Gibson, J.J.: The Ecological Approach to Visual Perception. Houghton Mifflin, Boston (1979)
31. Glaser, B.G.: Theoretical Sensitivity: Advances in the Methodology of Grounded Theory. Sociology Press, Mill Valley (1978)
32. Glaser, B.G., Strauss, A.: The Discovery of Grounded Theory; Strategies for Qualitative Research. Wiedenfeld and Nicholson, London (1967)
33. Goldberg, H.I., Ralston, J.D., Hirsch, I.B., Hoath, J.I., Ahmed, K.I.: Using an Internet CoManagement Module to Improve the Quality of Chronic Disease Care. Joint Commission Journal on Quality and Patient Safety 29(9), 443–451 (2003)

34. Greene, J.A., Choudhry, N.K., Kilabuk, E., Shrank, W.H.: Online Social Networking by Patients with Diabetes: A Qualitative Evaluation of Communication with Facebook. Journal of General Internal Medicine 26(3), 287–292 (2011)

35. Greenhalgh, T.: Patient and Public Involvement in Chronic Illness: Beyond the Expert Patient. BMJ 338, b49 (2009)

36. Hackworth, B., Kunz, M.: Health Care and Social Media: Building Relationships Via Social Networks. Academy of Health Care Management Journal 6(1), 55–68 (2010)

37. Han, W.T., Collie, K., Koopman, C., Azarow, J., Classen, C., Morrow, G.R., ... Spiegel, D.: Breast Cancer and Problems with Medical Interactions: Relationships with Traumatic Stress, Emotional Self-Efficacy, and Social Support. Psycho-Oncology 14(4), 318-330 (2005)

38. Hara, N., Hew, K.F.: Knowledge-Sharing in an Online Community of Health-Care Professionals. Information Technology & People 20(3), 235–261 (2007)

39. Hesse, B.W., Hanna, C., Massett, H.A., Hesse, N.K.: Outside the Box: Will Information Technology Be a Viable Intervention to Improve the Quality of Cancer Care? JNCI Monographs 2010(40), 81–89 (2010)

40. Hutchby, I.: Technologies, Texts and Affordances. Sociology 35(2), 441–456 (2001)

41. Jain, S.H.: Practicing Medicine in the Age of Facebook. New England Journal of Medicine 361(7), 649–651 (2009)

42. Jennings, A., Powell, J., Armstrong, N., Sturt, J., Dale, J.: A Virtual Clinic for Diabetes Self-Management: Pilot Study. Journal of Medical Internet Research 11(1), e10 (2009)

43. Kane, G.C., Fichman, R.G., Gallaugher, J., Glaser, J.: Community relations 2.0. Harvard Business Review 87(11), 45–50 (2009)

44. Keckley, P.H., Hoffmann, M.: Social Networks in Health Care: Communication, Collaboration and Insights. Deloitte Center for Health Solutions, New York (2010)

45. Koch, H., Gonzalez, E., Leidner, D.: Bridging the Work/Social Divide: The Emotional Response to Organizational Social Networking Sites. European Journal of Information Systems 21(6), 699–717 (2012)

46. Korda, H., Itani, Z.: Harnessing Social Media for Health Promotion and Behavior Change. Health Promotion Practice 14(1), 15–23 (2013)

47. Layder, D.: Sociological Practice: Linking Theory and Social Research. Sage (1998)

48. Leonardi, P.: Materiality, Sociomateriality, and Socio-Technical Systems: What Do These Terms Mean? How Are They Related? Do We Need Them? In: Leonardi, P.M., Nardi, B.A., Kallinikos, J. (eds.) Materiality and Organizing: Social Interaction in a Technological World, pp. 25–48. Oxford University Press, Oxford (2012)

49. Li, J.: Improving Chronic Disease Self-Management through Social Networks. Population health management 16(5), 285–287 (2013)

50. Lincoln, Y.S., Guba, E.G.: Naturalistic Inquiry. Sage, Beverly Hills (1985)

51. Lindholm, C., Burstro, M., Diderichsen, F.: Does Chronic Illness Cause Adverse Social and Economic Consequences among Swedes? Scandinavian Journal of Public Health 29, 63–70 (2001)

52. Lorig, K., Ritter, P.L., Plant, K., Laurent, D.D., Kelly, P., Rowe, S.: The South Australia Health Chronic Disease Self-Management Internet Trial. Health Education & Behavior 40(1), 67–77 (2013)

53. Majchrzak, A., Faraj, S., Kane, G.C., Azad, B.: The Contradictory Influence of Social Media Affordances on Online Communal Knowledge Sharing. Journal of Computer-Mediated Communication 19(1), 38–55 (2013)

54. Majchrzak, A., Markus, M.: Technology Affordances and Constraints Theory of Management Information Systems. In: Kessler, E. (ed.) Encyclopedia of Management Theory, pp. 832–836. Sage, Thousand Oaks (2013)
55. Maloney-Krichmar, D., Preece, J.: A Multilevel Analysis of Sociability, Usability, and Community Dynamics in an Online Health Community. ACM Transactions on Computer-Human Interaction 12(2), 201–232 (2005)
56. Marriott, L.K., Nelson, D.A., Allen, S., Calhoun, K., Eldredge, C.E., Kimminau, K.S., ... Varanasi, A.P.: Using Health Information Technology to Engage Communities in Health, Education, and Research. Science Translational Medicine 4(119), 119mr1 (2012)
57. Marshall, L.A., Williams, D.: Health Information: Does Quality Count For The Consumer? How Consumers Evaluate the Quality of Health Information Materials across a Variety of Media. Journal of Librarianship and Information Science 38(3), 141–156 (2006)
58. Merolli, M., Gray, K., Martin-Sanchez, F.: Health Outcomes and Related Effects of Using Social Media in Chronic Disease Management: A Literature Review and Analysis of Affordances. Journal of Biomedical Informatics 46(6), 957–969 (2013)
59. Mo, P.K., Coulson, N.S.: Empowering Processes in Online Support Groups among People Living With HIV/Aids: A Comparative Analysis of 'Lurkers' and 'Posters'. Computers in Human Behavior 26(5), 1183–1193 (2010)
60. Moorhead, S.A., Hazlett, D.E., Harrison, L., Carroll, J.K., Irwin, A., Hoving, C.: A New Dimension of Health Care: Systematic Review of the Uses, Benefits, and Limitations of Social Media for Health Communication. Journal of Medical Internet Research 15(4), e85 (2013)
61. Murray, E., Burns, J., See, T.S., Lai, R., Nazareth, I.: Interactive Health Communication Applications for People with Chronic Disease. Cochrane Database of Systematic Reviews 4, Article CD004274 (2005)
62. Myers, D.M.: Qualitative Research in Information Systems. MIS Quarterly 21(2), 241–242 (1997)
63. Nakayama, T., Takahashi, Y., Shimbo, T., Uchida, C., Miyaki, K., Sakai, M.: Potential Benefits and Harms of a Peer Support Social Network Service on the Internet for People with Depressive Tendencies: Qualitative Content Analysis and Social Network Analysis. Journal of Medical Internet Research 11(3), e29 (2009)
64. Nordfeldt, S., Hanberger, L., Berterö, C.: Patient and Parent Views on a Web 2.0 Diabetes Portal – The Management Tool, the Generator, and the Gatekeeper. Journal of Medical Internet Research 12(2), e17 (2010)
65. O'Connor, D.: Apomediation and the Significance of Online Social Networking. American Journal of Bioethics 9(6-7), 25–27 (2009)
66. O'Connor, D.: Apomediation and Ancillary Care: Researchers' Responsibilities in Health-Related Online Communities. International Journal of Internet Research Ethics 3, 87–103 (2010)
67. O'Keeffe, G.S., Clarke-Pearson, K.: The Impact of Social Media on Children, Adolescents, and Families. Pediatrics 127(4), 800–804 (2011)
68. Orlikowski, W.: CASE Tools as Organizational Changes: Investigating Incremental and Radical Changes in System Development. MIS Quarterly 17(3), 309–340 (1993)
69. Orlikowski, W.: The Sociomateriality of Organisational Life: Considering Technology in Management Research. Cambridge Journal of Economics 34(1), 125–141 (2010)
70. Orlikowski, W., Scott, S.: Sociomateriality: Challenging the Separation of Technology, Work and Organization. Academy of Management Annals 2(1), 433–474 (2008)
71. Pink, B.: 2009–10 Year Book Australia. Australian Bureau of Statistics, Canberra (2011)

72. Pousti, H., Burstein, F.: Barriers of Using Social Media to Support Health-Related Decisions: A Sociomaterial Perspective. In: Phillips-Wren, G., Carlsson, S., Respicio, A., Brezillon, P. (eds.) DSS 2.0 – Supporting Decision Making with New Technologies, pp. 545–556. IOS Press, Amsterdam (2014)

73. Ressler, P.K., Bradshaw, Y.S., Gualtieri, L., Chui, K.K.H.: Communicating the Experience of Chronic Pain and Illness through Blogging. Journal of Medical Internet Research 14(5), e143 (2012)

74. Samoocha, D., Bruinvels, D.J., Elbers, N.A., Anema, J.R., van der Beek, A.J.: Effectiveness of Web-Based Interventions on Patient Empowerment: A Systematic Review and Meta-Analysis. Journal of Medical Internet Research 12(2), e23 (2010)

75. Setoyama, Y., Yamazaki, Y., Namayama, K.: Benefits of Peer Support in Online Japanese Breast Cancer Communities: Differences between Lurkers and Posters. Journal of Medical Internet Research 13(4), e122 (2011)

76. Stellefson, M., Chaney, B., Barry, A.E., Chavarria, E., Tennant, B., Walsh-Childers, K., ... Zagora, J.: Web 2.0 Chronic Disease Self-Management for Older Adults: A Systematic Review. Journal of Medical Internet Research 15(2), e35 (2013)

77. Strauss, A.: Qualitative Analysis for Social Scientists. Cambridge University Press, Cambridge (1987)

78. Thompson, L.A., Black, E., Duff, W.P., Black, N.P., Saliba, H., Dawson, K.: Protected Health Information on Social Networking Sites: Ethical and Legal Considerations. Journal of Medical Internet Research 13(1), e8 (2011)

79. Treem, J., Leonardi, P.: Social Media Use in Organizations: Exploring the Affordances of Visibility, Editability, Persistence, and Association. Communication Yearbook 36, 143–189 (2012)

80. Urquhart, C.: Grounded Theory for Qualitative Research: A Practical Guide. Sage, Thousand Oaks (2012)

81. Urquhart, C., Lehmann, H., Myers, M.: Putting the 'Theory' Back into Grounded Theory: Guidelines for Grounded Theory Studies in Information Systems. Information Systems Journal 20(4), 357–381 (2010)

82. Vaast, E., Walsham, G.: Grounded Theorizing for Electronically Mediated Social Contexts. European Journal of Information Systems 22(1), 9–25 (2013)

83. Van Uden-Kraan, C.F., Drossaert, C.H., Taal, E., Seydel, E.R., van de Laar, M.A.: Participation in Online Patient Support Groups Endorses Patients' Empowerment. Patient Education and Counseling 74(1), 61–69 (2009)

84. Van Uden-Kraan, C.F., Drossaert, C.H., Taal, E., Shaw, B.R., Seydel, E.R., van de Laar, M.A.: Empowering Processes and Outcomes of Participation in Online Support Groups for Patients with Breast Cancer, Arthritis, Or Fibromyalgia. Qualitative Health Research 18(3), 405–417 (2008)

85. Vilhauer, R.P.: Perceived benefits of online support groups for women with metastatic breast cancer. Women & Health 49(5), 381–404 (2009)

86. Walsham, G.: Interpretive Case Studies in IS Research: Nature and Method. European Journal of Information Systems 4(2), 74–81 (1995)

87. Wellman, B., Haase, A.Q., Witte, J., Hampton, K.: Does the Internet Increase, Decrease, or Supplement Social Capital? Social Networks, Participation, and Community Commitment. American Behavioral Scientist 45(3), 436–455 (2001)

88. Wicks, P., Massagli, M., Frost, J., Brownstein, C., Okun, S., Vaughan, T., ... Heywood, J.: Sharing Health Data for Better Outcomes on PatientsLikeMe. Journal of Medical Internet Research 12(2), e19 (2010)

89. Yoo, Y., Alavi, M.: Emergent Leadership in Virtual Teams: What Do Emergent Leaders Do? Information and Organization 14(1), 27–58 (2004)
90. Zammuto, R., Griffith, T., Majchrzak, A., Dougherty, D., Faraj, S.: Information Technology and the Changing Fabric of Organization. Organization Science 18(5), 749–762 (2007)
91. Zhao, S., Grasmuck, S., Martin, J.: Identity Construction on Facebook: Digital Empowerment in Anchored Relationships. Computers in Human Behavior 24(5), 1816–1836 (2008)

ASTERIX and 2.0 Knowledge Management

Exploring the Appropriation of 2.0 KMS via the Myth of the Gaulish Village

Aurélie Dudezert, Pierre Fayard, and Ewan Oiry

Laboratoire CEREGE, Institut d'Administration des Entreprises de Poitiers,
Université de Poitiers, Poitiers, France
{ADudezert,PFayard,EOiry}@iae.univ-poitiers.fr

Abstract. Knowledge Management Systems (KMS) in companies have profoundly changed in recent years. They have become KMS 2.0 that aim to transform the firm and are driven by a new relationship to knowledge in line with 2.0 organisations. These 2.0 KMS have implemented modes of organisation that disrupt those that previously guided firms' performance. This can sometimes lead to paradoxical organizational dysfunctions as witnessed by the difficulties faced by some traditionally hierarchical French companies. Through a case study of *Constructor* and a theoretical background on IS appropriation in organizations and myths in management, we show how the Asterix myth contributes to understanding how 2.0. KMS are appropriated in such companies. We find evidence of similarities regarding knowledge and Knowledge Management between the Asterix' myth and the behaviours and practices concerning knowledge management within *Constructor*. As a result, the Asterix' myth may be a relevant perspective for understanding the obstacles, advantages and appropriations of 2.0. KMS within French organizations.

Keywords: knowledge management, knowledge management systems, organization 2.0, appropriation, myths.

1 Introduction

Approaches to Knowledge Management within firms have evolved considerably over the past few years. From practices focused on setting up Knowledge Management Systems (KMS) as "types of information systems devoted to the management of organisational knowledge" [1, p. 114], (i.e., IS for the support and improvement of the process of creating, stocking, transferring and using/exploiting knowledge), they have become KM 2.0 processes, seeking an overall transformation of the firm and affirming a new relationship to knowledge [2, 3].

This translates into a change in the nature of KMS. They appear today less as information systems enabling knowledge to be managed as a resource or exploited as a "traditional" asset, and more as platforms for interactions involving knowledge (social networks) at the service of a total mutation of the organisation towards a knowledge market: KMS 2.0 [4]. These processes also translate into a profound demand for

B. Doolin et al. (Eds.): IS&O 2014, IFIP AICT 446, pp. 186–206, 2014.

transforming the organisation which is now supposed to correspond to a 2.0 model inspired by the culture and literature of the IT world at the origin of an "organizing vision" [5]. This perspective relies on four characteristics: (1) an individual view of knowledge where employees are seen as entrepreneurs of their own knowledge. (2); a group project defined according to ad hoc requirements, structured as an organic network that is subject to constant reconfiguration (3); new forms of work supervision based on actors' collaboration and self-organisation and (4) group action no longer regulated by hierarchical supervision but by social control [4, 6-8].

By setting up the processes of knowledge management known as 2.0, firms were obliged to transform themselves according to modes of organisation that sometimes disrupted those that had, until then, constituted the basis of their performance. As mentioned in works on the appropriation of IS in organisations [9; 10], introducing IS naturally resulted in questioning and transforming modes of collective action; however it also gave rise to questioning the very meaning of that action (structuring meaning). When introducing KMS 2.0, this questioning may run particularly deep, because KMS 2.0 means not only recreating sense through collective action but also, at times, changing the way the firm conceives of organisational knowledge and its management. When KM 2.0 processes are set up in organisations that do not possess this relationship to knowledge, such firms may suffer many paradoxes in their work practices [11, 12].

Unless firms are aware of these traps and if they do not make necessary and suitable transformations, KM 2.0 may lead to failure. This is the case of certain French companies that have been focused on industry for many years and whose modes of organisation are very hierarchical. Even if these firms have recently become strongly international, they exist within a specific historical and cultural context that mixes national objectives for development, State support and entrepreneurship. These industrial firms remain focused on mastering risk and optimising production; their conception of organisational knowledge is mainly collective, embodied in well-established routines and standards. However, for a number of them, entering the knowledge economy led them towards more service-focused activities. They were thus highly interested by modes of knowledge management that would make them more creative and innovative. Nevertheless, we have to observe the lack of any "handbook" to guide the essential organisational changes for these companies suspended between past and future. These firms realised that their past modes of organisation were unseaworthy in the deep global waters of the current economic scenario – a scenario that is highly competitive, highly uncertain and severed from past traditions. Our paper adopts their viewpoint and proposes the myth of Asterix as a means to understanding the emerging tensions in these companies as they engage in KM 2.0.

Since 1961 and the publication of the first book of the adventures of Asterix and Obelix, the Asterix myth has often been used to understand and decode certain behaviours and traits characteristic of the French, including their relationship to themselves and others. The myth has been summoned in the analysis of the French political character [13] and of leadership [14]; however, until now it has been little cited in the domain of management. Is this because Asterix was not judged "serious" enough for that – especially since the strip cartoon is not exactly academic? We might also see the postulate of a managerial imperative where reason exists precisely to avoid actors being imprisoned by myths [15]. In fact, the works of [16] on myths and neo-institutionalist theory [17] do illustrate that the strength of such schemas of thought sometimes undermines actors' performance. However, myths are part of our lives and also contribute to the creation of meaning. As Burkert mentions:

> Adults and children like them and, in a sense, need them. For these stories, by seeking to give things meaning, speak of a human world that is impossible to analyse as one could do for a mere collection of electronic components. [18, p. 9]

Myths contribute to understanding an environment that does not end at the company door. Sharing a myth can certainly be a prison for thought, but it may also be cathartic [19], serving as an intermediary translator for creating meaning in a process of appropriating an innovation or a transformation [20]; a shared myth may enable actors project their emotions, understand each other and share tacit but commonly held sensations, references and landmarks. How can we avoid seeing Asterix's village as a symbol of the "French cultural exception", besieged by the invading powers in the camps of Delierium, Laudanum, Compendium and Aquarium? After all, spontaneous opposition to any dominant view imposed without taking account of "French" specific characteristics is an integral part of the French cultural heritage. It matters not whether this imposition be from Rome (Julius Caesar), the House of Austria, Perfidious Albion or, closer to our times, North America. Whether mirror or reality, this myth structures French schemas of thought. The work of Goscinny and Uderzo is an expression of this "Frenchness" [21] inhabited by the Gauls, and it reflects constants of French geopolitics and strategic thinking [22].

In this phase of deep change, using a powerful myth like Asterix can help understand the emerging tensions in French firms when they implement KMS 2.0. This article proposes to study how far this myth constitutes a tool for exploring the appropriation of KMS 2.0 in these firms today.

This contribution is in five parts. The first discusses the theoretical bases of research and the problem of appropriating KMS 2.0 inside firms. The second develops how the Myth of the Asterix Village can be a tool for exploring the appropriation of KMS 2.0 in certain firms. The third part presents the research methodology based on a case study at Constructor. The fourth part analyses this case in the light of the Asterix Myth and the final part presents the contributions and implications of the research.

2   Theoretical Bases: Knowledge Management, KMS 2.0 and Its Appropriation

If for some, knowledge is value added information [23, 24], for others, it is an asset of the firm [25], an individual cognitive process [26], know-how, an individual's particular experience and way of doing things that is hard to render explicit [27] or even a working practice developed by an individual in a given position [28-30]. This resource that is crucial for the firm has multiple dimensions and therefore requires specific processes to encourage its development, exploitation and value. Knowledge management thus relates to a dynamic, continuous set of distinct but interdependent processes of creating, stocking, transferring and applying knowledge [1]. It is supported by information technologies whose objective is to (1) codify and share best practices, (2) map out internal expertise and (3) create networks of knowledge to facilitate knowledge exchange among individuals [1]. In the 1990's, KM primarily focused on the technologies enabling knowledge to be stocked in the form of structured documents (Knowledge bases). In the last few years, Knowledge Management practices have evolved in organizations. Due to the introduction of Web 2.0 technologies, new usages of information and knowledge sharing have emerged. A new generation of employees (Generation Y or Milennials) has new habits at work. They use everyday Web 2.0 technologies (Blogs, Wikis, RSSi, Folksonomy, social networking platforms, Mashups, Podcasting, etc.) in the private arena, and therefore, consider that such technologies for e-collaboration and self-organizing are the best means/methods to work. Thus, the concept of KM has been impacted and has evolved towards more human interactions management and interpersonal networking, in addition to traditional information and knowledge processing. Organizations are currently developing a new type of KM which is social-based using Web 2.0 technologies and called KM 2.0 [31]. Thus KMS evolved towards more collaborative technologies. Such deployment of KMS 2.0 implies that actors appropriate specific collective modes of action as well as a particular relationship to knowledge. The KM 2.0 perspective considers the firm as a knowledge market that is based on four characteristics: (1) an individual view of the firm where employees figured as entrepreneurs of their knowledge, in other words, individuals who had the capacity to create knowledge for their own account and whose main objective was to develop this knowledge (understood as an asset they should make the most of). (2) A collective project defined according to *ad hoc* requirements and structured as a constantly reconfigured network. (3) New forms of work supervision based on actors' self-organisation and collaboration. (4) Collective action no longer regulated by hierarchical supervision but by social control [6-8, 32-35].

KMS 2.0 are thus inspired by a vision of knowledge and management that is above all centred on individuals: the firm becomes a platform for relationships among knowing individuals. Collective or routine knowledge [36], is no longer considered important in KMSs focused on encouraging new forms of organisation that free knowledge creation. The prevailing view is then that the optimal organisation of work should not be strictly planned, organised and systematised from above, but self-organised by individuals according to requirements and their evolution. In this configuration, the only "stable structure" is the firm's social network, based on informal relationships and social exchange. This mode of organisation would be more efficient for generating knowledge contributing to competitive advantages for the firm. The philosophy of these KMSs holds that for efficient knowledge creation, collective action should no more be regulated by hierarchical supervision but only by social control [4].

Now, this relationship to knowledge inspired by KM 2.0 does not necessarily make sense in all firms whose specific history, job and values may have led them to construct a different relationship to knowledge. Like all approaches for deploying Information Systems, setting up Knowledge Management Systems in organisations results in real organisational transformations requiring meaning to be reconstructed. Making use of the new technology (appropriation) arises from sense making resulting from a complex social construction whose outcome is often impossible to define a priori

[37-39]. In studies more specifically focused on the introduction of KMS [10, 40], holds that this sensemaking [41] is essential to appropriating a KMS. This author underlines that when a KMS is introduced, the different practices in and around the technology reproduce or reinforce the firm's social structures. Those structures that hold meaning are particularly modified by the arrival of a new technology. The recent work of [12, 42, 43] underline the extent to which, when a KMS 2.0 is introduced into an organisation, collective sense making around the technology and its associated new modes of action, is crucial for successful implementation. For Fayard [22], this collective sense making around KMS implementation in firms is partly influenced by country's national myths that structure employees' relationship to knowledge. Thus in order that KMS 2.0 be appropriated in an organisation, it is relevant to explore the country's national myths that structure employees relationship to knowledge in an firm and identify the potential paradoxes/tensions between this relationship and that implied by 2.0 KMS.

3   Using the Myth of the Gaullish Village to Explore the Appropriation of KMS 2.0

Like all human communities, organisations convey imaginary stories and symbolic forms steeped in references to myths [44]. Neo-institutionalist approaches, especially in the works of [17] underline that organisations are the reflection of myths rationalised by their environment. Institutional rules function as myths which organisations incorporate, gaining legitimacy, resources and stability. Certain products, services, techniques and policies are institutionalised to the point of becoming tacit rules that speak for themselves spontaneously and are never questioned nor made explicit. These rules function like powerful myths that are omnipresent in the environment, and their integration into the organisation in turn strengthens the organisation's legitimacy.

3.1   Approaches to the Myth in Management

To understand how this works, a first approach is to deconstruct the myth as far as this is understood as a source of alienation for the individual and non-performance for the firm. Adopting these institutionalised objects is seen as potentially harmful to the criteria of efficiency and effectiveness. This approach joins the viewpoint of R. Barthes in *Mythologies* [16]. In this work, the author describes himself as a "*mythologist*" whose role is to decode myths in order to free individuals from the alienation they create. For Barthes, myths are driving forces. The analysis of "*petit bourgeois*" myths aims to make individuals aware of those myths' effects on actor-consumer behaviours. This is the perspective developed by March [15] in his works on management sciences that decode the great myths of management in order to encourage innovation (Rationality, the Hierarchy, the Leader and Historical Efficiency). Along this line, Grimand [45] deconstructs organisational myths in Knowledge Management within organisations. He presents the myths and discourse constructed to diffuse Knowledge Management practices within firms. In fact, current discourse about 2.0 KMS can be seen as institutionalising these practices. This discourse develops an *organising view* (OV) around 2.0 KMS that interprets, legitimises and mobilises the actors of an organisation around the information System (IS) [5].

Myths can thus imprison the organisation in a logic that is not one of efficiency but of legitimacy. However, myths can also have virtues. When Jean-Pierre Vernant wrote *L'univers, les dieux, les hommes. Récits grecs des origins (The Universe, the Gods and Men. Greek Creation Myths)* in 1999 [46] he, like Barthes, also described himself as a mythologist, but one whose role was not to deconstruct, but rather to transmit ideas over time. He saw the need for this in a context when things change rapidly and references are lost. Transmitting ancient Greek myths was for him a way of making sense and reminding people of what has linked Western peoples for millennia. Burkert says the same thing when he writes, that in his opinion,

> A myth is an "applied fairy tale": not necessarily about origins, but a narrative that offers a meaning to our lives in a given society and an explanation of the world we live in. [18, p. 6]

Myths allow us to reconcile contradictions and are necessary to create meaning, solidarity and certainty [47]. According to Bowles [48], in an environment where Church and Religion do not play a structuring role anymore, myths have developped in work organization and are required to allow people to participate more fully in their work lives and social lives generally. In IT management, myths, symbolisms and cultural assumptions are thus naturally implicated [49]. Especially in IS Development, Hirschheim and Newman demonstrate that they offers simplifications, and allow actors to better cope with their world:

> By patterning behavior and responses to others' behavior, symbolism reduces a messy, complicated world to a simplier one. It also facilitates cohesion, permitting individuals to become accepted members of a group. [50, p. 57]

In Knowledge Management practices and KMS appropriation, symbolisms, myths and metaphors play also a determinant role [51-53]. Country's national myths play in particular a determinant role in KMS appropriation in organizations. In a research work on KM practices and KMS in Asia, Fayard shows that the Samouraï's myth structure employees' relationship to knowledge and KMS appropriation in Japan [22]. Chinese employees are for themselves quite influenced by the Mandarin's myth. In this research, Fayard suggests that the Asterix's myth may also influence the relationship to knowledge in French company and thus impact KMS implementation. This property of the myth of Asterix seems quite relevant for exploring the appropriation of KMS in French companys inclined to "*ethnocentrism*" [54].

3.2   ASTERIX and the Gaulish Village: A Myth for Exploring the Appropriation of 2.0 KMS

Asterix was born in 1959 by pure chance. The businessman Georges Dargaud asked René Goscinny and Albert Uderzo to create a cartoon for childrens' magazine entitled "*Pilote*". The authors created two emblematic key characters Asterix and Obelix; the series quickly became successful. Readers were easily won over because the series corresponded to the aspirations of post-war France. By embodying the "David and

Goliath" ideal of the weak versus the strong, resistance against imperialism (the Roman Empire), totalitarianism (the Goths and the Normans) and the defence of individual freedom against any form of uniformisation and oppression, Asterix contributed to a new French myth: France would be no longer sovereign of its overseas empire, but an independent non-aligned nation standing for anti-colonialism and anti- imperialism, a force between the two cold-war blocs [21, 55].

Based on comedy and satire, the series relies on a stereotype of a national mentality that is less important for its basis in reality than for its effect on the social integration of readers [55]. The "Frenchness" evoked by Rouvière highlights the image of a Franco-Gallic population, that is jovial, quick to object and easy to provoke, that expresses its taste for conviviality through good food and love. The success of Asterix over the years show that Asterix remains a myth that is a powerful creator of meaning in France. So much so, that for [22] it partially reflects French strategic thought and may lie behind the meaning of collective action, the relationship to knowledge and the type of Knowledge Management Systems set up in firms whose background is historically and culturally French. This is why it can be used as a framework of analysis for exploring the appropriation of KMS in companies.

Knowledge and Knowledge Management in the Gaullish Village. Our analysis of Knowledge and KM draws extensively on Rouvière's in-depth studies about the Gaullish Village.

Firstly this is a world that is anti-elitist[1]. In Asterix, nothing separates the elite of those with superpowers from the rest of the tribe. *Asterix* and *Obelix* are not heroes, but *"a couple of villagers"*[2] who can't do anything without each other. *Asterix* is certainly intelligent, but not strong. *Obelix* is strong, but not intelligent. As for the village chief, *Vitalstatistix*, he is no hero either: although he has the attributes of a true leader, the villagers treat him as one of them. *Cacofonix*, the bard who claims an elitism related to his art, is regularly gagged for making the distinction between "highbrow culture" and the festive, noisy and popular culture of his compatriots, the Gauls! As for *Getafix* the Druid, if his wisdom and his magic potion seem mysterious, his vast knowledge and magic powers do not make him a character separate from the rest of the villagers. He is not infallible and his tendency to self satisfaction, fanned by his inflated ego is rapidly called into question[3].

Thus in this village, each person's specific knowledge is valued. The villagers respect others' knowledge, but refuse to allow knowledge to become a basis for the superiority of one member of the community over another. As soon as any of the characters take themselves too seriously, they are immediately ridiculed and put in their place.

In the Gaullish village, community life is built on the basis of common values: convivial and good-natured equality. Individual knowledge is valued, but only in the context of shared conditions. In the village, conviviality and the respect of the community create knowledge and valued group routines such as banquets, quarrels, making-up, attacks by Romans and the anniversary of the Battle of Gergovia[4].

---

[1] Which is quite surprising, given that France is a country marked by its world of elites.
[2] See frontespiece of each album.
[3] See *Asterix and the Big Fight* or *The Mansions of the Gods*.
[4] See *Asterix in Corsica*.

This knowledge is developed around a shared common project ("ba" [56]) which is long term and structured by profound values. The squabbles are ever present, but everyone gets together to defend the common values of equality and respect of freedom from oppression for individuals and the group. These values and shared meaning uphold the whole Village throughout the series of volumes, and this despite any changes in the outside environment. The collective is supported by the community structure; there is a strong distinction between those who are both physically and culturally part of this community and....the others, all the others, who are not part of the Gaullish Village group. The fence that protects the village's life space is significant from this point of view for raises a distinction between the Village community and the rest of the world. Thus, the arrival of outsiders such as *Geriatrix* and his wife in *Asterix and Cesar's Gift* or *Justforkix* in *Asterix and the Normans* is not immediately seen as positive. The community needs time to accept other lifestyles.

Beyond this, the Village refuses to accept any project that is not its own idea. This does not mean that it is hermetically sealed: it does not hesitate to share its values and competences with other peoples outside Gaul who appear to suffer from absolutist[5] or totalitarian[6] oppression. Given time, the village welcomes members outside the community and respects their integrity. In *Asterix in Corsica*, all those who arrive in the Village from outside, or whom members of the village community have met, are warmly welcomed to celebrate the anniversary of the battle of Gergovia. Even Caesar and the Romans are not rejected as individuals. As [55], the Village is not against Caesar in order to eliminate him and does not propose itself as the liberator of Gaul; for the Village, resistance is simply a matter of honour. It is a matter of infuriating Caesar by preventing him from claiming to have conquered the whole of Gaul! History is on the march, and the Gaulish resistance is not trying to halt the general process of modernity: even the villagers know it is inevitable. However, they want to have time to adapt so that this modernity can be accepted on their own terms and reconciled with their profound values of equality and the respect of freedom.

The third structural feature in this world is the leadership of collective action by a democratically elected hierarchy. In the Gauls' Village, not everything relies on individual decisions; this does not mean that people do exactly as they please, but that everyone is respected. In particular, the democratically elected[7] Chief (*Vitalstatistix*); even if he is sometimes ridiculed, he is accepted as the leader of group action. Whenever there is a problem, a meeting takes place in his hut to decide what the group should do. The leader listens to the different protagonists, makes comments based on his own knowledge of the situation, puts things into perspective taking account of the Village values and way of life, then decides and gives the orders for action. *Vitalstatistix* shows and possesses all the attributes and qualities of a true leader, he knows about the outside political situation, takes responsibility in times of crisis and acts in the collective interest[8]. He possesses the symbols of authority, responsibility and unity in his legendary shield and the armchair/throne in his house. In return, the community cannot imagine life without him and

---

[5] See *Asterix in Switzerland, Asterix in Britain, Asterix in Spain.*
[6] See *Asterix and the Normans, Asterix and the Goths, Asterix and the Picts, Asterix and the Magic Carpet.*
[7] See *Asterix and the Big Fight.*
[8] See especially *Asterix and the Big Fight.*

when he goes on a health cure for his liver[9], *Asterix* and *Obelix* go with him to make sure he returns safe and sound.

In fact, in the Gaullish Village, collective action is never regulated by an autonomous individual or on a self-organised basis; it relies on democratically established rules that are respected by all. The Gaullish Village is not a happy go lucky free for all where there are no rules. The Villager-citizens all respect established customs and habits. This is particularly evident in *Asterix and the Big Fight. Vitalstatistix* submits to the rules of electing a leader even if this is not to the Village's advantage. In contrast to this the Gauls reject out of hand ideas that seem absurd and that have not been established democratically. Thus in *Asterix the Legionary*, to save *Tragicomix*, *Panacea*'s fiancé, *Asterix* and *Obelix* enlist in the Roman army. At first, wishing to remain inconspicuous, they line up to enlist like everyone else, then accept the jobs they are given. However, when this absurd way of doing things recurs, they spontaneously make use of the French speciality known as *"system D[10]"*. This means getting round any system of rules, or bending them to suit oneself.

As the myth of Asterix unfolds, we notice that certain principles are commonly considered basic to collective action: the respect of each individual and his/her qualities, respecting individual and collective freedom from oppression, anti-elitism, conviviality and neighbourliness, the leader's legitimacy combined with the rejection of absolutism, reliance on common sense and the importance of experience.

These principles of the Asterix myth offer a way to analyse the relationship to knowledge and knowledge management conveyed by KM2.0 practices in certain French firms.

The Gaulish Village and KM 2.0. With regard to the relationship to knowledge, in KM 2.0 approaches, what counts is less the respect of individual differences and actors' having an equal capacity to create knowledge, than individuals being able to create knowledge themselves. It appears that firms implementing KM 2.0 rarely emphasise the collective aspect of this implementation. Rather than being seen as a group project, KM 2.0 is usually set in motion as requirements come up – this is unlike the collective project of the Gaullish Village, which is long-term and based on deep values firmly grounded in custom. Then, KM 2.0 processes are based on the idea that efficiency supposes the absence of hierarchical supervision (the boss/chief). Instead of this, the "collaborative" process is led by a "facilitator" The functions of exercising authority, encouraging unity and taking responsibility are never invested permanently in one individual. Finally, the rules of social life conveyed by KMS 2.0, (inspired by the 2.0 organisation), are not pre-defined and democratically discussed, but come from social control that may result in oppression and the denial of individual freedoms. The rules are not constructed democratically. They are constructed around certain groups of actors who share a similar viewpoint. These rules are not explicitly expressed and are therefore not discussed in the whole group. They are rather informal, contract or market type arrangements based on the exchange of gifts

---

[9] See *Asterix and the Chieftan's Shield.*

[10] The "D" in this French expression comes from the word "Débrouille" ("système Débrouille" has become "système D"). This expresson means getting round any system of rules, or bending them to suit oneself.

and counter gifts (reciprocity/mutual gifts). We can see here that it is difficult to reconcile the relationship to knowledge and its management implied by a 2.0 KMS and the relationship to knowledge and its management conveyed by the Asterix myth when both are seen as important myths that influence the sense of collective action.

Table 1. Comparison of the relationship to knowledge and knowledge management in KM 2.0 processes and in the Asterix myth

	2.0 KM	ASTERIX MYTH
Knowledge	Knowledge issues Knowledge Entrepreneur: An individual capable of creating knowledge for his/her own good	Village issues and group routines: Individuals' own knowledge, respect of their specific characteristics and all considered equal (anti elitist) but also collective knowledge that structures the group.
Collective project	Defined according to ad hoc requirements Structured in a network	Upheld by the whole village over the long term, based on deep values. Structured around the community but not hermetically sealed off.
Leadership of collective action	Actors organise themselves collaboratively The manager is the "leader" of the collaboration	Leadership through a democratically elected chief who assumes responsibility authority and group unity.
Regulation of collective action	Social control: contractual arrangements among actors	Democracy: Explicit rules democratically decided with conviviality and neighbourliness Otherwise: "System D" (getting round/bending the rules to suit ones own purpose)

4   Research Methodology

As an illustration of how looking at the myth of the Gaullish Village of Asterix can help to analyse how KMS 2.0 are appropriated in firms with a French background and culture, we shall use a case study of the firm *Constructor*. Choosing a case study is justified by the exploratory nature of our research that aims to examine a contemporary phenomenon in its real context [57]. Focusing on a particular case enables us to make an in-depth analysis of the appropriation of KMS. This research aims to understand and translate the organisational reality as experienced by the actors.

4.1   *Constructor* and Knowledge Management

This industrial group *Constructor* was founded in 1952 and has been developed in a French historical and cultural context. In 1952, the founder took the opportunity offered by the country's post-war reconstruction, to found his company, specialised in the building industry in the Paris region. In 1955, he started to build social housing projects as part of the largely State funded programme to counter the housing shortage. In 1959, the firm developed industrial prefabrication while still enjoying public funding. In 1970, the company was floated on the stock market. In the following years, it diversified and developed new activities.

Constructor is now the French and European market leader of the construction industry and is present on every continent. The group employs over 54 000 collaborators worldwide over half of whom are outside France. Although originally a construction company, today *Constructor's* business model also extends to services such as communications, logistics etc.

Since 2005, the IS Department of *Constructor* had set up knowledge sharing tools and processes for the Group's collaborators. Several technologies were deployed amongst which a directory in 2006, a search engine in 2007 and a collaborative work platform between 2008 and 2012. *Constructor* doubled its number of collaborators between 2005 and 2013 by taking a deliberate step towards internationalisation. In May 2011, the head of Knowledge Management for the Group suggested exploring the idea of deploying a social networking tool internally in order to foster ties and improve knowledge sharing (KMS 2.0). In 2013 the knowledge sharing department changed. All its activities were combined into one skills centre. The KM tools were deployed, but little used by collaborators. In order to better meet needs and define new developments, *Constructor* decided to carry out an assessment of the Group's KM practices.

4.2   Collection and Analysis of Data

This research was undertaken in two phases. The first from May to October 2011; the second in January 2013. We used different methods of data collection (interviews, meetings, observations etc.). According to Eisenhardt [58], this variety in data collection methods is considered a necessary triangulation for the consolidation of research results [59].

The programme began in May 2011. It aimed at understanding how Group members perceived the idea of deploying a company social network. Data was collected through semi-directive face-to-face or telephone interviews. We questioned 26 participants for an average of about an hour each. The sample was made up of collaborators mostly working at the company's headquarter. The majority of those we met were familiar with IT, for example laptops, smartphones, VPN access, web based administration tools etc. Participants were distinguished by their type of expertise, level of responsibility and age group.

After informal exchanges during 2012, the project continued in 2013 in order to obtain a more precise idea of the needs and obstacles linked to adopting the 2.0 KMS. A second data collection phase took place in January 2013. This was led by the company's head of KM and concerned 17 participants. This panel consisted of directors and assistant directors, department heads, technical experts, engineers, site foremen and administrative assistants. All were executives from different hierarchical levels. The interviews lasted an average of one hour face-to-face or by phone and were transcribed in writing. Observation data were also collected.

We then coded these data using open coding [60]. Three researchers carried out a content analysis to explore the appropriation of the KMS in the organisation. The list of themes was enlarged as the coding process advanced. Two significant themes then emerged from the discourse:

- The expression of and claim to having a specific culture concerning work practices and knowledge.
- The expression of numerous paradoxes/tensions concerning the place and role of the KMS in work practices.

This analysis was given to *Constructor*. In a second phase and in order to better understand the tensions and paradoxes expressed, three researchers undertook a second coding of the data. This was based on the comparison between knowledge management 2.0 and the Asterix Myth presented above. Making use of this myth seems justified by the first analysis that showed the claim to a specific culture, but also because *Constructor* is a company strongly rooted in a French cultural and historical background.

5   Analysis of Tensions Emerging during the Appropriation of the KMS 2.0 at *Constructor* via the Myth of the Village of Asterix

5.1   Knowledge in the *Constructor* "Village"

The typical *Constructor* collaborator is described as a highly autonomous individual who finds meaning through maintaining social exchanges. These individuals are entrepreneurs who are proud of their company's achievements, always seeking success and pushing themselves ever further. As one participant put it, "On the sites, we redesign the world". A typical *Constructor* collaborator considers that "Your value is largely related to what you know and the information you have". *Constructor* collaborators also tend to avoid being explicit about any problems they encounter; they are not very open to sharing knowledge about problems: "There is a certain pride in solving problems oneself" as one interviewee described it. This may lead some to brag about individual knowledge and this is not always looked upon favourably: "In traditional companies like this one, results and action are always combined with a lot of noise and movement".

In fact at *Constructor* the knowledge described as being valuable and in need of management, is above all collective, technical and procedural (codified technical documents describing all the job processes, financial documents, job descriptions etc.). Consequently, knowledge management is seen by company actors as managing information in order to optimise information search, standardise work processes and capitalise on experience. This formalisation and sharing is largely carried out using tools that are deployed in the different entities of the Group: "The site documents are on an internal network...."; "In terms of formalisation of procedures, Constructor is one step ahead"; "We have a data base.... all the documents are there".

The relationship to knowledge is thus very close to that found in the Asterix Village myth. Actors are left to be largely autonomous in order to develop expertise that is recognised, but that must not lead making any individual stand out. The knowledge that is valued is built up gradually and is at the service of the *Consctructor* project, a project proudly upheld by these actors. It should be mentioned that outside contributions are not mentioned. Knowledge is conceived in the ring-fenced environment of the *"Constructor Village"*.

5.2   Project, Conviviality, Stockade: The Village Boundaries

Constructor employees have a culture of "sound workmanship". The constructions are a success story shared by all company actors.

The organisation emphasises the conviviality and human dimension of the job: "It's the characteristic of jobs in construction where the human element and team work are very important"; "I think you must not forget the heart of our job where relationships are very important....in construction, human contact is essential. We need to discuss things...." Collaborators value interactions and informal exchanges about (non virtual) social networks. For some of them, informal discussion is "a lot better" than the technology available: "In the company, when you're talking about knowledge sharing, human contact is still the most important thing"; "we prefer to spend time with someone who explains something than be all alone in front of a screen" or "over a meal rather than with one of those long sagas written up and posted on Vega". One of the symbols of the importance of knowledge transmission through informal exchange, human relationships and shared work practices is a company "guild" created by *Constructor's* founder. It is an organisation internal to the Group whose objective is to encourage loyalty and reward the best workers. In 2010 the organisation had 1 105 members belonging to 17 Orders.

There is an absence of knowledge sharing practices among different entities: "Knowledge sharing is not at all in the company's mentality. There are still a lot of barriers between the different entities....information remains within each entity". Likewise, knowledge-sharing experiments between departments enabling transversal collaboration within the company are little used.

The result is that the collaborators we questioned do not spontaneously feel the need for a KMS 2.0 of the social network type, because they consider that they already have one that they know how to work. These networks are built up partly through each individual's professional experience, but also because the individuals concerned come from the same higher education establishment: "At *Constructor*, I know my colleagues well, but I also know friends of friends who work at *Constructor* and the alumni network of my university". This "old boy network" culture is maintained by the firm in as much as the company creates specific training processes whose objective is to group young graduates from *Grandes Ecoles* who have the potential to do well in the group (High Potentials). The fact that these graduates attend these courses together helps to maintain this social network.

In this context, the deployment of the 2.0 KMS is described as a necessary process but one that is nevertheless resisted. It is necessary in order to meet the needs of future collaborators: "Something has to be done on the level of intra company communication. Young people are more and more capable of having on-line exchanges and if 10 years from now everything is the way it is now, *Constructor* will no longer be an attractive company for recruits". According to the interviews, KMS have two other uses: getting information from the ground to reach those in charge of overall coordination, and avoiding "reinventing the wheel". Collaborators would like *Constructor* to go further technically speaking. They do not understand that the tools available are not 2.0, because they are used to using these tools outside the company: "We hear about Web 2.0 everywhere but in our company. It's a pity". Collaborators explain the "Problem of attractiveness" of KMS because these systems are technically inefficient compared with the tools they use outside in their private life: "What we need is a search engine a bit like Google, something efficient".

Here we find similarities with the Village of Asterix: a project upheld by the community for many years unites actors around strongly shared values such as teamwork and good workmanship. We also observe that this common viewpoint may lead to the erection of barriers between departments, and groups ("old boy" networks maintained by the organisation, strong identity of belonging to various entities within the organisation etc.) or even erecting stockades and having a knee-jerk rejection of what comes from outside (such as the social network). However, as in the Asterix Village, it is not so much a matter of fighting against modernity, (seen as inevitable given changes in the external environment), as finding a way to implement these modern processes while reconciling them with the *Constructor* Group values and way of functioning. Interviewees made remarks implying this. However, there is one notable difference with the Asterix Village: collaborators of *Constructor* do not mention their capacity to contribute knowledge from outside the company and/or to benefit from such an exchange. The climate evokes something more akin to wishing to remain safely behind the Village stockade and a fear that the outside world will disrupt the community inside.

5.3   Hierarchy and Explicit Rules – Recognised and Accepted to Lead and Regulate Collective Action

Constructor is a reassuring organisation described as having a highly structured hierarchy where managerial responsibilities are recognised and accepted. According to those interviewed, collaborators' level of acceptance of the KMS depends on how far Top Management encourages them to use the tool. As one interviewee put it: "If collaboration is not explicitly or officially recognised, people find it hard to take the time to get involved".

In *Constructor*, information flow processes are all highly formalised. In order to be relevant for collaborators, information has to be traceable and shared formally. The principal is "controlled sharing" of "worthwhile" information. This formalism of exchanges is considered to be a specific characteristic of the *Constructor* Group.

As a result, everyone interviewed mentioned the adverse effects of the KMS 2.0, evoking danger if the Group's informal functioning became visible: "If everyone could see everything, some entities or teams would try to make themselves look better than they really are to win prestige or even to get bonuses". This refers to the positions taken by some social groups towards others. With this type of KMS, the rule is no longer explicit and formalised, but depends on mutual adjustment and negotiation between groups of actors. The risk of disseminating information or losing control of it are evoked as factors that might destabilise the organisation, and this is also mentioned with regard to cases experienced on outside social networks. Thus one collaborator asked the following: "What would happen if a collaborator is fired and can transmit messages that are negative for the organisation on an information system like a social network? The same thing goes for salary reductions". Another expresses fears of "Information leaks to the competition". Finally, almost all of those interviewed emphasised the risk of confusion between private and professional life: "The idea of using a social networking tool is interesting and can be useful, but I have no clear view of how we can draw the line between what is private and what is work related." Another collaborator adds: "If you want to implement such a tool into a working milieu, there has to be a real distinction between private and professional life."

The people we met call for the definition of "procedures" and "directives" in order to guide and standardise knowledge sharing practices. Some think that knowledge sharing practices should be written within a formal framework like other existing work procedures. The collaborators of *Constructor* feel that they are drowning in information and lost when faced with the multiple KMS currently available: "There's too much information for us to have time to read it"; "Too much information kills information." Today, the high number of sources of data and overload are an obstacle to integrating knowledge as well as to seeking and sharing it: "The problem is that once all these tools become available, they ask collaborators to work more and more." However, these KMS are also described as "Potential gold mines".

Collaborators are prepared to use KMS, but they also want to continue working in the current mode. The KMS has to be integrated into existing practices without threatening these: "I'm in favour of this type of tool because they mean you are proactive. However, the tool's implementation can only be successful if it is focused on work, on professional needs and if it is easy to use with plenty of guidance". Appropriating this tool requires specific training so that the technologies can be effectively integrated into work practices. Collaborators count on training sessions: "There is a lack of publicity and communication so that people know about these tools. There is also a lack of training so that problems can be communicated. Sometimes there's nobody available to train people about new tools". They emphasise that the appropriation of the tool also depends on the Group's capacity to prove that using it is an advantage.

Since the training mentioned above is not very clearly proposed today, many collaborators tend to return to former knowledge management practices (system D/getting round the rules with a "personalised" solution), especially by stocking their files on personal servers or archiving them in their computers: "A lot of departments capitalise their experience by creating files on their personal servers, under their name, where they could just as well put them on Vega"; "There is such a lot there and what we are looking for doesn't come up; so I just archive it myself on my computer and I classify all the files that are relevant.....I must have over ten thousand files". Confronted with information overload, many people also prefer human contact for managing knowledge: "It seems easier to find the right person than to find the information yourself." Seeking and exchanging information might be done face to face, by telephone and/or email: "A lot of subjects are exchanged and discussed informally with mail or phone discussions."

The respect of hierarchy and what it implies, such as that clear rules on knowledge sharing will be made explicit, echo the modes of leadership and group regulation described in the myth of the Asterix Village. Hierarchical supervision is accepted and recognised as the means of leading collective action. Moreover, these procedures are desired. They are mentioned as explicit rules that can be controlled or even opposed in what is a form of democratic decision-making. They are decisions for action that are constructed together.

Table 2. Relationship between knowledge and knowledge management evoked by collaborators at *Constructor*

	KM 2.0	Constructor	ASTERIX Myth
Knowledge	Knowledge issues Entrepreneur: An individual capable of creating knowledge for his/her own good	Individual issues and group routines (collective, technical and procedural knowledge). Individuals should not make themselves stand out too much.	Village issues and group routines: Individuals' own knowledge, respect of their specific characteristics and all considered equal (anti elitist) but also collective knowledge that structures the group.
Collective project	Defined according to ad hoc requirements Structured in a network	Upheld by a group of actors over the long term structured around strong community values (teamwork, good workmanship etc.)	Upheld by the whole village over the long term, based on deep values. Structured around the community but not hermetically sealed off.
Leadership of collective action	Actors organise themselves collaboratively The manager is the "leader" of the collaboration	Lead by a respected supervisory hierarchy	Lead by a democratically elected chief who assumes responsibility authority and group unity.
Regulation of collective action	Social control: contractual arrangements among actors	Procedures: a form of democratic construction of decision-making and action. Explicit controllable rules desired – which can if necessary be opposed. Otherwise: System D.	Democracy: Explicit rules democratically decided with conviviality and neighbourliness Otherwise: System D (getting round/bending the rules to suit one's own purpose)

Finally, the individuals we met do not reject the idea of change, but want change within the rules of the "*Constructor Village*" and not that imposed by the KM 2.0, inspired by the organisation. Confronted by the rules of KM 2.0, "system D" takes over: the *Constructor* Villagers construct their own mode of functioning on the basis of the new opportunities offered by KMS 2.0.

6   Contributions and Implications

This article explores the appropriation of KMS 2.0 through an analysis based on the Myth of the Village of Asterix. It contributes to understanding the gap found in certain companies (French companies in particular) between the adoption of KMS 2.0 by managerial or Information System departments and the appropriation of these KMS by collaborators. In line with the works of Feldman and March (Signal and Symbol Theory), it contributes to appreciating the symbolic dimension in IT Management and in IS appropriation [31, 38, 39, 49-52, 61, 62].

Using myths as tools of analysis can be useful for understanding the appropriation of KMS inside an organisation. By recalling what makes sense to the collective entity, this approach helps to better understand the tensions and objections expressed when a KMS is set up. In this article, we have chosen to analyse these tensions by referring to the "Gaulish Village" whose vision of knowledge and knowledge management differ from that conveyed by 2.0 organisations. These different viewpoints have different appreciations of collective action. Collective action in Asterix involves the reflection of social values which can be either an impetus for action or an obstacle. Through the case of the *Constructor*, we highlight the similarities between the attitudes, postures and functions of the Asterix Village inhabitants concerning knowledge, and those described by the company actors concerning knowledge management. These provide a supplementary key to understanding the obstacles to appropriating KMS 2.0.

The study carried out here in no way claims to be a generalisation. We do not consider the Myth of Asterix as a single analytical tool for decoding the behaviour of collaborators in all French companies introducing KMS 2.0. Each enterprise has its own founding myths, history and imaginary narratives that structure the meaning of collective action in each case. The company studied here is very specific. Its history is one of a series of founding myths according to which the Asterix myth seems to provide a relevant basis for exploration. However, in some companies, the appropriation of KMS 2.0 probably depends on creating new hybrid forms of collective action, inspired by 2.0 organisations, but supporting pre-existing values, projects and structural modes of collective action. From this point of view, it may be interesting to use myths that structure collective action as tools for understanding. Beyond this, resorting to myths can also be a way of creating sense out of KMS deployment processes. For Barthes, the myth is a language that relies on discourse and words as well as on objects, forms and images. What is important is the value of the verbal or visual sign. The myth is a semiological system based on a signifier (the verbal or visual unit) a signified (what is meant by this sign) and finally a sign that combines and transcends the signified and the signifier to create meaning. Each of these is used to convey a *"mythical concept"*, for example "Frenchness" in Asterix [21]. When the concept becomes mythical, the meaning of its basic nature is immediately appropriated by each of those who bear it. Certainly, this meaning is not always identical for each individual – there are variations depending on different sensibilities. Nevertheless, a common meaning emerges that enables individuals to identify with their community [18], a discussion, a shared language and collective action. Resorting to this type of referential narrative can create a space for discusion about the tensions that arise when a KMS is set up; such discussion may then result in the emergence of ways of using the KMS that make it easier for actors to appropriate [63]. One of the perspectives of this work is thus to study the pertinence of employing myths as an instrument for dialogue and sensemaking relative to KMS

This work also underlines the importance of taking account of the values and culture of the organisation if its members are to appropriate the KMS. It is not only a matter of taking account of the so called "technological" culture and the climate of technology management [64] but more generally to taking into consideration the actors' shared representations about their work practices and the organisation. This perspective is found in works on the social dynamics of appropriating IS, and particularly on socio-materiality [65]. However, such studies give scant attention to representations related to "belonging" to a country. Even if these are only one type of representation shared by organisational actors, it nevertheless seems important to take them into account. In particular, in the context of Knowledge Management, the works of [22] show how far Japanese and Chinese views of KM are influenced by shared national representations such as the myth of the samurai or the Mandarin. It would be interesting to look more deeply into the role played by shared national representations on KM practices in organisations.

Finally, this work highlights how far ITs convey meaning. These technologies can even be seen as a sign/vehicle of a myth. In the case presented here, 2.0 KMS convey a representation of work and collective action constructed in a specific "field" (in the sense of Meyer and Rowan). This representation or organising view could be developed around KMS by IS departments, computer service providers, consultants, journalists, professional associations and researchers, and might be helpful in involving actors and legitimising KMS projects. In particular it makes explicit the objectives behind the deployment of KMS in terms of improving work processes. However, the representation of work and collective action conveyed by the KMS is an idealised mythical representation that may conflict with other representations of what collective action is, or should be within an organisation. This is even more so when the actors who choose to adopt the technology are not always aware of the representations it conveys. In the case presented above, the Information Systems Department was not aware that the KMS conveyed a representation of work and collective action inspired by the model of 2.0 organisations. For the IS Department of *Constructor*, it was a matter of providing users with the most recent technologies in order to provide the best response to their requirements. Also, *Constructor* was unaware of the conflicting representations that the deployment of the KMS aroused and hence did not understand the obstacles to its adoption. However, *Constructor* had understood that certain discourse should not be associated with the deployment of these IS. It thus explained that the expression "*Knowledge Management*" could not be used at *Constructor*; instead the KM deployment processes were referred to as "*knowledge sharing*". This deliberate choice of vocabulary shows some understanding of the conundrum of introducing KMS 2.0 into previously non - 2.0 organisations. It would be interesting to explore further the links between IT appropriation, cultural myths and organisational transformation. Indeed, there may well be lessons to be learned from examining firms where this transformation has had less happy results than in the case of *Constructor*, and where the implementation of KMS 2.0 has ignored the paradox of the Asterix myth – a myth that is at once so quintessentially French, yet that is at the same time based on shared human values.

References

1. Alavi, M., Leidner, D.E.: Knowledge Management and Knowledge Management Systems: Conceptual Foundations and Research Issues. MIS Quarterly 25, 107–136 (2001)
2. Davenport, T.: Enterprise 2.0: The New, New Knowledge Management? Harvard Business Online (2008), http://blogs.hbr.org/2008/02/enterprise-20-the-new-new-know/
3. Boughzala, I., Dudezert, A.: Knowledge Management 2.0: Organizational Models and Enterprise Strategies. IGI Global, Hershey (2011), doi:10.4018/978-1-61350-195-5

4. Dudezert, A.: La Connaissance dans les Entreprises. Éditions La Découverte, Paris (2013)
5. Swanson, E.B., Ramiller, N.C.: Innovating Mindfully with Information Technology. MIS Quarterly 28(4), 553–583 (2004)
6. Boughzala, I., De Vreede, G.-J.: Vers l'Organisation 2.0: Un Nouveau Modèle Basé sur l'Intelligence Collective. In: Actes de la 15ème Conférence Internationale de l'Association Information et Management, La Rochelle, France (2010)
7. Roulleaux Dugage, M.: Organisation 2.0: Le Knowledge Management Nouvelle Génération. Groupe Eyrolles, Paris (2007)
8. Deschamps, C.: Le Nouveau Management de l'Information. La Gestion des Connaissances au Coeur de l'Entreprise 2.0. FYP Éditions, Limoges (2009)
9. Orlikowski, W.J.: The Duality of Technology: Rethinking the Concept of Technology in Organizations. Organization Science 3(3), 398–427 (1992)
10. Orlikowski, W.J.: Improvising Organizational Transformation over Time: A Situated Change Perspective. Information Systems Research 7(1), 63–92 (1996)
11. Fayard, P., Blondeau, E.: La Force du Paradoxe. En Faire une Stratégie? Dunod, Paris (2014)
12. Gaumand, C.: Système de Gestion des Connaissances Dédié à la Chaîne Logistique Intra-Organisationnelle: Une Recherche Intervention au Sein de l'Entreprise Bonfiglioli Transmission. Thèse de Doctorat en Sciences de Gestion, Ecole Centrale Paris (2014)
13. Duhamel, A.: Le Complexe d'Astérix. Essai sur le Caractère Politique des Français. Gallimard, Paris (1985)
14. Enrègle, Y.: Du Conflit à la Motivation. Editions d'Organisation, Paris (1985)
15. March, J.: Les Mythes du Management. Gérer et Comprendre 57, 4–12 (1999)
16. Barthes, R.: Mythologies. Seuil, Paris (1957)
17. Meyer, J.W., Rowan, B.: Institutionalized Organizations: Formal Structure as Myth and Ceremony. American Journal of Sociology 83(2), 340–363 (1977)
18. Burkert, W.: Qu'est-ce qu'un Mythe. Les Grands Mythes de l'Humanité. Le Monde des Religions, Hors Série (21), 6–9 (2013)
19. Schmidt, J.: Entretien: Nos Références Sont Mythologiques. Les Grands Mythes de l'Humanité. Le Monde des Religions, Hors Série (21), 96–97 (2013)
20. Igalens, J.: Le Talent du Griot: L'Art de Transmettre une Représentation, de Partager une Vision. Le Talent Majeur du Responsable Hypermoderne. Revue Internationale de Psychosociologie 17(41), 131–145 (2011)
21. Rouvière, N.: Astérix ou la Parodie des Identités. Champs-Flammarion, Paris (2008)
22. Fayard, P.: Le Réveil du Samouraï: Culture et Stratégie Japonaise dans la Société de la Connaissance. Dunod/Polia Ed., Paris (2006)
23. Fahey, L., Prusak, L.: The Eleven Deadliest Sins of Knowledge Management. California Management Review 40(3), 265–276 (1998)
24. Grover, V., Davenport, T.: General Perspectives on Knowledge Management: Fostering a Research Agenda. Journal of Management Information Systems 18(1), 5–21 (2001)
25. Dzinkowski, R.: The Measurement and Management of Intellectual Capital: An Introduction. Management Accounting 78(2), 32–36 (2000)
26. Schubert, P., Lincke, D.-M., Schmid, B.: A Global Knowledge Medium as a Virtual Community: The NetAcademy Concept. In: AMCIS 1998 Proceedings, Paper 207 (1998), http://aisel.aisnet.org/amcis1998/207
27. Nonaka, I., Takeuchi, H.: The Knowledge-Creating Company. Oxford University Press, New York (1995)

28. Cook, S., Brown, J.: Bridging Epistemologies: The Generative Dance Between Organizational Knowledge and Organizational Knowing. Organization Science 10(4), 381–400 (1999)
29. Brown, J.-S., Duguid, P.: Organizational Learning and Communities of Practice: Toward a Unified View of Working, Learning and Innovation. Organization Science 2(1), 40–57 (1991)
30. Wenger, E.: Communities of Practice: Learning, Meaning and Identity. Cambridge University Press, Cambridge (1998)
31. McElroy, M.E.: The New Knowledge Management: Complexity, Learning, and Sustainable Innovation. Butterworth-Heinemann, New York (2002)
32. McAfee, A.: Enterprise 2.0: The Dawn of Emergent Collaboration. IEEE Engineering Management Review 34(3), 38 (2006)
33. McAfee, A.: Enterprise 2.0: New Collaborative Tools for Your Organization's Toughest Challenges. Harvard Business School Press, Boston (2009)
34. Tapscott, D., Williams, A.D.: Wikinomics: How Mass Collaboration Changes Everything. Penguin, New York (2006)
35. Hamel, G.: The Future of Management. Harvard Business School Press, Boston (2007)
36. Nelson, R.R., Winter, S.G.: An Evolutionary Theory of Economic Change. Belknap Press of Harvard University Press, Cambridge (1982)
37. Pinch, T.J., Bijker, W.E.: The Social Construction of Facts and Artefacts: Or How The Sociology of Science and the Sociology of Technology Might Benefit Each Other. Social Studies of Science 14(3), 399–441 (1984)
38. Pinch, T.J., Bijker, W.E.: The Social Construction of Facts and Artifacts: Or How the Sociology of Science and the Sociology of Technology Might Benefit Each Other. In: Bijker, W.E., Hughes, T.P., Pinch, T.J. (eds.) The Social Constructions of Technological Systems: New Directions in the Sociology and History of Technology, pp. 17–50. MIT Press, Cambridge (1987)
39. De Vaujany, F.X.: Pour une Théorie de l'Appropriation des Outils de Gestion: Vers un Dépassement de l'Opposition Conception-Usage. Management & Avenir 3(9), 109–126 (2006)
40. Orlikowski, W.: Using Technology and Constituting Structures: A Practice Lens for Studying Technology in Organizations. Organization Science 11(4), 404–428 (2000)
41. Weick, K.: Sensemaking in Organizations. Sage, Thousand Oaks (1995)
42. Sellin, C.K.: Des Organisations Centrées Processus aux Organisations Centrées Connaissance: La Cartographie de Connaissances Comme Levier de Transformation des Organisations. Le Cas de la Démarche de "Transfert de Savoir-Faire" Chez Total. Thèse de Doctorat en Sciences de Gestion, Ecole Centrale Paris (2011)
43. Khalil, C., Dudezert, A.: Entre Autonomie et Contrôle: Quelle Régulation pour les Systèmes de Gestion des Connaissances. 18ème Conférence Internationale de l'Association Information et Management (AIM), Lyon (2013)
44. Cabin, P.: Les Mythes de l'Entreprise. In: Cabin, P. (ed.) Les Organisations: État des Savoirs, pp. 279-284. Éditions Sciences Humaines, Paris (1999)
45. Grimand, A.: De l'Emergence de Mythes Gestionnaires: Une Déconstruction du Knowledge Management au Travers de la Philosophe de Roland Barthes. In: Actes de la 14ème Con-férence Internationale de Management Stratégique (AIMS), Angers (2005)
46. Vernant, J.-P.: L'Univers, les Dieux, les Hommes. Le Seuil, Paris (1999)
47. Bolman, L., Deal, T.: Modern Approaches to Understanding and Managing Organizations. Jossey-Bass, San Francisco (1984)

48. Bowles, M.: Myth, Meaning and Work Organization. Organization Studies 10(3), 405–421 (1989)
49. Kaarst-Brown, M.L., Robey, D.: More on Myth, Magic and Metaphor: Cultural Insights into the Management of Information Technology in Organizations. Information Technology & People 12(2), 192–218 (1999)
50. Hirschheim, R., Newman, M.: Symbolism and Information Systems Development: Myth, Metaphor and Magic. Information Systems Research 2(1), 29–62 (1999)
51. Andriessen, D.G.: Stuff or Love? How Metaphors Direct Our Efforts to Manage Knowledge in Organisations. Knowledge Management Research and Practice 6, 5–12 (2008)
52. Andriessen, D.G.: Metaphors in Knowledge Management. Systems Research and Behavioral Science 28, 133–137 (2011)
53. Nonaka, I.: The Knowledge-Creating Company. Harvard Business Review 69(6), 96–104 (1991)
54. Perlmutter, H.: The Tortuous Evolution of Multinational Enterprises. Columbia Journal of World Business 1, 9–18 (1969)
55. Rouvière, N.: La France des Lumières Est Tout Entière dans Astérix. In: Astérix, Notre Héros: La Saga, pp. 42–47. Le Point, Hors Série Novembre-Décembre (2013)
56. Nonaka, I., Konno, N.: The Concept of "Ba": Building a Foundation for Knowledge Creation. Californa Management Review 40(3), 40–54 (1998)
57. Yin, R.K.: Case Study Research: Design and Methods, 3rd edn. Sage, Newbury Park (2002)
58. Eisenhardt, K.M.: Building Theories from Case Study Research. Academy of Management Review 14(4), 532–550 (1989)
59. Benbasat, I., Goldstein, D.K., Mead, M.: The Case Research Strategy in Studies of Information Systems. MIS Quarterly 11(3), 369–386 (1987)
60. Corbin, J., Strauss, A.: Grounded Theory Research: Procedures, Canons, and Evaluative Criteria. Qualitative Sociology 13(1), 3–21 (1990)
61. Dudezert, A., Leidner, D.: Illusions of Control and Social Domination Strategies in Knowledge Mapping System Use. European Journal of Information Systems 20(5), 574–588 (2011)
62. Karoui, M., Dudezert, A.: Capital Social et Enjeux de Pouvoir: Une Perspective Socio-Politique de l'Appropriation d'une Technologie de Réseaux Sociaux au Sein d'une Collectivité Territoriale. Systèmes d'Information et Management 17(1), 49–80 (2012)
63. Callon, M., Latour, B. (eds.): La Science Telle qu'elle se Fait. Anthologie de la Sociologie des Sciences de Langue Anglaise (Nouvelle Édition Amplifiée et Remaniée). La Découverte, Paris (1991)
64. Boynton, A.C., Zmud, R.W., Jacobs, G.C.: The Influence of IT Management Practice on IT Use in Large Organizations. MIS Quarterly 18(3), 299–318 (1994)
65. Orlikowski, W.: Sociomaterial Practices: Exploring Technology at Work. Organization Studies 28(9), 1493–1448 (2007)

Communication Roles in Public Events –

A Case Study on Twitter Communication

Milad Mirbabaie[1], Christian Ehnis[2], Stefan Stieglitz[1], and Deborah Bunker[2]

[1] University of Muenster, Muenster, Germany
{milad.mirbabaie,stefan.stieglitz}@uni-muenster.de
[2] University of Sydney, Sydney, Australia
{christian.ehnis,deborah.bunker}@sydney.edu.au

Abstract. Whilst many studies have looked at the characteristics of effective communications via social media platforms, their use during public events for people to communicate and organize is still relatively uncharted. We have even less understanding of the roles that public event participants play in their use of social media, and this study seeks to address this gap in our knowledge. We analyse the Twitter data related to the 1st May 2014 event (Labour Day) in Germany to identify participant roles in this event, and the impact their tweets had on other participants. From this analysis we draw some tentative conclusions about participant roles in public events and their impact and highlight areas for further investigation.

Keywords: social media analytics, Twitter, public events, emergency service agencies (ESA), social network analysis.

1   Introduction

There is no doubt that social media has been adopted by many people in order to exchange information that is both timely and topical. The mass usage of social media is of course underpinned by the low transaction cost for the sharing of information (i.e. ubiquitous access, negligible monetary costs of devices and telecommunications, low time investment). The emerging and swift diffusion of mobile devices, such as smartphones, further lower these costs and lead to increasing rates of ad-hoc information being shared [1].

As a result social media is having an increasing impact on communication during public or extreme events. Examples of such events could be public holiday celebrations, public disturbances and demonstrations, or large public crowd incidents such as the Boston Marathon bombings in 2013 [2]. Witnesses to a public event often share text based information or use their smart phones to share photos within seconds of an incident occurring. From our current understanding of social media use for personal communication we know that social media are not a one-directional information channel. Increasingly, social media communication has a material effect on unfolding events, and for better or worse this has an impact on the management of, and response

B. Doolin et al. (Eds.): IS&O 2014, IFIP AICT 446, pp. 207–218, 2014.
© IFIP International Federation for Information Processing 2014

to an event. In this sense, social media increasingly becomes an additional source of information that must exist beside traditional "command and control" systems.

It is now becoming critical to understand underlying principles and knowledge about social media communications and how these impact and affect the participation in and management of public events. Until now, there has been very little research conducted to better understand the role of event participants when they communicate via social media i.e. it is unclear if social media communications by individual event participants have differing levels of influence or impact on other individual event participants. To this end, our study analyses the "1st of May" public event (German Labour Day 2014) Twitter data to identify participants and the roles that they played in the event via social media. We decided to analyse this public event, because it has characteristic of an extreme event, but is predictable in its unfolding through experience from previous years. The paper proceeds as follows: Section 2 outlines related work in the field. Section 3 describes the 1st of May case; Section 4 explains our research design; we then present our analysis in section 5 and our findings in Section 6. The paper ends in Section 7 with conclusions and an outlook for further work in the area.

2   Using Social Media to Communicate during Extreme Events

We are observing an emerging trend for individuals and groups to use social media to communicate during extreme events and crises [3]. Social networking platforms (Facebook and Twitter), mapping (Ushahidi and Google) and wiki and mash-up technologies; have enabled one-to-one, one-to-many and many-to-many communications frequently resulting in collaborations. For example we have seen the adoption and use of these platforms and technologies by NGOs, for eco-collaboration activities [4]. These collaboration technologies were used in a structurally dynamic manner depending on the NGO national context (Thai, Lebanese and Australian). We have also witnessed individuals and groups using social media platforms during the civil uprising of the "Arab Spring" i.e., Tunisia 2010/11 and Egypt 2011 [5] and the current uprising in the Ukraine and Crimea 2014.

As a result, traditional centralized "command and control" systems, used by government agencies during events, crises and disasters, must now deal with, make sense of and utilize the proliferation of information generated by organizations, groups and individuals on open and freely available communication and collaboration platforms. Indeed, in order to ensure successful event, crisis and disaster management outcomes, it is imperative that non-agency organizations, groups and individuals constantly provide accurate and reliable information to government agencies, and receive accurate and reliable information from these agencies in return [6]. For example, during the 2011 Queensland Floods [7], there were reports of the difficulties of government agencies in communicating with and engaging local communities to firstly obtain and then incorporate local knowledge on floods, into emergency agency decisions. This may have contributed to higher than necessary the loss of life and property for some communities [8].

The case of the formation and role of the Student Volunteer Army (SVA) during the Christchurch Earthquakes (2010/2011), is one of many cases that motivate us to examine how to best encourage effective communications between government agencies, organizations, communities, groups and individuals during an extreme event [9]. In the case of the SVA we see the development of situational awareness, utilization of resources and optimization of crisis management outcomes through the inter-play of communications via social media platforms and the subsequent input of the resulting information input into proprietary (and closed) government systems. The SVA was formed by the use of social media in the wake of the Christchurch earthquakes (September 2010 to June 2011). Bunker et al. [9] studied and analysed the first few weeks of Facebook and Twitter activity by the SVA after the February 2011 Christchurch Earthquake (the major disaster event in the earthquake series throughout 2010/2011). This analysis highlighted the power of harnessing community ethos, goodwill, motivation and momentum through open communications via social media, as the prime focus of interactions between the SVA and disaster management agencies.

A recent European example of the complex impact of social media on participant communications are the London riots of August 2011, which saw four days of the worst violence and destruction in the UK's recent history [10]. These riots have been seen as a response to the perceived neglect of public needs by a government implementing severe austerity measures [11] and were triggered by the shooting of Mark Duggan by the London Metropolitan Police. In the course of these riots, social media were used both by rioters to purposefully organise unrest and looting by UK citizens, and by law-abiding individuals to purposefully share advice about the safety of local areas, organising the post-riot clean-up, and to support local businesses whose shops had been looted or torched. The UK government admitted that it was unable to effectively monitor social media services, and briefly considered shutting down access to Facebook and Twitter [11, 12].

Data analysis from all of these case examples clearly highlight that during public events, effective communications via social media platforms must be:

- Accurate, reliable, timely and two-way (between agencies, organizations, groups and individuals);
- Influential and capable of harnessing positive thoughts and ideas (business and community ethos and goodwill as well as individual motivation); and
- Purposeful and intentional (for well-organized activity).

This of course helps us to understand the characteristics of effective "messages" and communications propagated through the use of social media platforms during extreme events. We know very little, however, about the characteristics of, or roles played by event participants when they communicate through the use social media platforms.

Barley [13] discusses a role-based approach to the impact of technology on work tasks which is grounded in Nadel's [14] work into relational and non-relational roles. He argues that roles:

- Are grounded in daily–life interactions;
- Are intimately bound to social relationships;
- Are partially defined by task performance (but subsumed an individual's skills);
- Allow an analysis of not only technological material implications but also how technological constraints are transformed into social processes; and
- Offer a set of inter-related concepts to help define links between adjacent levels of analysis [13, p. 68].

A role focussed approach to the analysis of social media use for public events, would allow researchers to focus on how event participants use such technological platforms to interact and communicate; carry out social relationships (and social processes); and perform various tasks against the background of specific events.

Relational roles (as defined by Nadel) must have a "specific other" e.g. a son must have a mother, while a *non-relational role* exhibits behaviours that are indicative of that role e.g. a professional class such as an accountant, lawyer etc. Barley concludes, however, that all roles are "bundles of non-relational and relational elements [13, p. 68] so it is difficult to arbitrarily separate the two.

In the case of a public event, we would assume that various participants would have roles to play, some of which would be relatively predetermined and well defined i.e. government agencies, and some of which would have emergent characteristics i.e. self-organising community groups, social activists etc.

Barley highlights that researchers studying the impact of technology on role-based (organisational) structures must focus on 3 elements which directly impact roles: 1) how technologies influence tasks, skills, and other *non-relational aspects of roles*; 2) how these changes influence the *relationships between roles*; 3) how properties of the social network determine *role relations and the structure's* (network) *configuration*. These 3 elements, he argues "either sustain or modify" structures such as networks as they are the "blueprints for ongoing action" [13, p. 70].

So what role does the "messenger" play in these communications? In order to address this shortcoming in our knowledge, our study has looked at participant roles and the use of social media during the "1st of May" Labour Day public event in Germany.

3   Case Study

The 1st of May is a public holiday in Germany celebrated as Labour Day. Traditionally there are Labour Day rallies and marches in many German cities. Most of the rallies and marches are peaceful events, however, historically several radical groups become violent in some of these marches. The city districts of Berlin and Hamburg specifically have a history of marches that have turned into violent riots. Because of this history the local police forces in these two cities are always supported by federal and other state police forces to contain any potential violence.

In contrast to previous years, besides a few local incidents, the 1st of May 2014 Labour Day marches were generally peaceful events [15]. In the evening a march in Hamburg turned violent and was ended by the police [16]. In Berlin the two biggest 1st May related events were a march with about 19,000 participants and the festival "myFest" with about 40,000 participants. The police in Berlin were pleased with the peaceful atmosphere of both events [17].

4   Research Design

In order to understand the different participant roles in the '1st of May' event and their use of social media to communicate, collaborate and organize, we use an exploratory research approach for data collection and analysis. We firstly accessed Twitter, a widely-used and popular micro-blogging platform according to the "total number of active registered Twitter users" [18], to collect the data for our dataset. We did this by utilizing a self-developed software tool, which collects data through the Twitter Search API by using specified keywords in order to find relevant tweets (on the 1st of May topic). Data tracking started on the 28th of April 2014 and ended on the 5th of May 2014. This timeframe ensured that the most important content regarding the 1st of May topic was collected over a time period leading up to and after the event. All keywords were tracked and merged into a single dataset for further analysis. As the selection of keywords directly influences the data that are collected we ensured that our keywords were carefully selected to effectively target the relevant data for the event. For example it is very important not to choose keywords that have different meanings in different contexts. Furthermore, the Tweets (in this case) were required to be directly linked to the event to avoid including any unrelated data. For this study we selected 6 keywords: 3 of these describe the event itself; and 3 described locations that were related to the event. Our keywords are presented in Table 1.

Table 1. Keywords for Twitter data collection (by category)

Category	Keyword	Reason / Meaning
Event	1Mai	Main topic/date
Event	1Mai_nazifrei	National socialists use this day in order to demonstrate. This keyword is used by individuals who to oppose the Nazi movement
Event	Tag_der_Arbeit	Labour movement
Location	Feuerwehrbrunnen	Hot spot for demonstration in Berlin, Germany
Location	Mariannenplatz	Hot spot for demonstration in Berlin, Germany
Location	Rote Flora	Hot spot for demonstration in Hamburg, Germany

Our data set included a total number of 13,413 Tweets generated by 7,734 accounts (participant nodes). After collecting the data, we prepared them in Excel in order to investigate the influence of certain participants in the event and the role they played i.e. ESA, organization, community group, individual etc. related to communication via social media.

5   Analysis

We conducted a social network analysis (SNA) to get an overview of the data and to detect the most important participant nodes in the network by role. To visualize the network, we used Gephi, a tool that is available as open source software for graph visualization. The participant nodes of the network reflect the primary sources of tweets and the edges of these nodes were defined as re-tweets.

The following Figure 1 represents the SNA, which illustrates the participant nodes and the edges as the re-tweets. One of the "Individual" accounts for example has re-tweeted most (indicated by the size of the bubble), but was re-tweeted from small number of participant nodes (indicated by the gray gradation). Another example would be the account "Emergency services agency" (here the Police of Berlin) that represents a node, which has been re-tweeted very frequently by other accounts and which re-tweeted other postings very rarely.

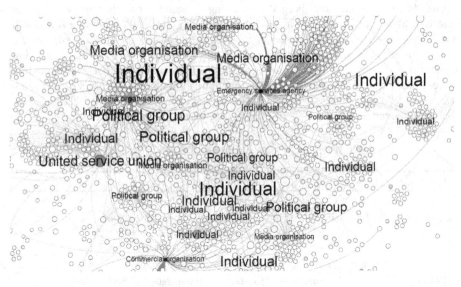

Fig. 1. Social network analysis - 1st of May (Labour Day)

By manually analysing the Twitter accounts contained in our dataset we found five primary roles that 1st May event participant nodes played:

- Emergency services agencies (police)
- Media organizations (including journalists and bloggers)
- Political groups and unions
- Individuals (politically engaged / personal experiences about 1st of May (Ausflug))
- Commercial organizations

In order to obtain a clearer overview of the data we then ran an algorithm (ForceAtlas 2) in Gephi and used the participant node tweet in- and out- degree functionality. The in-degree implies the degree of how much a participant node *has been re-tweeted*, whereas the out-degree describes the degree of how much a participant node *has re-tweeted*. In our network analysis we defined the node in-degree in the colour grey (the bubbles and arrows) with the size of the bubbles signifying the node out-degree. Table 2 illustrates our analysis of the dataset as it relates to key Twitter accounts (participant nodes).

Table 2. Data analysis

TwitterAccount (participant node)	Number of tweets	In-degree (was retweeted)	Out-degree (has retweeted)
Sorted by in-degree			
Media organisation	42	266	1
Emergency services agency	31	238	0
Commercial organisations	1	137	0
Political group	25	105	1
United service union	28	102	18
Media organisation	7	80	1
Media organisation	12	77	1
Individual (politically engaged)	47	76	3
Media organisation	7	70	0
Individual (politically engaged)	37	69	15
Sorted by out-degree			
Individual (politically engaged)	52	0	52
Individual (politically engaged)	67	0	45
Individual (politically engaged)	64	2	39
Political group	36	0	35
Individual (politically engaged)	38	1	31
Individual (politically engaged)	29	0	29
Political group	57	19	27
Media organisation	22	0	22
Individual (politically engaged)	23	0	21
Political group	34	8	21

Based on our analysis we have highlighted the following influential network participants based on the number of re-tweets (Table 3).

Table 3. Key findings

Influential Network Participants	Description	Example Tweets	Further Information
The account of a Media organisation was re-tweeted most	The node represents a left-oriented newspaper named "neues deutschland" (English: "The New Germany")	".@*GregorGysi: Botschaft des #1Mai lautet, „dass man sich nicht länger alles bieten lassen darf*'" (English: The message of the '1st May' is that you do not have to put up with everything) "*#1Mai: Polizei kesselt in Plauen Gegner der Nazidemo ein #pl1mai*" (English: Police encircled in Plauen opponents of the Nazi demonstration)	It was twittered most by a politically engaged individual, which is also the account that re-tweeted most in our dataset. It is not clear, if this node is a single person or a media outlet, but it was very active regarding political topics
The account 'PolizeiBerlin_E' (a emergency services agency) was re-tweeted second most, but twittered only 31 times	This account represents the official account of the police of Berlin	"Ca. 10.000 Teilnehmer/innen der „Revolutionären #1Mai Demo" erreichen gleich den Hermannplatz." (English: Around 10,000 participants of the" revolutionary '1st Mai' Demonstration are going to reach the Hermann Square)	The account was twittered most by a media organisation (18 retweets of "PolizeiBerlin_E"), a boulevard newsmedia outlet which is a 100% subsidiary of the Axel-Springer AG (B.Z. Ullstein GmbH 2014) The account was twittered second most by a single person who also retweeted "PolizeiBerlin_E" 9 times
There was participation of a grocery store node that can be categorised as a commercial organisation	There was a single tweet in the dataset, with a high re-tweet rate	"Für alle, die am #1Mai eine Überdosis Pfeffer erwartet, wir haben auch Salz!" (English: For those who will have an overdose of pepper at the '1ˢᵗ Mai', we also have salt!)	The grocery store used the attention of the crowd in order to make some advertising
There was a participation of a real estate company node which represents a political group	They are highly motivated to stop rising rents in Hamburg, Germany	"Welcome center im karoviertel eröffnet! Hamburgs größte Hausbesetzung! #1Mai #1maihh" (English: "Welcome center opened in Karoviertel! Hamburg's largest house squatting!)	The account tries to get some attention of the people, during the '1ˢᵗ of May' issue, towards the rising rents in Hamburg. Therefore they call the people occupying some houses in Hamburg

Table 3. (*continued*)

The united service union node was re-tweeted fifth most	It is the official account of ver.di, a united service union	#Bsirske zum #1Mai: Für ein soziales und solidarisches Europa. #Mindestlohn schnell auf 10 Euro erhöhen. (English: For a social and solidary Europe. The minimum wage must be quickly increased to 10 euros)	During the German Labour day, this account tries to motivate the participants of the demonstration and describe their demands for working conditions
		Ob auf dem #Taksim, in #Berlin oder #Madrid. Wir wünschen euch einen tollen & kämpferischen #1Mai. #MayDay is ours (English: It doesn't matter where you are, whether on the Taksim Square, in Berlin or in Madrid. We wish you a great & struggling '1st of Mai')	

6   Discussion

Our findings reveal interesting communication behaviour and emerging participant roles during the 1st of May event. The results of the SNA, the statistical analysis and further analysis of the primary participant roles indicate that ESA (in our study PolizeiBerlin_E) are central to the event and are frequently re-tweeted on Twitter. The Berlin Police while generating the 4th largest number of tweets (Table 2) actually generated the 2nd largest number of re-tweets (Table 3).

The Berlin Police have a non-relational role to play in the 1st of May event exhibiting behaviour that is typical of Police communications with the wider community. This is manifested in the topics and content of Police tweets. The characteristics of the Police tweets in this dataset (table 2) can be classified into following types:

1. Event Information:

• Start and end of a demonstration:

"Der 18 Uhr-Aufzug hat soeben mit einer Kundgebung am Lausitzer Platz begonnen."

• Number of active police officers:

"...6.400 Polizistinnen und Polizisten sind heute rund um den #1Mai im Einsatz."

• Number of participants:

"Die „Revolutionäre #1Mai Demo"befindet sich aktuell mit ca. 19.000 Personen..."

- Location:

"...*auf der <u>Zossener Str.</u> in Richtung <u>Hallesches Ufer</u>.*" (English: address-names)

2. Traffic Information

"*<u>Der Görlitzer Bahnhof ist momentan noch gesperrt</u>. #1Mai #MyFest #BVG*"
(English translation: Goerlitz central station is closed at the moment…)

3. Warning

"*Aus der „Revolutionären #1Mai Demo heraus werden vereinzelt Pyros gezündet, Flaschen und Steine auf Polizist*innen geworfen.*"
(English translation: Pyrotechnics are used in the 1May demonstration…)

4. Behaviour influencing

"Bitte meiden Sie den #Hermannplatz ab 18:30 Uhr weiträumig, da er für eine Demo komplett gesperrt wird. #Neukölln #Verkehr #1Mai"
(English translation: Please avoid the #Hermannplatz (location) from 6:30 pm widely, since it is completely blocked for a demo…")

The Police communications behaviour in turn influenced the relationship between various participant roles in the Twitter network as both the SNA and the statistical analysis indicate a "Megaphone Effect" of Police communications i.e. twittering a few tweets which are then re-tweeted by many participant nodes very often.

Another important finding shows the relationship of the top 5 participant roles and the number of their tweets (Table 2). This list is dominated by media (news), but none of the media participants have a significant effect on the 1st of May topic as highlighted by their low tweet in-degree. Only the left-oriented media roles, have a highly significant effect on the tweets and thus on the participants who re-tweet their tweets.

We also identified some individual participants and small groups who were very active according to the number of their tweets but which were not re-tweeted at all. An interpretation of this finding might be that, they were not noticed by other participants in the event because their role (and communications) in the event had no meaning to other participants. There was also a very low participation rate in the event (at least via Twitter) of extreme right-wing participants. Most of the active participants in our dataset seemed to be strongly left-wing oriented. This may be accounted for by the role of mainstream political organisations and the willingness (or otherwise) of non-mainstream participants to public commitment to beliefs.

Finally, we found that a European supermarket used the event and participation in it via Twitter, to advertise for their brand. With a single tweet, which was re-tweeted 137 times, they were able to attract highly effective attention to their products without incurring the usual advertising costs. Their role as a commercial business was effective in using the network to propagate marketing information.

As we can see by this analysis, the properties of the Twitter social network (the notion of tweeting and being retweeted) have an effect on the role relations and the network configuration.

7   Conclusion

Our analysis gives an initial overview of how participants in the 1st May 2014 event in Germany used social media (Twitter) to communicate. We have also been able to highlight 1) how Twitter influenced the behaviour of the non-relational Police role; 2) how this non-relational role (in the network) influenced the relationships between participant roles; and 3) how properties of this Twitter network (the notion of tweets and re-tweets) have determined role relations and network configuration.

We are currently performing a more detailed analysis of the communication practices of participants in this event as well as their role characteristics (emergency services agencies, media organisations, political groups and unions, individuals and commercial organization). We are specifically analysing what kind of messages are most often generated and shared and what kind of messages are ignored (and by whom).

So what of the 'messenger'? From our initial analysis we can now better understand that roles, their relationships and the social network structure in the use of social media platforms (in this case Twitter) during an event such as the 1st of May. We also understand that the volume of tweets by an event participant does not necessarily translate into attention or influence as defined by re-tweeting (and in- and out-degrees). Obviously there is some interplay between the role played by the event participant and the characteristics of effective social media communications. Our further research and analysis will focus our investigations on this interplay.

As with every study there are limitations. The event we have chosen to analyse is a public event which is relatively planned and well-controlled. It has given us an opportunity to evaluate roles through the use of social media with a smaller scale dataset, which may not be able to be effectively scaled up to a less controlled and more chaotic event (such as a riot or crisis event). Our initial analysis has also been based on the identification of tweets and re-tweets by keyword. Whilst this can be helpful to gain an initial understanding of event participants and their roles and influence via Twitter, it gives us none of the subtle understanding or context behind the contents of each tweet. The next stage in our analysis will seek to address this limitation. We must also understand the roles of event participants who did not seek to communicate via Twitter (for example right-wing political groups) and why this was the case, so as to better understand the reasons for, and motivations behind event participant selection and use of social media such as Twitter

References

1. Stieglitz, S., Dang-Xuan, L., Bruns, A., Neuberger, C.: Social Media Analytics: An Interdisciplinary Approach and Its Implications for Information Systems. Business and Information Systems Engineering 6(2), 89–96 (2014)
2. Ehnis, C., Bunker, D.: The Impact of Disaster Typology on Social Media Use by Emergency Services Agencies: The Case of the Boston Marathon Bombing. In: Proceedings of the 24th Australasian Conference on Information Systems, Melbourne, Australia (2013)
3. Stieglitz, S., Krüger, N.: Analysis of Sentiments in Corporate Twitter Communication – A Case Study on an Issue of Toyota. In: Proceedings of the 22nd Australasian Conference on Information Systems, Sydney, Australia (2011)

4. Aoun, C., Vatanasakdakul, S., Bunker, D.: From Cloud to Green: E-Collaboration for Environmental Conservation. In: Chen, J., Dou, W., Liu, J., Yang, L.T., Ma, J. (eds.) Proceedings of the IEEE 9th International Conference on Dependable, Autonomic and Secure Computing (DASC 2011), including the 1st International Conference on Cloud and Green Computing (CGC 2011), pp. 705–712. IEEE Computer Society, Los Alamitos (2011)
5. Bunker, D.: Serendipity in Disaster and Complex Scenarios. In: Makri, S., Toms, E.G., McCay-Peet, L., Blandford, A. (eds.) Proceedings of the 1st International Workshop on Encouraging Serendipity in Interactive Systems, 13th IFIP TC13 Conference on Human-Computer Interaction, Lisbon, Portugal, pp. 7–10. Springer (2011)
6. Sydney Alliance: Half a Million Sydneysiders to Create Change and Opportunity and Improve the City (2011) (press release),
   http://www.sydneyalliance.org.au/news/2011/09/14/
   sydney-alliance-the-way-to-have-your-say/
7. Ehnis, C., Bunker, D.: Social Media in Disaster Response: Queensland Police Service – Public Engagement During the 2011 Floods. In: Proceedings of the 23rd Australasian Conference on Information Systems, Geelong, Australia (2012)
8. Campbell, J.: Local Knowledge Needed in Grantham. The Chronicle (April 28, 2011),
   http://www.thechronicle.com.au/story/2011/04/28/flood-
   survivor-martin-warburton-grantham-flood/
9. Bunker, D., Ehnis, C., Seltsikas, P., Levine, L.: Crisis Management and Social Media: Assuring Effective Information Governance for Long Term Social Sustainability. In: Proceedings of the 2013 IEEE International Conference on Technologies for Homeland Security (HST 2013), Boston, United States, pp. 246–251. IEEE (2013)
10. The Guardian: Reading the Riots: Investigating England's Summer of Disorder (December 14, 2011),
    http://www.theguardian.com/uk/interactive/2011/dec/14/
    reading-the-riots-investigating-england-s-summer-of-
    disorder-full-report
    Payne, S., Quilty-Harper, C.: London Riots: Incidents and Suspects Mapped in the UK. The Telegraph (August 9, 2011), http://www.telegraph.co.uk/news/
    uknews/law-and-order/8689355/London-riots-all-incidents-
    mapped-in-London-and-around-the-UK.html
    Halliday, J.: Facebook and Twitter to Oppose Calls for Social Media Blocks during Riots. The Guardian (August 24, 2011), http://www.guardian.co.uk/media/2011/
    aug/24/uk-riots-facebook-twitter-blackberry
11. Barley, S.R.: The Alignment of Technology and Structure through Roles and Networks. Administrative Science Quarterly 35(1), 61–103 (1990)
12. Nadel, S.F.: A Theory of Social Structure. Cohen and West, London (1957)
    Spiegel Online: Demonstrationen zum 1. Mai: Bürger feiern, Gewerkschafter mahnen, Demonstranten stören die NPD. Der Spiegel (May 1, 2014), http://www.spiegel.
    de/politik/deutschland/erster-mai-zusammenstoesse-bei-
    gegendemos-gegen-npd-a-967151.html
    Berliner Morgenpost: Polizei setzt Wasserwerfer gegen Demonstranten ein. Berliner Morgenpost (May 1, 2014), http://www.morgenpost.de/nachrichten/
    article127526047/
    Polizei-setzt-Wasserwerfer-gegen-Demonstranten-ein.html
13. Hasselmann, J.: Polizei "zufrieden und glücklich" nach Großeinsatz. Der Tagesspiegel (May 2, 2014), http://www.tagesspiegel.de/berlin/1-mai-in-berlin-
    polizei-zufrieden-und-gluecklich-nach-
    grosseinsatz/9833138.html%2016.07.2014
14. Statisticbrain: Twitter statistics, http://www.statisticbrain.com/
    twitter-statistics/

Design Theory Projectability

Richard Baskerville[1,2] and Jan Pries-Heje[3]

[1] Georgia State University, Atlanta, USA
[2] Curtin University of Technology, Perth, Australia
baskerville@acm.org
[3] Roskilde University, Roskilde, Denmark
janph@ruc.dk

Abstract. Technological knowledge has been characterized as having a scope that is specific to a particular problem. However, the information systems community is exploring forms of design science research that provide a promising avenue to technological knowledge with broader scope: design theories. Because design science research is materially prescriptive, it requires a different perspective in developing the breadth of applications of design theories. In this paper we propose different concepts that embody forms of general technological knowledge The concept of *projectability*, developed originally as a means of distinguishing realized generalizations from unrealized generalizations, helps explain how design theories, being prescriptive, possess a different form of applicability. The concept of *entrenchment* describes the use of a theory in many projections. Together these concepts provide a means for comparative discussions of the importance of design theories. Projectable design theories guide designers in the design of artifacts similar in principle, but different in context. These can also help design researchers understand interrelationships between design theories.

Keywords: design science research, design theory, technological knowledge, generalizability, research methodology.

1   Introduction

At a recent design science conference Pries-Heje and Pries-Heje [1] presented a 6-by-6 framework based on a design theory regarding physically distributed project teams. The design theory premised that such project teams would achieve improved cooperation when social capital is systematically built in six different ways during six phases of a team's life-cycle. An instance of this framework was evaluated in a banking project, and subsequently new instances are now being rolled out to 100 other projects. In the work below, we consider the question, "does such widespread replication of the theory across many different instances qualify the design theory as an *important* theory?" In what ways does it have consequences? As a prescriptive design theory, it is clearly different from the descriptive theories traditional in social science. Should we instead consider, "is it an important *design* theory?" In what ways does it have consequences for design?

B. Doolin et al. (Eds.): IS&O 2014, IFIP AICT 446, pp. 219–232, 2014.

There is a continuing interest in design science that are well anchored to seminal publications [e.g., 2, 3, 4, 5, etc.]. It has a presence in the top journals [6]. But its value as an academic enterprise is debatable [7, 8]. Is design science truly "science"? Is design science a proper activity for leading information systems scholars? Is design science "research"? If the answer to the first question is "yes", then at least scientists are likely to answer the other two questions "yes" as well. But how do we compare the scholarly importance (or significance) of design science research studies? In this paper we consider one characteristic that can help distinguish an important or significant design science study from a trivial or insignificant study.

Generalizability is one measure of the intellectual usefulness of scholarly knowledge, even though it may take different forms [9]. It provides one indication of the importance of the particular findings from a research study. We usually assume that a generalizable study is important because it offers wider consequences in the future. The usefulness of design science knowledge has a more practical character and is often directed to a narrow context. If design science knowledge is to have wide consequences, there must be a means for assessing its value not merely descriptively in its own design context, but prescriptively for future contexts.

In this paper, we borrow the concept of projectability [10] from the philosophy of science and develop it as a design science alternative to generalizability. As with generalizability in descriptive research, projectability offers a frame for comparing the consequences of such prescriptive research methods as design science research. We develop this concept in the following way. First we distinguish projectability from generalizability. Next we describe the projection of technological knowledge (and design science results in particular). We then illustrate the use of these concepts in comparing the projectability of four design theories. After a brief discussion of the implications of the illustration, we conclude.

2   Generalizability versus Projectability

The scientific enterprise seeks "to discover and to formulate in general terms the conditions under which events of various sorts occur, the statements of such determining conditions being the explanations of the corresponding happenings." [11, p. 4] The notion of "general terms" is important. Like an experiment, a design can be highly localized and particularistic. But the scientific public is not interested in a particular, past, local design. They want to learn about larger policies and interesting theoretical constructs. They want to connect the results of design science to broad conceptual applicability, requiring "generalization at the linguistic level of the constructs" rather than their operationalization in a particular design [12, p. 18].

Simply borrowing the concept of generalizability from other sciences may be problematic in design science. The phenomena in the natural sciences "have an air of 'necessity' about them in their subservience to natural law. The phenomena in design science "have an air of 'contingency' in their malleability by their environment." The genuine problem in design science is to show how general empirical propositions can be made about designs that, "given different circumstances, might be quite other than they are." [13, p. xi] This problem does not just inhabit the science aspect of the enterprise, for the wider practical value of design studies lies in their consideration for applicability beyond a single environmental example [14]. For design science to be truly science, research, and a proper activity for leading information systems scholars, it should ideally produce generalizable knowledge.

There are different ways in which researchers may choose to generalize their findings from the study of one phenomenon to explain other, perhaps similar, phenomena [9]. For example, studies that focus on a phenomenon in a sample of instances where that sample has been randomly selected from the population of such instances; such studies will often adopt a statistical frame of generalizability that will project an expectation that characteristics found in the sample will also inhabit the population. For these studies, the characteristics of the population are subject to prediction or controls. The *context* of generalization is subject to prediction or control.

Context, at a fundamental level, might be either theoretical or empirical. Different contexts can shape different forms of generalizability. This diversity leads to different and sometimes conflicting definitions. In information systems, one analysis of the different ways to achieve generalizability in scientific studies involves distinguishing between theoretical and empirical statements [9]. This analysis developed four types of generalizability: generalizing from empirical statements to theoretical statements (Type ET), generalizing from empirical statements to empirical statements (Type EE), generalizing from theoretical statements to empirical statements (Type TE), generalizing from theoretical statements to theoretical statements (Type TT).

But because design science is not the same kind of science as, for example natural science, we should admit the possibility that generalizability of design sciences might be altogether different in nature than previous forms of generalizability. For example, in design science the future context for using design knowledge can be unpredictable and beyond control because it may not yet exist. Design science is materially prescriptive in the sense that its theories prescribe as-yet unconstructed artifacts. In design science research, design theories provide theoretical explanations that are usually functional rather than deductive [13, 15] and theoretical statements in design science tend to be prescriptive rather than descriptive [2, 16]. Generalizability in design science tends to be of a different nature, prescriptive rather than descriptive.

Transferability is a conceptual alternative to generalizability that is sometimes associated with forms of naturalistic inquiry such as action research [17, 18]. But a requirement for transferability is a deep knowledge of both the "sending" and "receiving" contexts in order to determine adequate congruence [18, p. 124]. In contrast, design science assumes that its theories can be applied in designing as-yet immaterialized future artifacts in as-yet unknown contexts.

Existing notions of generalizability and transferability are less suitable for the highly contingent notions of future applicability inherent in the materially prescriptive nature of design science. For example, an underlying principle of generalizability in social or natural science is the principle of abstraction. Abstraction involves a logical determination of the "universal" on the grounds of the "particular" [19, p. 158]. Abstraction is "a putative psychological process of the acquisition of a concept x either by attending to the features common to all and only x's or by disregarding just the spatio-temporal locations of x's" [20, p. 3]. Lockean abstraction is a process of discovering the idea of general types of objects from observations about individual material objects, such that a "type" is equivalent to a "generalization" so that a word is, in itself, a generalization [19, p. 403]. Abstraction is a process that separates a particular existence or instantiation from the idea, word, or general name for it and, at the same time, separates this idea from other ideas. We exclude some parts of a particular while retaining some other parts, yielding a general idea [21]. While abstraction operates well in descriptive science, it is less suitable for use in prescriptive science. Loss of the particular existence involves loss of the context of an instance.

While abstraction as a basis for generalizability might be useful in descriptive theory, generalizability for prescriptive theory must take a quite different form in order to promote the integrity of design science as a future source of general technological knowledge. Rather than adopt or adapt the notion of generalizability from the descriptive sciences, design science calls for a prescriptive form of general technological knowledge that can operate across different (perhaps presently non-existent) contexts.

Goodman's [10] concept of *projectability* provides such an alternative. Goodman originally developed this concept as a means of distinguishing realized generalizations from unrealized generalizations. It is useful in design science because it helps explain how design theories, being prescriptive, possess a different form of applicability.

Rather than attempting to focus on the history of regularities or consistencies that currently exist, or predetermination of the relevant abstract characteristics, *projection* involves determining possible regularities or consistencies that could be created in the future. A *projection* is any relevant instance that supports a theory. A theory is *actually projected* when some (but not all) of its possible instances have been examined. A theory is *projectable* if it is capable of being projected, has no known violations (observations that oppose the theory), and not all possible instances have been examined. When the terms of the theory have been used in many projections, it is said to be *entrenched* [10, pp. 80-81].

Goodman's concept fits particularly well for conceptualizing the applicability of design theories. This fit is because empirical design studies will *actually project* a design theory by instantiating it, and future instantiations will serve to *entrench* the design theory.

Thus this focal shift turns our attention away from the act of confirming or falsifying a descriptive theory, and toward the act of entrenching a prescriptive theory using future instantiations (actual projections). For design theories, determining their prescriptive projectability may be more relevant than determining their descriptive generalizability. This determination regards the consequence of the theory for further designs. The status of what we know about a design theory's projectability provides one criterion for the importance of the theory. We may know that a projectable theory is important, but we would know that one that has been projected is more important. Evaluation of an instantiated artifact is critical because it means the design theory is actually projected. Similarly, a design theory that has become entrenched as a result of a wider scale of projection would be known to be more important still. Its consequences are broader.

The projectability of a design theory depends on the way in which the terms of its statements are anchored to actual or possible projections. The most limited design theories may not be projectable beyond the actual projection empirically demonstrated in the originating research. More typically, design theories can be projected to instances defined by a class of possible projections available (but not yet actualized).

In some cases, the title of the design theory suggests its projectability. For example, in "Building an information system design theory for vigilant EIS", the projectability extends (at least) to future instantiations of vigilant executive information systems [5]. Another example is "A theory of decision support system design for user calibration" where the projectability allows for future instantiations of decision support systems [22]. A third example is "A design theory for systems that support emergent knowledge processes", where the projectability is future instantiations of knowledge management systems [23].

For design science, projectability on a very broad scale implies a design theory that could possibly be projected to an infinite number of future design problems; we characterize such a design theory as a *projectable design theory*.

Returning to the example introduced at the beginning of this paper [1], we propose an answer to the "important theory" question in at least one way. Since the design theory has actually been *actually projected* across many instances of projects in an organization it has proved important in terms of its *projectability* within this organization. We propose that there is a further process to make *projections* in other organizations leading to a process to *entrench* the theory. Hence it is clearly a *projectable design theory*.

3   Projecting Design Theory as Technological Knowledge

We can expect that the nature of a projectable design theory would be different from the nature of a generalizable theory in natural or social science. This is because one way in which design science differs from social or natural science is its stronger dependence on functional explanations. This kind of explanation is grounded on the relationship between functional requirements and the prescriptive components of the design. While authorities in the philosophy of science might disagree about whether functional explanations should be regarded as scientific or non-scientific [cf. 11, 24], functional explanations form the core of theories in design science [13, 15].

Because design theories engage functional explanations, a projectable theory in design science may also be able to encompass a family of other, perhaps more material, design theories that involve values, decisions, games, operations research, etc. These design theories are all operative or technological theories that other sciences (like natural or social science) might regard as dependent on non-scientific or ordinary knowledge:

> In a conceptual sense, the theories of technology are definitely poorer
> than those of pure science: they are invariably less deep, and because
> the practical man, to whom they are devoted, is chiefly interested in
> net effects that occur and are controllable on the human scale: he
> wants to know how things within his reach can be made to work for
> him, rather than how things of any kind really are. [24, p.123]

Such representations of technological theories as inferior no longer stand well against critical scrutiny. For example, one acknowledged form of technological or design theory is the *technological rule* [25, 26]. Rules prescribe a form of practical action. One important form of rule, *rules of science and technology*, are the norms for scientific research techniques as well as other advanced production techniques [25, p. 132]. But scientific knowledge itself is not distinguished from ordinary knowledge by its rationality, objectiveness, nor its regard for substance. Ordinary knowledge can also be rational, objective, and substantial. What distinguishes scientific knowledge is its scientific approach: the scientific method and goal [24, p. 6]. Because this scientific method is encoded by technological rules, such a fundamentally distinctive character of science cannot be regarded as "poorer" or "less deep".

4   Comparing Projectability of Design Theories

In this section, we will compare the importance of four design theory examples. The first two examples are declared design theories in the sense that the underlying research studies explicitly proposed these theories as *design theories*. These illustrate design theories that are *projectable* and *actually projected*. But these examples are too recent to illustrate the concept of a design theory that has become *entrenched* by numerous actual projections. It may be the case that design science is itself too new in information systems to permit such examples. So we will use two further examples of theories that were not originally proposed as *design theories* but can be easily recast as such. This *post hoc* reconceptualization of these as design theories provides an indication of how we might recognize design theories that are projectable, actually projected, *and* entrenched.

4.1   Vigilant Executive Information Systems

While often cited as the seminal source of design theory itself, Walls et al. [5] also illustrated their proposal with an example of a design theory for a Vigilant Executive Information System (VEIS). The example may never have been *actually projected*, but it held promise for being *projectable* to the range of VEIS as proposed in the descriptions. It was logically evaluated in the research, but not reported as instantiated for evaluation. [The works predated the notions of build and evaluate that followed, 3, 4]

This design theory suggested that the environment of many organizations had become "turbulent" and proposed "vigilance" as newly required functionality in order for executive information systems (EIS) to remain appropriate. The theory prescribed changes in the EIS interface to incorporate new inputs such as templates, triggers, and twitches. A template is the frame of reference with which an executive perceives an issue domain. A trigger is a stimulus causing a template to shift. A twitch is a short movement with a sudden motion leading to a template modification. The theory prescribed changes in the EIS functionality to incorporate such features as rapid response through open loop control. Open loop control is faster because it does not necessarily depend on a control feedback loop.

While the Walls et al. paper had a tremendous consequence through its proposal for a concept of design theory, the VEIS example seems less important. The authors proposed conservatively that it was projectable so far as adding vigilance to information systems. This VEIS design theory was narrowly projectable, not actually projected, and not entrenched. In terms of its actual consequences, we might conclude that our knowledge so far suggests that the VEIS design theory was not very important.

But as a prescriptive theory, this conclusion could change. It is always possible that the projectability is better than described. For many organizations, the turbulence has only increased. The information available from this environment has also increased with data arising more online activity. There is new science emerging aimed at discovering useful knowledge for decision making in organizations [27]. It is at least feasible that the functions and interface involved in the VEIS design theory may be projectable into this new data science. Its projectability may have increased, and its importance may rise as a result. But we must wait until there is knowledge from actual projections before the consequences might be descriptively known. Actual projections and entrenchment conceptualize the history of projections. The concept of projectability is itself much broader, and encompasses both history and future projections in undetermined new contexts.

4.2   Theory Nexus

A design theory nexus is an artifact that improves the search for design solutions among contrasting alternatives using the principle that these are based on distinct kernel theories [the underlying psychosocial theories, natural theories, computing theories, etc., cf. 5]. Carroll and Kellogg [28] used the term *nexus* to describe the interactive nature of such kernel theories when used to design artifacts. Using examples from human computer interface design, they explain how the use of multiple psychological theories specify in too much detail the designed artifacts, and that the exact effects of an artifact in relation to the theories underlying its design can only be realized by experience with the artifact; or in Goodman's terms, its *actual projection*. The empirical design will actually project the design theory by formalizing it or instantiating it and thereby understanding exactly how the theories determine the artifacts.

A theory nexus emerges when multiple kernel theories drive the design of an artifact. As the artifact becomes formalized, it articulates these theories in such a way that any conflicts that inhabit the theories make the formalization or instantiation of the design problematic. In such settings, designs emerge from an iterative process in which design theories are re-articulated in the presence of the artifact and competing design theories.

Pries-Heje and Baskerville [29] used the nexus concept as a basis for a *design theory nexus* as an approach to designing artifacts that help solve wicked problems. A wicked problem is an incomplete and contradictory problem that changes over time and for which no classic linear decision model can be found. Many social, commercial or financial planning problems will be wicked "because they won't keep still" [30]. Such problems are often refined, rather than solved, by alternative solutions. We can work towards a solution if not solve it. Wicked problems have some of the following five characteristics [31]: (1) There is no definitive formulation of the problem. We need to understand the problem (better) through working with the solution. (2) There is no stop signal embedded in the problem. This is because the process by which we solve the wicked problem is identical to the process by which we understand the problem. (3) There are no true or false solutions but only solutions of varied goodness. (4) Any solution to a wicked problem is a unique one-time solution. (5) You cannot list – or number – a finite set of solutions.

The design theory nexus pulls the wicked problem itself into the theory nexus. Not only are the kernel theories and the design artifact re-articulated in this nexus, but the problem itself is rearticulated in the process.

The study reports two instantiations of the design theory nexus: One for a wicked problem (organizational change) and one for the problem of user involvement. The two instantiations were intended to demonstrate how the design theory nexus operated with wicked kinds of problems and more normal kinds of problems. In this case, the study is claiming that the nexus design theory is projectable across a very wide range of problem solving settings. It has been actually projected into two instances. The projectability suggests that this theory has potential to be very important. However, the actual projections provide only the limited knowledge about its consequences in two instantiations. While we have more knowledge about this design theory's projectability than we do about the VEIS design theory, neither of these two theories is known to be entrenched.

4.3   Pattern Design Theory

The examples of the explicit design theories above help us differentiate between design theory projectability, actual projection, and entrenchment, and to evaluate the value of such knowledge in determining the importance of the design theory. But neither design theory above was entrenched. In order to gain a sense of how an entrenched design theory might appear, we will consider the concept of a pattern as a design theory. Aside from its explicit use as a design theory [15], Vaishnavi and Kuechler [32] inspire such recognition by applying pattern theory as a framework for design science.

The influential book *Notes on The Synthesis of Form* opens with, "These notes are about the process of design: the process of inventing things which display new physical order, organization, form, in response to function" [33]. This responsive relationship between inventions and function is a *pattern*. For example, Alexander went on to show how to express pattern theory using a pattern language where he *projected* exact methods for constructing practical, safe and attractive designs at every scale, from entire regions, through cities, gardens, buildings, and down to the doorknob of a door in the building [34]. Today, we might characterize Alexander's notions about a meta-language for construction as a design theory, and recognize it as an obvious instantiation of general pattern design theory.

This theory of patterns – providing rules and pictures - is a projectable design theory because it explains why and how certain kinds of subject design theories are generated. For example, pattern theory justifies the use of patterns in the IT development arena such as the use of reusable solutions by object-oriented software development when encountering a commonly recurring problem [35]. We can even characterize this notion of reusable solutions as a design theory in its own right: A prescriptive framework consisting of *Problems and Constraints* followed by *Solution and Pattern*. Gamma et al. [35] project this fundamental patterns design theory to 23 areas of object oriented development. Two examples of such object patterns include a *Singleton* and a *Proxy*. A Singleton pattern is one in which object creation is restricted. The object class is allowed to have only one instance. In personal records, for example, there will be only one surname, but multiple forenames. The surname object would be a Singleton pattern. A Proxy pattern that provides a placeholder for another object thereby controlling access and allowing substitution of parts of the system as long as they interface in the same way with the placeholder. In shopping systems, a verify credit proxy object might always respond "unverified credit" for privacy purposes until the user is logged in; after which a completely functional verify credit object is engaged instead. From this perspective, a pattern design theory has been actually projected in object oriented design. Object oriented design has subsequently been projected further to innumerable instances of software designs.

Pattern theory inhabits methods in design science research as problem solving patterns for different phases of design. In this sense, pattern theory can support a form of subject design theory for DSR, that will provide "... a methodology for the practice of DSR that is keyed to the patterns" [32, p. 3]. In this work, there are problem solving patterns for different phases of design. For example this work details patterns for the "build" and "evaluate" phases of DSR, and provide meta-patterns (such as brainstorming) that can be used across multiple DSR phases. This study actually projected the pattern design theory into a design science methodology, which in turn has been further projected to instances of design science studies.

In this case, such a supposed pattern design theory has vast projectability and countless actual projections. In the two examples above, the projections themselves have further projections. Such a pattern design theory is solidly entrenched by the variety and enormity of the actual projections. A well-entrenched design theory appears likely to have projectability not only into instances of artifacts, but into other subsequent design theories. An entrenched design theory may have "children" as it were; regenerations of itself as a design theory in newer forms with more current applications.

4.4   Contingency Design Theory

As a fourth example of how a massively projected design theory might become known to be important, we will consider how contingency theory might appear as an entrenched design theory. The core idea in contingency theory is that organizations that want to optimize performance need to adopt the structure that fits best with the situation they are in - the contingencies given them. "At the most abstract level, the contingency approach says that the effect of one variable on another depends on some third variable ..." [36, p. 5]. Contingency theory arises in a broad array of studies. For example, it has been *projected* into vague and ambiguous situations, where the information available could be interpreted in many ways depending on perspective [37]. Contingency factors have included leadership style [38, 39], formalization and centralization of organizations depending on the uncertainty of the environment [40], communication support, process structuring and information processing [41, 42], as well as task complexity and whether the technology is appropriate for the task [43].

Contingency theory in management is sometimes formalized as technological rules, expressing a decision design as, "A technological rule follows the logic of 'if you want to achieve Y in situation Z, then perform action X'. The core of the rule is this X, a general solution concept for a type of field problem." [44, p. 23]. The "Z" in such technological rules embodies the contingencies. Technological rules need grounding: "Research that intends to ground a technological proposition to explain why and how it produces certain outcomes will typically have to draw on survey-based field studies" [45, p. 9]. Hence, grounded technological rules need at least one *actual projection* (the field study).

Our supposed contingency design theory is projected into the concept of technological rules, which in turn can be used as a design theory for designed organizational decision heuristics. This regeneration is the projection of the contingency design theory into technological rules as a design theory. The highly projectable design theory is the overall contingency theory, and it is projected as Van Aken does it – If Y in Z do X – or as Donaldson puts it – effect of 1 or 2 depends on 3. In both cases the underlying level embodies the contingencies in situ and the theory applied for a specific instance. An example of the latter is the expression of different sets of technological rules for different management areas.

Like pattern design theory, such a contingency design theory has vast projectability and is deeply entrenched by countless actual projections. It has regenerated with its actual projections into other design theories. As a result, we have considerable knowledge about the importance of such a theory.

5   Discussion

The examples in the previous section included declared design theories and *post hoc* reconceptualized design theories. The declared design theories were declared and presented as design theories in research. The *post hoc* theories were constructed as an argument to illustrate how we might know about important design theories that are not only projectable, but have been actually projected and entrenched.

The examples have also shown how design theories are not only projectable into material artifacts as design instances, but also into future design theories. It is also possible to project a design theory backward in time in order to gain better knowledge about why a past design or a design theory succeeded. An example in this discussion was our projection of the pattern design theory into object oriented design methodology. This specific projection is interesting because a design theory is normally thought to be prescriptive, but it also has a descriptive component that can be used for better understanding past design successes and failures. This descriptive component involves the functional explanations within design theory that justify the various components in the design [15]. In the Design Theory Nexus, the theory rearticulation structure is functionally explained by the particular nature of wicked problems.

Additional insight into the projectability of a design theory can arise because actual projections should not be logically reversible. In the nexus example, we considered a post-hoc projection of the design theory nexus that was logically consistent in recasting all psychologically overspecified designs as wicked problems. The projection cannot be reversed because all wicked problems are not psychologically overspecified designs. This one-way nature of actual projects between design theories helps us determine which design theory in the pair is more projectable (and therefore more important).

Similarly, Goodman's notion of projectability helps identify interesting situations where design theories are projectable into instances (actual projections) of another. For example, one interpretation holds that the more projectable contingency design theory inhabits both the vigilant executive information system (VEIS) design theory [5] and the user calibrated decision support system (UCDSS) design theory [22]. In VEIS design theory, the executive process is contingent on triggers from the environment. In UCDSS design theory, the locus of symbolic representation is contingent on problem novelty. Contingency design theory is so projectable that it can be easily projected to instances of UCDSSs instantiated with the design theory for UCDSS as well as to instances of VEISs instantiated with the design theory for VEIS. But the design theory for UCDSS cannot easily be projected into a VEIS design, or vice-versa. Contingency as a design theory is entrenched and more projectable than both UCDSS or VEIS.

It is likely that there are many cases where multiple cases of entrenched design theories actually projected into a less projectable design theory. For example, we might use patterns for contingency, or build methods that rearticulate technological rules in a nexus. The VEIS design theory uses contingency triggers and patterns coded as executive process templates for determining managerial processes. Entrenched design theories are not necessarily mutually exclusive when actually projected into another design theory.

We recognize the two forms of projectability of design theory. In form one, the design theory may be actually projected into instances of some operational artifact. For instance, in our opening example, a six-phase social capital project team design theory has been actually projected into operating instances of more than 100 project teams. In form two, the design theory may be actually projected into another design theory. For instance, we earlier proposed actually projecting pattern design theory into the VEIS design theory. The distinction between forms one and two has parallels in the kinds of generalizability in descriptive science. Actually projecting a design theory to operating instances is parallel to generalizing from theoretical statements to empirical statements [described as type TE generalizability in 9] while actually projecting a design theory to another design theory is parallel to generalizing from theoretical statements to empirical statements [described as type TT generalizability in 9]. However, the materialization of design theories as prescriptive, functional projections makes design science projections rather different in operation than descriptive science generalizations.

Like generalizability, it is unlikely we will ever develop absolute or relative scales of projectability. It cannot be meaningful to decide that VEIS has scale-3 projectability while UCDSS has scale-4 projectability. The prescriptive nature of design science means that projectability assessments are subject to massive revision in cases where a design theory proves more useful in the future than now. However, Goodman's concept of projectability provides a language for discussing the character of a design theory as general technological knowledge, and to compare those characteristics among quite different design science studies. It provides the means to begin discussing in design science terms the ways in which one design science study could be seen as more important than another.

For example, in the introduction, we asked about the importance of a six-phase social capital project team design theory. We can say that it has been actually projected into operating instances of more than 100 project teams. We can assess that the theory is certainly projectable because it has been actually projected many times. While it has not been actually projected beyond one organization, it is clearly projectable to other contexts. It may even be said to be entrenched (at least in one organization) given the large number of actual projections. We might also characterize it as more entrenched than either VEIS or the Theory Nexus, but not so vastly entrenched as our contingency or pattern design theories.

While using the concept of projectability in design science has many rational justifications discussed earlier, it is also useful for helping to distinguish design science from other forms of science. Projectability is rooted only in the philosophy of science, and is perhaps less confused with the statistical concept of the generalizability of a sample to a population. The class of possible projections cannot be equated to a population, because the class is, at least partly, non-existent. A design theory is not projected to a population. The confusion over the applicability of statistical generalizability concepts in non-quantitative research settings has fueled debate in the field of information systems [46, 47].

6   Conclusion

The distinct and often material way in which design science makes prescriptive design theory projections illuminates two distinctions between our consideration of general technological knowledge and other forms of knowledge. On the one hand, we acknowledge how technological knowledge is different from knowledge in the natural and social sciences. On the other hand, the ability to develop broadly projectable design theories means that design science can develop more general technological knowledge. This change in the development of technological knowledge production is rather fundamental, perhaps even revolutionary. This innovation is actually taking place in the information systems community; occurring so gradually that this important achievement may go unnoticed by the field itself.

The notion of projectability provides a means to assess and discuss the comparative importance of different design science research studies. It is different from generalizability because of its prescriptive and more context-independent characteristics. It enables us to distinguish design theories that feature characteristics of projectability, actual projections, and entrenchment. Actual projections and entrenchment are historical characteristics of the design theory's past projections. Importantly for a prescriptive science, projectability is itself the conceptualization of the consequence of a design theory in unplanned, uncontrolled, future contexts.

References

1. Pries-Heje, J., Pries-Heje, L.: Designing a Framework for Virtual Management and Team Building. In: Peffers, K., Rothenberger, M., Kuechler, B. (eds.) DESRIST 2012. LNCS, vol. 7286, pp. 256–270. Springer, Heidelberg (2012)
2. Gregor, S., Jones, D.: The Anatomy of a Design Theory. Journal of the Association for Information Systems 8(5), 312–335 (2007)
3. Hevner, A.R., March, S.T., Park, J., Ram, S.: Design Science in Information Systems Research. MIS Quarterly 28(1), 75–105 (2004)

4. March, S.T., Smith, G.: Design and Natural Science Research on Information Technology. Decision Support Systems 15(4), 251–266 (1995)
5. Walls, J.G., Widmeyer, G.R., El Sawy, O.A.: Building an Information System Design Theory for Vigilant EIS. Information Systems Research 3(1), 36–59 (1992)
6. Baskerville, R., Lyytinen, K., Sambamurthy, V., Straub, D.: A Response to the Design-Oriented Information Systems Research Memorandum. European Journal Information Systems 20(1), 11–15 (2011)
7. Junglas, I., Niehaves, B., Spiekermann, S., Stahl, B.C., Weitzel, T., Winter, R., Baskerville, R.: The Case for Design Science Research in Europe. European Journal Information Systems 20(1), 1–6 (2011)
8. Österle, H., Becker, J., Frank, U., Hess, T., Karagiannis, D., Krcmar, H., Loos, P., Mertens, P., Oberweis, A., Sinz, E.J.: Memorandum on Design-Oriented Information Systems Research. European Journal Information Systems 20(1), 7–10 (2011)
9. Lee, A.S., Baskerville, R.L.: Generalizing Generalizability In Information Systems Research. Information Systems Research 14(3), 221–243 (2003)
10. Goodman, N.: Fact, Fiction, & Forecast. Harvard University Press, Cambridge (1955)
11. Nagel, E.: The Structure of Science: Problems in Scientific Explanation. Routledge and Kegan Paul, London (1961)
12. Shadish, W.R., Cook, T.D., Campbell, D.T.: Experimental and Quasi-Experimental Designs for Generalized Causal Inference. Houghton Mifflin, Boston (2002)
13. Simon, H.A.: The Science of the Artificial, 3rd edn. MIT Press, Cambridge (1996)
14. Williams, R., Pollock, N.: Moving Beyond the Single Site Implementation Study: How (and Why) We Should Study the Biography of Packaged Enterprise Solutions. Information Systems Research 23(1), 1–22 (2012)
15. Baskerville, R., Pries-Heje, J.: Explanatory Design Theory. Business & Information Systems Engineering 2(5), 271–282 (2010)
16. Walls, J.G., Widmeyer, G.R., El Sawy, O.A.: Assessing Information System Design Theory in Perspective: How Useful Was Our 1992 Initial Rendition? Journal of Information Technology Theory and Application 6(2), 43–58 (2004)
17. Guba, E.G., Lincoln, Y.S.: Epistemological and Methodological Bases of Naturalistic Inquiry. Educational Communications and Technology Journal 30(4), 233–252 (1982)
18. Lincoln, Y.S., Guba, E.G.: Naturalistic Inquiry. Sage, Newbury Park (1985)
19. Walmsley, J.: The Development of Lockean Abstraction. British Journal for the History of Philosophy 8(3), 395–418 (2000)
20. Priest, S.: Abstraction. In: Honderich, T. (ed.) The Oxford Companion to Philosophy, p. 3. Oxford University Press, Oxford (2005)
21. Walmsley, J.: Locke on Abstraction: A Response to M.R. Ayers. British Journal for the History of Philosophy 7(1), 123 (1999)
22. Kasper, G.M.: A Theory of Decision Support System Design for User Calibration. Information Systems Research 7(2), 215–232 (1996)
23. Markus, M.L., Majchrzak, A., Gasser, A.: A Design Theory for Systems That Support Emergent Knowledge Processes. MIS Quarterly 26(3), 179–212 (2002)
24. Bunge, M.: Scientific Research I: The Search for System. Springer, New York (1967)
25. Bunge, M.: Scientific Research II: The Search for Truth. Springer, New York (1967)
26. van Aken, J.E.: Management Research Based on the Paradigm of the Design Sciences: The Quest for Field-Tested and Grounded Technological Rules. Journal of Management Studies 41(2), 219–246 (2004)
27. Davenport, T.H., Barth, P., Bean, R.: How Big Data Is Different. MIT Sloan Management Review 54(1), 43–46 (2012)

28. Argyris, C.: The Discipline of Managment and Academic Defensive Routines. In: Mansfield, R. (ed.) Frontiers of Management, pp. 8–21. Routledge, London (1989)

29. Pries-Heje, J., Baskerville, R.: The Design Theory Nexus. MIS Quarterly 32(4), 731–755 (2008)

30. Ritchey, T.: Wicked Problems: Structuring Social Messes with Morphological Analysis (2011), http://www.swemorph.com/pdf/wp.pdf

31. Rittel, H., Webber, M.W.: Dilemmas in a General Theory of Planning. Policy Sciences 4, 155–169 (1973)

32. Vaishnavi, V.K., Kuechler, W.: Design Science Research Methods and Patterns: Innovating Information and Communication Technology. Auerbach Publications, Boca Raton (2008)

33. Alexander, C.: Notes on the Synthesis of Form. Harvard University Press, Cambridge (1964)

34. Alexander, C., Ishikawa, S., Silverstein, M.: A Pattern Language: Towns, Buildings, Construction. Oxford University Press, New York (1977)

35. Gamma, E., Helm, R., Johnson, R., Vlissides, J.: Design Patterns: Elements of Reusable Object-Oriented Software. Addison-Wesley, Reading (1995)

36. Donaldson, L.: The Contingency Theory of Organizations. Sage Publications, Thousand Oaks (2001)

37. Galegher, J., Kraut, R.E.: Computer-Mediated Communication for Intellectual Teamwork: An Experiment in Group Writing. Information Systems Research 5(2), 110 (1994)

38. Hersey, P., Blanchard, K.H.: Life Cycle Theory Of Leadership. Training and Development Journal 23(5), 26–34 (1969)

39. Hersey, P., Blanchard, K.H.: So You Want to Know Your Leadership Style? Training and Development Journal 35(6), 34–54 (1981)

40. Lawrence, P.R., Lorsch, J.W.: Organization and Environment: Managing Differentiation and Integration. Harvard University, Graduate School of Business Administration, Division of Research, Boston (1967)

41. Zigurs, I., Buckland, B.: A Theory of Task/Technology Fit and Group Support System Effectiveness. MIS Quarterly 22(3), 313–334 (1998)

42. Zigurs, I., Buckland, B.K., Connolly, J.R., Wilson, E.V.: A Test of Task/Technology Fit Theory for Group Support Systems. Database for Advances in Information Systems 30(3/4), 34–50 (1999)

43. Van de Ven, A.H., Drazin, R.: The Concept of Fit in Contingency Theory. Research in Organizational Behaviour 7, 333–365 (1985)

44. van Aken, J.E.: Management Research as a Design Science: Articulating the Research Products of Mode 2 Knowledge Production in Management. British Journal of Management 16(1), 19–36 (2005)

45. van Aken, J.E., Romme, G.: Reinventing the Future: Adding Design Science to the Repertoire of Organization and Management Studies. Organization Management Journal 6, 5–12 (2009)

46. Lee, A.S., Baskerville, R.L.: Conceptualizing Generalizability: New Contributions and a Reply. MIS Quarterly 36(3), 749–761 (2012)

47. Tsang, E.W.K., Williams, J.N.: Generalization and Hume's Problem of Induction: Misconceptions and Clarifications. MIS Quarterly 36(3), 729–748 (2012)

Designing Artifacts for Systems of Information

Richard Baskerville[1], Robert Davison[2], Mala Kaul[3], and Louie Wong[2]

[1] Georgia State University, Atlanta, USA
baskerville@acm.org
[2] City University of Hong Kong, Kowloon, Hong Kong
isrobert@cityu.edu.hk, louiehmwong@gmail.com
[3] University of Nevada, Reno, USA
mkaul@unr.edu

Abstract. This paper reports an exploratory study of information systems (IS) design professionals that offers insight into the evolution of the systems concept in systems design practice. The analysis distinguishes the current object of this design effort as *systems of information* (SI). SI differs from IS in that SI seeks to maintain the necessary degree of integrated systematicity while retaining or acquiring the necessary technology. IS, in the past, had an implied capacity to build a complete system from the ground up. SI has an implied constraint that certain technological components must be "taken as given" and the design problem becomes one of maintaining an ideal socio-technical system as the various technologies evolve within and around the system.

Keywords: information systems, information technology, design.

1 Introduction

Information Systems and Technologies should lie at the heart of both the research and the practice that comprise the discipline and profession of information systems. The elaboration of information systems (IS) with information technologies (IT) can perhaps be traced to Orlikowski and Iacono's [27] authoritative and widely cited 'desperate search' for the IT artifact in IS research. Many current researchers now seek to ensure that the IT artifact is so central to their research that the systems in which these artifacts should be embedded are simply omitted. Lee [20] listed system as one of the key concepts in the field of information systems research that has been taken-for-granted and has fallen into neglect (the others included information, theory, organization, and relevance). The extent of the problem can be readily perceived in contemporary discourse about cloud computing, service science, experiential computing, and the waves of 'apps' that flood our personal devices – for in all of this, there is little explicit regard for systems.

Where are the systems then? Taken for granted as a tacit assumption? Forgotten or abandoned? Shunted aside or obscured by the clouds? Socially deconstructed, reconstructed or transmogrified into something else? Or are they still here, even though ignored in much of our research and discourse and thus invisible to the audience? Further, what are the consequences of the disappearance or invisibility of systems?

B. Doolin et al. (Eds.): IS&O 2014, IFIP AICT 446, pp. 233–245, 2014.

Does their absence empower us to new creative heights or impoverish our understanding of how the various components of what we used to call IS fit together? By substituting systems with seductively metaphorical terms like 'clouds' or 'solutions' [24], have we deliberately reinvented ourselves as purveyors of delusive simplicity even as we remain custodians of the complex [19]?

In this article, we explore these systems concepts and their entanglement with our current practice of IS research. We challenge the assumption that IS and IT are identical and instead assert that technology, including design science, technology artifacts and materiality, share the center of the field with socio-technical information systems. We first engage in a review and interpretation of the way IS is conceptualized in the literature. This material is organized into four views, which we term: design engineer, design guide, design gardener, and design therapist. These views, and the common role of designer in these views, resulted from a qualitative study where we explore the perceptions of IS practitioners with respect to the way technology artifacts and information systems are designed and developed. *System design* was not among the original assumptions when this research was formulated. The role of the practitioners as designers of systems and artifacts arose from the data as a central, shared and defining activity that contextualised widespread practitioner thinking about today's systems and artifacts. Through this process, we reveal current views of technology and systems that will help us to reconceptualize both the technology and the systems of information in contemporary practice. Through an extended discussion, we further reflect on the implications of these views for IS practice and consider future research directions that build on our assertion of the primacy of the system in IS.

2   Conceptualization of Information Technology and Information Systems

Wikipedia defines information technology as "the application of computers and telecommunications equipment to store, retrieve, transmit and manipulate data, often in the context of a business or other enterprise. The term is commonly used as a synonym for computers and computer networks, but it also encompasses other information distribution technologies such as television and telephones". Oxford English Dictionary [25] defines it as the "branch of technology concerned with the dissemination, processing, and storage of information, esp. by means of computers". The concept has a long history, encompassing developments as old as, for example, the telegraph [14].

The systems concept is well established with a broad agreement on its general meaning. An analysis of the definitions for the concept finds that the most common textbook definitions are very similar. A system is an assembly or set of interacting entities or elements with relations between them [8]. In a system, the behavior of each element has an effect on the behavior of the whole, and these behaviors are interdependent. Elements can form subsystems, and these subsystems also affect the behavior of the system as a whole. The connectivity is such that independent subsystems cannot form. A system is a whole that cannot be divided into independent parts. Interaction is important: one element's behavior is influenced by another. The relationships between elements in a system are defined by behavior, and such behavior means each element has significant properties that may change. For an element to be considered as being inside a system, it means that the element must affect parts of the system and also must be affected by parts of the system [8].

From an IS perspective, the systems concept is anchored in general systems theory [6, 9] and systems science [2, 17]. Systems theory was quickly adapted as information systems theory [1, 18], especially in its "soft" variety that merged action research and systems science into a form of systems thinking and soft systems methodology [11]. The application of systems theory as a means of coping with complexity emerged as a central purpose of the concepts [7, 12]. Open, biological, and social systems concepts provide attractive explanations for behavioral changes arising in the social-technical nature of the use of information technologies in the workplace [32]. The notion that communication is the defining operation in a social system offers an essential justifying role for information systems [23]. Also thematic is the notion that systems, once created, can have a certain autonomy and durability, meaning they can be self-organizing [5, 30] and self-reproducing (autopoietic) [22, 31].

Despite the fairly broad agreement on the defining aspects of a "system", there are rather more diverse definitions of information systems. For example, there are different kinds of things that have been labeled as information systems, such as: organizations that deliver information to their clients; systems of active elements that deal only with symbolic objects (i.e., information); the subsystem within any self-governing system that enables communication between the managerial or operational subsystems of an organization [10]. Lee [20] divided the information system into three interacting and constituent subsystems: the organization system, the data system, and the technology system. A study of more than 20 published definitions of IS confirms this potential disagreement. Most include references to computers or technology, and most refer to organizations; and while some mention society or social aspects, a few entirely ignore IT, organizations and society, taking for example a database perspective. In general, what agreement can be found in the literature suggests that IS are systems in which human participants and/or machines use information, technology, and other resources to produce informational products and/or services [4, p. 451].

One reason for this diversity in the conceptualization of IS may partly lie in the relegation of the systems concept into the background as part of the IS assumption ground. This relegation can be useful when the purpose is to understand the consequences of the IS in its context, i.e., what the IS contributes or creates. As an example, Riemer and Johnston [29] explain the IT artifact as a kind of Heideggerian *equipment* that, while co-constituting practice and social identity, fades from notice as it is absorbed into use. Its role as the embodiment of a system or as a component of a system is lost to the preeminence of its consequences. It is mainly argued as either distinct from other components or hopelessly entangled with other components such that its role may only be to materialize social purpose without necessarily taking notice that a social-technical system exists. We see similar effects from the debates over whether social and material aspects of information systems are separable or inextricably entangled [21, 26]. The latter position effectively black-boxes the social technical system as a somewhat impenetrable sociomaterial system in order to add clarity to its socially constructive consequences. For example, Pentland [28] employs the social materiality concept to help us more clearly observe the ability of a system to retain patterns of action.

The systems aspect of IS is assumed, at best, to be shared and taken-for-granted when in fact there may be some disagreement about just which aspects of the systems concept are more dominantly valued in a particular IS perspective. Based on systems theory, there are two key dimensions along which the systems perspective can vary [3, 17]. One dimension aligns with the distinction between the elements of a system versus the relations between, or interactivity of, those system elements [8]. A designer might dominantly value the discrete information technologies that make up the system. Such a component-focused designer would approach a system design task as one of integrating available components. We will designate this approach as an integrating components viewpoint.[1] Alternatively, a designer might dominantly value the relationships and interactions between these technologies, the accompanying data and the people who constitute the system. Such a relationship-focused designer would approach a system design task as one of growing or nurturing a healthy or sustainable ecology within (and perhaps in the outside environment of) the system. We will designate this approach as fitting an emergent ecology viewpoint. To an important degree, this dimension represents a contrast between an IT assumption and an IS assumption.

The second dimension considers the behavior of the elements within a system in affecting the behavior of the system. At an organizational level, this dimension aligns with a design distinction between the ways in which the system interacts with the complex aspects of its environment (such as culture). For our purposes, this dimension is helpful in distinguishing between a 'controlling-the-complexity' design culture versus a 'coping-with-complexity' design culture. For the control perspective, a designer might dominantly value the importance of the system in controlling the complexity of its organizational environment. For example, the system designer might aim to prevent diverse cultural settings from affecting system performance. Such a control-focused designer would approach their design task as one designing a system where the system may help manage and control. This view is consistent with Boulding's lower levels of systems complexity and is exemplified by control mechanisms in cybernetic systems, such as a thermostat [9]. We will designate this extreme approach as a control the complexity viewpoint. Opposite this viewpoint, a designer might dominantly value the importance of the system in matching and interoperating with the complexity of its organizational setting. At this perspective, the designer would view the cultural context of an organization as one that is adaptable to the system, where the system does not deterministically control how work is done. This view is consistent with Boulding's higher levels of systems complexity and is exemplified by societal systems made up of communicating, autonomous human beings [9]. We will designate this approach as a coping with complexity viewpoint.

Collectively, these two dimensions provide indications of the "how" and "why" of systems designers. The vertical axis suggests why systems designers take various design decisions, and the organizational cultural contexts wherein those design decisions

---

[1] While the primary elements of systems used in this paper are consistent with existing systems literature, the labels and terminology used in this paper for the various dimensions and viewpoints of systems emerged from the data analysis described later in the paper.

are made. The design decisions may be influenced by a flexible organizational culture and environment where systems must be dynamically adaptable to the infinite variety of circumstances. Alternatively, the design decisions may be driven by a corporate mandate to control the behavior of an organization (and its various component parts, including people). The second dimension helps explain how a system is being designed. For example an emphasis on a solution using discrete components represents an IT-centric design decision. On the other hand, an emphasis on the interrelationships between such components, as well as the data, models, procedures and people who use them represents an IS-centric design decision. These two dimensions help define four divergent design views of designing the systems aspect of information systems, which we discuss next.

Table 1. Different system viewpoints

View toward Interacting with The Environment	Dominant Designer Value	
	Integrating Components	Fitting Emergent Ecology
Control the Complexity	Design Engineer	Design Guide
Cope with the Complexity	Design Gardener	Design Therapist

We consider these four design views first from the Complexity-Controlling aspect. Where there is a mandate to control organizational behavior, an emphasis on discrete technological components implies a system design view we call *Design Engineer*. An emphasis on the interrelations between these components implies a system design view we call *Design Guide*.

System Designer as Design Engineer: The system is assumed to be the amalgamation of a set of discrete technologies and people. Their ability to interact is less important than their discrete capabilities. This viewpoint involves the assumption that the setting for the system is an organization that can be built and controlled. Centralization is frequently a core attribute in this control setting, with the system helping organize and control the organizational complexity.

System Designer as Design Guide: The system is assumed to be the interaction of the whole set of interconnected system technologies and people. The individual capability of each system element is less important than its contribution to system activities as a whole. This viewpoint involves the assumption that the setting for the system is an organization that can be built and controlled. In order to achieve this, system designers must guide the organization in order to discover the strong shared-purpose in connecting technologies and people. The system is designed to organize and control the natural complexity of the organizational context, but is done through relationship-building (both within the technical system and the human community).

Where there is a design culture that places less emphasis on controlling organizational behavior and more emphasis on adaptation between system and organization, an emphasis on discrete technological components implies a design view we call *Design Gardener*. An emphasis on the interrelations between these components implies a view we call *Design Therapist*.

System Designer as Design Gardener: The system is assumed to be the amalgamation of a set of independent technological artifacts or people. Their ability to interact with each other or with other system components is less important than their discrete capabilities. Like a gardener choosing which plants to grow in which corners of a garden, this viewpoint involves the assumption that the setting for the system is a dynamic organizational environment that will operate more-or-less independently of control mechanisms. Design decisions must provide an avenue to cope with the infinite variety of circumstances in this environment. The goal of the system designer is to choose the right system elements that will best adapt to organizational complexities, rather than to control them.

System Designer as Design Therapist: The system is assumed to involve emergent interactions among interconnected sets of system technologies and people. The individual capability of each system element is less important than its dynamic integration in system activities as a whole. This viewpoint involves the assumption that the setting for the system is a changing ecological environment that operates more-or-less independently of control mechanisms. The goal of the system is to cope with and adapt to the natural complexity of the environment, rather than to control it. Like a therapist who helps a patient change holistically to a better state, this system design viewpoint is characterized by highly organic assumptions about both technical and human systems. The designer helps the system holistically to cope with change through emergence.

3   Methodology

We developed our theoretical framework using logic and analysis of concepts in the literature. In order to determine if it reflects design viewpoints held in practice, we planned a qualitative field study using interview guidelines. The choice of a qualitative form of such a field study is driven by the exploratory nature of the framework. Because the systems concept is open to interpretation by the respondents, it was important to trap richer qualitative data at this stage of the development of the theoretical framework (i.e. allow researchers to be surprised by the data), rather than incorporate an attempt to nail the study to a single conceptualization of the systems idea [16, 33].

The field study reflects the selection of firms and practitioners who assume differing roles in designing information systems. It is important to retain qualitative values for this study because a single actor may enact multiple roles. When this occurs, the researchers require the latitude to offer interpretations of the role assumed by a subject in relation to offering a particular reflection for the study, relying on cues that may be in the margins of the qualitative data. While we cannot experimentally manipulate the role assumed by the respondents, we can select respondents that represent differing roles. Because this selection process involves interpretation, the qualitative nature of the study remains continuous [33].

Similarly, the design views must also be captured qualitatively. It requires conceptualizations described by respondents of (1) their system setting and (2) their focus given to either the discreteness of technologies or the integrated nature of systems. In this sense, our respondents are selected on the basis that they constitute natural hosts for four viewpoints about technology and the settings in which technology is situated.

4   Research Procedure

We examined 12 cases, each representing a practicing IS professional involved in system design in the various roles described. We collected data aiming to assess three cases in at least four different roles (vendor, CIO, consultant, etc.). Three cases provide sufficient confidence that design viewpoints discovered would be present in multiple cases (i.e., more than one). Our objective is not to prove any universality, but only to detect cases of the four expected design viewpoints (design engineer, design guide, design gardener, and design therapist). Three cases in each category provide three opportunities to find the expected effects.

Further, in the 12 selected cases, we examined cases in two geographic regions in order to reveal possible cultural differences. For each role, at least one case was examined in Hong Kong and at least one case in the USA.

We used a semi-structured interview guide that (1) collected simple demographic information to provide a sense for possible alternative explanations for the conditions; (2) offered the subject an opportunity to describe and explain their role in relation to systems and systems design; (3) offered the subject an opportunity to describe and explain their assumptions about the systems setting; and (4) offered the subject an opportunity to describe and explain their assumptions about technology and its relations. In the interview guide, section (2) was explicit about the role enacted by the subject (the expected independent condition), however both (3) and (4) were intentionally less direct, intending to provide an ideal setting for the subject to reveal the presence in their design thinking of their attitude about the two dependent conditions.

5   Examples from the Findings

The analysis of the interview data provided illustrations of the way our information systems practitioners conceptualize systems along the dimensions described above.

5.1   Design Gardener View

Dave, Business Intelligence Manager in a US Manufacturing Firm of some 21,000 employees, provided indications of this view. The system is assumed to involve the amalgamation of a set of discrete technologies or people. Their ability to interact is less important than their discrete capabilities. Dave described a litany of incompatible systems that were pasted together *post hoc*:

> We have the finance system; we have a plant maintenance system
> …we have time management systems, and…our HR is really out-
> sourced, so I shouldn't count that. We do have billing, ordering, and
> picking up systems – so that's all in one area. We do have data ware-
> house. There's a lot of use of access databases … So most of them are,
> let's say, I want to use the word, artificially put together. What that
> means is we found solutions to transfer data from one to another
> if they are not originally directly compatible.

5.2   Design Guide View

Horace, a CTO and Chief ERP Architect for a Hong Kong manufacturing firm of some 28,000 employees provided indications of this view. The system is assumed to be the interaction of the whole set of interconnected system technologies and people. Even though, historically, individual technology silos may have existed, the individual capability of each system element is now less important than its contribution as a participant in system activities as a whole. For Horace, this is about the value of ERP systems and how the standardizing systems fit the business need for sharing information:

> ERP is centralized. The reason to centralize is we want to share in-
> formation, not because we want to control. A good example is we do
> internal transfer of raw materials. If we transfer fabric from one fac-
> tory to another, the system will handle all the inter-company charges
> automatically. But if you use two separate systems, you need to build
> your own interfaces. Another example is we share fabric. So one cus-
> tomer has orders in both plants. And if we need fabric, plant A can
> check their inventory for plant B. So for technical reasons, we cen-
> tralize.

5.3   Design Therapist View

The system is assumed to be the interaction of the interconnected set of system technologies and people. The individual capability of each system element is less important than its contribution to system activities as a whole. This viewpoint involves the assumption that the setting for the system is a changing ecological environment that will operate more-or-less independently of control mechanisms. The setting is complex, but the goal of the system is to cope with the complexity rather than to control it.

Jerzy, an IT services manager for a small Hong Kong IT services firm of about 10 employees, expressed opinions consistent with this view; particularly noting the tensions between users and the technology. These tensions moderate the way each system component can contribute to the larger system as a whole.

> The information system helps us retain memories about previous
> projects. Ultimately, we want to have the system acting as the com-
> pany's memory on all existing and historical projects and help recall
> what we did in the past and facilitate reuse of previous works. This
> is just like a large search engine for the company.

Although the system can operate quasi-independently, in an SME there needs to be a reasonably tight hold on systems and procedures:

> However, management and control works are still there. We can't pass that to the information system and people do not 100% trust the system.

5.4   Design Engineer View

The system is assumed to be the amalgamation of a set of discrete technologies and people. Their ability to interact is less important than their discrete capabilities. This viewpoint involves the assumption that the setting for the system is an organization that can be built and controlled. The setting is complex, and the system can help organize and control this complexity.

Alice, a CIO of a US manufacturing firm of about 30,000 employees, provided an indication of this view. She points out that technologies and people are entities that must be controlled. Systems provide the means for controlling these discrete elements:

> Major systems such as ERPs are the life blood of compliance within our organization and are on the critical path to management and control. In our business, the consequence of putting the wrong technology or people into operation can be catastrophic – it can lead to loss of face with customer, missing out on contractual obligations and missing on commitments to shareholders.

6   Discussion: Systems of Information

The data provided many further indicators of concepts illustrated in the examples above. Our positioning of the statements above should not be taken as instances of positioning each respondent neatly and holistically into one of the quadrants. Indeed, three of the respondents provided bifurcated perspectives. These comments can be interpreted as a respondent whose perspective is in motion, a possible transition from one viewpoint to another. Rather, we argue that the statements likely represent a moment-of-reflection that fits the noted position. We are mapping these moments-of-reflection rather than mapping people. While these positions may indeed suggest a general orientation of the person who made the statement, it is quite possible that the mapping would be quite different if the individual reflected on a different situation.

We are also investigating the presence of systems concepts among the reflections of information specialists. Such systems-oriented reflections are not the bailiwick of information systems alone. From the outset of the IS field, we have understood that systems concepts broadly inhabit diverse disciplines. For example, when Thomas Haigh asked Charles Bachman about "systems people" in the early days of computing at Hewlett-Packard; Bachman replied,

... they were certainly concerned with systems, but they weren't generic systems people. They were functionally specialized. I guess
they were all systems people, whatever they had to do. They were
concerned with: 'How to manufacture things?' 'How to ship things?'
'How to pay for things?' People were specialists in 'how to do it.' If
that makes you, a systems person, so be it. It was not specialized to
information systems. It could be whatever, but it was a way to handle
professional specialization. [15, p. 42]

As a consequence, it is likely that the grid in Table 1 can also be used to map reflections from a complexity-control, complexity-coping, component-integrating, and
ecology-emerging perspective across a diverse range of human occupations. Our particular interest however, was observing information specialists reflecting on systems
concepts, as opposed to other kinds of specialists.

We sought to discover the ways in which IS management employed the systems
concept. We began with the apparent conflation of IT and IS. In this area, we sought
to discover the ways in which the systems concept was currently used by information
specialists, and whether this could be distinguished from the technology concept.

We found indications that an entanglement between IT and IS was less of an issue
than an entanglement of practice and design within current IS management thinking.
Surprisingly, the respondents were generally focused on how to organize and execute
transitions from current systems to future systems. They were designing future systems, given the constraints and affordances of their current technologies and people.

We distinguish the object of this design effort as *systems of information* (SI). SI
differs from IS in that SI seeks to maintain the necessary degree of integrated systematicity while retaining or acquiring the necessary technology. IS, in the past, had an
implied capacity to build a complete system from the ground up. Even if this capacity
is not a necessity, SI has an implied constraint that certain technological components
must be "taken as given" and the design problem becomes one of maintaining an ideal
socio-technical system as the required technologies evolve in and around the system.
The reconceptualization of IS as SI reflects the *reversal of field* that is taking place in
the practice of systems design. It involves the practice of experiential design, a form
of design and redesign that is contemporaneously integrated with the lived experience
of the object-of-design.

For example, the presence of an ERP (or ERP-like) system at the enterprise level is
often taken for granted in the systems reflections of our respondents. Their challenge
is to acquire new capabilities (i.e., new technologies) while maintaining systematic
qualities such as efficiency, effectiveness, usability, etc. The problem, from the CIO
level down, is how to satisfy new demands from internal stakeholders or external
clients by acquiring and integrating new technologies without compromising the
enterprise's essential socio-technical systematicity. They were thus engaged in the
difficult design problem of getting from here to there without wrecking the overall
system's benefits. The technological problem can be viewed most vividly as a cutting-
edge new component ("a trendy new app"). The systems problem is most typically
viewed as one of integration ("how can I add this trendy new app and keep my enterprise up"). This is the design focus of SI, making integrated systems out of commodi-
tized components. SI is oriented to the ideal design of technological mash-ups [13].

The SI design problem is no less socio-technical than the IS design problem. IS designers focused on building usable information systems with ideal social and technical characteristics. The SI design problem is different in that it is more similar to architectural programming because of the mash-up constraints. Certain technological features are given and the population of users is given. The SI challenge is to program the entanglement between these people and that technology as well as the entanglement between that technology and the pre-existing system – and data.

As a consequence, the entanglement artifact is different from other kinds of artifacts. The SI designer is designing not only the typical artifacts, such as technologies, models and processes, but also the entanglement (programming the mash-up). This new kind of artifact, the programmed entanglement, presents a more complex systems problem to the designer, who needs to exercise not only considerable care and innovation, but also wisdom and contextual intelligence. The large number of predefined constraints and affordances that arise when programming (or reprogramming) a mash-up in the presence of a new technology or component constitute a significant issue. It appears that this new kind of SI design is being carried out at widely varying levels of the IS function within the organization.

The results of the foregoing study have limitations. As an interpretive and qualitative study it does not respond to typical positivist criteria such as repeatability and reliability. The respondents, their positions and the firms represented in the cases were not random, but were intentionally selected to provide a diversity of viewpoints on the discrete complexity-control, complexity-coping, component-integrating, and ecology-emerging. Our aim was not to study designers *per se*, choosing instead to focus more on managerial positions. The validity of theoretical generalizability arises in the care in the design of this diversity, not from the limited quantity of respondents. While we were certainly successful in achieving an ideal spread of reflections, the data did not support classifying a respondent entirely in one quadrant or another. Rather, respondents appeared to situate themselves in whichever quadrant was appropriate for the moment at hand. Thus, given an infinite variety of organizational circumstances, each with its own technologies, problems and people, so an equally infinite variety of positions can be proposed in order to ensure optimal organizational functioning. The dynamic flexibility and contextual intelligence that this requires of the SI designer implies that any design space within the systems quadrant may be inhabited at any one time by the same designer, depending on the circumstances. The implication for IS researchers is that they need to be more sensitive to organizational circumstances (people, problems, technology) when they analyze either the behavior of designers or the artifacts that they design. A purely design guide perspective, for instance, cannot hope to meet the exigencies of all conditions. In different circumstances, and in particular as an organization evolves, so perspectives can shift. As Leonard pointed out, as his company has grown from a local to a global logistics provider, so his view of systems has shifted from one of gardening to one of guiding. Other companies may see the reverse, or something different: there is no ideal state that can apply to all companies in all circumstances. However, benchmarking against the competition can be a useful exercise.

7   Conclusion

Our research indicates that the conceptual conflation of information systems and information technology is misleading. Information specialists reflect differently on their work using these two concepts in distinctive ways. From this perspective, little has changed in the way IS and IT concepts are present in practice. However, we did discover that the way information specialists are conducting design in their work is quite surprising. Rather than designing information systems in holistic ways, information specialists are designing system usage programmatically, being very careful to preserve the systematicity of information practices, while acquiring the necessary current technologies. We term this new aspect of design practice *systems of information* to distinguish the particular practice of programming the entanglement of new technologies with old technologies and the entanglement of technologies with people.

This entanglement is a *reversal of field* in the practice of systems design. Designers are experiencing their lives within an environment that is defined by previous systems designs while concomitantly experiencing their own designs as new technologies are inserted, appended, or overlapped with old systems. The need to maintain integrated systematicity while retaining or acquiring the necessary technology is central to SI. System design today only rarely evokes a capacity to build an entire new system from the ground up. That form of systems design is the "old" IS. Today, systems design operates on a platform constrained by a set of technological components must be retained in and for the new system. The design problem has become one of maintaining an ideal socio-technical system as the required technologies evolve in and around the system.

References

1. Ackoff, R.L.: Management Misinformation Systems. Management Science 14(4), B147–B156 (1967)
2. Ackoff, R.L.: Science in the Systems Age: Beyond IE, OR, and MS. In: Klir, G. (ed.) Facets of Systems Science. Plenum Press, New York (1991)
3. Ackoff, R.L.: Creating the Corporate Future: Plan or Be Planned For. Wiley, New York (1981)
4. Alter, S.: Defining Information Systems as Work Systems: Implications for the IS Field. European Journal of Information Systems 17(5), 448–469 (2008)
5. Ashby, W.R.: Principles of the Self-Organizing Dynamic System. Journal of General Psychology 37, 125–128 (1947)
6. Ashby, W.R.: General Systems Theory as a New Discipline. In: Klir, G. (ed.) Facets of Systems Science. Plenum Press, New York (1991)
7. Ashby, W.R.: Requisite Variety and its Implications for the Control of Complex Systems. In: Klir, G. (ed.) Facets of Systems Science, pp. 405-417. Plenum Press, New York (1991)
8. Backlund, A.: The Definition of System. Kybernetes 29(4), 444–451 (2000)
9. Boulding, K.: General Systems Theory – The Skeleton of Science. Management Science 2(3), 197–208 (1956)

10. Carvalho, J.A.: Information System? Which One Do You Mean? In: Falkenberg, E.D., Lyytinen, K., Verrijn Stuart, A.A. (eds.) Information Systems Concepts: An Integrated Discipline Emerging, pp. 259–280. Kluwer, Leiden (2000)
11. Checkland, P.: Systems Thinking, Systems Practice. Wiley, Chichester (1981)
12. Flood, R.L., Carson, E.R.: Dealing with Complexity: An Introduction to the Theory and Application of Systems Science. Plenum Press, New York (1988)
13. Gamble, M.T., Gamble, R.: Monoliths to Mashups: Increasing Opportunistic Assets. IEEE Software 25(6), 71–79 (2008)
14. Gleick, J.: The Information: A History, A Theory, A Flood. Pantheon, New York (2011)
15. Haigh, T., Bachman, C.W.: Charles W. Bachman Interview: Tucson, Arizona. In: ACM Oral History Interviews, Tucson, Arizona, September 25-26, ACM, New York (2006)
16. Klein, H.K., Myers, M.D.: A Set of Principles for Conducting and Evaluating Interpretive Field Studies in Information Systems. MIS Quarterly 23(1), 67–93 (1999)
17. Klir, G. (ed.): Facets of Systems Science. Plenum Press, New York (1991)
18. Langesfors, B.: Information Systems Theory. Information Systems 2, 207–219 (1977)
19. Law, J., Mol, A. (eds.): Complexities: Social Studies of Knowledge Practices. Duke University Press, Durham (2002)
20. Lee, A.S.: Retrospect and Prospect: Information Systems Research in the Last and Next 25 Years. Journal of Information Technology 25(4), 336–348 (2010)
21. Leonardi, P.M., Barley, S.R.: Materiality and Change: Challenges to Building Better Theory about Technology and Organizing. Information and Organization 18(3), 159–176 (2008)
22. Luhmann, N.: The Autopoiesis of Social Systems. In: Geyer, F., van der Zouwen, J. (eds.) Sociocybernetic Paradoxes: Observation, Control and Evolution of Self-Steering Systems, pp. 172–193. Sage, London (1986)
23. Luhmann, N.: System as Difference. Organization 13(1), 37–57 (2006)
24. Morgan, G.: Images of Organization. Sage, London (2007)
25. Oxford English Dictionary OED Online. Oxford University Press (1989)
26. Orlikowski, W.J.: Sociomaterial Practices: Exploring Technology at Work. Organization Studies 28(9), 1435–1448 (2007)
27. Orlikowski, W.J., Iacono, C.S.: Research Commentary: Desperately Seeking "IT" in IT Research – A Call to Theorizing the IT Artifact. Information Systems Research 12(2), 121–134 (2001)
28. Pentland, B.T., Feldman, M.S., Becker, M.C., Liu, P.: Dynamics of Organizational Routines: A Generative Model. Journal of Management Studies 49(8), 1484–1508 (2012)
29. Riemer, K., Johnston, R.B.: Rethinking the Place of the Artefact in IS using Heidegger's Analysis of Equipment. European Journal of Information Systems 23(3), 273–288 (2014)
30. Varela, F.: The Principles for Self-Organization. In: Ulrich, H., Probst, G.J.B. (eds.) Self-Organization and Management of Social Systems: Insights, Promises, Doubts and Questions, pp. 25–32. Springer, Berlin (1984)
31. Varela, F., Maturana, H., Uribe, R.: Autopoiesis: The Organization of Living Systems, Its Characterization and a Model. Biological Systems 5, 187–196 (1974)
32. Von Bertalanffy, L.: The History and Status of General Systems Theory. Academy of Management Journal 15(4), 407–426 (1972)
33. Walsham, G.: Doing Interpretive Research. European Journal of Information Systems 15(3), 320–330 (2006)

Author Index

Printed in the United States
By Bookmasters